GOD'S WOUNDED WORLD

# GOD'S WOUNDED WORLD

*American Evangelicals and the Challenge of Environmentalism*

Melanie Gish

BAYLOR UNIVERSITY PRESS

*Cover and book design* by Kasey McBeath
*Cover photo* by Olivier Mesnage/Unsplash

Library of Congress Cataloging-in-Publication Data

Names: Gish, Melanie, 1976- author.
Title: God's wounded world : American evangelicals and the challenge of
  environmentalism / Melanie Gish.
Description: Waco : Baylor University Press, 2020. | Includes
  bibliographical references. | Summary: "Traces the evolution of creation
  care and environmental advocacy movements within American
  evangelicalism in the late twentieth and early twenty-first centuries"
  --Provided by publisher.
Identifiers: LCCN 2020022045 (print) | LCCN 2020022046 (ebook) | ISBN
  9781481311731 (hardcover) | ISBN 9781481313346 (pdf) | ISBN
  9781481313339 (mobi) | ISBN 9781481311755 (epub)
Subjects: LCSH: Environmentalism--Religious aspects--Christianity. |
  Evangelicalism--United States.
Classification: LCC BT695.5 .G57 2020  (print) | LCC BT695.5  (ebook) |
  DDC 261.8/80973--dc23
LC record available at https://lccn.loc.gov/2020022045
LC ebook record available at https://lccn.loc.gov/2020022046

*God's Wounded World* has been made possible in part by a major grant from the
National Endowment for the Humanities: NEH CARES. Any views, findings,
conclusions, or recommendations expressed in this book do not necessarily
represent those of the National Endowment for the Humanities.

Printed in the United States of America on acid-free paper with a minimum
of thirty percent recycled content.

The evangelical faith reaches beyond belief to behaviour; it brings with it a multifaceted challenge to live accordingly.

John Stott, *Evangelical Truth*, 85

# CONTENTS

# PREFACE AND ACKNOWLEDGMENTS

The origin of this book can be traced to a Google search of the terms "environmental" AND "conservative," performed early in 2008. What has captivated my attention since then is an organized movement of environmentally active evangelicals, wrestling not only with ecological degradation and an interrelated set of culture war issues, but also with what it means to be "evangelical" in this day and age.

Despite previous personal encounters with ecologically sensitive German evangelicals, biblical Christianity was not even remotely on my mind when I initially searched for potential misfits in the American culture war paradigm. As I immediately learned, however, green evangelicals were a sensation in George W. Bush's America. One journalist of the *New York Times* had gone so far as to call them "human hybrid[s]," thereby implicitly suggesting that being evangelical and environmentally concerned probably required very special breeding—perhaps in a lab? Admittedly, this conspicuous variety of religiopolitical actor seemed much more interesting in the American context than the mere "Republicans for Environmental Protection" that Google's algorithm included among my initial search results as well.[1]

I approached the topic of this book as an outsider in several ways: non-evangelical, non-environmentalist, non-American. For almost a year I observed textual sources of data from across the Atlantic, following hyperlink trails and newspaper headlines, scanning organizational websites and publicly available tax forms, reading blogs, articles, and books. Although it has grown in volume and academic breadth since then, the body of scholarly sources on evangelical environmental engagement was scant at the time. Two organizations dominated the extent of coverage and public attention back then (and have gotten the largest share of scholarly attention since 2008): the Evangelical Environmental Network (EEN), which had initiated the Evangelical Climate Initiative (ECI) in 2006, and the Cornwall Alliance for the Stewardship of Creation (CA), which had immediately opposed it. There seemed to be other evangelical environmental organizations connected with the EEN, though, and in August 2009 I was able to gain participant observer access to a gathering of their leaders at Judson University in Elgin, Illinois. There I finally got a better understanding of the different groups and leaders who belonged to the creation care advocacy community—fittingly, the informal gathering at Judson operated under the name "Creation Care Community Consultation" (CCCC)—and also the chance to set up further one-on-one encounters for extensive semi-structured interviews.[2]

What followed were ten months spent in the United States, between November 2009 and August 2010, during which I conducted interviews at various locations across the country; attended another meeting of the CCCC, this time in Washington, D.C.; visited churches, events, and cultural institutions; and talked to everybody who was willing about faith, the environment, and the culture war/s. The interviews with creation care leaders and with the national spokesman of the CA, as much as the participant observations at the CCCC, were conducted in the structured way detailed in the introduction and appendix of this book. My rather ethnographic observations and informal conversations happened at random and were not performed or documented in an academically structured way. Although they have not directly shaped the argument of this book, they nevertheless challenged my preconceived notions about religious America, environmental activism, and the nuances between the front lines of the culture war/s. Moreover, they added cultural texture to a topic I approached from the outside rather than with an insider's perspective.

Not only does the topic of this book cut across the generally contentious minefield of religion and social/political engagement, at the root of its argument lies a fault line within American Evangelicalism for which I use the short-hand description green gap. It is therefore important to emphasize that my primary goal has been to gain and foster understanding, not to take a position on either side of this gap. Consequently, I have aspired to conduct this research in a manner as impartial and value free as possible, regardless of my own religious beliefs or the ideological convictions I personally hold. Furthermore, I have attempted to treat all the data with equal fairness and respect, and to keep an academic yet benevolent distance which overall follows the "critical empathy" approach popularized by R. Marie Griffith and employed by other scholars of lived religion.[3]

---

No academic work arises in a vacuum, and this book came out of my dissertation written at the Heidelberg Center for American Studies (HCA) of Heidelberg University in Germany. There are many individuals who contributed in one way or another, primarily among them my doctoral advisers, Martin Thunert and Günter Leypoldt. At the HCA my fellow alumni Maria Diaconu, Barbara Kujath, and Styles Sass provided many critical insights, emotional support, and ongoing friendship. My research would not have taken the shape it did without Hans Krabbendam either, who was formerly at the Roosevelt Institute for American Studies in Middelburg, Netherlands. Hans connected me with Janel Curry, who sat on the EEN's board at the time and in turn introduced me to the CCCC. In addition, Lou Petterchak, Evi Klett, and Gerd Müller, retired librarians/teachers and social activists at heart, immersed themselves much more deeply into this project than can be expected of politely interested family or friends. I greatly benefited from our conversations and from Lou's suggestions and comments on my early drafts. Thanks to all of you.

Most importantly, I am deeply indebted to the people who granted me interviews, as much as to those who facilitated them in the first place: Peter Bakken; Calvin Beisner; Nelson Bock; Ed Brown; Rand Clark; Janel Curry; Calvin DeWitt; Peter Illyn; Jim Jewell; Kendra Juskus; Alexei Laushkin; Ben Lowe; David Neff; Dean Ohlman; Nancy Sleeth; and Jeremy Weber. Without you this book would certainly not exist. Thank you for your help. Thank you for taking time out of your busy schedules to meet and answer my questions. Thank you for sharing coffee, lunch, or dinner. And thank you for being honest, patient, and kind.

Without funds from various sources, I would not have been able to pursue this endeavor. My research was generously supported by the Curt Engelhorn Ph.D. Scholarship of the HCA, by grants from the Jolanta and Soheyl Ghaemian Travel Fund for Scholars, and the Graduiertenakademie of Heidelberg University. In addition, Hannah Klett donated a flight from Denver to Portland. Thank you.

Thanks also to my husband, Chuck, and to our families for their love and support, in particular to Cassaundra Gish and to my parents, Wilfried and Irmgard Hofmann. Apart from Chuck, who has probably shaped my understanding of "America" more than any textbook ever will, my grandmother Maria Fleck and my brother, Chris, were truly encouraging during times when encouragement was needed the most. In addition, many dear friends and coworkers accompanied this endeavor with supportive inquiries and joyful distractions over the years, thank you.

Lastly, thanks to Baylor University Press: first of all to former Director Carey Newman for his interest in my manuscript and then especially to David Aycock, Cade Jarrell, and Jenny Hunt for guiding this project to completion. It goes without saying that any mistakes and shortcomings of this book are mine alone. My hope is that it will be of interest to an academic audience as much as to a wider readership that includes environmental practitioners, religionists, and skeptics of both alike. Moreover, my deepest hope is that it lives up to the Press' mission and turns out to be a "book for good" after all.

# ABBREVIATIONS

| | |
|---|---|
| ASA | American Scientific Affiliation |
| BE | Blessed Earth |
| CA | Cornwall Alliance for the Stewardship of Creation |
| CCCC | Creation Care Community Consultation |
| CEC | Christian Environmental Council |
| CES | Christians for Environmental Stewardship |
| CFACT | Committee for a Constructive Tomorrow |
| CNF | Christian Nature Federation |
| CoC | Care of Creation, Inc. |
| COEJL | Coalition on Environment and Jewish Life |
| *CT* | *Christianity Today* |
| COR | Coalition on Revival |
| ECI | Evangelical Climate Initiative |
| EDCC | Evangelical Declaration on the Care of Creation |
| EEN | Evangelical Environmental Network |
| EPA | Environmental Protection Agency |
| ESA | Evangelicals for Social Action |
| FoF | Focus on the Family |
| ICES | Interfaith Council for Environmental Stewardship |
| ISA | Interfaith Stewardship Alliance |
| NAE | National Association of Evangelicals |
| NCC | National Council of Churches of Christ |
| NRPE | National Religious Partnership for the Environment |
| PWP | Plant with Purpose |
| RE | Restoring Eden |
| RGD | Resisting the Green Dragon |
| SSA | Seminary Stewardship Alliance |
| TJP | The James Partnership |
| USCCB | U.S. Conference of Catholic Bishops |
| Y.E.C.A. | Young Evangelicals for Climate Action |

# INTRODUCTION

*An Unlikely Alternative*

Amid a series of scandals eventually leading to former Environmental Protection Agency (EPA) Administrator Scott Pruitt's resignation in July 2018, an article in *Slate* magazine wearily declared that environmentalism and American evangelicals were "like oil and water"—the two simply did not mix very well. Pruitt, a Southern Baptist and a Republican climate change skeptic with a penchant for environmental deregulation and fossil fuel industry money, is an obvious case in point. A decade prior, however, one could just as easily get the impression that the opposite held true when news about the greening of American evangelicalism spread fast and far beyond the confines of national media outlets, first in the wake of the What Would Jesus Drive? campaign (WWJD?) in 2002, and then with the ECI in 2006.[1]

Initiated as a grassroots effort by the EEN under the umbrella of the National Religious Partnership for the Environment (NRPE) (the latter is an interfaith organization founded, like the EEN, in the early 1990s), the WWJD? campaign linked transportation choices to questions of faith and morality. In tandem with partner organizations from other faith traditions, initial campaign activities included a convoy of nuns driving hybrid cars through Detroit and meetings of Jewish, Catholic, mainline Protestant, and evangelical leaders with executives of motor city's Big Three (General Motors, Ford, and Chrysler) to advocate improvements in fuel efficiency. Apart from directly lobbying the Big Three, another goal of this effort was to frame carbon dioxide emissions as a legitimate moral concern and, alongside abortion, a pressing "life issue." Furthermore, the EEN raised awareness about global warming within the evangelical community specifically by placing ads in Christian magazines, showing television spots in four states, and sending educational materials to thousands of congregations. Following the initial activities of the campaign, EEN Executive Director, the Rev. James (Jim) Ball, and his wife, Kara, went on a "What Would Jesus Drive?" tour of the Bible Belt in their Toyota Prius. Along the way, Ball spoke at a variety of events and on Christian radio stations and to numerous mayors, state representatives, and city council members. The drive ended with a booth at Creation Festival, the largest Christian music festival in the United States, where the EEN had introduced a recycling program the year prior.[2]

By the time the new millennium began, environmentalism as a cultural space and social movement had become as closely associated with political progressivism or liberalism and aligned toward the Democratic Party as evangelicals had, in turn, become associated and aligned with religiopolitical conservatism and the Republicans, making news about evangelical efforts to reduce greenhouse gas emissions more than surprising. Due to its unwontedness, the WWJD? campaign yielded about three to four million dollars' worth of free media, including approximately 1,900 articles in U.S. newspapers, five hundred television and radio stories, all-day coverage on CNN, and a mention on Jay Leno's night show. It was also mentioned in Michael Crichton's controversial thriller *State of Fear* (2004). Moreover, non-American observers perceived the campaign to have a lasting impact on the climate change debate in the United States. German journalist Markus Becker opined in an article about America discovering her green conscience in the wake of Hurricane Katrina: "Four words illustrate where debate about climate change is headed in the United States: 'What would Jesus drive?'"[3]

Whereas the EEN's role in the WWJD? campaign had largely been to sensitize and mobilize the evangelical grassroots with regard to transportation choices and their environmental impact, the network's subsequent ECI started at the grasstops. Originally signed by eighty-six influential evangelical public leaders in 2006—among them megachurch pastor and bestselling author Rick Warren, who had prayed with George W. Bush the evening prior to the president's second inauguration—the ECI was a direct "Call to Action" on America's most contentious and partisan environmental problem: global warming. Noncompatible with the "war on science" that Republicans were increasingly accused of waging, it declared climate change real and mainly human-induced. Signatories of the ECI also admitted that the issue posed a moral dilemma for Christians because although largely caused by the rich, it affected the global poor the most. Therefore, the problem had to be addressed immediately by individuals, churches, businesses, and governments. Such a stance was rather sensational considering Evangelicalism's and environmentalism's politicization along opposing partisan lines. Since it was immediately countered by other evangelicals associated with the Religious Right, the ECI also appeared to expose a noteworthy crack in the evangelical-Republican coalition.[4]

With the presidential election of 2008 coming up, the prospect of a greener and potentially more progressive Evangelicalism on the rise thus loomed large. Expectations were buoyed by polls suggesting that, albeit with caution, "millions of evangelicals . . . [had] become more environmentally conscious in the last year." Moreover, according to other research noting change within American Evangelicalism, the majority of evangelicals did *not* identify with the Religious Right. Young evangelicals in particular disapproved of George W. Bush and the strong alliance their faith community had forged with the Republican Party since the late 1970s. In addition, several older evangelical leaders who had signed the ECI were also publicly voicing concerns about the evangelical–Republican alignment and the narrow agenda of the Religious Right, thereby prompting *Time* magazine to declare the "birth of the new evangelicalism" among the Top Ten Religion Stories of 2008.[5]

As NPR's Gregory Warner reminisced in July 2019, however, "If you paused at this moment in history, it could really seem like Christians would be ready to not only sign on to the environmental movement but even take the lead. So what happened?" Needless to say, an evangelical green revolution has not happened since then. Neither have evangelicals prevented the election of Donald J. Trump and the furtherance of a Republican agenda unmatched in its antienvironmental sentiment and deregulation efforts since the presidency of Ronald Reagan. Like any emulsion conventionally created from water and oil, the mix of Evangelicalism and environmentalism turned out to be unstable in the long run. Or so it must certainly seem if we overlook the small but still persistent movement behind initiatives such as the ECI.[6]

---

This book is about evangelical environmental leaders and the organizational place, as much as the discursive space they have created at the intersection of American Evangelicalism and environmentalism since the late 1970s. It analyzes the evolution of this particular advocacy community since the establishment of the first evangelical environmental organization in 1979–1980, until 2009 and 2012–2013, respectively, when the newest group at that time was founded and then temporarily disbanded. Although its analysis ends before the election of President Trump, the actors portrayed as alive in this book are active to this day, deeply committed to the long haul and intent on stirring the fickle blend of American Evangelicalism and environmentalism until "creation care" does become an accepted value of the larger evangelical church. Because to them, being evangelical *and* environmental is a religious and civil obligation much more than an ideological challenge in politically and culturally polarized America.

While this book cannot weigh in on immediately contemporary evangelical (environmental) matters due to the time frame covered, it nevertheless owes its existence and arguments to a green gap within American Evangelicalism older than the internecine conflict over global warming—and deep enough to persist in the future, too. Unlike the so-called "God gap" or "religion gap" in the American electorate, which crudely divides more religiously vocal Republicans from overall less religiously committed Democrats, the intra-evangelical green gap crudely divides environmentally concerned evangelicals from environmentally skeptical and dismissive evangelicals. Theirs is a division having to do with ideology as well, yet it cannot be reduced to politics. Science, economics, and theology all play additional roles too, but the fault zone at the bottom of the green gap is more complex still, including upthrows and downthrows of cultural posture, religious tradition, and individual biography.[7]

The movement creation care leaders have built because of—not to mention despite—the green gap has thus had to grapple with more than one dilemma over the course of its existence. Consequently, in terms of movement organizations, it is tiny compared to both mainstream environmentalism on the one side and the larger evangelical community in the United States on the other. As we shall see, however, evangelical environmentalists have nevertheless succeeded in the establishment of an organizationally anchored, non-fundamentalist "in-between-but-still-within" space at the intersection of American Evangelicalism and environmentalism. A site of creative negotiation and diplomatic wrestling for a more environmentally conscious, ideologically transcending, and culturally bridging evangelical alternative, this space and its occupants are misfits indeed in an increasingly polarized two-party political system and corresponding cultural climate of antagonism.[8]

Its ensuing partisan homelessness and small size may not render the creation care movement a more politically fruitful ally for transpartisan coalitions, which had been a hope that had arisen with the ECI and all but crashed a few years later. As this book shows, however, the creation care movement must nevertheless be seen as a crucial mediating actor between religious and ideological poles and as an important addition to American environmentalism. Moreover, as an alternative to an increasingly partisan, nationalistic, and culturally combative political Right, the creation care movement may also turn out to be a significant site of resistance for the preservation of a less belligerent and more holistically oriented Evangelicalism instead.[9]

## DEFINITIONS AND METHODOLOGY

Social movements form when cultural agreement is challenged by dissonance over issues of profound importance, such as environmental degradation, sexual morality, and economic, racial, and gender inequality. At these "cracks of culture," movements arise like "prophets" to identify what is wrong, why that is, and what should be done about it. As "embryos of a new society," social movements embody and articulate the visions of alternatives. They aim to change not the peripheral and the routine, but the institutions and behaviors of central importance to society. Within the political process in America, "Movements are not an aberration but a regular part." Naturally, their academic conception has been disputed and changed over time.[10]

Drawing on a body of literature from multiple disciplines, I understand social movement—or, public interest—organizations as makers of meaning and rather tangible embodiments of ideas and ideologies in pluralistic democracies. Although social movements are collective actors and larger in the sum of their participatory scopes than their individual organizational building blocks combined, movement organizations are crucial for the mobilization of resources. If they evolve into stable advocacy communities, they also are indispensable for the embedding of certain values into society. Taken together, movement organizations can be understood as the organizational backbone of social movements, marking distinctive public spaces where ideas, ideals, and identities are collectively generated, negotiated, and disseminated. Their better tangibility—as opposed to that of the broader movements they belong to—largely results from the fact that movement organizations are visibly and legally organized as groups who facilitate organizational websites and must comply with state laws of incorporation and the tax code of the Internal Revenue Service (IRS).[11]

As movements persist throughout time and grow in size, the difficulty to conceptualize and analyze them *as such* inevitably increases. While there is no "environmental movement" incorporated in the United States, there are thousands of organizations operating under the banner of environmentalism alone. No qualitative analysis can include all of them, let alone any unorganized or loosely organized movement of actors. In addition, their very name attests to the fact that movements are changeful by default and thus in "continuous flux." What we describe with the convenient shorthand of "Religious Right," for instance, has experienced several cycles of decline, presumed death, and eventual rebirth since its ascendancy in the late 1970s. Likewise, the modern environmental movement that emerged in the 1960s has ebbed and flowed through its own rhythms of change. Any qualitative movement analysis is therefore not only based on a construction of the observer to some degree (who must decide whom to include and whom not) but also on a temporal construction at that.[12]

The roster of organizations on which this analysis rests was compiled in a methodological process reflecting the eventual transition of my own position from a nonparticipant to a participant observer in the CCCC. The idea was to find as many U.S.-based evangelical environmental or creation care organizations with a national or global outlook as possible. Ideally, the selected organizations should understand themselves as networking partners toward a common goal so that, taken together, they could be regarded as a movement or advocacy community. The organizations analyzed here fulfilled this latter requirement by participating in the CCCC, "a friendly gathering of like-minded people" organized infrequently by evangelical environmental leaders. The first meeting I attended was organized by Janel Curry, chairwoman of the EEN's board at the time, and took place at Judson University in Elgin, Illinois, from August 6 to 7, 2009. The second meeting took place at Western Presbyterian Church in Washington, D.C., from August 2 to 3, 2010, and was organized by Edward Brown, founder of Care of Creation, Inc. (CoC). To ensure that I would encounter their founders and/or major spokespersons there, the organizations included in this study had to be founded before the CCCC 2009 or 2010 meetings.[13]

By applying admittedly rather strict selection criteria, which are further specified below and extensively detailed in the appendix, I found a small sample of eight national evangelical environmental organizations, one of which was disbanded in 1992 but whose founder was still connected to the CCCC. Compared to the larger environmental movement in the United States, this number is tiny. Nonetheless, it has continuously risen since the establishment of the first evangelical environmental organization in 1979–1980 and is growing still. Moreover, the fact that these organizations exist(ed) at all is significant in itself. As Christopher Bosso reminds us, advocacy organizations share one crucial characteristic: they are not made in jest. Rather, they are deliberately created by people who "decided that [they were] necessary, that there was a reason to create [them] in the first place." Considering the myriad environmental (and evangelical) organizations, instead of creating a viable new organization, which ultimately fails in many cases, every new group's leader(s) could have also invested their resources in ventures already established. Polemically speaking, environmentally concerned evangelicals could have joined the Sierra Club or the National Wildlife Federation. Or, similar to the environmental justice advocates who initially hailed from within mainline Protestant denominational bodies, creation care advocates could have also worked out their environmental aspirations from within already established evangelical churches and other institutions. Instead, they have started founding exclusively "evangelical" environmental parachurch nonprofits since 1979. However few in number, these organizations' existence therefore points to an advocacy need that their founders deemed necessary of separate organizational incorporation.[14]

In order to make the case for a national evangelical environmental or creation care advocacy community, the following could not be included in this book: regionally confined volunteer groups, affiliates of international organizations, creation care programs maintained by churches or other denominational institutions, and evangelical social justice or relief and development organizations supportive of environmental protection. Although there is a community of widely Christian and generally Protestant environmental organizations in the United States as well, those were not included either, even though they may have evangelicals among their leaders and/or supporters.[15]

While religiously motivated environmentalism in general is an important area of study too, the focus of this book remains on the evangelical tradition because of evangelicals' specific role within American culture and politics, especially in the past four decades. There is no doubt that such an approach can seem myopic in the spiritually diverse arena of environmental engagement. Or, perhaps worse, it may seem misguided in the murky waters of lived religion, especially at a time when the definition of "evangelical" appears to be more intensely debated than ever. Nonetheless, a selective strictness was necessary in order to credibly answer the question of whether an *evangelical* environmental (mini-)movement has indeed developed at the intersection with American environmentalism before embarking on a subsequent analysis of its religiopolitical space in politically and culturally polarized America.[16]

As for the much-debated term "evangelical," this study follows a layered definitional approach accounting for self-identification, denominational belonging, core religious beliefs and practices, and historical lineage. The actors portrayed in this book therefore identify themselves as "evangelical" and worship at congregations within the evangelical tradition. Furthermore, and as detailed throughout, their collective social engagement as much as their individual biographic backgrounds conform with historian David Bebbington's quadrilateral of evangelical hallmarks, namely activism, conversionism, biblicalism, and crucicentrism. In addition, the evangelical identity of creation care leaders is expanded beyond self-identification, beliefs, and practices. It also includes a historical and cultural dimension based on a sense of belonging to the larger religious tradition that started with the Protestant Reformation in sixteenth-century Europe and has, in the American contemporary context, been shaped by the generally more accommodating (neo-)evangelical departure from fundamentalism in the middle of the twentieth century.[17]

In particular, when it comes to Evangelicalism's more recent history and present situation, an association with right-wing politics seems to have become the norm among many white evangelicals. According to some observers, theologically grounded definitions like Bebbington's are therefore obsolete to a certain extent. The etymological root of the term "evangelical," however, remains the Greek word for *gospel* or *good news*. Historically, the word has thus been used to designate a religious and not a political and/or racialized identity. Moreover, it has been used to describe a set of beliefs and practices uncoupled from a certain national or cultural context, and as such, it is in my opinion still valid. This does not negate the fact that Evangelicalism in America has been divided along racial and political lines, of course. Neither can it be denied that the politicization of American

Evangelicalism has affected the meaning and usage of the term itself. In fact, considering Seth Dowland's claim that self-identified American evangelicals today do not hold evangelical beliefs and that "a significant number of evangelical believers reject the term *evangelical*," it seems plausible that the label "evangelical" may have turned into a second-order semiological system in the American context, whose original meaning has become superseded by a politically very effective "myth." More qualitative research in this direction could perhaps help to explain the support for Donald J. Trump by people who claim the evangelical label but do not conform and align with its theological beliefs and historical background. Nonetheless, creation care leaders, who are predominantly older, white, male, and rather conservative on certain issues, insist on a religiously grounded definition of their evangelical identity. While they do not reject the term itself, they consciously challenge and critique its ideological connotations and cultural presuppositions, as discussed throughout this book.[18]

Regarding environmentalism specifically, the term "environment"—derived from the French *environner*, meaning *to surround* or *enclose*—did not come into common use until the mid-twentieth century. With the increase of pollution and ecological degradation, it has since been employed "as a synonym for the words nature, or milieu, or ecosphere inasmuch as they are influenced or threatened by human activity or have some impact on that activity." Primarily for reasons of variation, I largely use the terms "environmentalism" and "creation care" interchangeably when it comes to designations such as "evangelical environmentalist" or "creation care activist," and "evangelical environmental movement" or "creation care movement." According to creation care advocates, however, they are only interchangeable to some extent because unlike the term "environment," "creation" refers to much more than that which surrounds us. To evangelical believers, "creation" does not exist as detached in source, form, and meaning from its "creator." Hence and as we shall see, evangelical environmentalism is not simply environmentalism done by evangelicals. It is indeed the *care of creation*, and underlying the activism of evangelical environmentalists is therefore a specific, religiously embedded motivational stimulus and a distinctive creation care theology.[19]

Another reason why the leaders and organizations portrayed in this book prefer the term "creation care" over "environmentalism" is more strategic. Although from a political theory perspective environmentalism is neither inherently conservative nor inherently liberal, environmentalism in America has become a domain of the political Left rather than the Right. Consequently, the number of Americans who generally define themselves as "environmentalists" has steadily declined from a high of 78 percent in 1991 to 42 percent in 2016. While in 1991 the same high percentage of Republicans and Democrats identified as environmentalists, in 2016 56 percent of Democrats identified with this label vis-à-vis only 27 percent of Republicans. Moreover, studies on social movement identity show that the support for the environmental movement itself seems to have become politically polarized too. Creation care, therefore, is not only the theologically more apt term for evangelicals to use, it also appears to have less ideological baggage and fewer cultural and political connotations attached to it.[20]

In this book we will extensively explore and discuss the ideological locus of the creation care movement specifically. Beforehand, however, it is also important to note that this study does not start from the assumption that evangelical environmentalism ought to be a movement on the more liberal or progressive side of the ideological spectrum simply because most environmentalists in America are located there. Neither can creation care advocates necessarily be regarded as "conservative environmentalists" simply because most evangelicals can be found to the right of the political center. Although religions may indeed have a tendency to move toward the Left as they turn green, in theory, at least, environmentalism transcends political boundaries because it "is neither left nor right in the sense that environmental policy tools can have a left, right, or centrist character." That said, however, my aim is *not* to reduce Evangelicalism's internal political diversity and fluidity to a Left-Center-Right trichotomy in order to locate evangelical environmentalists within a rather broad and characterless "evangelical center." Instead, the goal of this book is to better understand the creation care movement and the religiopolitical space it occupies on its own terms, through the motivations and visions of its leaders and their organizations, and through the positions they take on certain issues that are considered to be in tension with each other according to the binary culture war paradigm. Not understanding the creation care movement better in its own right came at the cost of inflating its political potential based on an alleged ideological locus in a more liberal or progressive evangelical center. We should not risk the additional fare of deflating—if not ignoring—the movement's cultural potential as a mediating current within an ever more polarizing America.[21]

## SCOPE OF THE STUDY

After a contextualizing overview of both Evangelicalism and environmentalism up until the 1980s (chapter 1), the tentative convergence of the two movements in the shape of an evangelical ecotheology is detailed in chapter 2. Chapters 3 to 6 then provide a qualitative interdisciplinary analysis of organized creation care, which is shaped by social movement theory and the population ecology of interest representation. From an evolutionary point of view, three distinct phases of organization founding can be discerned: the 1980s are the founding time of what I call "pioneer creation care organizations" (i.e., the Au Sable Institute of Environmental Studies,

Floresta/Plant with Purpose, and the Christian Nature Federation [CNF], as discussed in chapter 3). The 1990s are the founding time of "politically unafraid evangelical environmental organizations" (i.e., the EEN and Christians for Environmental Stewardship [CES], as explored in chapter 4). And, after the founding of the countervailing environmentally skeptical CA in 2000 (see chapter 5), the mid- to late-2000s are the founding time of "apolitical creation care organizations" (Care of Creation, Inc.; Blessed Earth; and Creation Care, Inc., as analyzed in chapter 6). Since the development of the creation care movement is seen through an evolutionary lens, chapters 3 to 6 build upon and relate to each other, hence the inclusion of the CA in the analysis of this process even though it does not belong to the creation care advocacy community represented by the CCCC. As a countervailing force, however, it must be regarded as a shaping factor of the overall evolution of creation care since the movement's early days, as argued and detailed in chapter 5. Moreover, an analysis of the CA and its discontent with creation care reveals several characteristics of the green gap, which helps us better understand the particular "in-between-but-still-within" space environmentally active evangelicals have built against the opposition of their internal critics and the backdrop of the larger culture war.[22]

Each of chapters 3 to 6 addresses questions of organizational origin, founding motives, means, and opportunities. All chapters present individual strategies and tactics employed by the respective organizations and their leaders, and deal with the question of resources. In addition, all of the organizational analyses contain elements of the respective individual founder's and/or leader's biography, which are intrinsically connected to—and thus inseparable from—the corresponding organization's founding mission and preferred advocacy strategy. For reasons of methodology and practicality, the organizational studies are understood as exemplary and cumulative instead of individually exhaustive.[23]

In order to conclusively explore the overall religiopolitical locus of the movement, attention is also paid to positions on a set of contentious issues at the intersection of Evangelicalism and environmentalism. For reasons which will become more transparent in chapter 1, I chose the issues of science versus Scripture; (over)population versus abortion; anti-consumerism versus (free-market) capitalism; and government regulation versus individual responsibility as particularly potent for this purpose. Furthermore, the conclusion expands on this set by means of additional parameters accounting for self-understanding of the occupied religiopolitical space; partisanship and ideology; and overall posture toward pluralism and cultural mediation.

# 1
# EVANGELICALISM AND ENVIRONMENTALISM

## *A Contextualizing Overview*

The current U.S. environmental movement is a confusing patchwork of overlapping discourses and organizations that, over 150 years, have developed into communities with disparate goals, issue focuses, and organizational structures. Despite attempts by conservationists and reform environmentalists, no master frame has emerged that can unite all these factions into a cohesive political movement.

Robert J. Brulle[1]

We are troubled by the fact that the confusions and corruptions surrounding the term Evangelical have grown so deep that the character of what it means has been obscured and its importance lost. Many people outside the movement now doubt that Evangelical is ever positive, and many inside now wonder whether the term any longer serves a useful purpose.

"An Evangelical Manifesto"[2]

Environmentalism has been called "the most significant social movement in America." Likewise, Evangelicalism passes as the most socially important religious movement in America. Within their larger historical contexts in the United States, both Evangelicalism and environmentalism have been predominantly white and predominantly shaped by men rather than women. Both share a transnational orientation; environmentalism because ecological problems do not stop at national borders, Evangelicalism because the saving of souls is an equally global endeavor. While environmentalism has been compared to a religion, Evangelicalism has been criticized for its overt politicization over the past forty years.[3]

Despite a generally prevalent tendency to view both of them as universal or unified phenomena, American Evangelicalism and environmentalism are both internally diverse and fluid in terms of doctrine and ideology. As the quotes cited above underscore, there is an element of "confusion" in both the definitions of what it means to be evangelical and in what it means to be an environmentalist. In addition, both movements have long and complex histories that cannot be unrolled by quick pulls on single skeins, much less woven together seamlessly as one singular tale. Although there are points of contact and convergence before the rise of a few pronounced evangelical environmental organizations late in the twentieth and early in the twenty-first centuries, the longer part of environmental thinking and acting in the United States has not seen much *explicitly expressed* overlap with evangelical Christianity. If anything, philosophical disagreement and ideological clashes have become the norm after the emergence of the modern environmental movement in the 1960s and evangelicals' intense politicization in the opposite direction since the late 1970s. Hence there is the need to outline some of the major developments in the histories of both Evangelicalism and environmentalism up until the 1980s within a contextualizing frame in order to establish the necessary background for the later chapters.

## EVANGELICALISM AND ENVIRONMENTALISM IN THE EIGHTEENTH AND NINETEENTH CENTURIES

Evangelical Christians have played a crucial role in shaping American culture and politics since the early eighteenth century, when "the three P's" within Protestantism (i.e., Scots-Irish Presbyterianism, Continental Pietism, and New England Puritanism) came together, and believers started to discover a "true religion of the heart" during the First Great Awakening. This religious revival movement—yielding between twenty-five thousand and fifty thousand converts in New England in the years 1740–1742 alone—is most closely associated with preachers such as Jonathan Edwards (1703–1758) and George Whitefield (1714–1770) and their fiery sermons condemning rationalism and human depravity. A second, more populist awakening, the Great Revival, followed in the late eighteenth and early nineteenth centuries, and turned Evangelicalism into the dominant religion of the 1800s. In the South, Methodists and Baptists "'colonized' the frontier regions . . . so thoroughly and effectively that the region bears the unmistakable stamp of evangelicalism to this day." In the North, evangelicals got zealously involved in the various reform movements of their time, such as abolitionism, the temperance movement, and women's suffrage.[4]

In the history of environmentalism, on the other hand, the nineteenth century is closely associated with the discourse of "Manifest Destiny," arguably the dominant American "environmental" narrative to this day. Conceptualized as a discursive frame, Manifest Destiny is used by sociologist Robert J. Brulle as a summary term for the overarching economic and moral rationale that has guided and justified Americans' "exploitation" of nature since 1620. As such it roughly corresponds with what environmental historian John Opie calls "American triumphalism" and political scientist John Dryzek refers to as "Promethean" or "cornucopian discourse"—a confident understanding of the limitlessness of nature and human progress. According to this rationale, nature has no value in itself, and the sole purpose of natural resources, which are perceived as abundant, is to assure human welfare.[5]

Overall, American environmentalism can be seen as rooted in protests against the discourse of Manifest Destiny. A growing concern with progress and modernity interlaced with a nostalgic reverence for nature dates back at least to the beginning of the Industrial Revolution and the Romantic countermovement it inspired. As the American landscape changed from an agricultural to an industrialized one, transcendentalists such as Ralph Waldo Emerson and Henry David Thoreau were among the first to identify the problematics of those changes. Over the course of the nineteenth century, the transcendentalists were joined by early conservationists like George Perkins Marsh (1801–1882), who published *Man and Nature*—"the first comprehensive description in the English language of the destructive impact of human civilization on the environment"—in 1864, as well as preservationist and Sierra Club founder John Muir (1838–1914), to name only the most prominent examples.[6]

Toward the end of the nineteenth century, three ecologically more sensitive counter-narratives to Manifest Destiny could be discerned: Wildlife Management, Conservation, and Preservation. The efficient management of wildlife had become necessary due to uncontrolled hunting practices and a decreasing wildlife population. As a reaction to these problems, the newly evolving discourse framed wildlife as a crop that could be harvested; thus, Wildlife Management became popular as a scientific attempt to manage ecosystems. Similarly, the utilitarian frame of Conservation sought to find ways in which natural resources could be technically managed to assure human health and welfare.[7]

Preservation, on the other hand, comes discursively closest to the transcendentalist movement and differs from Wildlife Management and Conservation mostly in its ethical orientation. Being biocentric rather than anthropocentric, it acknowledges an intrinsic value of nature and emphasizes its spiritual importance. As its signature trait, Preservation stands for the promotion and the development of national parks and other areas where wilderness and wildlife should be preserved without being disturbed by human activity. Not in line with the overt Republican anti-environmentalism of today, the first national parks and forests in the United States were established under Republican presidents Ulysses S. Grant and Benjamin Harrison. Still existing environmental organizations that were founded by preservationists are older than the ones that employed the discursive frames of Wildlife Management and Conservation, respectively. However, Conservation was the dominant discourse of the Progressive Era, hence the sometimes sole reference to nineteenth- and early twentieth-century conservationism vis-à-vis twentieth-century environmentalism.[8]

Nineteenth-century transcendental thinkers, nature enthusiasts, conservationists, and preservationists were all loosely connected in their appreciation of America's "wild places," their concern with diminishing forests and wildlife populations, and their overall skeptical stance toward Manifest Destiny. Unlike modern, twentieth-century environmentalism, though—and with a few exceptions like John Muir's founding of the Sierra Club in 1892, for instance—this early movement largely remained an intellectual one and did not consolidate as a program of political reform that expressed and demanded clear environmental policies.[9]

## SCIENCE, MODERNITY, AND FUNDAMENTALISM

Dominated by a generally evangelical religious consensus in America, the nineteenth century also gave birth to the term "ecology" and to modern science as a profession. As is known, tensions ensued. In particular Charles Darwin's *On the Origin of Species*, published in 1859, challenged believers' focus on biblicalism and orthodoxy. In the United States the forces of modernity thus not only prompted rising environmental sensitivities but eventually also the unfolding of the "Great Reversal" of Evangelicalism's previous societal dominance.[10]

Positivism and evolutionary theory in particular, and an increasing theological liberalism triggered by German higher criticism in general, made it difficult for some Protestants to maintain the biblical view of human origins, the Genesis account of creation, and other essential tenets of their faith. Another group of Protestants reacted in the opposite way, though, emphasizing that a strong focus on the Scriptures and their infallibility was more important than ever in those modern times. The tensions between these two currents eventually led to a split between "modernists" and "fundamentalists." Modernists read the biblical books more critically, welcomed modernity, and became overall more religiously liberal and worldly oriented. Fundamentalist Protestants, on the other hand, rejected modernism and concentrated on *The Fundamentals* and the "truth" of their faith, hence the name. They largely embraced a premillennial dispensational eschatology that emphasized the nearing end times and the importance of evangelism and conversionism as opposed to the social reform efforts of their theologically more liberal modernist brethren.[11]

Modernists and fundamentalists were particularly divided over the Darwinian theory of human evolution, "and the rift was aggravated by the seeming rise in agnosticism among the cultural and scientific elite." Symptomatic of "a new and profound cleavage between traditional values and modernity," the controversy had started in the pulpit and was carried into biology classrooms of public schools by the 1920s. From there fundamentalists took to legislative lobbying in 1922, which resulted in the passage of the Tennessee Butler Act in 1925. The Butler Act forbade the teaching of human evolution in public schools and was immediately challenged by the American Civil Liberties Union (ACLU), which found a teacher (John Thomas Scopes) in the small town of Dayton, Tennessee, who was willing to purposely break the law. The controversy thus climaxed in one of the most famous and bizarre lawsuits in American history, the "Scopes Monkey Trial."[12]

Defended by Clarence Darrow of the ACLU, Scopes was prosecuted by former secretary of state, three-time Democratic nominee for president, and populist evangelical, William Jennings Bryan. After Scopes, the Tennessean Butler Act was upheld until its repeal in 1967. However, the verdict was a Pyrrhic victory as the trial was a major public relations disaster for the fundamentalist movement. While the nation was listening to live radio broadcasts of the proceedings, and journalists like H. L. Mencken "mercilessly lampooned the denizens of eastern Tennessee" in the press, the intellectual foundations of fundamentalism seemed quite questionable after Darrow had asked Bryan several "village atheist questions" and concluded that "no intelligent Christian on earth" believed his "fool ideas." The trial had ended quite abruptly with Darrow demanding that Scopes be charged guilty so that a higher court could take on the matter, while Bryan died within six days of the sentence.[13]

After their embarrassment in Tennessee, fundamentalists retreated from the public sphere. To fend off ridicule and compensate for their loss of cultural power and intellectual credibility, they created their own conservative Christian subculture of Bible schools, seminaries, colleges and universities, missionary organizations, radio stations, and publishing houses. Those institutions drew clearly demarcated boundaries from the rest of American society and largely concentrated on evangelism and revival efforts instead of social reform and political action. Fundamentalists' detachment was reinforced by religious principles and biblical prophesies providing explanations for the crisis, and to this day born-again Protestants feel alienated from a culture in which they once enjoyed the status of being among the most respected members of society. Moreover, the creationism versus evolution debate has remained a source of actual social conflict in the United States since then and has impacted the creation care movement as well, as addressed in more detail in later chapters.[14]

## (NEO-)EVANGELICALISM AND ENGAGED ORTHODOXY

Whatever feelings of defeat and alienation fundamentalist Protestants may have felt after the Scopes Trial, they were not intense enough to keep the entire community disengaged for long. Instead of being "true outsiders" in a culture for which they felt a strong sense of guardianship and patriotism, fundamentalists had reacted more like "wounded lovers" when they temporarily went into subcultural exile. It is therefore not surprising that roughly twenty years after Scopes, a new cadre of more moderate leaders began to emerge out of the fundamentalist movement, and they were poised to leave their resentment behind.[15]

Assembled under the leadership of the Rev. Harold J. Ockenga (1905–1985) in St. Louis, Missouri, on April 7, 1942, the primary motivation of those fundamentalists who initiated what is often referred to as modern "neo-evangelicalism" was the desire to develop a "more intellectually respectable, culturally engaged, and socially responsible alternative" to fundamentalism. As a first step on the way to achieving this goal, they founded the National Association of Evangelicals (NAE) in 1942. Programmatically situated between the theologically liberal Protestant mainline represented by the Federal (later National) Council of Churches (FCC) on the one side, and the separatist American Council of Christian Churches (ACCC), founded by fundamentalist Carl McIntire the year prior, on the other side, the NAE strove "to present a positive testimony to the gospel without directly confronting the Protestant establishment in fundamentalist fashion." Unlike ACCC, the NAE welcomed non-fundamentalists from other Christian traditions, such as Pentecostals and Anabaptists, in order "to pull together a new coalition of conservative Protestants."[16]

Another influential figure involved in spawning and supporting this new evangelical movement was Billy Graham (1918–2018). While the NAE concentrated on networking and infrastructure concerns more than actual evangelistic outreach, Graham would become the primary evangelist and "standard bearer for the evangelical movement" between the 1950s and 1980s. In this capacity he ventured widely across traditional ecclesiastical and national boundaries with his crusades and, later, the Lausanne Committee for World Evangelization. Together with his father-in-law, L. Nelson Bell, Graham also launched what would become "mainstream evangelicalism's flagship journal," *Christianity Today* (*CT*) in 1956. Apart from the NAE and *CT*, various other educational, evangelistic, and cultural institutions and organizations were either newly founded or drawn into Evangelicalism from within the fundamentalist subculture.[17]

Overall, the (neo-)evangelicals were much more reform-oriented than the fundamentalists, albeit not as strongly as their theologically more liberal Protestant brethren who had propagated the social gospel at the turn of the twentieth century. *CT*'s founding editor Carl F. H. Henry (1913–2003), for instance, was convinced that the Bible asked for cultural engagement and thus passionately decried the "apparent lack of any social passion in Protestant Fundamentalism" in his influential book *The Uneasy Conscience of Modern Fundamentalism* (1947). Social passion, however, does not cogently lead to political action, nor did evangelicals give up their orthodoxy and the strong notion of sin as the root cause of all ills, social or other. Additionally, not all evangelicals were as reform-minded as Henry. Henry's successor at *CT*, fellow Wheaton College graduate Harold Lindsell (1913–1998), for example, still believed that upholding biblical inerrancy had to be evangelicals' primary concern, and that social and political questions were secondary to this task. But Lindsell and others within the movement thought so mainly because they were strongly convinced that spiritually transformed, God-centered lives of individual Christian men and women had a positive impact on society. Therefore, "Service in one's occupational calling was often the very best thing one could do both to serve God and to aid mankind." Hence, the transformation of society through individual salvation and responsibility must not necessarily be seen in conflict with cultural engagement and social or political action. Both were and still are important complementary expressions of what Henry had termed modern evangelicals' "engaged orthodoxy," albeit evangelicals have displayed individual preferences when it comes to placing either one in the foreground. This holds true for their creation care organizations as well, as detailed in later chapters.[18]

While separatism and "militant anti-modernism" have long been regarded as the primary trademarks of fundamentalism, evangelicals in the mold of Ockenga, Henry, and Graham have largely adapted to the pluralism and functional rationality of modernity and engaged in coalition building with non-evangelicals. Their higher level of tolerance for scriptural ambiguity has also made evangelicals less concerned with the fulfillment of prophesy and the "correct" belief about Jesus Christ's second coming. Fundamentalists, on the other hand—especially in their "ideal-typical" occurrence—"are more likely to insist on dispensational premillennialism as the only correct belief about Christ's Second Coming. In fact, fundamentalists are likely to see that belief as a key test as to whether a person 'really believes the Bible' . . . [whereas] evangelicals take a generally more accommodating stance on nearly everything."[19]

## ENVIRONMENTALISM IN THE FIRST HALF OF THE TWENTIETH CENTURY

If American religious history of the first half of the twentieth century can be characterized by a period of relative evangelical quiescence before more "restless" fundamentalist leaders like Ockenga and Graham emerged with a renewed zeal to engage American society and beyond, two environmentalist shifts took place during the time of the evangelical retreat. On the one hand, the conservation discourse spread from the West and East Coasts across the nation. On the other, several new environmental advocacy organizations were established, some with close ties to Washington, especially as the federal government became increasingly involved in conservation efforts with the New Deal economic programs (1933–1939). In terms of their environmental ethics, the interwar organizations expanded their view of nature from scientific manageability and nature's embedded aesthetic value to an appreciation of nature's *"recreational* benefits and opportunities." In short, "Nature was not just to be managed and admired, but enjoyed as another consumer good."[20]

The interwar period is not to be dismissed in its importance for the further development of American environmental activism and politics, especially since the major environmental laws of the late 1960s and early 1970s "were erected upon the legal platform of the New Deal." Moreover, much of the conservative resistance toward federal (environmental) regulation has its roots in the Franklin D. Roosevelt administration, which expanded the authority of the federal government and protected the interests of farmers, workers, and other citizens against business interests.[21]

While environmentalism was temporarily dormant during World War II, the value of nature as a recreational commodity also played a role in the postwar era of rising consumerism. Tied in with nature's commodification as beneficial to human health was a concern with the ecological degradation directly caused by warfare and the production of war supplies. Hence, environmental advocacy organizations created between the late 1940s and early 1960s had to deal with a broadened agenda of concerns. Overall though, the 1950s were a decade of civil religious consensus rather than stirring environmental sentiments.[22]

## (CIVIL) RELIGION AFTER THE SECOND WORLD WAR AND THE SHOCKING 1960s

With hindsight it seems like the traumatic experience of World War II led to a revival of religion and a surge in religious observance. This surge occurred especially among the younger generation, who attended service weekly in large numbers after the war. According to the polls of the time, those young, college-educated fathers and their wives went to church mainly for spiritual guidance but also because "churchgoing was the thing to do." After all, this was one of the prime times of "civil religion" in America—a term originating with Rousseau but used and popularized by sociologist Robert N. Bellah to designate the specific, publicly expressed, and widely accepted blend of Judeo-Christian values and archetypes considered to form the spiritual and moral foundation of America and her institutions.[23]

Civil religion has been an integral part of the American political-cultural fabric since the nation's founding. The upsurge it experienced after the war was largely due to the threat of the Soviet Union and the "Red Menace" of atheistic Communism, against which America offset herself by emphasizing her religious roots and heritage. So Americans attended church dutifully throughout the 1950s. They added "under God" to the Pledge of Allegiance in 1954 and "In God we trust" on their coins in 1956, and mostly there was no public outcry about this mix of faith and patriotism. Moreover, religion itself was not a partisan activity at the time; denominational ties were still stronger than the cohesion produced by shared religiopolitical identities would eventually become. President Eisenhower and Billy Graham neither agreed on theology nor foreign policy, "but they agreed on the place of religion in what both considered perilous times. They agreed that America was fighting atheistic Communism and that national survival rested on the belief of Americans in God." Although evangelical churches were growing at the time as well, the surge in church attendance was mostly felt in mainline Protestantism and Catholicism.[24]

The "era of sex, drugs, and rock 'n' roll" that would follow the complacent Eisenhower years, however, "represented a perfect storm for American institutions of all sorts—political, social, sexual, and religious." Sexual mores changed rapidly and radically, and church attendance quickly dropped among the age cohorts that were so dutifully attending worship services throughout the 1950s. Secular authority was questioned across the board, but in particular cosmic and ecclesiastical authority was doubted, which not only produced a post-Christian "death of God movement" but also a more individualist seeker spirituality. The revolutionary climate of the time thus pushed the dominant American churches into the double crisis of questioned authority and uncertain identity. Evangelicalism, which had not gained as many new attendants as Catholicism and mainline Protestantism throughout the 1950s, also did not feel the extent of apostasy as much in the 1960s.[25]

Although evangelicals were more prominent in American culture and politics again, especially compared to their retreat following the Scopes Trial, "Jane Fonda and Malcolm X grabbed headlines much more frequently than Billy Graham or his contemporaries did" during the sixties. On the environmentalist front, however, the cultural revolution of the 1960s marked the dawn of a new era of concern and action. In the historiography of the environmental movement, it is therefore commonplace to distinguish rather broadly between at least two different waves of environmentalism: environmental thinking and conservation efforts before the Second World War, and the "more reformist—even revolutionary—impulses that erupted in the 1960s."[26]

## THE BIRTH OF MODERN (REFORM) ENVIRONMENTALISM

The beginning of modern environmentalism in America is usually correlated with Rachel Louise Carson's (1907–1964) condemnation of DDT and other pesticides in her book *Silent Spring* (1962). A marine biologist by training, a longtime employee of the U.S. Fish and Wildlife Service, and an avid conservationist, Carson conducted and presented government-funded research for most of her career. Subsequently, she turned her scientific findings into a rather poetic and activist prose, which was critical of modern science and its aggressive advances. The culprits in *Silent Spring* are the hundreds of new chemicals that "come from our laboratories in an endless stream" and are used relentlessly in "man's war against nature," a war that, according to Carson, "is never won" but instead has caught "all life . . . in its violent crossfire." Accusing agricultural scientists and the government of "the contamination of man's total environment," Carson saw chemical pollution as potentially as threatening to life on earth as nuclear war. In accordance with her ecological worldview, humans and nature were intrinsically connected and thus the so-called "insecticides" deserved the more appropriate label of "biocides."[27]

Emphasizing the delicate balance of ecosystems and criticizing the overuse of new chemicals without warning the public about their possible impacts on human health, Carson's book consolidated the discourse of Reform Environmentalism. This discursive frame is informed by utilitarian philosophy and aware of the dependence of human survival on functioning ecosystems. It has its intellectual roots in the nineteenth century as well and was initially concerned with the health-threatening impacts of urbanization and the capacity of the planet to sustain all its inhabitants. Drawing on this discursive source, postwar environmental health concerns are thus also rooted in a particular type of "antimodernism" that opposes the long unquestioned benefits of modern society, such as economic growth, consumerism, and, as very well reflected by Carson, the negative ecological consequences of certain scientific advancements. Early Reform Environmentalism had not evolved into a larger movement and "failed to connect with either the conservationist or the preservationist movement until the 1960s." Revitalized by economic growth and its widespread effects on the environment after the Second World War, it was then able to function as a bridge between older discursive frames. The term "environment," which came into common usage in the 1960s, and the general label of "environmentalism," which added to the consolidation of preexisting discourses, enabled Reform Environmentalism to become the most dominant and overarching discursive frame of contemporary environmentalism.[28]

Only a few years after Carson's *Silent Spring*, another "apocalyptic narrative" of impending eco-crisis further galvanized American environmental attitudes and actions: *The Population Bomb* (1968) by Stanford biologist Paul

R. Ehrlich. The book tapped an additional source of reform environmentalists' fear—the carrying capacity of the earth—and drew a gloomy picture of an overcrowded planet ravaged by imminent mass starvation and environmental desolation, set to happen as early as the 1970s. An extraordinary piece of activist scholarship geared toward a popular audience, it sold three million copies within the first ten years of its publication.[29]

Influenced by Malthusian theory, Ehrlich (1932–) perceived population growth as the root cause of environmental problems: "The causal chain of the [environmental] deterioration is easily followed to its source. Too many cars, too many factories, too much detergent, too much pesticide, multiplying contrails, inadequate sewage treatment plants, too little water, too much carbon dioxide—all can be traced easily to *too many people*." Too many people, therefore, not only led to food shortages but also to a "dying planet." In order to halt the catastrophic development that had been going hand in hand with ever growing population numbers, *The Population Bomb* advocated strict population control measures.[30]

According to Ehrlich, population control had to be exercised on a national as much as on a global level. Nationally the United States was urged to set "a goal for a stable optimum population size" and to move toward fulfilling it "rapidly." The same was to be demanded from other nations by means of a "do as we do" foreign policy position.[31]

In order to fulfill the U.S. population goal, Ehrlich did not shy away from considering an encroachment of the state on individual liberties for the sake of more collective "reproductive responsibility," if necessary. To avoid controversy and resistance, however, he suggested "a series of financial rewards and penalties designed to discourage reproduction" as a more "workable" solution. Concrete suggestions included an income tax reversal for families with children; luxury taxes on cribs, diapers, etc.; responsibility prizes for childless couples; subsidization and simplification of the adoption process; and mandatory sex education before junior high school to discuss the need for population control and birth planning techniques as much as the nonreproductive and pleasurable functions of sex. An anathema to the religious community (of which he most directly criticized Roman Catholics for their opposition to birth control), Ehrlich also sanctioned abortion as "a highly effective weapon in the armory of population control." Moreover, the governmental agency he envisioned with the oversight of these population control measures, a "federal Department of Population and Environment (DPE)," was supposed to aid Congress with the establishment of federal laws guaranteeing extensive abortion and voluntary sterilization rights.[32]

*The Population Bomb* sounds extreme today, especially since many of its dire predictions did not unfold as prophesied. Though Ehrlich has been widely challenged and criticized, including by cornucopian economist Julian L. Simon and by fellow environmentalist Barry Commoner, his text nevertheless prompted the establishment of the United Nations Population Fund (UNFPA) in 1969. Similar to the Club of Rome's publication *The Limits to Growth* (1972), it also articulated a strong critique of the capitalistic economic system and thus broke with the most salient idea of the twentieth century, our "economic growth fetish."[33]

While the originator of population theory, Thomas Robert Malthus (1766–1834), appeared apologetic about the "melancholy hue" with which his understanding of population dynamics and the future of mankind was tinted, Ehrlich self-confidently flaunted his pessimism as the only rationally and environmentally sensible option. In the 1960s and 1970s, this posture was concurrent with the rising sense of environmental concern and exigency that was being felt by an increasing segment of the American population. Highlighted in their significance by the powerful "Earthrise" image taken from space in 1968, environmental disasters like the Santa Barbara oil spill and the Cuyahoga river fire in 1969 all but underscored the urgency of the claims about a fragile and ecologically imperiled planet. This climate of urgent eco-crisis and the coming together of different shades of green after World War II eventually culminated in the first Earth Day on April 22, 1970, when about twenty million Americans gathered for national teach-ins on the environment, and it became obvious that environmentalism had turned into a social movement.[34]

Earth Day 1970 was the brainchild of then Senator Gaylord Anton Nelson (1916–2005), a Democrat from Wisconsin. Nelson was inspired by the student anti-war protests and deemed a broad-based movement necessary in order to tackle pressing air and water pollution problems. Especially compared to now, the late 1960s and early 1970s were still a time of bipartisan consensus on environmental protection. Earth Day was thus permeated by a unified environmentalist spirit and succeeded in achieving "a rare political alignment [by] enlisting support from Republicans and Democrats, rich and poor, city slickers and farmers, tycoons and labor leaders." Hence, it also prompted President Nixon, certainly "no 'green' radical but [a politician] keenly attuned to the political zeitgeist," to create the EPA by executive order in 1970.[35]

Subsequently, various major pieces of legislation like the Clean Air Act (1970), an update and expansion of the Clean Water Act (1948, 1972), and the Endangered Species Act (1973) authorized the EPA to control, regulate, and set standards regarding pollution, toxic wastes, pesticides, and biodiversity. Requiring "billions of dollars of public and private investment," those laws "prioritized clean air, water, or the recovery of an endangered species over economic interests." Moreover, they enabled citizens to legally challenge the government in case of non-enforcement. Needless to say, proponents of private enterprise and small government were not happy about them, and in his 1979 memoir Gerald Ford went so far as to disavow the EPA as a creation of Lyndon B. Johnson's Great Society.[36]

## THE (RE)BIRTH OF POLITICALLY AND SOCIALLY ACTIVE EVANGELICALISM

In retrospect, grassroots activism on behalf of the environment was most intense and successful in demanding environmental policies between the late 1960s and the late 1970s, a decade often called the golden age of environmentalism. Many new environmental interest groups formed during that time as well, a development that corresponds with an overall rise in citizen advocacy organizations lobbying on behalf of public interests and quality-of-life concerns. This surge was connected to an increasing political participation of the middle classes, a trend toward issue politics, and economic and technological advances fostering postmaterialist values and the mass politicization of the citizenry, which has arguably contributed to the culture wars as well.[37]

In their encompassing study of the American religious landscape after the Second World War, *American Grace* (2010), social scientists Robert D. Putnam and David E. Campbell pose that America's recent religiopolitical struggles and conflicts have resulted from "three seismic societal shocks" since the 1950s: the social and political upheaval of the sixties, and then the "two major aftershocks" this "earthquake" triggered in the form of (1) the rise of conservative religion, and (2) the countermovement among young adults in the 1990s and 2000s into a more nonreligious (or decidedly politicized anti-religious) direction that the first rise provoked.[38]

The evangelical "counterattack" that followed the "religious crash" of the sixties came in the late 1970s and 1980s. Student radicalism had climaxed in the late 1960s and then declined. Nationwide religious observance numbers stabilized, and in particular the number of young, educated people who attended church rose again, from about 24 percent to about 32 percent between the early 1970s and the mid-1980s. This in itself does not solely account for the unfolding of the first "aftershock," though. Rather, it is the fact that young, educated people did not only start going to church more often again, but also that they favored evangelical Protestant churches, and that their preference for conservative religion went hand in hand with a preference for conservative politics.[39]

Although the majority of evangelicals and fundamentalists had not participated in the environmental debates and activism of the 1960s, they were neither oblivious to nor totally dismissive of the burgeoning environmental movement. Obviously influenced by Carson's advocacy efforts, Billy Graham had acknowledged a connection between DDT and the industrial nations' destructive ecological attitude in 1965, for instance. On the occasion of Thanksgiving in 1966, *CT* had followed suit with an editorial stating that "despoiling nature," "killing wildlife," and "polluting streams" was not consistent with a thanks-giving spirit. Unlike Rachel Carson and the reform environmentalists, however, Graham, the editors of *CT*, and other evangelicals who referred to critical ecological conditions during that time mainly used environmental problems to illustrate "cultural decline" and the human "need for Christ." Moreover, throughout the "long sixties" evangelicals assembled their own set of grievances revolving around "moral pollution" rather than eco-crisis, which eventually propelled them into broad-based political and social action as well.[40]

Concrete manifestations of the societal trends that irked evangelicals at the time reached from the "statism" of Lyndon B. Johnson's Great Society to forced racial desegregation. They included changing gender roles as well as Supreme Court decisions that restricted the public role of religion and expanded the rights of women, such as *Engel v. Vitale* (1962) and *Roe v. Wade* (1973). Most importantly, the move toward "moral decadence" and sexual permissiveness provoked resistance from conservative Christians because it was (and still is) deeply connected with the emotionally charged issues of abortion, homosexuality, premarital sex, and pornography. Intellectually the decade between 1966 and 1976 must be understood as the formative period of modern Evangelicalism, because not since the Civil War had evangelicals engaged the political and social issues of the day with such energy and effort. Although the movement exhibited a pluralism of political thought at the time as well—including reform-minded governmental solutions to tackling social justice and environmental problems—it was mostly united in its belief in the central role of the family and tilted toward conservative ideas. As Hart observes, in the 1950s and 1960s "the political aims of the neo-evangelical leadership . . . were to contribute to the health of the nation." But this goal would narrow during the 1960s, when evangelicals focused more on protecting the family and thus shifted in their concerns from "domestic issues (in a national sense) to issues of domesticity."[41]

As a political force, American Evangelicalism was "born again" in the mid- to late 1970s. In particular two events re-catapulted evangelicals "on the American cultural and political map, [on which] they have remained conspicuous throughout the decades since then": the election of Southern Baptist Jimmy Carter for president in 1976 and the fundamentalist Rev. Jerry Falwell's founding of the Moral Majority organization in 1979. Needless to say, it was Falwell's fundamentalism and the Moral Majority that eventually came to define the public face of modern Evangelicalism and not Jimmy Carter's more progressive peace, justice, and environmental policy efforts.[42]

In the post-Watergate climate of distrust, Carter was certain that his religious conviction would be an asset to his politics and dauntlessly referred to himself as "born-again" on the campaign trail in 1976. In the same year former

Nixon aide and Watergate convict Charles (Chuck) Colson's (1931–2012) conversion narrative with the same title sold more than 500,000 copies. Though the media was initially confused regarding Carter's usage of the term "born-again," Gallup's polling eventually revealed that about 50 million Americans were familiar with such a spiritual experience. Thus, the bicentennial year was soon dubbed "the year of the evangelicals," the news media started to pay more attention to the evangelical phenomenon, and, consequently, "evangelicals began to feel they had come into their own once again, and to dream about further power and glory." The prospect of having an honest fellow believer in the White House, who would potentially fill other positions in his administration with fellow evangelicals, must have indeed seemed like a historic opportunity to repeal what evangelicals perceived as unchristian trends set in motion during the cultural revolution of the 1960s.[43]

Over the course of Carter's election campaign, however, it became obvious that Carter's Evangelicalism was not as evangelical as some had hoped. For one, Carter did not espouse an inerrantist view of Scripture. Neither was he outspokenly against abortion, which "suddenly surfaced as a campaign issue" late in the summer of 1976. In addition, admitting that he had "committed adultery in his heart many times" in an interview with *Playboy* magazine—"the cultural embodiment and advocate of a lifestyle about as unevangelical as one could adopt"—did not help much either.[44]

Evangelicals were thus divided in their support for the peanut farmer and Sunday school teacher from Georgia. Billy Graham, who had been a strong advocate for Richard Nixon prior to the Watergate debacle, was reluctant to endorse the Democratic candidate. Charismatic Pat Robertson, on the other hand, who would campaign for the Republican Party nomination for the presidency in 1988, initially had great hopes that Carter would finally "inject some morality into politics." On a less elitist level within the evangelical community, Republican Dean Ohlman, who would be one of the first evangelicals to join the organized creation care movement in the 1980s, decided to stick with Gerald Ford. But Jim Jewell, who would later spend many years as Chuck Colson's chief-of-staff before becoming gradually involved in creation care with the EEN's ECI, was so enthusiastic about Carter that he "delayed [his] final college work to become part of his Iowa campaign staff."[45]

His victory notwithstanding, Carter received much less of the evangelical vote than his predecessor had in 1972 (51 percent as opposed to Nixon's 84 percent). He hardly appointed any fellow believers as officials in his administration. Once in office, he also "turned out to be less a born-again Christian than a born-again liberal," alienating evangelicals even more over the course of his presidency with his stances on abortion, homosexuality, and school prayer. Most detrimental to his support from within Evangelicalism, however, was Carter's association with the Internal Revenue Service's

(IRS) plan to revoke the tax-exempt status of private schools that did not comply with the goals of racial desegregation.[46]

Beginning in the mid-1960s, many fundamentalist and evangelical churches had established private schools to cater to their congregants' children. Although some of those schools were indeed established to circumvent desegregation, "they were never simply refuges from racial integration." More encompassing, they were designed as Christian alternatives to the public school system, which evangelicals deemed necessary in order to shelter their offspring from irreligiosity and youth hedonism. Apart from its financial and racial implications, conservative Christians thus also considered the IRS plan as undue governmental expansion. Moreover, they perceived it as an attempt to further spread "secular humanism," their shorthand for a worldview devoid of God, meaning, and moral values. Although Carter had nothing to do with the proposed IRS ruling, which was based on a 1972 district court decision, he was nevertheless blamed for it by those who disliked his policies.[47]

The concept of "secular humanism" as a worldview that has no place for God and holds that only "man is the measure of all things" was successfully popularized by evangelical public theologian Francis A. Schaeffer (1912–1984) as the new ideological enemy of evangelicals in the latter half of the twentieth century. Born in Philadelphia, Pennsylvania, in 1912, Schaeffer is perhaps best known for starting L'Abri Fellowship in the Swiss Alps together with his wife, Edith. Set up as a "shelter from the pressures of a relentlessly secular 20th century" (and at times resembling a hippie commune rather than a religious study center), L'Abri has attracted streams of international seekers and walkers of the Christian way of life since 1955. Convinced that Christianity was objectively true and permeated all aspects of life, in the United States Schaeffer "almost singlehandedly alerted evangelicals to the dangers and virtues of art, philosophy, and music, [and thus to] realms of life previously neglected by born-again Protestants." The populist Religious Right movement that would arise toward the end of the Carter presidency had "very few systematic thinkers" and among them "only two of cross-denominational importance." Schaeffer was the more popular and publicly visible of the two.[48]

From Schaeffer's point of view, secular humanism was the root cause for America's moral decadence. Evidence of secular humanism's destructive influence was the issue of abortion in particular, which divided those who believed in the sanctity of life from those who did not, and which Schaeffer thus "specifically targeted" in the book and companion film series *Whatever Happened to the Human Race?* (1979). With his conviction of their "cobelligerency" in a secular and immoral culture, Schaeffer sought to inspire both American fundamentalists and evangelicals to action in order to curtail the rampant disregard for life and the family, and the moral corruption of a nation originally erected upon Christian principles. According to conservative political strategist and Heritage Foundation cofounder Paul Weyrich (1942–2008), it was this threat of secular humanism, tied to the IRS plan to revoke the tax-exempt status of racially discriminating schools, that galvanized the Christian community in the late 1970s more than any of the specific socio-moral hot button issues.[49]

If the evangelicals and fundamentalists of the 1970s mostly feared the spread of secular humanism and the federal government's intrusion into their separative educational institutions, to American business leaders "the rise of the environmental regulatory state" was an unwelcome additional restraint to the free market system, especially at a time when America's economy was in the grip of an oil crisis. Jimmy Carter aggravated both religious and corporate interests. Not only was he too libertine, progressive, and falsely associated with the IRS plan to revoke the tax-exempt status of evangelical and fundamentalist schools; perhaps worse, he also did not appear to be a believer in unlimited economic growth and the environmentally detrimental discourse of Manifest Destiny, which jibes in many ways with evangelical ideas about the divine provenance of America's resources. Moreover, Carter seemed to lack a quintessentially American "vision of abundance," instead promoting sacrifice, discomfort, gasoline rationing, and higher energy prices. In short, Carter followed a "conservation, not consumption" strategy as reaction to the energy shortages of the 1970s and dared the nation to face limits, problems, and "mistaken idea[s]," among them the understanding of "freedom" as "the right to grasp for ourselves some advantage over others." Americans did not respond well to his message of malaise. Consequently, the Iran hostage crisis (November 4, 1979–January 20, 1981) sealed Carter's fate as the only one-term Democratic president of the twentieth century, all while Ronald Reagan's jolly embrace of American exceptionalism won the day.[50]

## THE RISE OF THE RELIGIOUS RIGHT

Put in perspective with the rising tide of political conservatism, abortion may not have been the definitive issue that sparked the formation of the Religious Right, which lobbied hard to get Reagan elected in 1980 and 1984. Appalled by the advances of secular humanism and disturbed by "moral shocks" such as the Supreme Court's *Roe v. Wade* (1973) decision, however, evangelicals and fundamentalists had gradually become more open toward political involvement and social activism. In addition, they were also consciously pulled into a more organized engagement by, among others, New Right strategists such as Paul Weyrich, who were eager to utilize the already existing communications networks within the evangelical and fundamentalist Christian community for a larger movement on the political Right.[51]

One activist account that is equally fascinating and illuminating when it comes to the convergence of Christian moral grievances and conservative political strategy in the early days of the Religious Right movement is Richard Viguerie's *The New Right: We're Ready to Lead* (1980). Here Viguerie (1933–), another leading conservative activist and pioneer of direct mail methods, emphasizes the importance of single-issue groups and coalition politics for the future success of the conservative movement. As he writes about Weyrich's efforts, "Paul is constantly looking for new groups to add to the growing New Right coalition—anti-abortion groups, veterans' groups, religious groups, tax groups, small businessmen, etc. He believes that family-oriented issues will be the key issues of the 1980s." For co-optation, as Weyrich understood all too well, is not possible with just about any communications network. As sociologist Jo Freeman explains, "To be cooptable, it must be composed of like minded people whose backgrounds, experiences, or location in the social structure make them receptive to the ideas of a specific new movement."[52]

That there was a large pool of like-minded Americans, and that evangelicals and fundamentalists fell into that category, was not doubted by Weyrich and other New Rightists. Reality had proven that those who eventually came together on the religiopolitical Right in the late 1970s and early 1980s were the ones the Rev. Jerry Falwell identified as "the backbone" of America in the foreword to Viguerie's book. Namely, "those citizens who are pro-family, pro-moral, pro-life, and pro-American, who have integrity and believe in hard work, those who pledge allegiance to the flag and proudly sing our national anthem." Weyrich would call them the "moral majority," a name that stuck. Giving up his previously held culturally and politically separatist stance to some degree but nonetheless sticking to a fundamentalist jeremiad, Falwell lamented that for too long those moral citizens had "stood by and watched as godless, spineless leaders have brought our nation floundering to the brink of death." Now, at the turn of the 1980s, it was imperative for them to band together to fight depravity, decadence, and demoralization, and to "guide America back to a position of stability and greatness." From today's perspective, we could call Falwell Sr.'s vision for America MAGA 1.0.[53]

To accomplish this goal Falwell put considerable energy into various organizing efforts throughout the 1980s, most notably the registration of millions of new Christian voters. Readily, Weyrich and others around him lent their support in the founding processes of some of the premier Religious Right movement organizations, such as the Christian Voice (1978), the Religious Roundtable (1979), and the Moral Majority (1979). Through Falwell's engagement, not only with the Moral Majority but also with his television program *Old Time Gospel Hour* and his "I love America" rallies, he functioned as an important bridge between fundamentalism and Evangelicalism. Not only that, but like the neo-evangelicals in the 1940s and 1950s, Falwell initially shocked other, more separatist-oriented fundamentalists with his espousal of Francis Schaeffer's thesis that their "co-belligerency" in a secular and immoral culture justified a more inclusive orientation across theological discrepancies within American Protestantism. Eventually this strategy bore fruit within quite a remarkable segment of Christianity in America. By 1982 it did not appear to make much sense anymore to distinguish between evangelicals and fundamentalists as two separate sociological categories.[54]

As a movement of "cultural defence" and an advocate of a particular conservative ideology and lifestyle, the New Right and the Religious Right did more than bring evangelicals and fundamentalists closer together again on the basis of a common political agenda largely focused on Judeo-Christian values and morality. Also, and in a rather exceptional manner, conservative Protestants, Catholics, Jews, and other religious groups joined and eventually produced what Putnam and Campbell call the "coalition of *most* of the religious." The glue that has held this coalition together has been two social issues in particular—abortion and homosexuality—and ever since Ronald Reagan's presidency, this coalition has become strongly aligned with the Republican Party.[55]

## RONALD REAGAN, CONSERVATIVE BACKLASH, AND ALTERNATIVE ENVIRONMENTAL DISCOURSES

A strong advocate of conservation, alternative energy sources, and independence from Middle Eastern oil, Jimmy Carter installed thirty-two U.S.-made solar hot-water panels on the roof of the White House during his presidency. But this symbolic environmentalist gesture barely survived the Reagan Revolution, perhaps most tellingly in the shape of a Swiss documentary film entitled *A Road Not Taken* (2010). After the roof of the White House was resurfaced in 1986, Reagan refused to have Carter's solar panels reinstalled in an equally symbolic manner. Salvaged from a dusty federal warehouse by the director of a financially struggling environmental college in Maine in the 1990s, a small number of the original panels were eventually turned into educational artifacts. In 2010 one of these was sent to a science museum in China.[56]

If 1976 was "the year of the evangelicals," then the year of Reagan's election for president was "the year of evangelical politics." A crucial event in the history of modern Evangelicalism and the politicization of conservative religion, Reagan's victory over Carter was significant for the development of the culture wars far beyond the 1980s. Moreover, a "polarizing figure in himself," Reagan set the course for further fragmentation, including the disparate political alignments of Evangelicalism with the Republican Party and environmentalism with the Democratic Party. While evangelicals mobilized to form the Religious Right and largely sided with Reagan during the 1980s, the environmental movement experienced a backlash after its golden years of environmental legislation, which ushered in a "third wave" of environmentalism in the United States.[57]

Starting with Ronald Reagan's presidency, political conservatives and corporate America—which favored reduced government, states' rights, and free market capitalism—heavily and successfully opposed environmental regulation. As governor of California Reagan had a record of deriding environmentalists as exaggerating "doom-cryers," opposed to both economic progress and freedom. His "blithe nonchalance" toward environmental problems extended "toward the scientific facts about them," thus setting an early example for the Republican dismissal of scientific expertise. During the presidential election campaign in 1980, Reagan did not keep his antienvironmental sentiments a secret and openly sympathized with the interests of business leaders, loggers, ranchers, and miners. He also actively courted conservative Christians. Once in office, he filled executive positions crucial for the furtherance of a federal green agenda with right-wing officials skeptical of the magnitude of environmental problems and opposed to governmental regulation, such as evangelical Secretary of the Department of the Interior James G. Watt (1938–) and EPA Administrator Anne Gorsuch Burford (1942–2004).[58]

Environmentalists were appalled. Alarmed by Reagan's antienvironmental rhetoric during his election campaign, the leaders of the ten most powerful environmental organizations in the United States met shortly after the president's inauguration to discuss the future course of the environmental movement. During their meeting they agreed to combine forces by forming the "Group of Ten," which originally consisted of the Kendall Foundation, the Sierra Club, the National Audubon Society, the Natural Resources Defense Council, Friends of the Earth, the Environmental Policy Institute, the Izaak Walton League, the Wilderness Society, the Environmental Defense Fund, and the National Wildlife Federation. As a collective strategy they consented to spending most of their resources on lobbying the environmentally unfriendly administration in Washington. The "Environmental Decade" of the 1970s thus "became the opening chapter in an ongoing political contest."[59]

During the 1980s the Group of Ten became "synonymous with mainstream environmentalism and represented what the American media meant when they referred to the environmental movement." Membership in the national organizations surged during that time, not only due to environmentalists' discontent with the Reagan administration, but also due to fears of environmental disasters stoked by concrete incidents such as the Chernobyl nuclear power plant accident in Ukraine (1986) and the Exxon Valdez oil spill in Alaska (1989). Provoked to counteractive insider lobbying, the ensuing professionalization of the larger national environmental organizations made them a regular part of the policy process. However, it also chipped away their revolutionary edge. In addition, and much to the dismay of many grassroots activists and more radical environmentalists, the Group of Ten formed alliances with major corporations like Amoco, Coca-Cola, and Exxon, thereby undermining the grassroots efforts of smaller environmental interest groups.[60]

On a discursive level, four alternatives to Reform Environmentalism have arisen from the 1970s onward: Deep Ecology, Environmental Justice, Ecofeminism, and Ecotheology. In particular the "deep ecologists" have been very critical of the "shallow" environmentalism of mainstream organizations. Drawing on the writings of Norwegian philosopher Arne Naess (1912–2009), they charged that the larger environmental organizations had been neglecting the moral and ethical dimensions of their cause. Deep Ecology's goal has thus been to achieve a radically biocentric understanding of the human–nature relationship. Hence, deep ecologists have not merely advocated preservation, but also the restoration of complete ecosystems. Moreover, Deep Ecology groups like the "nonhierarchical 'anti-organization'" Earth First!, founded in 1980, have not shied away from employing drastic tactics, such as tree spiking and other types of "monkeywrenching" or "ecotage." In the western United States, where much of the land is owned by the government, many battles between environmentalists and economic interests have ensued over matters of biodiversity, land development, and the extraction of natural resources in wilderness areas since the 1980s.[61]

Compared to Deep Ecology, the Environmental Justice discourse that arose as another alternative to Reform Environmentalism has not primarily focused on injustices done to nature by humans. Rather, it has drawn attention to the degree to which environmental degradation and health risks, such as toxic wastes and pollution, threaten and affect mainly the poor and racial or ethnic minorities. As environmental justice advocates charge, in a society based on the domination of humans over other humans, the poor and minorities are exploited in the same way as nature is. Employing strong notions of justice and environmental racism, this discourse appears closer to the civil rights movement than to mainstream environmentalism, especially since many historically black and mainline Protestant churches have played a role in shaping it. We will therefore return to Environmental Justice's more ecotheological variant in chapter 2.[62]

Similar to environmental justice advocates, ecofeminists have linked the control and exploitation of nature by humans to the control and exploitation of women by men. Feminist environmental activism thus strives to liberate both nature and women by changing human consciousness and moving toward a nature-based spirituality. Like the fourth alternative to Reform

Environmentalism—Ecotheology—Ecofeminism, Environmental Justice, and Deep Ecology strongly emphasize the societal, moral/ethical, and spiritual dimensions of environmental degradation.[63]

Before we move on to the discourse of Ecotheology and a more specific convergence of environmental concern and evangelical religion, the diversity of the environmental movement in terms of movement organizations and discursive frames needs to be stressed again. Likewise, the diversity within Evangelicalism needs to be stressed as well, not to mention its internal ideological fluidity despite an overall strong partisan alignment with the Republican Party since the 1980s.

While Brulle's model of environmental discourses as counter-narratives to Manifest Destiny helps to discern the major shades of green that have colored the American environmentalist imagination since the late nineteenth century (including the evangelical stewardship or creation care ethic detailed in the next chapter), we have to keep in mind that in reality there are many shades of green, and that they also blend into one another. From a critical theory perspective, this diversity may be detrimental to the overall political and cultural effectiveness of the environmental movement, because so far it has hampered the establishment of an encompassing "master frame." Viewed through an evolutionary lens, though, discursive, organizational, and ideological diversity are positive qualities of a mature advocacy community, whose survival depends upon "breadth and variety." Despite internal divergences and inner competition with American environmentalism, this variety has ensured the movement's stability. A few organizational deaths here and there notwithstanding, so far, the movement has not experienced a shortage of "rebels [and] frustrated believers determined to challenge the status quo by starting their own groups." Most likely, this is not going to change in the future either, thus guaranteeing the endurance of environmental values in American society and culture.[64]

That said, the drawing of different conclusions from different theoretical approaches to social movement activism should not distract us further. What is surprising, especially from the vantage point of our current moment in American history and politics, is that since 1979 evangelical Christians have been among those "rebels [and] frustrated believers determined to challenge the status quo by starting their own groups," and this in defiance of the political and cultural polarization that has increasingly pitted evangelicals and environmentalists against each other since then. True to their faith, though, evangelicals turned to theology before they embarked on the founding of specifically evangelical environmental organizations.

# 2
# THEOLOGY FIRST!

*The Beginnings of Green Evangelicalism*

With respect to virtually any issue, evangelicals instinctively turn to the Bible for insight and direction. Indeed, for evangelicals the Bible is not just one of the places to go—along with tradition, reason, and experience—when seeking knowledge of God or guidance on how to live. The Bible is the source and norm that takes precedence over all others. To use the classical terminology, the Bible is the *norma normans*—the ultimate norm, that which trumps all other authorities.

Steven Bouma-Prediger[1]

Then God blessed them, and God said to them, "Be fruitful and multiply; fill the earth and subdue it; have dominion over the fish of the sea, over the birds of the air, and over every living thing that moves on the earth."

Genesis 1:28 NKJV

## CHRISTIANITY AND ECO-CRISIS: THE "WHITE THESIS" AND THE DISCOURSE OF ECOTHEOLOGY

When the environmental movement became visible as a mass movement on the first Earth Day in 1970, many organizers and supporters hailed the inclusive quality of environmentalism and its ability to cut across ideological and social divisions. Even intellectual conservative leader Russell Kirk, who could hardly be called an environmentalist, wrote in 1971, "The issue of environmental quality is one which transcends traditional political boundaries. It is a cause which can attract, and very sincerely, liberals, conservatives, radicals, reactionaries, freaks, and middle-class straights."[2]

Religious voices, in particular those speaking in an unmistakably evangelical tone, however, were largely missing among those speaking out against environmental degradation in the 1960s and 1970s. *The Environmental Handbook* for the first Earth Day, copublished by Sierra Club dissident David Brower's newly founded organization, Friends of the Earth (1969), provided a text giving one explanation for this conspicuous absence: historian Lynn White Jr.'s essay "The Historical Roots of Our Ecologic Crisis" (1967) blamed none other than the Western world's Judeo-Christian heritage for the globally evolving eco-crisis.[3]

In a rather simplistic but compelling "update" of Max Weber's linkage between Protestantism and capitalism, White posed that human ecology was "deeply conditioned by beliefs about our nature and destiny—that is, by religion." He then pointed to the Judeo-Christian creation story, the dominion mandate in the book of Genesis, and the values of medieval Christianity, which had destroyed pagan animism and thus desacralized the natural world. Hence, White concluded that Christianity, "the most anthropocentric religion the world has seen," had not only established a dualism of man and nature but also insisted that it was "God's will that man exploit nature for his proper ends." In conjunction with the Western world's advances in technology and science, which White saw rooted in Judeo-Christian teleology and its "faith in perpetual progress," this "exploitive attitude" was responsible for the ecologic crisis the world was facing by the mid-twentieth century. In short, the ecologically unconcerned discourse of Manifest Destiny in America was an outgrowth of the Judeo-Christian religious tradition. According to this reasoning, it is no small wonder that in particular those who took the teachings of the Bible literally were not a more visible presence in the environmental movement at the time.[4]

White was not the first to accuse Judeo-Christianity of anthropocentrism and antagonism to nature. Neither was he the only one drawing a connection between the Christian faith and eco-crisis in the 1960s and 1970s. Still, the "White thesis" caused a stir among historians, theologians, social scientists, and environmentalists. Many accepted—or empirically verified—White's line of argument as a plausible explanation either for the desolate condition of the environment and Western environmental ethics, or for Christians' lack of environmental concern and activism. Some remarked that things were actually worse than White had pointed out because he had failed to mention Christianity's "pervasive otherworldliness" and the "traditional Christian view of wilderness as a cursed land," which only reinforced Christianity's ecologically destructive potential. Others, however, also criticized White's generalizations and attempted to modify or refute his claims, either with social-scientific studies or from theological and other perspectives. Even now, references to White are still common and seem almost inevitable when we talk about the intersection of religion and ecology.[5]

There are several reasons for the salience of the "White thesis." One of them may be the ambiguity of the text itself, as much as the overall ambivalence of the studies conducted to test White's hypothesis. Most importantly, though, White did more than charge Judeo-Christianity and its followers with "a huge burden of [potential ecologic] guilt." On the contrary, he contended with equal passion that religion held the key to solving the modern eco-crisis. "Since the roots of our trouble are so largely religious," reasoned White, *the remedy must be essentially religious, whether we call it that or not.*" Hence, White is largely credited with sparking the discourse of Ecotheology—the (re)examination of faith through the lens of ecology and environmental responsibility—with his thought-provoking thesis.[6]

To make his case for religion as a remedy to ecological degradation, White did not reject Christianity as an antienvironmental belief system per se, but mostly "the Christian axiom that nature has no reason for existence save to serve man." Alluding to a distorted quote by Ronald Reagan speaking before the Western Wood Products Association in San Francisco as gubernatorial candidate on March 12, 1966 ("If one had seen one redwood tree, one had seen them all"), White insisted, "To a Christian a tree can be no more than a physical fact. The whole concept of the sacred grove is alien to Christianity and to the ethos of the West." Even among "post-Christians," including Marxists, claimed White, this axiom was still "almost universally held." Therefore, the modern eco-crisis could not be solved by means of a rational and technological policy approach. Instead, a critical makeover of Western ideas about the human relationship to nature was crucially necessary: "What we do about ecology depends on our ideas of the man-nature relationship. More science and more technology are not going to get us out of the present ecologic crisis *until we find a new religion, or rethink our old one.*" Though White acknowledged that Eastern religions such as Zen Buddhism and Hinduism, for which the "beatniks and hippies" displayed a "sound instinct[ual]" affinity, could help Westerners improve their relationship with the natural world, he was "dubious of their vitality among us." Personally, he thus favored a rethinking of Christianity instead of cross-culturally adapting to—or creating—an entirely new belief system. For guidance on how to improve the man-nature relationship from within a Christian theological framework, White suggested turning to "the greatest spiritual revolutionary in Western history," St. Francis of Assisi (1181/1182–1226), because to St. Francis the virtue of humility had been closely linked to the idea of "democracy among God's creatures" instead of man's "monarchy over creation."[7]

Granted, not every adherent to the discourse of Ecotheology necessarily agrees with White's proposal of St. Francis "as a patron saint for ecologists" and his suggestion that the man–nature relationship should be rethought from within a Christian theological framework. In addition, the theological diversity *within* American Christianity makes it impossible to imagine a unified and generally agreed upon framework among Christian environmentalists since their differences in theology potentially provide for at least as many different ecotheologies. Consequently, in the aftermath of White's accusations, three basic "ethics" or "modes" of Ecotheology—reflecting the theological differences among the main branches of Christianity—began to emerge in America, which we shall address in more detail below.[8]

## EVANGELICAL REACTIONS TO THE "WHITE THESIS"

As believers in the ultimate truth and authority of the Bible, evangelicals perhaps felt even more accused and challenged by Lynn White than theologically less orthodox Christians. At least this would help explain the widespread reactions the "White thesis" triggered in evangelical and fundamentalist circles.[9]

Immediate responses came from *CT* and the American Scientific Affiliation (ASA). *CT* discussed White's arguments in some of its editorials and continued the debate in a conference financed by the Pew Charitable Trusts in May 1967. The participants in this conference were unwilling to accept White's blame but equally unable to reject the cultural mandate in the book of Genesis. They seemed open to a more moderate understanding of dominion along the lines of stewardship, however. Evangelical scientists affiliated with the ASA, a network founded in 1941 in order "to integrate, communicate, and facilitate properly researched science and theology in service to the Church and the scientific community," continued the debate in a panel discussion of White's essay in 1968. Here, panelists agreed that the problem of environmental degradation did not arise from the biblical text but rather from a misunderstanding of the dominion mandate. Properly understood, though, the Genesis command itself did not foster human exploitation of nature, according to ASA scientists.[10]

The growing public attention to ecological issues also led the NAE to publish its first-ever resolutions on the environment in 1970 and 1971. According to those, the NAE deemed the thoughtless destruction of the "God-ordained balance of nature" a "sin against God's creation." Therefore, the association pledged its "cooperation to any responsible effort to solve critical environmental problems and [its] willingness to support all proven solutions developed by competent authorities." Moreover, the NAE's constituency was asked to do the same. Hence, former NAE Vice President for Governmental Affairs Richard Cizik's turn toward the creation care movement in the beginning of the twenty-first century and his attempt to have the NAE support the ECI collectively cannot be regarded as a completely individual move without institutional precedent, as implied by the critiques leveled by his opponents.[11]

But just like the ECI more than thirty years later, the publication of White's essay in the handbook for the first Earth Day in 1970 sparked a series of outright dismissive responses among evangelicals as well. Anticipating some of the criticism the CA and its affiliates would later pronounce against environmentalism and the creation care movement, the *Christian Beacon* went so far as to condemn the entire environmental movement as "communist" and "anti-Christian." Interestingly, considering his subsequent role in mobilizing Jerry Falwell and other evangelicals and fundamentalists toward the formation of the Religious Right, it was no other than Francis Schaeffer who provided the first evangelical answer to the "White thesis" that went beyond blame-shifting and defending the teachings of the Bible, instead moving toward the formulation of an evangelical ecotheology.[12]

---

Although Schaeffer's *Pollution and the Death of Man* (1970) is the most encompassing and direct response to the "White thesis" penned by an evangelical in the 1970s, evangelical creation care advocates bemoan that this book, unlike Schaeffer's other works, has largely been "overlooked, or perhaps more correctly, ignored, as an aberration of an otherwise astute thinker."[13]

Equally convinced that worldviews have important social consequences, Schaeffer wholeheartedly agreed with White that human ecology was deeply conditioned by thoughts and beliefs, and thus by religion: "Men *do* what they *think*. Whatever their world view is, this is the thing which will spill over into the external world. This is true in every area, in student revolt and sociology, in all science and technology, as well as in the area of ecology." Citing the work of ornithologist and conservationist David B. Wingate on biodiversity loss related to DDT, and Tokyo's pollution problem specifically, Schaeffer neither questioned the scientific truth of ecological problems nor the reality of a (global) eco-crisis. Although he seemed quite utilitarian and more pragmatic in his ecological outlook than many reform environmentalists at the time, he nevertheless condemned modern "greed" and "haste"—and hence human sinfulness—as bearing some responsibility for environmental destruction. In addition, Schaeffer lamented the "death of 'joy' in nature" and the "death of nature itself." He did not refrain from connecting this death to the Darwinian worldview, though, *and* from simultaneously accusing fellow orthodox Christians of a similar joyless attitude toward the natural world.[14]

While Schaeffer agreed with White in many respects, however, he deemed "St. Francis's concept . . . that everything is equal and everything is spiritually autonomous" profoundly inadequate as a guiding concept for the reexamination of the human-nature relationship. Being a theologically conservative Christian, to Schaeffer the only solution to eco-crisis could be provided by the "Christianity of the Reformation" and a "genuine biblical view" of nature.[15]

A theologically correct view of nature, according to Schaeffer, could *not* dismiss man's "special and control role in nature." Nature, on the other hand, was valuable "not in itself autonomously" but because of its status as creation, and thus something that deserved the respect of its fellow human creatures. While both humans and nature were equal in this sense and bound by a "covenant of creation," only humans were created in the image of God, thus the cultural mandate in the book of Genesis could not be ignored. However, dominion was not to be exercised as exploitative domination. Instead, the cultural mandate had to be modified along the lines of the servant or stewardship model exemplified by Jesus' Parable of the Talents in Matthew 25:14-30. Schaeffer wrote, "Nature belongs to God, and we are to exercise our dominion over these things not as though entitled to exploit them, but as things borrowed or held in trust, which I am to use realising that they are not mine intrinsically. Man's dominion is under God's dominion and under God's domain." Hence, abuse or exploitation of nature was unbiblical. If the individual Christian did not act accordingly, he or she was "more wrong than the hippie who has no real basis for his feeling for nature and yet senses that man and nature should have a relationship beyond that of spoiler and spoiled."[16]

Despite some of his utilitarian reasons why modern Christianity ought to care about matters of ecology, Schaeffer emphasized that to Christians environmentalism could neither be a biocentric nor a wholly anthropocentric endeavor. Rather, as evangelical ecotheologians and creation care activists would later stress as well, environmentalism had to be God-centered, because only a theocentric environmental vision could "do justice to the testimony of Scripture." Especially regarding the more ecologically sensitive—and less religiously inclined—younger generation that had come of age during the 1960s, Schaeffer added that evangelicals would do well if they accepted their biblical responsibility "to help man save the earth." Not only was the failure to do so an opportunity missed, but worse, a missed "evangelistic opportunity" at that.[17]

Apart from Schaeffer's book no other evangelical ecotheological monograph was published throughout the 1970s. Unlike the mainstream environmental movement, which was characterized by an upbeat grassroots activism and organizational expansion, no evangelical environmental organization emerged during the 1970s, and evangelical thinking about environmental problems decreased toward the end of the decade. Coincidentally or not, this decrease in evangelical concern correlates with a decline in public environmental concern. Moreover, chronologically it also correlates with an increasing ideological polarization of the American citizenry and the ascendancy of the Religious Right. The latter "neglected environmental matters altogether" and followed "the conservative and business-friendly orthodoxy of the Reagan administration" instead.[18]

## EVANGELICAL ACADEMICS AND THE INTELLECTUAL FOUNDATION OF CREATION CARE

The rise of the evangelical political Right notwithstanding, however, a small circle of evangelical academics kept attending to environmental issues throughout the 1970s and in the shadow of the Republican antienvironmental and pro-business climate of the 1980s. Among others, this group included philosopher Loren E. Wilkinson and several scientists affiliated with the ASA, who published scholarly articles in favor of environmentalism regularly in the organization's magazine, *The Journal of the American Scientific Affiliation* (now *Perspectives on Christian Science & Faith*). Most influential in the formulation of a biblically rooted "creation-care theology"—a need that had to be fulfilled sufficiently before evangelicals could become socially and politically more active with regard to the environment—was biologist Calvin B. DeWitt, whom his followers endearingly call the "grandfather" of creation care.[19]

DeWitt notes three specific events that constituted important pillars for the academic creation care movement of the 1980s: first, the publication of *Earthkeeping: Christian Stewardship of Natural Resources* (1980); second, the establishment of an environmental education program at the Au Sable Institute of Environmental Studies in Mancelona, Michigan; and third, Au Sable's Forum on Environmental Stewardship.[20]

The five authors who collaborated on the first edition of *Earthkeeping* were initially brought together in the late 1970s under the auspices of the Calvin Center for Christian Scholarship (CSSS), an affiliate of the evangelical Calvin College in Grand Rapids, Michigan. Scholars involved included DeWitt and Loren Wilkinson, and they came together from different academic disciplines to study the relationship between Christian stewardship and natural resources. *Earthkeeping* expanded Francis Schaeffer's ecotheological proposal with a more nonutilitarian understanding of nature, a concern with the health of the entire planet, and with an emphasis on "human-subduing-which-is-service." Furthermore, the authors showed distress about the fate of the poor and the fact that they suffered from environmental problems more than the affluent. In retrospect, *Earthkeeping* would turn out to be the book that "most clearly defined the evangelical environmental theology of the 1980s."[21]

The Au Sable Institute in rural northern Michigan, on the other hand, is largely regarded as "the first evangelical environmental organization" in the United States. Founded in 1961 and initially called Au Sable Trails Camp for Youth, the nonprofit used to be an evangelical science camp and biological field station for college students until oil was discovered on its premises in 1975. Somewhat paradoxically considering the problem of climate change and other environmental issues related to oil development, with the help of additional money from two oil wells, the trustees of Au Sable decided to broaden the camp's agenda in order to put a stronger emphasis on ecology and environmental stewardship. To assist them with this effort, Calvin DeWitt, professor of environmental studies at the University of Wisconsin–Madison, was hired as an adviser in 1979. Shortly thereafter, in 1980, the institution changed its name to the Au Sable Institute of Environmental Studies, redefined its goal to promote environmentalism among evangelicals by training students from Christian colleges, and appointed DeWitt as executive director.[22]

Starting in 1980, the institute also organized its first forum on ecotheology. While participants agreed on the need to confront a globally evolving eco-crisis from the perspective of faith, this first meeting was overall characterized by a lack of consensus regarding the differing eschatological and philosophical views of its participants. Nonetheless, subsequent forums were organized annually and "established Au Sable as the most consistent and fruitful source of evangelical reflection on environmental issues during the 1980s." Even though not all of the attendees had the same understanding of what an evangelical environmental ethic should entail, consensus grew over time, and a distinct evangelical stewardship ethic and creation care theology developed in consistency with the book *Earthkeeping*.[23]

## THE EVANGELICAL STEWARDSHIP ETHIC AND CREATION CARE THEOLOGY

The evangelical stewardship ethic and creation care theology that developed under the patronage of DeWitt's Au Sable Institute over the course of the 1980s is best illustrated by contrasting it with two other modes of Christian ecotheology that advanced during that time as well: "eco-justice" and "creation spirituality." According to Laurel Kearns, sociologist and research pioneer in green Evangelicalism, the trio reflects "the differences and tensions among conservative, mainline, and liberal Christian theologies." Whereas creation spirituality and environmental stewardship mark the theologically liberal and conservative borders of Christian environmentalism, respectively, the eco-justice ethic of the Protestant mainline largely adds environmental concerns to a long-established social justice frame. Of the three, only creation spirituality has been "more oriented to a possible new religion," while the evangelical stewardship ethic and creation care theology have been attempts to rethink the man–nature relationship and the ecologic crisis strictly from within a theologically conservative Christian framework.[24]

Rooted in conservative theology, the evangelical stewardship ethic begins with the Bible and reconsiders the dominion mandate in the book of Genesis (1:26-28) "as a divine charge to be good stewards and to take care of and protect (but not rule or perfect, as in older interpretations of the passage) the Creator's creation." Hence, degradation and damage done to God's creation are regarded as sinful. Judeo-Christian Scripture is not seen as the cause of eco-crisis, but rather secular arrogance, ignorance, and greed, which have led to noncompliance with the teachings of the Bible. Therefore, proponents of the Christian stewardship ethic display a "desire to return to an early modern world where they think biblical values were more central." Even though Christian stewards counter the otherworldliness and creationism of fundamentalists and other ideologically and theologically more conservative evangelicals, they are wary of New Age nature spirituality, biocentrism, and the postmodern scientific worldview. However, they do not categorically oppose science. Rather, they view science—especially biology—as a tool to understand and care for God's creation.[25]

Very much like the supporters of the evangelical stewardship ethic, proponents of creation spirituality are "discontent with the secularization and differentiation of modern society" and "disturbed by the separation between religion and science." Thus, they emphasize the need to change ideas and worldviews. For both environmental stewardship and creation spirituality proponents, "creation" is a crucial term and concept. Both view ecological problems as resulting from "the lack of a more immanent sense of God in creation" and Western Christians' preoccupation with human salvation. Furthermore, the book of Genesis is important to creation spirituality as well, although the theologically liberal proponents of this ecotheology oppose notions of human superiority. Additionally, creation spirituality does not rely on the Bible as a basis for an environmental ethic but is more influenced by medieval mysticism and cosmological physics.

According to creation spirituality the dualisms of the Western worldview—and *not* human sinfulness—are the cause of environmental problems. Human beings are seen as only one equally important part of the whole creation; hence, creation spirituality proponents assert that anthropocentrism must be overcome by self-reflection. Likewise, the constraints of traditional Christianity must be overcome by an attempt to form a progressive, postmodern, and ecologically conscious religion. This discrepancy in theology between Christian environmental stewardship and creation spirituality is very well reflected in the religious backgrounds of the two early spokespersons for the two respective ethics: Calvin DeWitt self-identifies as evangelical Protestant, whereas Matthew Fox, the "founder of creation spirituality," had been a Dominican Catholic until he was silenced by the Vatican and left the Catholic Church.

On the organizational level, both Christian stewardship and creation spirituality proponents "work from parachurch groups outside of potentially related denominations." The mainline Protestant eco-justice ethic, on the other hand, is "firmly located in the mainline denominations and denomination-specific special purpose groups." Like their predecessors spreading the social gospel in the beginning of the twentieth century, eco-justice advocates concentrate on making societal structures and institutions more just. Hence, in the environmental arena they emphasize the real cost of environmental damage and the equal distribution of resources. Therefore, the eco-justice ethic can appear more as a variety of the larger environmental justice discourse than a specific type of Christian ecotheology, although it may be too faith-based and not political enough for some of the more secular adherents of the environmental justice movement.[26]

As much as this model is still helpful to distinguish three major currents within the broader discourse of Christian Ecotheology, it needs to be emphasized that: it is based on ideal-types of ecotheological frames emerging in the late 1980s; the discursive borders separating these frames have not been impervious; and there has been no consensus among Protestants on the meaning of the term "stewardship." Evangelicals around Calvin DeWitt and the Au Sable Institute may have considered "stewardship" along the lines of duty, "earthkeeping," and "caring;" thus, DeWitt speaks of a specific evangelical "creation-care theology" as the basis for evangelical environmental activism. Evangelicals affiliated with the CA, on the other hand, use the stewardship label primarily to justify their supposedly more "prudent" free market approach to environmentalism (see chapter 5). Furthermore, the Protestant mainline has not been restricted to the eco-justice position and neither does the creation care movement lack a justice component, which we shall see in the following chapters. Likewise, many mainline Protestants adhere to the stewardship ethic as well, although they tend to have a more celebratory and enthusiastic attitude toward nature than theologically more conservative Protestants. The latter have been—and still are—very cautious not to forget God within the man-nature relationship and not to confuse their caring for creation with nature worship.[27]

## EVANGELICALS, ENVIRONMENTALISM, AND THE POLITICAL AND CULTURAL CLIMATE OF THE 1980s

Whereas the evangelical Left of the 1970s and 1980s was generally supportive of the concept of environmental stewardship and appreciative of the budding creation care movement, evangelical environmentalists were not actively supported by more conservative leaders from within the larger evangelical community, especially during the Reagan years. Francis Schaeffer's ecotheological treaty notwithstanding, only a few evangelical public leaders accepted the reality and problematics of eco-crisis and acknowledged environmentalism as an issue needing to be dealt with. In his book *Approaching Hoofbeats: The Four Horseman of the Apocalypse* (1983), Billy Graham, for example, expressed that despite God's plan for the ultimate end of the world, evangelicals should not only concentrate on saving souls but also do what they could regarding environmental problems. Likewise, in 1986, Carl F. H. Henry told the International Council on Biblical Inerrancy, "No less than to the commission to preach redemptive good news worldwide, the believer must respond to the divine call to apply to the world the doctrine of creation and preservation of the universe and of mankind's stipulated role of stewardship." Most conservative Protestants outside the small circle of evangelicals actively involved in shaping the discursive foundation of the creation care movement, however, were either not responsive to environmental issues or simply denounced them.[28]

The latter—who seemed to be mostly of a more fundamentalist orientation and included President Reagan's Secretary of the Interior James G. Watt (1938–)—derided wilderness protection and environmental controls because, as critics charged, their other-worldly eschatology provided a compelling theological rationale for the exploitation of natural resources: if the world was going to end in destruction soon anyway, why even worry about environmental degradation and ecological sustainability? Although Watt has often been misquoted as saying, "After the last tree is felled, Christ will come back"—as if Christian fundamentalists saw the possibility of ushering in the second coming by recklessly engaging in premeditated acts of "divine destruction"—the original statement Watt made connecting his faith to his environmental outlook during a briefing before the House Interior and Insular Affairs Committee on February 5, 1981, does not exactly bespeak of a very ecologically sensitive perspective either. As Watt put it: "I do not know how many future generations we can count on before the Lord returns, whatever it is we have to manage with a skill to leave the resources needed for future generations." At best this statement displays a utilitarian embrace of conservation; at worst it points toward Watt's affiliation with the so-called wise use movement.[29]

The wise use movement developed out of the Sagebrush Rebellion in the western United States in the early 1980s. Putting a strong emphasis on states' and property rights, its supporters have been in favor of a "wise" but market-driven use of natural resources as opposed to environmental regulation. While the wise use rhetoric has drawn "on private militia, conservative Christian, and right-wing doctrines," the Religious Right increasingly promoted the importance of free markets for economic growth and societal welfare during the 1980s, and thus re-invoked John O'Sullivan's nineteenth-century understanding of America's Manifest Destiny. Even though Watt, who was an alleged supporter of the Sagebrush Rebellion, served as secretary of the interior for a short time only, the media readily accepted him as a compelling example of evangelicals' other-worldly unconcern with environmental issues. Within the evangelical community, on the other hand, "Watt was able to use these portrayals as proof that he was being persecuted for his faith rather than his environmental policies, thereby encouraging religious conservatives to view environmentalists as the enemies of Christianity."[30]

---

While end-time thinking and a fundamentalist, premillennial dispensationalist perspective may foster antienvironmental attitudes and behaviors, the Reagan evangelicals of the 1980s viewed environmentalism as dangerously enmeshed with pantheism, panentheism, and/or neo-pagan spirituality, thus fostering theological and spiritual corruption. With the controversy surrounding James Watt and the further rise of the New Age movement, a 1970s debate about the negative influence of New Age ideas was thus revived in conservative Christian circles, promoting the image of environmentalism as the movement of "the new pagans who worship trees and sacrifice people."[31]

Not very coherent and eclectically mixing several strands of faith, the New Age movement includes spiritually libertarian seekers who emphasize holism and the self, and who experience their being as connected to the world and to other human and nonhuman beings by an all-permeating divinity. To a great degree, New Age ideas about immanence overlap with neo-pagan theology, and at times it is difficult to discern between the New Age and neo-paganism. A contemporary "version of American nature religion," the New Age movement displays a strong affinity to ecology and the environmental movement. Like environmentalism, New Age and neo-pagan ideas date back to the nineteenth century, and to some extent all three movements can be seen as spiritual reactions to modernity and materialism.[32]

Concerned about cosmological healing and reconciliation as well, however, New Agers "had also aligned themselves with evangelical and social gospel themes that invoked a sense of collective moral responsibility." As it was growing in popularity, evangelicals thus increasingly perceived the New Age movement as a threatening alternative to their beliefs. Whether the evangelical fear of the New Age movement was proportional to the actual size of the movement or not, evangelical environmentalists have thus had to draw a clear discursive boundary between their ecotheology and New Age spirituality since the beginning of the creation care movement.[33]

An early impetus for this kind of boundary drawing was the publication of Constance Cumbey's book *Hidden Dangers of the Rainbow: The New Age Movement and Our Coming Age of Barbarism* (1983). A lawyer from Detroit, Cumbey strongly condemned the environmental movement, including its developing evangelical shade of green, as a movement of neo-pagans and New Age adherents whose aim was to create the "New World Religion" of the Antichrist. A few years later, Berit Kjos, a mother deeply concerned about New Age ideas permeating American culture and the public school system, would follow suit with *Your Kid and the New Age* (1990) and *Under the Spell of Mother Earth* (1992). The latter also condemns environmentalism and includes a short chapter on "How to Live Life Free from Demonic Oppression." Here, Kjos vividly illustrates what it means for more fundamentalist evangelicals to view themselves as being caught in "spiritual warfare" and exposed to "Satan's timeless bait" of "untamed lifestyles, hypnotic meditations, spiritism, various forms of divination, witchcraft techniques, and other occult forms of empowerment." Although books like Kjos' and Cumbey's may seem overblown if not bizarre to more secular audiences, in particular *Hidden Dangers of the Rainbow* was popular among conservative evangelicals during the 1980s. Evangelical environmentalists thus responded directly to Cumbey's accusations by discussing her book and creation care's association with New Age heresies during the Au Sable forum of 1984.[34]

During said forum, *Earthkeeping* editor Loren Wilkinson uttered caution about the possibility of New Age ideas potentially influencing evangelicals' environmental thinking as well. Even though evangelical environmentalists had derived their creation care theology from the Bible, what had triggered the evangelical engagement with environmental issues first had largely been "an almost unavoidable, irresistible cultural pressure." Whereas environmentally concerned evangelicals may have derived "the gospel of stewardship" from the Bible, as evangelical leftist David Oates concurred, it had "nevertheless required two thousand years to incubate. It [had taken] the broodings of Wordsworth, Thoreau, Muir, Leopold, Carson, and Commoner to bring it to the light of day." To provocatively place the matter within the framework of H. R. Niebuhr: in the case of the budding evangelical environmental movement, *Christ* had not transformed culture; rather, culture had started transforming *Christ*.[35]

So, on the one hand, creation care advocates at Au Sable understood very well that the criticisms of Lynn White and Constance Cumbey were not entirely far-fetched, and that the Bible had not necessarily been the "natural" starting point for the evangelical path toward environmental engagement. On the other hand, though, their careful study of the Judeo-Christian Scriptures through a green lens had also revealed to them the biblically embedded stewardship ethic and creation care theology previously described. Once discovered, evangelicals concerned about the environment found this ethic too compelling to ignore. Moreover, they have not only refined and defended it discursively over the course of the past four decades; they have also attempted to institutionalize it with the help of the evangelical environmental parachurch organizations discussed in depth in the following chapters.

# 3
# PIONEER CREATION CARE ORGANIZATIONS

In building the movement called evangelical environmentalism, there were two great needs, and both have been increasingly met over its twenty-five years of development: First, was the need to build . . . a creation-care theology. This had to be rooted in a thorough and scholarly biblical theology. Most importantly, it also had to be coherent with an integrated scientific understanding of the biosphere and the world. . . .

Second, was the need to find ways to put this evangelical creation-care theology into practice. Already, many organizations were engaging the world in practical ways: World Vision and MAP International, for example. Needed beyond these practical evangelical agencies, however, was that of networking evangelical practitioners around matters of creation-care.

Calvin B. DeWitt[1]

As ecological awareness was rising in America, concerned Protestants were contemplating three different strategies to tackle environmental problems: concentrating on change through the church and religion, government action, and politics. The latter was "a choice permeated with ambivalence" considering the Protestant commitment to the separation of church and state, which has often been interpreted as a separation of religion and politics. In particular evangelicals have historically held this separation in high regard, and after the fundamentalist–modernist schism in the beginning of the twentieth century, their movement was largely characterized by a cautious apoliticism until the rise of the Religious Right. Although changes in the political opportunity structure of the late 1970s and early 1980s encouraged the political mobilization of conservative Christians—and likewise compelled mainstream environmental movement organizations to become more focused on lobbying activities in the nation's capital—evangelical environmentalists favored the church and educational institutions as agents of change at least until 1990. The first evangelical environmental organization to emerge in America, the Au Sable Institute of Environmental Studies, thus reflects this preference of environmental advocacy through education very well.[2]

Au Sable's concentration on the ecotheological foundation of creation care and the education of evangelical students notwithstanding, however, evangelical environmentalists eventually realized that a larger and more practically oriented network of organizations and individuals was necessary to put their creation care theology into action. Apart from Au Sable, additional organizations have thus been founded during and since the 1980s, some of which have turned to politics as a means of change as well. Although the first three evangelical environmental organizations in America, founded over the course of the 1980s, have been quite different from each other and have largely refrained from political engagement, collectively these pioneers nevertheless resonated with the cultural climate out of which they arose. Moreover as we shall see below, they have carved out a discursive space at the intersection of Evangelicalism and environmentalism that expanded Au Sable's aim to overcome the divide between Evangelicalism and (environmental) science, with, on the one hand, Floresta's blend of spiritual, environmental, and economic relief efforts, and on the other, with the CNF's (failed) attempt at establishing an evangelical outdoors club untainted by New Age spirituality.

## BRIDGING THE FAITH–SCIENCE DIVIDE: CALVIN DEWITT AND THE AU SABLE INSTITUTE OF ENVIRONMENTAL STUDIES (1979/1980–)

Its financial backing by oil money notwithstanding, the re-branding of "Au Sable Trails Camp for Youth" as "the Au Sable Institute of Environmental Studies" signified a growing concern and engagement with matters of ecology and environmentalism primarily in the circle of Reformed evangelical academia in the northeastern United States of the late 1970s and early 1980s. This is not to say that Au Sable's reach has been restricted to the northeast, or that creation care is only a regional and denominationally confined phenomenon. Au Sable has catered to a diverse body of students from a variety of evangelical colleges across the country; likewise, creation care advocates hail from different denominations within the evangelical tradition across the United States. Nonetheless, it is important to emphasize that the first evangelical environmental organization in America was an educational institution that emerged at the intersection of Reformed theology and the natural sciences and has concentrated on shaping the discursive foundation of creation care and on educating students as its primary means of advocacy.

Although it is not a typical environmental (interest) organization, Au Sable filled a space at the intersection of Evangelicalism and environmentalism that had been created by an interplay of need and pressure. For one, there was the cultural and scientific pressure on evangelical Christians to engage in environmental issues. And for another, there was the community internal need to have an organizational place where ecological issues could be addressed from a biblical point of view and where an evangelical ecotheology could be integrated into the environmental science curriculum of evangelical students. However, since institutions are not only shaped by means and opportunities but also by the worldviews, motivations, and personalities of their leaders and the decisions they make, Au Sable and the creation care theology that developed at the Institute can hardly be separated from the relentless activism of former executive director and creation care pioneer Calvin DeWitt. No leader within the creation care movement personifies the activist scholar at the intersection of evangelical faith and environmental science better than he does, and a closer look at DeWitt's intention and motivation not only helps us understand the mission of the Au Sable Institute and its niche within the creation care movement better, but also why science and Evangelicalism must not necessarily be in conflict with each other.

Calvin DeWitt was born in 1935 and holds a Ph.D. in zoology from the University of Michigan. Environmentally active since the 1970s, he has left a tremendous imprint on the Au Sable Institute, evangelical ecotheology, and other groups and leaders within the creation care movement. In addition, DeWitt has shaped the education of numerous students during his tenure as professor at the Gaylord Nelson Institute for Environmental Studies at the University of Wisconsin–Madison, from 1972 until 2011. Speaking to DeWitt, a gentle but passionate man who exudes an intriguing air of humility and authority, one can easily get the impression that a reverence for nature and life—and, therefore, an inevitable concern with ecological problems and the environment—must be a deeply ingrained personality trait of every person studying any of the natural sciences, *especially* if he or she is an evangelical Christian.

When asked if he had had some kind of conversion experience that turned him into an "environmentalist," a label he accepts as long as it is not attached to "all sorts of other presumptions," DeWitt simply stated, "I had a turtle in my backyard at the age of three, and I have always been doing this. I mean, there are some people who think you have to go through a conversion in order to do what you are doing, but it depends on where you start." Whereas most of the other leaders in the creation care movement have indeed experienced what they refer to as conversions to creation care—or have accepted their environmentalist calling and the corresponding label of identification much more reluctantly and gradually, as we shall see—DeWitt, in the words of his former chief operating officer at Au Sable, "was born this way."[3]

Adding to DeWitt's personal predisposition toward an intrinsic concern for the natural world were his training as a scientist and, contrary to the "epistemological warfare narrative" prevailing in Western academic thought, the religious context he was raised in and has stayed faithful to throughout his life. As he emphasizes, the "world-and-life-view" that has compelled him "to love science and to practice joyful stewardship" has been profoundly shaped by the Reformed tradition, especially by the "two-books theology" derived from The Confession of Faith (or The Belgic Confession) of 1561. Here, in the oldest of the doctrinal standards of the Christian Reformed Church, the two means by which God is known are described as God's word and God's creation. Both Scripture and the text of creation thus reveal God in their own fashion. Creation—this "most elegant book" is how The Confession of Faith describes it—must, therefore, be safeguarded and kept, according to DeWitt, and not trashed, destroyed, or otherwise dominated. Since its "creatures, great and small" are "letters" expressing God's "eternal power and divinity," biodiversity loss and species extinction have been especially troubling and lifelong environmental concerns of DeWitt's. And since the spiritual and intellectual transition from Puritanism to the transcendentalist movement of the nineteenth century was rather gradual, it is not surprising that DeWitt sees himself as being kindred in spirit to preservationist pioneer and Sierra Club founder John Muir, whom he explicitly refers to as "another reader of the two books."[4]

To DeWitt, however, Scripture cannot be forgotten over the reading of the book of creation, as some charge had been the case for Muir. The Bible is not a book that compels believers to adopt an exploitative attitude toward nature, as Lynn White had claimed; instead, in DeWitt's view, it is a source of "wonderfully ecological" texts, provided that both creation and the Bible are read "coherently," meaning "*within* each and *between* the two." Only such a coherent reading then "fosters a conscious and deliberate world-and-life-view that seeks and finds a vocation of service to both science and faith . . . [and thus] a loving care for creation that is rooted in science and guided by ethics."[5]

According to DeWitt's understanding, science then becomes a tool that can help the believer better understand God *and* care for creation. Consequently, the scientist plays a special support role in the service of "the shepherd," or Jesus Christ. "As the shepherd seeks to lead," writes DeWitt in one of his numerous articles on the topic, "the scientist helps read the lettres, helps the image bearers once again to behold and wonder, helping us to ponder the works of God, to understand the degradation and destruction, to understand creation care."[6]

Neither science nor the stewardship ethic alone are sufficient in themselves, though. Both need to be tied to praxis, or "a proper understanding of living rightly in the world." Moreover, the three ought to be "ligated to form a science-ethics-praxis triad." If any ligament of this triad is severed, the result may be "a science unconstrained by ethics," "an ethics . . . uninformed about the material world," or "a praxis cut free from science and ethics"—all types of brokenness that make a wholesome and morally right life on earth impossible. For DeWitt, keeping this triad together is thus "a principal responsibility of religion and religious people," which evangelicals have so far failed to fulfill on a large scale.[7]

---

If movements are created and held together by "a reasonably coherent story about why what is wrong is wrong and what can be done about it," creation care movement leaders like Calvin DeWitt are certainly the ones who play a crucially influential role in specifying the reasons that have led into—and the strategies and tactics that will lead away from—eco-crisis. According to DeWitt, "two great divides" in America have so far hindered the larger evangelical community from engaging in a scientifically grounded and ethics-based creation care praxis at large—and thus have also impeded the development of a larger evangelical environmental movement. The first is "the divide between science and evangelicalism"; and the second is "the divide of 'people vs. the environment.'"[8]

The first divide between science and Evangelicalism began to form with the publication of Charles Darwin's *On the Origin of Species* in 1859. This divide deepened considerably with the Scopes Trial in the beginning of the twentieth century but was "temporarily bridged" in the early days of the modern environmental movement with Rachel Carson's *Silent Spring* (1962) and Francis Schaeffer's *Pollution and the Death of Man* (1970). In 1979, however, the divide "reappeared" with the rise of Jerry Falwell's Moral Majority, which DeWitt calls "a movement that helped 'burn' whatever remained of the bridge that had spanned this science-evangelical divide." Since then, this divide has persisted and is perhaps most clearly noticeable by the ongoing (young-Earth) creationism versus evolution debates in America.[9]

In addition to and as a "consequence of the first divide" between faith and science, a second "divide of 'people vs. the environment'" began to develop with the "poor replacement" of the term "creation" by "environment." This "linguistic divide" introduced by the modern environmental movement has, according to DeWitt, allowed for an unfortunate dichotomy of people and the environment. Or, to make a reference to *Pollution and the Death of Man* that DeWitt does not explicitly make, has discursively broken the "covenant of creation": whereas the term "creation" united people and their surroundings, making it obvious that both were dependent upon each other (and upon their creator), the term "environment" semantically—and thus spiritually—separated people from their surroundings (and thus from their creator).[10]

As a result of these two interwoven divides, DeWitt laments, evangelicals largely followed evangelists like Jerry Falwell, who excluded "the creation, the Creator, and caring for creation from their preaching and teaching" throughout the 1980s. Those evangelicals who followed the agenda of the Religious Right focused on people and families only and "quite unintentionally, helped bring about the decline and disappearance" of the term "creation." Thus, what has remained of the terminology due to the semantic shift surrounding the originally holistic understanding of "creation" is the term "creationist," a designation for a person who holds a certain perspective on the origins of life as opposed to a term that designates a person who cares for all of creation. In addition, the separation this shift created between people and the environment triggered the question of which was more important. Small wonder that family-oriented evangelicals automatically sided with the people side of the divide.[11]

The divide of people versus the environment may become especially apparent in culture war battles during which conservative Christians charge that environmentalists are pro-birds but anti-babies. Or, for instance, when pro-life activists mockingly deride the "liberal logic" that supposedly holds that "trees have souls but unborn babies are just blobs of tissue." According to DeWitt's understanding, however, neither conservative Christians skeptical of the environmental movement nor environmentalists subsuming the needs of people to those of nature have been able to develop an adequate environmental science-ethics-praxis triad so far, a comprehensive need he thinks the creation care movement is able to fulfill.[12]

It may have been politically expedient for Religious Right leaders such as James Dobson and Jerry Falwell to concentrate on family issues, a focus that was encouraged by Paul Weyrich and other political strategists who tried to get evangelicals involved in politics in the late 1970s. Creation care advocates like DeWitt consider this perspective myopic and incomplete, though. In addition to what he wryly calls Dobson's "focus problem," DeWitt also views evangelical leaders on the political Right as more "fundamentalist" and less "scholarly" in their religious tradition and academic training than he is. Although denominationalism lost its significance in America, and the distinction among believers within the wider evangelical fold has been blurred due to their political mobilization along an ideological binary exacerbated by the two-party system, to evangelical insiders like DeWitt, the distinct demarcations between the different movements within the larger evangelical Protestant tradition are obvious still. Moreover, they seem to be especially prominent when it comes to ignorant stances about environmental stewardship and creation care on the part of those who harbor more rigid views on ideology and biblical authority. To counteract the "trivialization of creation, and the jettison of the creation by the evangelicals due to the power of these preachers [i.e., Falwell and others], who did not know very much about the creation . . . [and] didn't even really understand very well that they depended on it for their own survival" thus became the central focus of DeWitt's work at Au Sable.[13]

In order to bridge the divide between Evangelicalism and environmental science, DeWitt, as director of Au Sable, would establish partnerships with evangelical colleges and universities, where he would find "at least one person, usually a scientist, who was interested in the world and interested in learning, and investigation." These scientists would come to Au Sable as representatives of their colleges and universities, develop an educational program together with DeWitt, and later send their students to the Institute where they could get credit for taking courses in environmental science and stewardship practices. Underlying this strategy was the idea that students trained at Au Sable would go back and teach in their respective colleges and universities and speak in their churches, thus developing a Christian environmental stewardship movement *from within* Evangelicalism. Additionally, Au Sable would organize the already mentioned forums and provide a meeting and exchange place for evangelicals interested in and involved with creation care.[14]

It is important to emphasize that when DeWitt became a creation care activist, he had no intention to criticize the evangelical church for its lack of ecological consciousness as Lynn White had done in the late 1960s. Not a biblical literalist but someone who "takes the Bible seriously" and tries to authentically emulate Christ, DeWitt did not see a problem with Scripture but rather with the parlous relationship between faith and science on the one hand, and in the rise of a politicized, theologically and culturally reductionist Evangelicalism on the other. Therefore, his aim has always been "to work within the church," teaching environmental stewardship and creation care from within the evangelical tradition, instead of breaking with his faith and starting a possible new religion like some of the religiously disenfranchised proponents of creation spirituality attempted to do.[15]

Over the past four decades, Au Sable has developed a variety of environmental science courses and catered to students from nearly sixty participating Christian colleges across the country. In 1999, in what the organization describes as "a bold move," DeWitt also purchased a wildlife preserve on Whidbey Island in the state of Washington, where a second campus, Au Sable–Pacific Rim, was established. Additional courses have taken place in India and Costa Rica, all geared toward the Institute's mission to "serve, protect and restore God's earth."[16]

Considering that DeWitt's activism has been holistically aimed at "bridge-building and a 'defragmentation' of the disciplines and our dealings with the world," his advocacy activities over the past forty years have stretched well beyond those of the Au Sable Institute. In fact, DeWitt repeatedly emphasized how crucial it was to realize that the saving of the world had to be a team effort. He thus took part in various organizing and counseling activities too numerous to mention, in particular establishing Au Sable as a "venue" and "support base" for leaders who eventually founded other evangelical environmental organizations. At around the same time when the EEN was established in the early 1990s, DeWitt also attempted to initiate an International Evangelical Environmental Network (IEEN) and a *Creation Care* newsletter produced by a British editor at the former publishing company Chapman & Hall. Although the IEEN did not take off as an organization and was soon "overshadowed" by the EEN in the United States, DeWitt worked closely with the EEN, and *Creation Care* became the title of the EEN's periodical in 1998. In addition, DeWitt has developed strong ties with ecologically concerned British evangelical theologians and scientists, including John Stott and Sir John Houghton, through the John Ray Initiative. They, in turn, were influential forces in getting the NAE more involved in the EEN's creation care efforts around climate change in the early 2000s. DeWitt's name will thus come up repeatedly in connection with other creation care groups, including the following organization on whose board of advisors he has served since 1993.[17]

## PLANTING TREES ("FOR JESUS"): SCOTT SABIN AND FLORESTA USA/PLANT WITH PURPOSE (1984–)

Whereas the primary motivation behind the Au Sable Institute was to foster ecological awareness and responsibility among evangelical students, the aim of the second creation care organization to emerge during the 1980s was to directly address the issue of deforestation as one of the root causes of global poverty. Floresta USA, officially renamed Plant With Purpose (PWP) in 2010, may thus fit the commonly imagined profile of an environmental (interest) organization better. By promoting global evangelism, though, PWP also puts an overt emphasis on spiritual renewal along with ecological restoration and economic relief. But as we shall see, the organization's focus on creation care is so central to PWP's overall goal and identity that it cannot be classified as an evangelical relief and development organization, either.

PWP was founded as Floresta USA in 1984 by Tom Woodard, a San Diego businessman and congregant of Mount Soledad Presbyterian Church in California. Woodard became concerned about environmental problems while volunteering for a Christian relief organization in the Dominican Republic in the aftermath of Hurricane David, which had severely hit the nation in 1979. During his work on the island, Woodard realized that food aid alone could not solve the problem of hunger and poverty in the long run; he recognized the direct link between poverty-related problems and environmental degradation, in particular deforestation, in third world countries. Convinced that the environment had "everything" to do with poverty, as one of PWP's informational brochures states, Woodard founded Floresta

USA to "address the environmental, economic, and spiritual needs of the rural poor throughout the world." In order to simultaneously address those needs, the organization developed a three-part approach to holistic transformation that would integrate environmental restoration, economic empowerment, and spiritual inspiration. As PWP's mission statement articulates, "We teach, we plant, we create enterprise, and we share the gospel."[18]

Although Floresta/PWP was first incorporated in California, Woodard also set up a Floresta team in the Dominican Republic as early as 1985. Considering the organization's mission and its founder's professional background, it should not come as a surprise that the organization's first initiative was to start a large for-profit tree nursery called Los Arbolitos. The aim of this initiative was to simultaneously provide high-quality tree seedlings for local reforestation efforts as well as jobs for Dominicans. In addition, the profits of the nursery were to be used for other initiatives of PWP.[19]

During its peak productivity, Los Arbolitos "was the largest tree nursery in the Caribbean, employing as many as a hundred people, with the capacity to produce up to ten million seedlings annually." Even though there had been a great need for reforestation in the Dominican Republic, and the nursery became part of a growing environmental movement in the area, there was little commercial demand for tree seedlings. In addition, and inspired by the example of Los Arbolitos, the Dominican government had started to produce its own tree seedlings, to be given free of charge to anyone willing to plant them, thus "making it virtually impossible for Los Arbolitos to remain profitable." Nonetheless, Los Arbolitos raised awareness regarding the issue of deforestation in the Caribbean and has remained in business by shifting its focus to the growing demand for ornamental plants in addition to processing the occasional governmental order for tree seedlings.[20]

Viewed with its eventual difficulties in mind, Los Arbolitos may not appear to be the best-chosen example of a project signifying PWP's otherwise successful founding story. However, even though it turned out not to be as profitable as its initiators had intended it to be, as the very first initiative of PWP, Los Arbolitos does exemplify very well how intricately linked environmental restoration and economic empowerment are according to the organization's philosophy and mission. Because apart from directly providing labor and producing tree seedlings for restoration purposes, the intended effects of Los Arbolitos and related PWP projects have been much further reaching than that. As PWP explains, planting trees "restores productivity of the land," which in turn "leads to a direct improvement in the quality of life," because it enables farmers to grow more crops and thus have more food and more money. As incomes start to grow, farmers can start to invest in their households and the infrastructure of their villages as well, thus producing wide-ranging synergy effects that ideally turn a bleak and barren "village without purpose" into a green and prosperous "village that plants with purpose." Seen from this vantage point, "Planting trees is sustainable development in its simplest form." Since its founding in 1984, the organization has thus facilitated the planting of over thirty million trees.[21]

PWP's programs have mostly been long-term and practical, hands-on projects, intended to empower local communities instead of creating more dependencies that only uphold the "vicious cycle" of poverty. In order to overcome this vicious cycle, PWP not only facilitates concrete agroforestry and reforestation efforts but also helps farmers start their own businesses. Supported by microcredit programs and other tools of economic empowerment, farmers can thus become independent (micro-)entrepreneurs, who in turn help "the community as a whole to diversify its economy."[22]

Other programs of the organization include the training of farmers in sustainable farming techniques, family garden initiatives, and the construction of compost heaps, cisterns, and fuel-efficient stoves. In addition, PWP supports local church outreach and services, including Bible study groups. It also organizes workshops on peace, reconciliation, and creation care. Last, but certainly not least, the organization provides disaster relief responses, such as in the aftermath of the Haitian earthquake on January 12, 2010. As an immediate reaction to this catastrophic event (which controversial evangelical leader Pat Robertson had publicly called the consequence of a Haitian "pact to the devil"), PWP donated over ninety tons of seeds instead of food, so that farmers could "begin to feed themselves again." Furthermore, PWP's local team enlisted over twenty-five hundred rural Haitians in a short-term employment program, planting six hundred thousand trees and constructing several hundred miles of soil conservation barriers on the devastated island.[23]

In addition to local teams in the Dominican Republic and Haiti, Floresta/ PWP partner organizations have also been established—or formed with other organizations—in Burundi, the Democratic Republic of Congo, Mexico, Tanzania, Thailand, and Ethiopia. While PWP's overseas partners mostly lead community sponsorship and service programs in cooperation with local churches and individuals, the San Diego office in California provides consulting, planning, evaluating, and monitoring services to each of these programs. Headed by Executive Director Scott Sabin since 1995, PWP's headquarters also serves as fund-raiser for donations from individuals, churches, foundations, corporations, and during special events, which are then distributed to members abroad. In 2011, PWP USA added a first regional representative position to its California main office, which has since been filled by Corbyn Small. Small is located in Denver, Colorado, and focuses on fund-raising and building partnerships throughout Colorado, Texas, and Arizona.

PWP is a partner of the EEN and has collaborated with the United Nations, World Relief (the relief and development arm of the NAE), and the Au Sable Institute, among many other evangelical and non-evangelical organizations. Since the early 1990s Sabin has participated regularly in meetings with other creation care leaders, who in turn have supported PWP in various ways as well. In the late 1990s, for instance, Calvin DeWitt traveled to the Dominican Republic to brief national leaders, lawmakers, and local Floresta staff on creation care, which resulted in the passage of "landmark legislation in 2000 for a nationwide emphasis on reforestation" in the Dominican Republic. Unlike DeWitt's straightforward and rather "natural" (in the sense of self-evident) creation care journey described previously, however, Sabin's career has been that of an "unlikely environmentalist" and thus provides an interesting yet synergistic contrast to DeWitt's initiation in—and motivation for—creation care.[24]

Scott Sabin grew up in Southern California and introduces himself—not without a refreshing dose of self-irony—as "a typical evangelical from the U.S. suburbs . . . [who] had grown up in the church and accepted Jesus at summer camp." After high school Sabin studied political science and aspired to be a diplomat. A Spanish language requirement for his master's degree in international relations brought him to an immersion program in Guatemala, however, where Sabin's haphazard "journey toward becoming an environmentalist" began.[25]

For one, although the Guatemalan Civil War (1960–1996) was winding down at the time, "injustice and poverty were impossible to ignore," making any "guilt-free enjoyment of privilege" impossible. Still, amid all the socioeconomic plight and squalor that surrounded him whenever he was not taking Spanish classes, Sabin met "missionaries, aid workers, local pastors and ordinary Christians who were beacons of light in the darkness," and whose presence showed him "that God was there, working through someone to bring redemption." Although he claims to be a person who is generally "skeptical of overly spiritual interpretations of events," to Sabin this time in his life seemed truly "miraculous." He felt that "God was guiding [his] every step" by introducing him to inspiring individuals who were "working with incredible courage to share the light of Christ's love" in order to alleviate poverty and desperation. Being around them, Sabin realized that "following Jesus could be far more exciting than [he had] ever imagined." Already skeptical about his previous professional aspirations due to these experiences, upon his return to California Sabin attended a talk given by evangelical sociologist and justice advocate Anthony Campolo. Inspired by Campolo's call to action and sacrificial love, he thus decided to "work with the poor" instead of pursuing a career in diplomacy and international relations.[26]

Floresta USA "was the Christian anti-poverty organization closest to [Sabin's] home." Although initially not convinced that "planting trees for Jesus," as his father supposedly mocked, was the right step toward his newly desired career in humanitarian work, Sabin nonetheless volunteered to stuff envelopes and call donors on behalf of the organization. His goal was to move on to another organization as soon as possible, but in 1995 he became Floresta's executive director instead. Moreover, after a trip to the Dominican Republic and Haiti during that same year, Sabin realized for himself that environmental issues were "foundational" in addressing the problem of poverty. As he emphasizes, he had "no intention of devoting [his] life to environmental issues" before this trip. It was only when he experienced firsthand that poverty and environmental degradation were interconnected that Sabin became as fully convinced of Floresta's holistic philosophy and mission as the organization's founder.[27]

While Sabin deems an overcoming of the evangelical "suspicion of science" an important step in an individual's response to eco-crisis, in his case poverty was the primary motivator for his activism. Related to Calvin DeWitt's view of the broken ligaments of the science-ethics-praxis triad, according to Sabin and PWP, poverty is "as much as anything else" a consequence of brokenness as well, namely that of the broken relationships among God, humans, and the rest of creation. This encompassing understanding of the "broken quality of life" is central to the evangelical worldview. Derived from humankind's fall described in the book of Genesis, its antidote is the biblical vision of *shalom*, or the healing of relational wounds and the restoration of peace, harmony, and balance.[28]

In order to foster *shalom* instead of brokenness, it is most important for Christians to focus on their relationships with God and others: they are to love God and their neighbor as they love themselves (Matt 22:34-40). But Sabin emphasizes that humans can only love if "we have an accurate view of who we are in God's universe" and do not "distort our self-worth." Discounting "our importance and giftedness . . . [therefore] leads to helplessness and disempowerment," which Sabin considers particularly strong amplifiers of spiritual and economic poverty. In addition, humanity's broken relationship with creation exacerbates the problem. Moreover, since it has been created by God, God has a relationship with creation as well. Therefore, humans ought to take their biblical responsibility as stewards of creation seriously not only in third world countries ravaged by rural poverty but also in wealthy industrialized nations like the United States and Canada.[29]

Under the directorship of Sabin, PWP has concentrated on "healing" these broken relationships in the holistic fashion Woodard envisioned when he first started the organization: sustainable agriculture and reforestation efforts are intended to heal humanity's relationship with creation. The encouragement and stimulation of local enterprise "addresses the relationships between people, as it levels the playing field for the disadvantaged and helps families stay together." And "discipleship focuses on our relationship with God. By helping others to follow Jesus and obey his commandments, thus fulfilling the Great Commission," Sabin explains, the organization "help[s] to create a foundation upon which future development can be built." Therefore, PWP does not only address poverty and environmental degradation as different aspects of brokenness, but it also emphasizes the importance of evangelism in order to bring about spiritual transformation.[30]

It is important to stress that according to PWP, economic empowerment and environmental restoration are inextricably intertwined with spiritual transformation, because "none of the physical and environmental changes would last if there wasn't also a change of heart and character." As Sabin explains, the root of this conviction lies in the organization's experiences in the Dominican Republic, where some of the farmers who had succeeded in Floresta's early programs had not only become more wealthy but also more prone to spending their newly earned money on excessive alcohol consumption and adultery, for instance. To avoid potentially negative side effects of its work, PWP is therefore not hesitant to facilitate Bible studies in cooperation with local churches in order to "share the gospel" with its program participants.[31]

Considering the typical evangelical conviction that "without Christ" any situation or effort is "hopeless," such an openly evangelistic stance should not disconcert more secular advocates, though. While Sabin is not the only creation care activist to advocate the saving of souls along with the planet, as we shall see, he does emphasize that evangelism is not the primary motivation for PWP's ecologically sustainable development work. If their environmental efforts were simply an ecologic means to an evangelistic end, they would be disingenuous. As Sabin explains by drawing a parallel to his parenthood, "I do not feed, clothe, and educate my children *so* I can share the gospel with them. I feed them, clothe them, educate them, *and* share the gospel with them because I love them."[32]

In addition, rather than making mere converts in "the insensitive way in which it is often done," for reasons of "pure practicality," Sabin and PWP focus on making disciples who attempt to imitate Christ and are actively involved in loving God and their neighbors. Conversion is thus regarded only as "a first step," whereas discipleship is a sign of a life transformed and dedicated to the kingdom of Christ. Only such a transformation seems spiritually—and thus economically and ecologically—sustainable to Sabin and PWP, hence the emphasis that their focus on discipleship is purely practical.[33]

Over the years PWP has become the most financially robust group within the evangelical environmental advocacy community. What the organization illustrates very specifically is that creation care is about much more than the environment. Creation care even extends to the interconnectivity of global poverty and ecological degradation, because "ultimately the problem [of environmental degradation] is a spiritual one."[34]

As Sabin has come to learn on his unlikely journey toward environmentalism, creation care must include the preservation of endangered creatures, the conservation of wilderness, and environmental health and safety issues. Additionally, a discursive proximity can be found with the environmental justice movement and Catholic social teaching in Sabin's conviction that "justice for the poor and oppressed should be a seamless part of creation care." Viewed as a sacred revelation of its creator, however, creation also demands and deserves care uncoupled from utilitarian and justice considerations. Being more than just a (re)new(ed) way of knowing or seeing God, creation care is "fundamental to proclaiming and demonstrating God's kingdom to all of creation." Therefore, a refusal to engage in the care of creation is essentially a refusal to reveal God's kingdom.[35]

## CELEBRATING THE WONDER OF CREATION: DEAN OHLMAN AND THE CHRISTIAN NATURE FEDERATION (1989–1992)

Arguably, the third evangelical environmental organization to emerge during the 1980s, the CNF, could not be more different from either the Au Sable Institute or Floresta USA/PWP. Founded by Dean Ohlman in 1989, it was consciously modeled after a secular environmental organization in order to provide "a 'safe' alternative" for evangelicals considering their theological and cultural reservations about environmentalism. Interestingly, it did not last very long, but during the short time of its existence, the CNF probably received more support from evangelicals associated with the Religious Right than any of the other creation care movement organizations so far. This fact alone provides for a remarkable case study despite the organization's short lifespan. What makes the case of the CNF even more extraordinary is its founder's personal journey from a "Republican, conservative, anti-environmentalist" with a "typical Baptist, premillennial, dispensational mindset" toward a life dedicated to creation care activism.[36]

It is not clear to what extent the overlap between New Age ideas and environmental engagement has made evangelicals uneasy about the environmental movement. Rather than politics and ideology, however, in the individual case of Dean Ohlman, the presence of the "hippies," "New Agers," and "secular humanists" within environmentalism indeed provoked resistance during the Reagan years.[37]

A writer by profession, Ohlman was researching Eastern religions and the New Age movement in his function as director of communication for the organization Bibles for India in the early 1980s. Originally from the Grand Rapids area of Michigan, where his family was deeply rooted in the land and the local religious community, Ohlman graduated from fundamentalist Bob Jones University in South Carolina in the 1960s and later moved to Southern California with his wife and children. Always a lover of nature and the outdoors, especially hiking and fishing, at some point he was a member of the National Audubon Society. What increasingly troubled Ohlman during the 1980s, however, was not the ecological problems that environmentalists and nature enthusiasts were lamenting but what he perceived as the negative influence of New Age mysticism on environmentalism. (Or, as he put it in a contribution to Berit Kjos' book *Under the Spell of Mother Earth* [1992], "the satanic deception in the environmental movement.")[38]

In particular the reading of a Sierra Club publication entitled *Well Body, Well Earth* (1983) eventually pushed him on a path toward creation care activism: "I was stunned by what I found in the book: it was a virtual manual for bringing New Age mysticism into resolving the world's environmental crises." He wondered how could "the granddaddy of environmental action agencies . . . publish a source book recommending our communicating with the 'spirit of the earth,'" and why there was no Christian alternative organization "that relates the biblical story of the earth" instead?[39]

Unlike his old friend Calvin DeWitt at the Au Sable Institute back home in Michigan, Ohlman was not primarily interested in bridging the divide between faith and science in order to inspire a sophisticated evangelical creation care theology. Neither was he concerned about the connection between environmental degradation and poverty in third world countries. Rather, after having read *Well Body, Well Earth*, Ohlman wondered about the lack of a theologically correct environmental organization catering to Christians appreciative of nature and the outdoors like himself.[40]

In the meantime, Ohlman had moved on to a position as a staff writer at Biola University. Since this contract was coming to an end, however, he decided to found such an organization himself. Thus, and in quite the fundamentalist–separatist fashion arguably reminiscent of the religious tradition he was raised in, Ohlman all but rebelled against mainstream environmentalism with the founding of his CNF in 1989.

---

The CNF started out small with a home office in Ohlman's Fullerton residence and only two other people on the board to fulfill the minimum requirements for incorporation. Financially backed by his older brother, Ohlman's "dream was to develop a sort of Audubon Society for Christians which would have a nice glossy magazine, have local chapters, do field trips, print pretty nature cards with Scripture verses, and even sponsor tours to exotic natural destinations for well-to-do believers who wanted a new Christian adventure." Perhaps the organization would "even address some genuine environmental problems—if there were any." While the National Audubon Society had originally been established in 1905 to outlaw the use of bird plumage in women's fashion (a concrete policy goal), Ohlman's initial conception of the CNF was not only a theologically correct version of the mainstream environmental model but also an apolitical one.[41]

The initial CNF information brochure reflected Ohlman's vision very well. It was glossy and included four color photographs depicting family outdoors scenes, the serenity of natural beauty, and, on its cover, a close-up of an iconic bald eagle. The latter towered over the organization's motto, "Celebrating the wonder of God in creation." Printed as a headline in the brochure's middle section, the reader would find a quote from Schaeffer's *Pollution and the Death of Man*: "The death of joy in nature is leading to the death of nature itself." As Ohlman had added to this quote, if there was "an overarching purpose for the CNF, it would no doubt be to restore that joy—joy based on the biblical view of nature." Further purposes underlying this overarching one, the brochure stated, were the reestablishment of the Christian worldview within the natural sciences and the enhancement of both the appreciation for and understanding of "God's handiwork evidenced in the natural world."[42]

Conceptualized as a federation of Christians who appreciated nature and put the creator "right up front," Ohlman's plan had been to eventually establish local CNF chapters. Membership in the CNF was open to organizational affiliates and individuals for an annual fee of twenty-five dollars. Both had to agree with the purposes of the organization and its creed. The latter, printed on the back of CNF membership cards, emphasized basic evangelical doctrine, mankind's superior position in the created order, and the member's "God-given authority and responsibility to care for [creation] as a good steward." While it acknowledged that humans could neither "fully comprehend the 'why' nor the 'how' of the creation process," members were nonetheless called upon to "thank God for the natural world that sustains life and [to] humbly submit [themselves] to the earthkeeping responsibilities handed down . . . [by] the caretakers of Eden."[43]

In the beginning it looked like Ohlman had discovered a very promising niche within the evangelical nonprofit world. Since Focus on the Family (FoF) was still located in Southern California at the time as well, Ohlman had immediately contacted the organization's vice president Peb Jackson. A "real outdoors man" himself, Jackson liked the idea of the CNF and pledged support. Coinciding with Earth Day in April 1990, FoF announced the CNF during its family news program, which ran several times that day, and kept advertising the organization for a week. Following FoF's introduction interested Christians started contacting Ohlman, and within a year the organization had six hundred members. Other prominent evangelical outdoors enthusiasts, such as Vernon Carl Grounds of Denver Seminary, would become lifetime members, and Ohlman gave interviews on Christian broadcasting stations across the country. It seemed reasonable to expect that the organization would reach its goal of twenty-five hundred dues-paying members before Ohlman's family funds ran out. A CNF bumper sticker with the motto, "Save the earth. Honor its Creator." confidently stated on its peel-off back, "The Christian Nature

Federation is a new organization that many believe will be one of the most significant Christian ministries of the 21st century."[44]

Though busy enlisting members and planning further steps and activities during the first year of the CNF's existence, Ohlman spent a lot of time reading environmental literature and revisiting his Bible as well. In addition to *Pollution and the Death of Man*, he recalls reading C. S. Lewis and several novels by George MacDonald, the Scottish minister and fantasy writer who had greatly impacted Lewis. Despite his skepticism Ohlman even subscribed to both the magazines of the Sierra Club and the National Audubon Society. Eventually, and for Ohlman unexpectedly, those readings would merge into two central insights that struck his conscience to the core. First, Ohlman realized that there was indeed a stewardship mandate in the Bible, and that for evangelicals creation care was not an optional adventure but a mandatory task. And second, despite their misguided spiritual orientation, environmentalists seemed to have a point when it came to the actual degraded state of creation.[45]

The moral shock of these two realizations bestowed something like a second conversion—or "born-again again"—experience upon him one afternoon in 1990. While sitting on a bench near the fenced off McColl Superfund site that had been contaminated by petroleum refinery waste during World War II, reading a George MacDonald novel, and glancing over the oil rigs of Orange County's Huntington Beach every so often, Ohlman all of a sudden "felt the movement of the Holy Spirit" and understood the "culpability of the evangelical, of the church as a whole, and Christianity as a whole, in allowing technology and our lifestyles to begin to damage the earth." Like any conversion moment, this changed the course of his life. Ohlman immediately wrote a "confession" in which he admitted "the reality of environmental degradation and the debauchery of materialism," shared it with his CNF constituency, and "began suggesting that Christians, of all people, should be supporters of genuine environmental protection."[46]

Ready to lead by example, after Ohlman's "born-again again" experience, the CNF began to advocate more environmental responsibility. Ohlman also took a stand in the spotted owl controversy, a pressing issue on the West Coast at the time, which pitted conservative economic interests against the ecological values of preservationists. He even started a local advocacy battle with Republican William E. Dannemeyer over the congressman's support for land development measures, which would endanger the natural habitat of coastal sage scrub and the blue-gray gnat catcher in California. Ohlman's vehement and biblically underlined criticism in the *Orange County Register* compelled Dannemeyer to call Ohlman into his office and ask him "not to rock the boat" and to "tone down" his rhetoric. Shockingly to himself and "everybody else," it also turned Ohlman into an "environmentalist!"[47]

Unfortunately, though, Ohlman's embrace of environmental responsibility would also usher in the demise of his CNF. As soon as he "dropped plans for all the glitzy things [he had] wanted to do" and started advocating for a more lifestyle-challenging approach to ecological problems, support for his organization started to wane. Hence, Ohlman never reached the goal of enlisting enough dues-paying members to financially sustain the CNF. Even though the evangelical relief and development organization World Vision would step in and employ Ohlman as a consultant on creation care for a while, in 1992, "after three thrilling, traumatic, spiritually fulfilling and financially devastating years," Ohlman had to file for bankruptcy and move back to Michigan to get started again with the help of his family.[48]

Most advocacy organizations do not survive beyond the first few years of their existence. The reasons for their high rate of death are many and include purely organizational factors, such as leadership skills, strategic planning, and fund-raising techniques. In particular organizations that advocate systemic social change usually "have a harder time getting funds from a mass base than do organizations dedicated to saving a particular species or landscape." In the case of the CNF, it appears that Ohlman's conservative evangelical supporters did not like to be "challenged to repent of their consumerist lifestyles and wasteful practices." This is understandable, considering that Ohlman's initial promise was merely a Christian outdoors adventure untainted by New Age spirituality and restricted to the joyful appreciation of God's handiwork. Whether his core constituency were politically and theologically conservative evangelicals or not, Ohlman's shift toward a more challenging creation care message—due to a very personal conversion experience during the critical stages of organizational establishment and member acquisition—may nonetheless have had a detrimental effect on the organization's growth. Especially by the end of the 1980s, however, both environmentalism and Evangelicalism had already become more politicized in opposite directions. Thus, the fact that Ohlman all of a sudden started openly confronting fellow Republicans like Congressman Dannemeyer must have also pushed the CNF into the same political camp as other environmental organizations, whether Ohlman was of an ideologically conservative orientation himself or not.[49]

The end of the CNF was not the end of Ohlman's career as a creation care activist. Returned to Grand Rapids in 1992, Ohlman first worked as director of creative services at Cornerstone College. Although not active in "direct creation care" at the time, he took part in the drafting process of "An Evangelical Declaration on the Care of Creation" (EDCC) and, together with Calvin DeWitt and others, participated in the EEN's unofficial steering committee, the Christian Environmental Council (CEC). Eventually, he became involved in another dispute, this time with E. Calvin Beisner and the Acton Institute, the latter a libertarian think tank also located in Grand Rapids. As a result of their disagreement over environmentalism, Ohlman left Cornerstone in 1996 and transitioned into a new position as editor for special projects at RBC Ministries. It was here where Ohlman was finally able to create a suitable creation care advocacy position for himself.[50]

Founded as a small radio station by pastor and Bible teacher Martin R. De Haan in 1938, RBC Ministries has turned into an "empire" in the world of evangelical parachurch organizations. Perhaps best known for the popular devotional guide "Our Daily Bread," it has several hundred employees and caters to an international mailing list of close to one million subscribers. Ohlman's parents had attended De Haan's church(es) in Grand Rapids, and Ohlman was a longtime friend of Martin R. De Haan II, who was presiding over his grandfather's ministry until his younger brother took over in 2011.[51]

Employed by RBC, Ohlman wrote a series of five booklets: *Celebrating the Wonder of Creation* (1998), *Celebrating the Wonder of a Tree* (2002), *Celebrating the Wonder of Water* (2003), *Celebrating the Wonder of Soil* (2006), and *Celebrating the Wonder of the Wilderness* (2007). Their overall message was simple: God's creation is wonderfully precious, and care for it a matter of love and obedience. In particular in the first booklet, Ohlman asserted that a theology of creation had been part of the Christian church since the fifth century after Christ. Quoting from T. S. Eliot's *The Idea of a Christian Society* (1939)—a "wrong attitude toward nature [implied], somewhere, a wrong attitude toward God"—Ohlman expressed the hope that a celebration of the wonder of creation would "stimulate in us the right attitude toward God and toward His handiwork upon which we depend."[52]

Through his position at RBC, Ohlman was able to reach a much larger audience than previously with the CNF. In particular his celebration booklets were so well received that some of them were transformed into a television series for RBC's *Day of Discovery* show, which was broadcast on PAX cable network and several independent stations. In 2008, RBC published another booklet of Ohlman's conceptualized to help "[defuse] the controversy" surrounding the creation account in the book of Genesis. In the same year the organization would launch his "webministry" called "The Wonder of Creation," through which Ohlman was able to directly spread his creation care message until his retirement in October 2013.[53]

Toward the end of his professional career, Ohlman emphasized that he still saw the fact that economically well-off and ideologically conservative evangelicals believed they deserved their high standards of living as the number one obstacle to a larger evangelical creation care movement. But despite his critical stance toward American materialism and consumerism, Ohlman has not become dismissive of capitalism and other ideological pillars of American conservatism. Quite similar to Scott Sabin and PWP, who "advocate for property rights" because in their understanding (land) ownership fosters (ecological) responsibility, Ohlman supports "robust free markets and property rights as they are properly understood and guided by Christian charity." In reliance on Francis Schaeffer's sermon "Ash Heap Lives," he thus proposes "the practice of 'compassionate capitalism' within responsible free markets," or the practice of a capitalism that is not "hard, cold, and unloving" but rather one that acquires and uses property "with compassion."[54]

In addition, Ohlman believes that "governments have an important regulatory and educational role in motivating their citizens to live—and their businesses and industrial corporations to operate—in a manner that safeguards the ecological integrity and fruitfulness of God's creation." Instead of running a Christian outdoors adventure organization or a politically activist environmental organization, however, Ohlman came to realize that for evangelicals to change their lifestyles—and to make corresponding political decisions—they, like himself before his conversion, first needed to be reminded of the fact that they had forgotten God's creation in their theology and had thus been "negative witnesses for our Creator and Savior." Hence his late focus on teaching principles and changing hearts and minds rather than making concrete environmental policy suggestions.[55]

In Ohlman's case it took many years to find an organizational niche conducive to his vocation and preferred style of advocacy. Although he started out as one of the evangelical environmental pioneers of the 1980s and initially attempted to establish an organization quite different from the Au Sable Institute, at the end of his career Ohlman followed a similar educational strategy, albeit one that catered to a different segment within the evangelical community and emphasized the awe and wonder of creation more than its scientific intricacies. What Ohlman's biography demonstrates for sure, however, is that feeling a call from God may not necessarily lead the believer along an easy path, but it certainly fosters perseverance. Like Scott Sabin and others who have had similar experiences, once converted to the cause, Ohlman has stayed faithful to and involved in the care of creation despite his initial skepticism toward environmentalism and the many obstacles the creation care movement has faced since the 1980s.

# 4

# POLITICALLY UNAFRAID EVANGELICAL ENVIRONMENTAL ORGANIZATIONS

When it comes to the environment, at some point you have to talk about the macro level. At some point you are talking about societal issues, at some point you are talking about legislation.

What about $CO_2$ emissions? What about air pollution? What about species becoming extinct? What about health impacts of environmental issues? At some point that reaches into the politics level, right?

What solutions are you offering?

You can't just say "I'm really interested in creation care" and it means practically nothing. So there has to be some teeth . . . it can't just be an emotional experience or a new way of seeing God, though that's important as well.

Alexei Laushkin, EEN[1]

According to commentators at the time, the twentieth anniversary of Earth Day on April 22, 1990, "united more people concerned about a single cause than any other global event in history." Despite two terms of the Reagan administration's dismissal, by 1990 environmental problems had moved to a more central position on the public agenda again. In addition to the disastrous Exxon Valdez oil spill in Alaska in 1989, further threats such as the "hole" in the stratospheric ozone layer and global warming had emerged over the course of the 1980s. Though not altogether new—the potential impact of rising carbon dioxide emissions on global temperatures had been predicted by a Swedish scientist as early as 1896—and primarily caused by industrialized nations, those issues were unexclusive in their consequences. Global in scope, their solution would demand international cooperation and regulation.[2]

Evangelicals, "like almost everyone else, . . . were swept into [this] heightened sense of ecological concern." The creation care theology that had developed at Au Sable throughout the 1980s thus began to spread beyond the circle of the predominantly Reformed academics and scientists at the Institute. Evangelical publications with environmental themes increased, ranging from practical how-to works to novels, children's books, and materials popularizing ideas developed by Au Sable affiliates.[3]

The growing popularity of creation care notwithstanding, however, the greater evangelical community was still wary of environmentalism. Although climate change had not become "a deeply partisan issue" yet, evangelical resistance toward environmentalism was prevalent. Moreover, in tandem with environmentalism's turn to the Democratic Party and Evangelicalism's ongoing mobilization toward the political Right, the green gap was growing, too.[4]

Perhaps the activism of the Religious Right emboldened evangelical environmentalists to become more politically daring as well. Perhaps it was the nudge from the Left. Perhaps environmental policy was simply inevitable after the Cold War. Recall the eventual politicization of the CNF at the turn to the 1990s and Ohlman's short-lived advocacy efforts against Congressman Dannemeyer. Although those proved ineffective in reaching ideologically conservative evangelicals and led to the demise of Ohlman's organization instead, the politicization of the CNF was nonetheless in tune with a changing political opportunity structure and the developments within both the environmental and the larger Evangelical movement at the time. That the CNF's logo was initially given over to the EEN, an act that Ohlman described as akin to "giving up [his] daughter in marriage," signifies more than a token of friendship.[5]

In addition to the EEN, two other politically unafraid evangelical creation care organizations emerged during the 1990s: Christian Environmental Association (1993; Target Earth International after 1998) and Christians for Environmental Stewardship/Restoring Eden (CES; 1996). Since nobody from Target Earth could be contacted via the organization's (outdated) website nor through the CCCC, this chapter's focus is on the EEN and CES.[6]

## A "CATALYST" FOR EVANGELICAL ENVIRONMENTAL ACTION: THE EVANGELICAL ENVIRONMENTAL NETWORK (1993/1994–)

The founding history of the EEN is complex and involves a diverse set of actors and midwife organizations, both from within and outside the evangelical community. It must be seen as an evolutionary step within organized creation care on the one hand. On the other hand, it must also be viewed against the backdrop of the culture wars of late twentieth-century America, when there has been a concerted effort on the part of scientists and environmentalists to foster a "greening of religion."[7]

The potentially crucial role of religions in solving environmental problems and ensuring human survival was publicly addressed during the Global Forum of Spiritual and Parliamentary Leaders on Human Survival in January 1990 in Moscow. About seven hundred political, scientific, and religious leaders from various parts of the world attended, among them Soviet President Gorbachev and popular American scientist Carl Sagan. In an attempt to get believers in America more engaged in environmental concern and action, Sagan and other scientists issued an "Open Letter to the Religious Community" after the event. They called the environmental crisis "intrinsically religious" and strongly encouraged faith leaders to join their cause.[8]

As a result of the "Open Letter," the Rev. James Parks Morton, dean of the Cathedral of St. John the Divine in New York, and Paul Gorman, vice president for programs at St. John, decided to establish a "Joint Appeal by Religion and Science for the Environment" in May 1990. The Joint Appeal was to be formally launched in October that year, during a bipartisan congressional breakfast hosted by Senator Al Gore (D-TN). Although Gorman and other religious leaders behind the Joint Appeal effort were of a rather liberal theological orientation, they consciously promoted the participation of evangelicals and invited Ronald Sider (1939–), a professor of theology and ethics at Eastern University in Pennsylvania and the founder of Evangelicals for Social Action (ESA).[9]

Sider, a Canadian-born Anabaptist active in the civil rights movement during the 1960s, founded ESA in 1978. Often considered one of the primary organizations of the evangelical Left (though Sider is better classified as an ideologically bridging evangelical), ESA is a rather untypical organization in American political culture because of its emphasis on Evangelicalism, traditional values, *and* social justice. Sider had never heard of Gorman before he received the latter's phone call and invitation to the Joint Appeal in 1990; apparently Gorman had gotten Sider's phone number from a "mainline Protestant friend" of his.[10]

Most likely it did not require much persuasion to get Sider involved in the Joint Appeal effort. Sider "had long embraced a 'consistent pro-life agenda,'" and in his book *Completely Pro-Life* (1987), published several years before Gorman's call, he had argued that such an agenda "seeks fullness of life in every area." Abortion, economic justice, the family, and the nuclear arms race were "certainly among the pressing life concerns of [the] time." Nonetheless, "the list of issues . . . [was] almost limitless" and included at least "four other related areas," according to Sider: smoking, alcoholism, racism, and environmental destruction.[11]

Regarding environmental destruction Sider had not articulated a comprehensive ecotheology in *Completely Pro-Life*. Relying on the *Earthkeeping* book edited by Loren Wilkinson in 1980 instead, he affirmed that "dominion [was] not devastation," that "humanity [had] the special calling of gracious gardener of the good earth," and that "rape" and destruction of the environment was an "insult" to "the Creator of the garden." Insisting that environmental destruction was foolish and a matter of "life-and-death," Sider deemed "vigorous political action" crucial in addressing it.[12]

But in addition, Sider felt somewhat uneasy about environmentalism, too. More specifically, he saw a certain "theological confusion" surrounding the issue, evident for instance in Shirley MacLaine's New Age mysticism, Matthew Fox's creation spirituality, Peter Singer's speciesism, and evangelical fundamentalists' antienvironmental dispensationalism. Attending a conference in South Korea on justice, peace, and the integrity of creation in March 1990, Sider also realized that even environmentally conscious Christians seemed reluctant to acknowledge the *imago dei*, a problem he had already briefly identified as prevalent among secular thinkers in *Completely Pro-Life*. Despite all these departures from "historical, biblical theology" on the part of environmental advocates and their critics, however, the environmental movement clearly marked a cultural space of yearning. Similar to Francis Schaeffer, Sider thus also perceived it as a space rife with "evangelistic opportunities" not to be ignored by evangelical Christians.[13]

Inviting the theologically conservative but in some areas rather politically progressive Ronald Sider to the Joint Appeal was "a wise choice," because he "was sufficiently liberal to work comfortably with the leaders of the Joint Appeal while clearly retaining his evangelical credentials and the respect of prominent evangelical leaders." Sider was asked to bring other interested evangelicals to the event, and with him came Robert Seiple of World Vision USA, the evangelical relief and development organization that eventually stepped in to temporarily employ Dean Ohlman while he was struggling to keep the CNF alive.[14]

The Joint Appeal met again in Washington in May 1992. This time Calvin DeWitt was among the attendees as well. Noting that they did not have to agree on all points theological in order to be willing to work together, the Joint Appeal decided to establish the NRPE, an interfaith coalition that would represent the Judeo-Christian faith traditions in America. To provide an evangelical partner for the NRPE, Sider agreed "to assume primary responsibility for making the Evangelical Environmental Network (EEN) a reality as a ministry of Evangelicals for Social Action," whereas Seiple pledged financial support.[15]

A few months after the second Joint Appeal meeting, in August 1992 Calvin DeWitt's Au Sable Institute held an "International Consultation on Evangelicals and the Environment." This five-day event was attended by sixty individuals from eight countries, among them Ronald Sider. The participants agreed that efforts of environmentally concerned evangelicals had to extend beyond Au Sable's educational endeavors, and that specifically evangelical environmental advocacy organizations were needed. DeWitt asserts that during this consultation, the decision was made to create an International Evangelical Environmental Network (IEEN), which eventually "led to formation of the EEN in America." According to the EEN's self-understanding, however, the organization was founded by Ronald Sider and Robert Seiple.[16]

Discursive discrepancies regarding their founding geneses are not uncommon for organizations that are the product of several individuals and midwife organizations. To some extent they can also be the result of personal issues between the individuals involved in them. Unlike Ohlman's CNF, the EEN was not conceptualized as a membership group by one organizational entrepreneur but as a network. Networks, however, are essentially decentralized and consist of several individual actors and the relationships between them. Whether told by DeWitt, Sider, or another node within the EEN, what the founding history of the EEN nevertheless shows is that at the turn of the 1990s, secular environmentalists and scientists, as much as environmentally concerned mainline Protestants, encouraged a more politically active evangelical environmental partner organization. Most importantly, though, it was recognized as a necessity by environmentally concerned evangelicals like DeWitt, by social action and "completely pro-life"-oriented evangelicals like Sider, and by evangelical relief and development organizations such as World Vision. Ingrained in the EEN's DNA was thus not only an orientation toward (interfaith) cooperation and a concern for the impact of environmental degradation on the global poor but also an embrace of political action. When the NRPE was formally launched at a White House ceremony led by then Vice President Al Gore on October 4, 1993, the EEN was introduced as a "catalyst for a new outpouring of evangelical environmentalism."[17]

### "An Evangelical Declaration on the Care of Creation" (1994)

Unlike the NRPE's mainline Protestant or Catholic partners, the EEN initially lacked the institutional credibility within the evangelical community that the other organizations already enjoyed among their respective constituencies. In order to establish itself as a credible voice within the larger evangelical movement and to communicate the message of creation care more effectively to evangelical Protestants, the first activity of the EEN was to publicly announce "An Evangelical Declaration on the Care of Creation."[18]

Like the founding of the EEN, the drafting of the EDCC involved a number of people, most notably Loren Wilkinson, Calvin DeWitt, and Susan Emmerich. The drafting began at Au Sable in the summer of 1993.

A first version of the document was then sent to evangelical individuals and organizations potentially interested in signing the document, with a request for comments and suggestions. On October 30, 1993, the draft was edited in Chicago after a two-day symposium the EEN had held together with affiliates of *CT*. Early in 1994, the reviewed and edited document was supported by 150 signatories from the "mainstream evangelical establishment" and published in *CT*. With the help of the NRPE and together with a creation care starter kit, it was also sent to about thirty thousand evangelical congregations. Although initial signatories included key evangelical intellectual leaders like Nathan O. Hatch, Kenneth S. Kantzer, and Richard Mouw, signatories from evangelicals affiliated with the Religious Right were missing. Also missing was support from the NAE, the parachurch organization that comes closest to representing American Evangelicalism as a movement. Still, the EDCC provided the discursive glue to hold the growing creation care movement together. According to participants in the CCCC 2009, it has been the movement's theological core and practical guiding principle since its formulation.[19]

Overall, the EDCC reflects the Christian stewardship ethic and creation care theology as it has been shaped by the Au Sable Institute. Adhering to the evangelical centrality of the Bible, it declares the "full authority of the Scriptures" and asserts, like Schaeffer in *Pollution and the Death of Man*, that "biblical faith is essential to the solution of our ecological problems." It regards creation care as a crucial expression of worship and honor to the creator and sin as the reason why the creation has been "polluted, distorted, or destroyed."[20]

Alluding to the seven deadly sins, the EDCC lists seven "degradations of creation" specifically: 1) land degradation; 2) deforestation; 3) species extinction; 4) water degradation; 5) global toxification; 6) the alteration of atmosphere; and 7) human and cultural degradation. But it also shares the "Good News" by asserting that there is "hope" in Christ and God's work of redemption and renewal, "not only for men, women, and children, but also for the rest of creation." Since humans "have a unique responsibility for creation," they must support creation by reaffirming that it is God's and by reflecting on the biblical and theological teachings about creation, its scientific intricacies, and the "nurturing role of beauty." Moreover, they should actively engage in practical creation care measures as well, such as making lifestyle choices that combat overconsumption and wastefulness, fight poverty, support "the development of just, free economies," and shape public policies that reflect the Christian stewardship ethic.

Forestalling resistance against environmentalism the EDCC also bears witness to the fact that bridging the widening green gap within American Evangelicalism has not been an easy task. To emphasize that creation care does not encourage nature worship, for instance, the document ascertains that the creator is "prior to" and different from creation, and can only be known "dimly through creation." In order to counter the premillennial eschatology and focus on the new Earth prevalent in more fundamentalist circles, the EDCC stresses that it is wrong to neglect the biblical command to be faithful stewards, and equally wrong to destroy what God has created, regardless of when Christ will return "to reconcile all things." Aware of the anti-family and pro-abortion bias evangelicals hold toward the environmental movement, the EDCC also affirms respect for "the institution of marriage as the way God has given to ensure the thoughtful procreation of children." Nonetheless, like secular environmentalists concerned about the carrying capacity of the planet, the EDCC acknowledges that "we are pressing against the finite limits God has set for creation," and that a continued population growth worsens the already present degradation. The EDCC also adds, though, that the human responsibility extends from bearing and nurturing children to nurturing "their home on earth." On its final note, the EDCC invites individual Christians, congregations, and organizations to join the cause of biblical creation care and to cooperate with other environmentalists in order to learn from them and share the "Good News" with them.

### A Growing Network and the EEN's First Advocacy Success

Although the EDCC was immediately opposed, as detailed in the next chapter, the EEN was growing quickly. In June 1994, Baptist minister Stan L. LeQuire was hired as a separate director for the network because the EEN had exhausted ESA's staff resources. In October 1995, LeQuire helped establish the CEC as "leadership committee and public policy arm of the EEN." The CEC was presided over by Calvin DeWitt, and its meetings were regularly frequented by Susan Emmerich; Allen Johnson, who founded a regional and more broadly Christian organization dedicated to protest mountaintop removal in Appalachia called Christians for the Mountains in 2005; Scott Sabin of Floresta/PWP; Peter Illyn of CES; and Dean Ohlman. After a period of dormancy, starting in 2009 the CEC re-emerged, at least to some extent, as the CCCC.[21]

Given DeWitt's interest in biodiversity and his leading role within the CEC, the first public advocacy effort of the EEN was to defend the Endangered Species Act of 1973 against a Republican bill intended to weaken its provisions. Drafted shortly after the 1994 Republican takeover of Congress by Representatives Don Young (AK) and Richard Pombo (CA), "The Endangered Species and Conservation Act of 1995" (HR 2275) was designed to support the rights of property owners rather than the rights of the various endangered species inhabiting their lands. In particular God's covenant with Noah (Gen 9:8-16) set a compelling stewardship example in light of species extinction; therefore, the EEN declared the Endangered Species Act "Noah's Ark of our day" and issued a resolution in its defense in October 1995.[22]

In addition, the network sent press releases to the media, placed advertisements in *Roll Call* magazine, and ran thirty-second television announcements. Eighteen states were targeted with letters and about two thousand signatures were collected in support of the original Endangered Species Act before the EEN, together with leaders from their NRPE partner organizations, went to Washington for more direct lobbying activities on January 31, 1996. During their day on Capitol Hill, DeWitt, Sider, and LeQuire gave an interview on *Fox Morning News* and met with several Republican officials. At a press conference—to which the group had brought a live, endangered puma—Sider prayed and declared that they had come to Washington "because God the Creator cared about his creation and therefore evangelical Christians must care for the environment." Sider recalls that this "blew away all the current political stereotypes and [was] a top story on the evening news."[23]

HR 2275 was never introduced to the floor of the House of Representatives. Even though many environmental interest groups had worked toward its opposition, Sierra Club director Carl Pope acknowledged in 1997 that the EEN had been instrumental in defeating the Young-Pombo bill. During the CCCC meeting in 2010, Jim Ball proudly reminisced, "We were the main force that stopped the gutting of the Endangered Species Act!"[24]

### Jim Ball and Global Warming

The dramaturgy of the EEN's campaign against the Young-Pombo bill reveals a successful combination of insider and outsider lobbying tactics, which the network readily emulated in its subsequent initiatives geared toward the problem of climate change. The EEN's engagement with the issue started in 1997, gained momentum with the media savvy WWJD? campaign in 2002, and finally culminated in the ECI of 2006. Inside the EEN the issue of global warming has been inseparable from Jim Ball, who was hired in 1999 to replace LeQuire.[25]

Born in Baton Rouge, Louisiana, in 1961, Ball grew up in a suburb of Dallas, Texas, within "a moderate Southern Baptist setting heavily imbued with evangelical piety and a strong belief in biblical authority." He "accepted Jesus into [his] heart" when he was thirteen. After his ordination in 1989, Ball started graduate studies in theological ethics at Drew University, where he wrote his Ph.D. dissertation on the evangelical response to eco-crisis. While working on his dissertation, Ball was a participant in the EEN's CEC. After his graduation in 1997, he worked for the Union of Concerned Scientists in Washington, D.C., in order to "eventually be a bridge between [environmental organizations] and the Christian community" until he assumed directorship of the EEN in 2000.[26]

Although Ball's career as a creation care advocate seems quite straightforward, especially compared to Ohlman's or Sabin's, it was not until his time at Drew that Ball's "creation care awakening" began. Not triggered by a moral shock or a dramatic conversion experience, Ball nevertheless describes his turn to creation care significantly embedded in the rhetoric of evangelical religious experience: it was a gradually unfolding, life-changing "awakening" process that he experienced because of the conscious effort of another person. Like an evangelical Christian would share her love for Christ, Bonnie Gisel, a fellow student at Drew, had kept sharing "her love for God's creation" with him. As a child Ball may have harbored a love for trees in his heart, but "unfortunately . . . no one [had] actively nurtured [his] love for God's creation." He was thus more concerned about peace and justice issues as an adult and considered Gisel merely eccentric at first. But her slow and gentle teaching effort, and her ability to provide "new eyes" through which Ball would eventually perceive his faith, finally convinced him to extend his care to the rest of creation, too.[27]

Remarkable about Ball's early account of his creation care awakening is not only Gisel's role as an environmental missionary of sorts but also his assumption that concern for creation would require "nurturing." This idea may be outdated as a concept of behavioral psychology explaining the influence of environment versus heredity, but in the context of Ball's awakening, it does emphasize that a potential concern for creation has not necessarily come "naturally" to evangelical Christians. Rather, like the religious convert requiring an exposition of the word of God and the sharing of the love of Christ prior to his or her conversion, the average environmentally unconcerned evangelical may indeed require an evangelist like Gisel to awaken and biblically justify his love and care for creation (in addition to scientific confirmations and cultural reminders that environmental problems do indeed exist).

Once Ball understood "that Christ's reconciliation included all of creation" and that his faith therefore required him to care for creation, his interest in the religion and ecology nexus was piqued as well. Moreover, his concern about environmental problems awakened, becoming stronger and more focused on global warming with his reading of Al Gore's *Earth in the Balance* (1992), and has remained his "calling" since—a calling that is more extensive than it may sound because according to Ball, the issue of global warming "touches on many other concerns," including hunger, poverty, peace, security, and, ultimately, human freedom and love.[28]

In addition to his concern about climate change, when Ball joined the EEN he also brought with him the conviction that legislation was crucial in order to "bring about substantive, real changes." Rather than emphasizing "voluntary hardship" as an adequate measure to tackle environmental problems—an approach favored in many evangelical writings on eco-crisis, as he concluded in his dissertation—Ball deemed solutions "worked out in public life" much more effective. In particular, regarding the complexity and magnitude of global climate change, individual measures were not enough, and climate policy was indeed inevitable. While he would not deny the importance of individual responsibility and grassroots mobilization, it is beyond coincidence that the EEN eventually became the creation care organization nearest to Washington, D.C.[29]

Considering the growing importance of the climate issue at the turn of the twenty-first century, the politically unafraid DNA of the EEN, and the fact that Ball was the only full-time staff member of the network until September 2006, Ball's twin interest in climate and policy would become the EEN's defining niche within the creation care movement during his directorship.

### The ECI and Its Aftermath

The EEN's advocacy efforts regarding global warming climaxed with the ECI, which was launched on February 6, 2006. On March 26, *Time* magazine declared Ball one of the five most innovative contemporary "climate crusaders." Along with the Sierra Club, the National Wildlife Federation, and the National Resources Defense Council, the EEN also participated in the annual meeting of the Clinton Global Initiative in September that year. Guests included Al Gore, Laura Bush, Colin Powell, Bill Gates, Kofi Annan, and numerous other world leaders. Also among the participants was Richard Cizik, still representing the NAE, in a panel discussion about the dialogue among civilizations.[30]

To get the initial eighty-six supporting signatures from evangelical public leaders and turn the ECI into the "PR coup" it was, several years of rapprochement and careful cooperation with Cizik and the NAE had been crucial. So had ties to British theologian John Stott, who had recruited California-based Rick Warren. To fund the ECI, the EEN had received a $500,000 grant from the NRPE and additional contributions from non-partisan Hewlett Foundation, Rockefeller Brothers Fund, and The Pew Charitable Trusts; from the progressive Bauman Foundation and the Nathan Cummings Foundation; and from the conservative Stewardship Foundation.[31]

The network's expansion in terms of public visibility and support from leaders such as Cizik and Warren was internally mirrored by an increase in staff and independence from ESA: in November 2004 the EEN had become incorporated separately, and in February 2007 the organization received 501(c)(3) status from the IRS. By that time the network had added four full-time staff in addition to Ball, including natural resource economist Lowell

(Rusty) Pritchard and public relations specialist Jim Jewell, who would later found Creation Care, Inc., together. In addition, the EEN was relying on contract workers and independent consulting agencies such as Russ Reid Co., who lobbied the Senate on behalf of the network.[32]

Despite the eventual increase in staff, 2006 was such a busy year that the network did not manage to publish a single issue of its *Creation Care* magazine. Apologizing for this neglect early in 2007, editor Rusty Pritchard explained that the "past year [had] seen the creation care movement explode into the public consciousness," and that "the EEN [had] had an influence on public awareness of environmental issues far, far out of proportion with its staff and budget." According to former Director of Communications Alexei Laushkin (1984–), an evangelical political science graduate who joined the network in 2006, the ECI "shifted the discourse in the evangelical community significantly on creation care." Because of the ECI, "the question no longer [was] if [evangelicals] should care about creation," but rather "HOW and to what extent."[33]

In retrospect, however, the ECI also deepened the green gap within evangelicalism. Moreover, it conjured up political expectations that would remain unfulfilled. Not only was the publicity the ECI received out of proportion with the EEN's resources; the claims it made were also not representative of the larger evangelical community's environmental sentiments.[34]

---

If we take a more critical look at the EEN's major advocacy campaigns since the successful defense of the Endangered Species Act in the mid-1990s, it is hard to overlook that the network profited from its status of being an "unexpected voice" within both environmentalism and Evangelicalism in order to gain publicity and attract funding. Especially regarding its financial support, the EEN had early on tapped evangelical and non-evangelical sources in addition to direct contributions from individuals. Unlike Ohlman, whose goal it was to finance the CNF with membership dues and direct contributions from fellow believers, the EEN has heavily relied on support from the NRPE and on grant money from foundations across the ideological spectrum instead. This broad financial support base has allowed the network to survive over the past decades, while Ohlman's CNF closed up shop. Arguably, however, it also fostered a politically unafraid posture toward climate change out of touch with the evangelical grassroots. Either way, maintaining the EEN's narrow, grasstops-oriented climate policy focus became impossible after the ECI.[35]

On August 1, 2009, the EEN thus hired the Rev. Mitchell (Mitch) C. Hescox to take over Ball's former position as president and CEO of the network. Prior to hiring Hescox, the EEN's board had agreed on a strategic transition plan for 2009–2011. The plan identified two major areas of advocacy focus for the organization: first, "affecting legislation and policy on climate change," and second, "changing hearts and minds on creation care." This strategic reopening of the EEN's focus went hand in hand with Ball's transition into the position of the network's executive vice president for climate and policy, which would allow him to concentrate on the first area of focus. Hescox, on the other hand, was to lead the organization in the implementation of its new strategic plan and to concentrate on broader creation care efforts.[36]

In its 2011 year-end electronic newsletter, the EEN announced the adoption of the theme "Creation Care. It's a Matter of Life." While this reframing attempt has not reconciled the EEN's intra-evangelical critics, it is certainly reminiscent of Ronald Sider's original, more broadly construed "completely pro-life" approach to environmentalism. Before we can turn to a more detailed exploration of the countermobilization that the EEN has generated since its founding and to the post-ECI phase of the broader creation care movement, however, another organization that formed in the 1990s and deserves the label politically unafraid needs to be introduced as well.

## RESTORING EDEN: PETER ILLYN AND CHRISTIANS FOR ENVIRONMENTAL STEWARDSHIP (1996–2014; WITH CREATION CARE, INC., SINCE 2014)

CES was formed in the Pacific Northwest in the early 1990s by evangelical minister Peter Illyn. Illyn has endorsed the EDCC and partnered with the EEN, Au Sable, and other creation care organizations. However, if there is one person among creation care leaders who openly displays some of the traits that have made evangelicals nervous about environmentalists—despite his faith meeting "ninety percent of the evangelical standard" and the reservations he himself may have regarding non-evangelical environmentalists—it would certainly be him.[37]

Raised within his family's Russian Orthodox faith background in South Carolina, Illyn (1958–) holds an MBA from Portland State University in addition to his first degree from Rhema Bible Training College. The latter, a Pentecostal educational institution in Oklahoma, is located "down the street" from (charismatic) Oral Roberts University, where Illyn studied before he "kind of got in trouble for protesting a nuclear power plant" and thus had to switch schools. Upon his graduation from Rhema, Illyn and his wife moved to the West Coast, where Illyn would pastor a church within the Foursquare Gospel denomination throughout the 1980s.[38]

Unlike Dean Ohlman before his born-again again experience, Illyn could never be described as a typical conservative evangelical. On the contrary, Illyn always felt a "cultural gap" between himself and the larger evangelical community. Early on, his religiopolitical and cultural affinities had thus aligned more with the Jesus freaks and hippie Christians of the West Coast than with those evangelicals who bought into the "crew cut, flat top, Jesus is a Republican" narrative of the Religious Right.[39]

Quite similar to Ohlman, however, Illyn always felt a strong connection to America's wilderness and the outdoors. As a child he loved reading Jean Craighead George's adventure story *My Side of the Mountain* (1959). And as a Foursquare associate pastor one of his favorite activities was to go backpacking with his youth group and discuss the Russian mystics and "the paradoxes of faith" around the campfire—a practice not very well received by the rest of his congregation. In return, a decreasing "tolerance for theological deviation" and a "growing hypocrisy in the church" were the things that irked Illyn about the Reagan evangelicals of the 1980s. By the end of the decade, he had become so depressed with his vocation that he felt only a long wilderness trip could help him reconnect with God.[40]

After training two llamas for a year to carry his "luxuries," including a Bible and six fantasy novels by Stephen R. Donaldson, Illyn set out for a four-month, one thousand-mile hike along the Pacific Crest Trail through Oregon and Washington in the early summer of 1990. Not only would this trip heal his spiritual burnout but also, rather unexpectedly, turn him into an "environmental evangelist."[41]

In retrospect, two events proved crucial in Illyn's turn toward environmentalism. The first incident happened about three months into his hike, when Illyn was already "feeling a deep, deep spiritual contentment." One night he awoke to the walking sounds of something big outside his tent, suddenly accompanied by a "high-pitched, soulful cry." Fearfully considering even "Bigfoot . . . on the matrix of possibilities," Illyn crawled outside his tent, carrying not much more than his pistol. Instead of the anticipated horror, however, he encountered a scene of "wonder" instead:

> Standing in the shadows, with the fog reflecting the moonlight, I saw a herd of ten to twelve elk grazing. In the middle of the herd was a magnificent bull. His antlers were so large they reached halfway down his spine. Surrounded by his harem of cows, this beast of the forest lifted his head towards heaven. With the steam blowing out his nostrils, he let out another cry. What I had heard earlier was the rut of the bull elk; a primal cry of wild, of glory, of lordship.
>
> Standing there . . . I was reminded of the scripture in Genesis 1: "And God made the beast of the earth after his kind, and cattle after their kind, and every thing that creepeth upon the earth after his kind: and God saw it was good." . . . As I watched the elk, I was overcome by a sense of goodness. It was at that moment when I realized how deeply I loved nature, the stars, the elk, and the wilderness. It was an epiphany of the eyes of my soul.[42]

A few days later Illyn reached a part of the Pacific Crest Trail where the federally protected wilderness bordered on a clear-cut of Douglas fir stumps left behind by a logging company. Compared to the scene of wonder he had experienced a few nights prior, this "site of carnage" broke his heart. It was the largest clear-cut he had ever seen and "the greatest devastation [he] would see until the World Trade Center towers fell" more than ten years later. Illyn was "shocked at the amount of devastation" and had "this sense of unnecessary destruction, of people who have power over nature but no sense of limits." Sitting down on one of the tree stumps and turning to his daily Bible reading, "The words [of Proverbs 31:8] meant something different. 'Speak out for those who cannot speak for themselves.' Praying beseechingly, [Illyn] asked, 'Lord, who speaks for your spotted owls, your elk, and your ancient forests?'"[43]

Granted, the question of nature's standing in the case of humanity's boundless appetite for natural resources was not novel. It had already been addressed in a secular manner in 1972, through the famous Supreme Court case *Sierra Club v. Morton*. Although not speaking for the majority, dissenting Justice Douglas had defended the idea of a legally justified substitute agency on behalf of the "inanimate object" nature in order to constrain federal officials from approving an extensive skiing development in the Sequoia National Forest.[44]

According to Illyn's recent insights though, nature's standing rested upon much more than humans' relation to it. Nature, as he had felt deeply a few nights before, was wonderful and enjoyable indeed, but it was also thoroughly good and intrinsically valuable because God had made it, thus revealing its creator. It may have taken more than a reading of Proverbs 31:8, but surrounded by the remains "of what had clearly been an ancient forest," Illyn realized that nature's standing was biblically mandated as well and that creation was in need of protection against human sinfulness. At this site of devastation, he thus "made a covenant with God to speak out for the wilderness and for all the species that called it home."[45]

For his remaining time in the wilderness, Illyn read his Bible "with a deliberate desire to discover God's truths about caring for creation." This practice "gave new meaning to verses that [he] had read many times before but without an environmental perspective." Upon his return, and befitting his newly declared environmentalist covenant, he started a wilderness outfitting ministry, taking small groups and families to wilderness areas in Washington state to inspire their care for creation. Illyn also became the first regional director in the Pacific Northwest for Green Cross, an initially ecumenical creation care organization that Ronald Sider's ESA had taken under its wings until it merged with the EEN. Eventually, Illyn's various creation care efforts consolidated into the incorporation of CES in 1996, which, as its former website stated somewhat confusingly, "became Restoring Eden in 2001."[46]

---

To call CES's organizational architecture intricate is an understatement. In 1996, the organization received 501(c)(3) status from the IRS. As early tax returns show, CES was doing business as Creation Care Study Program

(CCSP) until 2007. In 2010, Illyn said that CES had "three programs": Restoring Eden (RE), CCSP, and Renewal. At the time Illyn headed the civic engagement program RE. His partner, Christopher Elisara, was (and still is) in charge of CCSP, which has offered student field trips designed to foster ecological consciousness and cultural immersion in Belize since 1995 and New Zealand since 2000. Renewal, a student-led creation care grassroots network launched in 2008 with the support of the EEN and integrated into CES in 2009, seems to have been disbanded since. Or, at least partially, Renewal has morphed into Young Evangelicals for Climate Action (Y.E.C.A.), established under the auspices of the EEN in 2012. In 2014, RE was transferred to Creation Care, Inc., another evangelical environmental organization introduced in chapter 6. Since then, CES has been headed by Elisara alone, who was less of a presence in the creation care community at the time I conducted primary research, hence my focus on Illyn.[47]

Congruent with Illyn's personal experiences and ecological conversion, RE's mission was "to make hearts bigger, hands dirtier, and voices stronger by rediscovering the biblical call to love, serve, and protect God's creation." The organization's work thus rested on the three pillars of nature appreciation ("love"), environmental stewardship ("service"), and public advocacy ("protection").[48]

As Illyn experienced firsthand, to love creation is the prerequisite for any kind of service and protection on behalf of the environment. And like Dean Ohlman and others had discovered, for evangelicals this love is biblically mandated. In addition, it needs to be experienced. Drawing an explicit parallel to the evangelical born-again experience, Illyn believes that a cognitive shift is required of most Christians to trigger an ecological conversion and thus any kind of environmental engagement on their part. In particular among the younger generations, intimacy with—and appreciation of—nature is an endangered spiritual value. Thus, RE's former website not only recommended the study of the biblical basis of creation care but also worship nights under the stars, prayer hikes, and other types of reflection and contemplation with God in creation.[49]

In order to serve creation, CES encouraged both environmental education and service projects that "enhance the fruitfulness of nature and bring life to all that depend on it." Recommended actions to get one's "hands dirty for God's creation" were involvement in energy conservation efforts, sustainable food and agriculture projects, and activities intended to restore beauty and ecology. Considering the crucial importance of community, the organization also encouraged and supported the establishment of creation care groups in churches, schools, and other communities. In addition, the CCSP enlisted about sixty students from approximately thirty colleges and universities per year.[50]

Last but certainly not least, the "protect" part of CES's mission entailed three types of public policy and grassroots advocacy: (1) speaking out in the public square; (2) letting "our dollars speak in the marketplace"; and (3) educating the policymakers in the halls of power. As Illyn emphasized, civic engagement is crucial because faith is not just a private enterprise. Because of religion's public dimension, evangelicals ought to speak out in the public square regarding their values and moral concerns, all within the constraints of civility and with an acknowledgment of pluralism, of course. In addition, and similar to Jim Ball and others involved with the EEN, for Illyn changing hearts and minds is not enough to tackle large-scale systemic environmental problems. Although he admits that there is a place and a need for individual environmental actions, such as changing light bulbs, recycling, composting, etc., he insists that "you don't individually stop a coal plant from coming into your community, or don't individually stop mountaintop removal."[51]

Under the auspices of CES, RE was engaged with issues of biodiversity loss, mountaintop removal (MTR), clean coal, and climate change. A particularly strong emphasis on justice was discursively embedded into notions of "just power" and "climate justice." Illyn's covenant to speak out for those who cannot speak for themselves was thus not restricted to wilderness areas and nonhuman species. It included justice-oriented activism on behalf of those negatively impacted by climate change, such as the global poor, tribal Christians in Papua New Guinea, inhabitants of the Arctic National Wildlife Refuge, or disadvantaged Americans in Appalachia.[52]

As for concrete advocacy efforts, Illyn traveled extensively within and outside the United States to deliver the mission of his organization and inspire creation care activism among college students, churchgoers, and community members. Following the holistic approach of his activism, Illyn would take twelve college students to the small town of Haines, Alaska, for example, to inspire and deepen their connection with God in nature in a setting of natural beauty. The purpose of a trip like that, however, would be much more encompassing as Illyn also had his students restore Native American totem poles in order to symbolically "apologize for the spiritual arrogance of the earlier missionaries." Moreover, Illyn conceptualized this and many of his trips as an opportunity to speak on behalf of the Christian stewardship mandate and to build grassroots support for the environment. He and the students around him also traveled to Washington, D.C., to speak out in the halls of power, and they set up creation care advocacy booths at large Christian rock music festivals in order to acquire new members and collect petition signatures for RE campaigns, such as JUSTpower, which advocates for clean and renewable energy. In addition, RE organized teachings on civic engagement and advocacy tools and facilitated tours to sites in the Appalachian mountain region devastated by MTR.[53]

---

With its focus on younger Christians in the Pacific Northwest and using advocacy tactics closer to those popularized by environmental groups such as Greenpeace, RE occupied a more "edgy" niche within the creation care advocacy community. After all, Illyn did come to Evangelicalism and creation care from out of the Jesus Movement. This "loose collection of activists, youth ministers, entertainers, and born-again hippies" espoused a "more relaxed brand of evangelicalism" than the older generation of evangelicals concerned about the social and cultural effects of the 1960s. Illyn thus scores on many of the characteristics attached to the label he once identified with as well: an educational transition because of protest politics; a fondness for rock music; and a verbal demonstrativeness that seeks to counter and unmask both liberal and conservative and secular and evangelical contradictions and hypocrisies. A countercultural current therefore transpired through CES in various forms, from the grants allocated by the band the Grateful Dead to the provocative RE bumper stickers sporting slogans such as "God's original plan was to hang out in a garden with some naked vegetarians."[54]

Since he is no biblical literalist, Illyn's "theology of wild" has been open to various influences from across the major branches of the church's family tree. Those seem to include the relational theology of liturgical churches, Russian mysticism, the non-Jimmy-Swaggert-type of American Pentecostalism practiced by the Foursquare Gospel, the Kuyperian theology of reconciliation popular in the Christian Reformed and creation care circles of the Northeast, and the early understanding of Celtic Christianity that in nature "the wall between you and God is thinner." While RE firmly condemned the worship of nature (just like the other organizations within the creation care advocacy community), Illyn has not been theologically distressed by what theologically more conservative evangelicals consider the rather pagan "belly-button Christianity" that his indigenous Christian friends and partners in Papua New Guinea embrace.[55]

Well aware of the fact that he could only reach a certain segment of American evangelicals, Illyn knew that in order to "make environmentalists out of Christians," RE would have to concentrate on the "emerging, post-evangelical, post-denominational, and to some degree post-colonial" younger generation of Christians in the Northwest.[56]

To this demographic the creation care movement of the twenty-first century may be somewhat comparable to the Jesus Movement of the 1970s, which did provide an alternative to conservative Christianity on the one hand *and* to a morally relative hedonism on the other. Likewise, caring for creation may allow in particular younger evangelicals to rebel against their parents' generation by addressing an issue largely dismissed as either controversial or unimportant while still demonstrating the relevance of their faith to their increasingly non-Christian peers.

Despite CES's theological openness and more regional, West Coast brand of creation care activism, Illyn's Evangelicalism and his understanding of the importance of institutions and coalitions are strong enough to tie him closely to the church and to other evangelical creation care leaders as well. Although RE built coalitions with mainstream environmental organizations and Illyn does not object to being called a "tree hugger," he nevertheless emphasized that RE affiliates hugged trees *for Jesus*. Additionally, Illyn negates radical forms of biocentrism and, alluding to the secular organization Earth First!, points out that the creation care movement is an "earth third movement"—because Christians must love God first, then their neighbors, and then creation.[57]

Although more politically unafraid than most of the other creation care leaders, Illyn has nevertheless collaborated closely with fellow evangelical environmental activists through strategic and tactical alliances, interlocking directorates, and other forms of exchange and mutual support. Like others in the movement, Illyn is convinced that Christian colleges and churches are key players in the desired culture shift toward a more ecologically conscious Evangelicalism. His task as an environmental evangelist thus goes far beyond lobbying and advocacy activities on behalf of specific environmental policies. Moreover, Illyn sees it as his duty to enable Christians to develop an emotive connection to nature *and* to foster an integrative and interconnected worldview within the evangelical community, which will eventually transcend the rift that has been created by the culture war.[58]

While Illyn deems civic engagement crucial, it is important to note that RE did not intend to use public policy as a tool to recreate an ecologically intact paradise on earth. Rather, "restoring Eden" means that people of faith have to—individually and collectively, personally and politically, and thus holistically—work toward *shalom* and the restoration of broken relationships. As a promise of "balanced harmony," *shalom* stands in contrast with the green gap between those "compartmentalized" Christians who are trying to uphold an "American exceptionalism" and those in the creation care movement, who have, according to Illyn's understanding, a more integrative and holistically oriented Christian worldview.[59]

# 5
# ORGANIZED EVANGELICAL ENVIRONMENTAL SKEPTICISM

To rape the environment is a sin. God calls us to be stewards of creation. But it does not follow that Christians who are concerned about the earth should get on board the latest environmentalist bandwagon.

D. James Kennedy[1]

What I have to confess is a basic skepticism. Whenever I see a claim of fact from an environmental advocacy organization, my immediate gut reaction is to be skeptical.

E. Calvin Beisner, Cornwall Alliance for the Stewardship of Creation[2]

If the 1990s were the time of a more concerted organization and politicization of creation care, by the end of the decade this trend within the evolution of the movement also triggered a more organized evangelical critique. Ultimately, environmentalism could not only be viewed as a religious obligation and a cultural space rife with evangelistic opportunities, but also as a site of political maneuvering and scientific "myth" propagation further chipping away at the theological and ideological pillars of Christian America.

Evangelicals skeptical of environmentalism criticized the creation care movement early on, but it was the formation of the EEN and the network's advocacy efforts around climate change that eventually sparked a more organized countermovement. Over the past decades since then, evangelical environmental skepticism has evolved and taken organizational root as well, mostly under the leadership of E. Calvin Beisner and the CA. A closer look at the roots of the discontent surrounding the creation care movement is crucial in order to gain a better understanding of the opposition's motivation, self-understanding, and relation to the creation care movement. Moreover, gaining a nuanced perspective on organized evangelical environmental skepticism is particularly important if we want to better understand the latest evolutionary phase of the creation care movement, which sparked the establishment of decidedly apolitical creation care organizations apparently eager to evade the intra-evangelical discord that has surrounded the EEN since its founding.[3]

## "EXAMINE EVERYTHING CAREFULLY; HOLD FAST TO THAT WHICH IS GOOD": EARLY SKEPTICAL RESPONSES TO CREATION CARE AND THE EDCC

In May 1990, right before Peter Illyn embarked on his life-and-ministry-changing wilderness trek through the Cascade Mountains and right after Dean Ohlman's CNF had been introduced by FoF the week following the twentieth anniversary of Earth Day, *The Coral Ridge Encounter* magazine dedicated that month's issue to an investigation of the Christian responsibility to tend the earth. Published by televangelist D. James Kennedy's (1930–2007) Florida-based Coral Ridge Ministries, the cover of this particular issue sported the most iconic environmental picture ever taken: Earth seen from space.[4]

Although Kennedy had been actively connected to Pat Robertson, Jerry Falwell, and others on the Religious Right since the early days of the Moral Majority, he was less publicly visible than his colleagues and was thus later mockingly called "evangelical Christianity's best kept secret." In his May 1990 *Coral Ridge Encounter* contribution, Kennedy acknowledged that the cultural mandate in Genesis 1:26-28 required Christians (a.k.a. "God's junior partners") "to care for—or tend—the earth in His name." Apart from affirming this basic, politically and practically unspecified, but biblically mandated responsibility for the earth—which he reaffirmed in one of his last books published shortly before his death—Kennedy's position on environmental stewardship remained vague. Displaying a rather rigid view on biblical authority, he came to the following conclusion: "The Lord has a direct answer to pollution, acid rain, nuclear meltdowns and other environmental threats—simply apply God's Word to God's world."[5]

The matter of biblical environmental stewardship was not resolvable by all evangelical Christians on such simplistic terms, however. This was not only testified to by the budding creation care movement. Roughly a dozen pages after Kennedy's article, theologian James B. Jordan probed more thoroughly: "Where does the Church stand on issues concerning our planet? How can the Christian community get involved and have a positive, balanced impact on the problem?" And, most importantly to evangelicals suspicious of the environmental movement and its claims, "Is the world really teetering on destruction due to human carelessness and overpopulation?"[6]

To respond to these questions, Jordan introduced two evangelicals professionally engaged in finding answers: Dean Ohlman of the CNF and E. Calvin Beisner, the man who would come to be known as the "primary opponent" of the EEN and evangelical climate change activism. At the time Beisner (1955–) held a B.A. in interdisciplinary studies in religion and philosophy from the University of Southern California and an M.A. in society from International College. He had just published a book dealing with problematic issues at the intersection of ecology and economics from a biblical perspective: *Prospects for Growth: A Biblical View of Population, Resources, and the Future* (1990).[7]

Jordan's article, visually offset by a background of frosty Arctic ice on which a solitary polar bear was treading, introduced both Beisner and Ohlman not only via their respective works—in Beisner's case his newly published book, in Ohlman's his newly founded CNF—but also via black and white portrait photographs. The photograph of Ohlman showed a middle-aged man wearing a collared shirt, holding a Nikon camera in front of his chest, and gazing rather seriously in the distance. Arguably, it evoked the image of a National Park ranger. Beneath it said, "As a Christian conservationist, Dean Ohlman uses the Bible to battle the pantheistic view of nature, which is prevalent in our society's thinking." In contrast, Beisner's photo showed a confident but sympathetically smiling young man wearing a suit and tie, accompanied by the words, "With a solid background in ecology, economics, and religion, E. Calvin Beisner is well qualified to expose some of the myths of the environmental movement."[8]

While Jordan acknowledged that Ohlman and Beisner came to the debate from different perspectives, his article gave equal space and appreciation to both men. Since the issue of the magazine contained separate advertisements for both Beisner's book and Ohlman's organization as well, we can assume that their work was regarded as complementary instead of antagonistic. Although Beisner was introduced first, and his photograph towered above Ohlman's, it seems that at that point in time, Ohlman was nonetheless recognized as a qualified evangelical authority to answer Jordan's second question in particular, namely how the evangelical Christian community could get involved in environmentalism and have a positive, balanced impact. In contrast, however, Beisner was introduced as an authority on the question of whether or not some of the alarming claims of the environmentalists regarding eco-crisis should be taken seriously by evangelical Christians.

As Jordan summarized the main premises of *Prospects for Growth*, Beisner's work asserted that "the earth was made for man," and that human needs rightly had to dominate those of "the lower order of creation." Furthermore, Beisner's book showed "that God created a world far more resilient and far less fragile than modern environmentalists want us to believe."

It thus exposed some environmentalist claims, especially those pertaining to population, as "greatly exaggerated." In addition, Jordan emphasized that Beisner deemed "freedom [from state intervention] . . . much better for the environment than slavery," and that he soundly applied biblical principles to current environmental concerns such as ozone layer depletion and global warming.[9]

If Jordan's most important question had been where the church stood on environmental issues, Beisner's answer to Jordan's third question regarding the problematics and urgency of environmental problems turned Ohlman's conservationist efforts more or less into a non-priority. If the world was inherently resilient, and there were only minor ecological problems and degradations, evangelical Christians did not necessarily have to get involved in the environmental movement, did they? In fact, would it not be best if they approached the movement with caution since it was apparently wrong about its claims and therefore misguided in its actions?

It is crucial to keep this early portrait of Beisner as environmentalist myth detector in mind. To the audience that Kennedy's Coral Ridge Ministries has catered to, an exposition of the myths allegedly spread by the environmental movement has since become more important than an engagement in environmental conservation efforts, let alone the support of the creation care movement. Although both Ohlman and Beisner were appreciatively treated in the May 1990 *Coral Ridge Encounter* magazine, Ohlman's Earth Day 1990 interview for Kennedy's national radio broadcast was never aired—back then an early sign to Ohlman "that all was not well with [him] in conservative evangelical circles." This discrepancy between evangelicals like Ohlman and those more skeptical of the evangelical entry into environmentalism is even more profoundly exemplified by Beisner's reaction to the EDCC in 1993.[10]

---

While EEN affiliates were still fine-tuning the drafting of the EDCC late in 1993, *World,* a biweekly evangelical news magazine, published an article on the newly founded EEN and included an extensive analysis of the EDCC. Here, Beisner critiqued the document on three points specifically: (1) "factual errors" regarding the state of the environment in the seven areas of degradation listed, which "illustrate[d] a disturbing tendency among the declaration's authors to mimic the claims of crisis current in the popular press and the secular environmental movement without checking the credibility of these claims"; (2) flawed economic theory, especially regarding the declaration's unspecified understanding of sustainable economies, which "probably exclude[d] the productive economies of the West"; (3) "theological weaknesses" exhibited by not recognizing the *imago dei* as a source of creativity and Christ's resurrection as having "set in motion the reversal of the curse." Bluntly, we could sum up Beisner's criticism as bad science, bad economics, and bad theology on part of the EEN and the declaration's endorsers.[11]

But Beisner also admitted that "the declaration [was] not all bad news." Positive in his view were the recognition of poverty as a cause of environmental degradation and the declaration's support of "'just, free economies.'" Furthermore, Beisner applauded the declaration's warning "that many people [were] turning, in vain, to non-Christian religions for guidance in thinking about the environment." Therefore, he also expressed content with the fact that the EDCC "firmly assert[ed] the distinction between Creator and creature that [had] crumbled in the minds of many environmentalists West and East."[12]

Nevertheless, Beisner's primarily dismissive critique of the EDCC angered the actively organizing creation care community. In its January 8, 1994, issue, *World* gave Ronald Sider the opportunity to openly respond to Beisner's analysis (not without granting Beisner the opportunity of a brief rejoinder in that same issue, however).[13]

According to Sider, Beisner was the one whose scientific claims were not in line with "the vast majority of responsible scientists," especially regarding the extinction of species. Furthermore, Sider countered Beisner's charge of theological error with the suggestion that Beisner himself may espouse "an unbiblical perspective of the fall." Perhaps it was his "overly optimistic postmillennialism" that "led [Beisner] to overlook the way economic injustice, greed, and narcissistic individualism trample[d] the poor and mar[red] the environment"? As to Beisner's assumption regarding the EDCC's economic position, Sider asserted that "stewardship" neither meant the exclusion of humanity's "stewardly ownership" (under God's command) nor "a complete abandonment of Western economics." In closing, he also emphasized that only the "truth" could set evangelicals "free from sloaganeering, free from polemical cheap shots and ad hominem argumentation, free from either ignoring or exaggerating the environmental problems . . . and finally free from causing unnecessary and harmful division in the body of Christ," of which he thus accused Beisner indirectly.[14]

In his defensive response to Sider, Beisner pointed out that the focus of most of his criticism had been the lack of scientific evidence with regard to the seven environmental degradations the EDCC listed. While he claimed not to be "in favor of extinguishing species" either, he dismissed the biodiversity loss studies of Harvard University biologist E. O. Wilson due to a lack of "hard, empirical field data." As for his and Sider's differences regarding eschatology, Beisner deemed those irrelevant to the debate. Moreover, he saw a point of agreement in his and Sider's belief in the finitude of the earth, although he emphasized that "finitude and exhaustibility [were] not synonymous." Tellingly, Beisner's rejoinder to Sider ended with the following sentence: "I'm just urging people to try, as I am trying, to do as Scripture commands: to 'examine everything carefully; hold fast to that which is good.'"[15]

## THE CORNWALL ALLIANCE FOR THE STEWARDSHIP OF CREATION (2000–)

Apparently, the EDCC presented a critical challenge to what Beisner and others around him deemed good. Shortly after the EEN's successful campaign in defense of the Endangered Species Act, Beisner published an equally critical but more extensive book on the evangelical entry into the environmental debate, *Where Garden Meets Wilderness* (1997). Similar to D. James Kennedy, with whom he had been connected since before the founding of the EEN, the only environmental ethic Beisner seemed to be able to approve of was a general affirmation of the importance of stewardship. Other than that, caution regarding environmentalism seemed paramount.[16]

Beisner's environmental skepticism was initially not backed by an organization such as the EEN, or a public declaration like the EDCC. In 2000, however, several conservative Christian and Jewish leaders were brought together by the Acton Institute for the Study of Religion and Liberty, a libertarian think tank located in Grand Rapids, Michigan, which had also published *Where Garden Meets Wilderness*. Those assembled drafted and agreed on "The Cornwall Declaration on Environmental Stewardship," which was, according to Larsen, more or less "a distillation of the arguments propounded by Beisner in *Where Garden Meets Wilderness*." The Cornwall Declaration was to be the founding document for a new organization called the Interfaith Council for Environmental Stewardship (ICES), which participants envisioned as a "free-market-friendly alternative to the National Religious Partnership for the Environment."[17]

Unlike the NRPE and its partner organizations, ICES initially did nothing but gather signatures for the Cornwall Declaration. While the latter affirmed the "moral necessity of ecological stewardship," it also emphasized that a "clean environment [was] a costly good." Hence only "well founded and serious" issues should be tackled, such as environmentally caused human health problems in developing countries, "distorted resource consumption patterns driven by perverse economic incentives," and nuclear and other hazardous waste disposal matters. Among the environmental problems that were "without foundation or greatly exaggerated," the declaration listed "fears of destructive man-made global warming, overpopulation, and rampant species loss"—which were the very concerns that environmentalists and creation care advocates had identified as crucially problematic throughout the 1980s and 1990s.[18]

The Cornwall Declaration was initially signed by sixty-six members of the Catholic, Jewish, and Protestant communities, who have been joined by thousands more since its release in 2000, according to the CA. Among the initial Protestant signatories were several evangelicals associated with the Religious Right, such as James Dobson, Chuck Colson, and D. James Kennedy. There was "virtually no overlap" with the signatories of the EDCC.[19]

Dormant regarding other activities, in the wake of the EEN's climate activism during the George W. Bush presidency, ICES was reactivated as Interfaith Stewardship Alliance (ISA) in 2005. In 2007, ISA was then renamed the Cornwall Alliance for the Stewardship of Creation (CA) and has since actively countered the EEN and the evangelical creation care movement on many instances. Whereas the initial self-understanding of the organization's religious identity was "interfaith"—as reflected in the names of its former incarnations ICES and ISA—the CA has embraced a more exclusive "evangelical" religious identity congruent with Beisner's faith background.[20]

Until it applied for independent 501(c)(3) status in 2019, the CA was a "project" of an organization called The James Partnership (TJP), on whose IRS forms Beisner is listed as founder/board member and as the only person receiving a reportable compensation. TJP is run by Christopher Rogers, a "Republican operative" who also owns a public relations firm (CDR Communications) that has several Religious Right organizations among its clients, including FoF, Prison Fellowship Ministries, and Coral Ridge Ministries. Since the interim of its pending IRS status, the CA has been "a project of a Committee for a Constructive Tomorrow" (CFACT), a D.C.-based think tank lobbying for free market solutions to environmental problems since 1985.[21]

According to its mission, the CA "seek[s] to magnify the glory of God in creation, the wisdom of His truth in environmental stewardship, the kindness of His mercy in lifting the needy out of poverty, and the wonders of His grace in the gospel of Jesus Christ." Arguably, the "truth in environmental stewardship" part of this mission has been in the foreground of the organization's advocacy, which resembles that of a think tank as well. The CA has thus mainly produced papers, articles, books, and videos in order to educate the public and influence policymakers. Since its inception as ISA in 2005, the group has also issued several open letters and calls to action opposed to the climate activism of the EEN, such as "An Open Letter to the Signers of 'Climate Change: An Evangelical Call to Action' and Others Concerned About Global Warming" (2006). The more encompassing but equally critical "A Call to Truth, Prudence, and Protection of the Poor: An Evangelical Response to Global Warming" has been renewed several times since its first publication in July 2006. In addition, Beisner has testified before the U.S. Senate Environment and Public Works Committee, briefed the White House Council on Environmental Quality, participated in conferences, and spoken on radio and television talk shows (such as the *Glenn Beck Program* among others) in the United States and abroad.[22]

Beisner claimed in 2010 that the CA's newsletter went to at least 22,000 people directly and that the CA represented the views of the evangelical community much better than any of the creation care movement organizations. In 2013 according to its website, the CA had twenty-two senior fellows, fellows, and adjunct scholars, forty contributing writers, and thirty-three advisors. If its recent move toward organizational independence is any indication, the organization has fared quite well over the past decade.[23]

While its politically unafraid stance toward climate change eventually became the EEN's defining niche within the creation care movement, the CA has become equally defined by its skeptical stance toward global warming and its allegedly close association with the "climate change denial machine." As explained in "An Open Letter," the scientific data—provided, alas, by contrarian scientists—compels evangelical environmental skeptics to present "extensive evidence and argument against the extent, the significance, and perhaps the existence of the much-touted scientific consensus on catastrophic human-induced global warming." Climate change may be happening to some extent but certainly not in alarming proportions. Therefore, and unlike the signatories of EEN's ECI, affiliates and supporters of the CA do not see an obligation to act upon the issue. Moreover, in line with Beisner's early EDCC criticism, they recommend caution and prudence in order to "effectively protect humanity—especially the poor" instead.[24]

---

It is empirically valid to associate skepticism about the reality and extent of anthropogenic climate change with the economic and political interests of the larger conservative movement and corporate America. The positions of Beisner and the CA have not only been critiqued for their embrace of free market capitalism and their equally strong dismissal of mainstream environmental science but also for their alleged darker motives.[25]

An early report by Right Wing Watch, for instance, found that the CA is closely linked to the "anti-environmental" CFACT, which is in turn a part of the Competitive Enterprise Institute's "climate change denialist network" and has received funding from ExxonMobil, Chevron, and Scaife Family Foundation. The signatories of the CA's position papers and calls include contrarian scientists, who are oftentimes well rewarded by the so-called "dark money" flow into the advocacy organizations that pay for their refutations of the scientific consensus. The authors of the CA's "Call to Truth" thus trigger "the most obvious objection to their enterprise," namely that they are "well-credentialed lobbyist[s] hired out by energy corporations to neutralize environmentalist concerns." Considering the intricate network of individuals and organizations on the political Right and the funding that connects them to corporations and right-wing foundations, "All of the antienvironmental groups associated with the Religious Right" must be deeply entangled in "a web of deception and subterfuge."[26]

CFACT is an element of what critics call the "climate change denial machine," and Beisner's further involvement with the CA was indeed prompted by an acquaintance of his who was affiliated with CFACT and concerned about the EEN's activism. Moreover, money certainly plays a crucial role in American politics. Especially around the issue of climate change, the number of—and the money spent on and by—actors attempting to influence Congress has risen sharply since 2003, when the U.S. Senate voted on the first comprehensive climate policy proposal. But not only climate change skeptics depend on—and are influenced to varying degrees by—the financial support they receive. Whether the money creates the cause or the cause attracts the money—and in each case, to what degree of influence—is hardly told objectively in the realm of interest group politics. Subjectively, it very often appears to be only the other side that is corrupted by manipulating interests, of course.[27]

Just as opponents of U.S. conservatism, the Religious Right, and the Tea Party movement have critiqued the funds that flow into advocacy organizations on the political Right, so have critics of the political Left and the environmental movement been quick to attribute guilt by association when it comes to the funding sources of politically more progressive organizations. In sync with the CA's intensifying countermobilization in 2006, for example, the Acton Institute and the socially and theologically conservative Institute on Religion and Democracy (IRD) (both of which Beisner has served as a fellow for) prepared a joint paper to expose the allegedly hidden agenda of the ECI. The authors charged that the EEN received donations from progressive foundations that otherwise support causes diametrically opposed to Christian morality, such as abortion and population control, thereby implying that the EEN would support those as well. According to Jim Jewell, who was responsible for the ECI's PR at the time, Acton Institute's "smear" portrait of creation care activists "in bed with the pro-abortion folks" worked very well and made evangelicals even more suspicious of the creation care movement.[28]

When asked directly about the funding of the CA, Calvin Beisner said he preferred not to know where the money for his organization was coming from so that when he was out on speaking engagements he did not "feel beholden to anybody." Such a decidedly ignorant position can arguably be interpreted as deceptive as well. Looked at from a value-neutral perspective, though, it does not seem much different from the EEN's Jim Ball's rather lighthearted view of funds without strings: "Anytime anybody wants to give me money to talk about what Jesus said we ought to be doing and the lordship of Christ, I'll take it." Both Ball and Beisner seem to purposely focus on the ends of their respective works rather than on the sources of their means (or, at least they both want to publicly appear that way).[29]

More importantly, however, the arguments against involvement in tackling the problem of climate change expressed in organizational statements such as the CA's "Open Letter" and "Call to Truth" are not entirely new. Nor are they surprising if we consider Beisner's response to the EDCC and the even earlier depiction of him as environmentalist myth detector. Recall that his EDCC criticism centered around disagreements regarding theology, science, and economics. Likewise, the CA's "Renewed Call to Truth, Prudence, and the Protection of the Poor" condemns the "idea" of what the organization calls "global warming alarmism" on three grounds specifically: "poor theology," "poor science," and "poor economics." The motivation for evangelical environmental skepticism thus appears to be more complex and faith-based as well. We would therefore be wrong to simply dismiss Beisner and the CA as "liar-for-hire." Moreover, only when we venture beyond a simplistic attribution to conservative ideology and/or fossil fuel money can evangelical environmental skepticism tell us more about the intra-evangelical boundaries of creation care than about its own connections to right-wing organizations and the so-called climate change denial machine.[30]

## CONTOURS OF FAITH-BASED EVANGELICAL ENVIRONMENTAL SKEPTICISM

### Theology and Economics

Attending Heartland Institute's "Global Warming Is Not A Crisis!" conference in 2008, journalist Eric Pooley observed that the work of many presenters was part of their identities: "Many . . . simply loved intellectual combat; they saw themselves as flinty truth tellers trying to stop the world from adopting solutions they hated in response to a problem they didn't think existed." A similar habitual demeanor can arguably be attributed to Beisner as well, who was among Heartland's speakers in 2008 and who has repeatedly emphasized the importance of truth, logic, and careful examination. In his own words, Beisner understands himself as a "fact-checker-type" rather than a person whose actions are driven by emotions. Losing an argument, especially about his faith, is not something he likes.[31]

When asked how and when he became interested in the intersection of environmental stewardship, economics, and poverty, Beisner mentioned Ronald Sider's book *Rich Christians in an Age of Hunger* (1977). A pastor friend had strongly recommended the book to Beisner while he was temporarily living in rural northwest Arkansas in 1980. At first Beisner refused to read it because at the time he "had no interest whatsoever in the economic issues." His friend was persistent, though, and Beisner eventually gave in.[32]

Beisner "had never studied any economics" prior to his reading of *Rich Christians,* so he did not feel qualified to evaluate the measures Sider recommended to alleviate poverty. But during "the first decade of [his] Christian life," which began in Southern California with a conversion during Billy

Graham's Anaheim Crusade of 1969, Beisner's "interest [had] almost exclusively [been] in Biblical studies, theology, and reasons for Christian faith, apologetics." Hence, he "recognized a great deal of misuse of Scripture in [Sider's] book, and a lot of illogical reasoning" and was therefore suspicious of Sider's grasp of economics. Moreover, he felt strongly compelled to learn more about economics and the history of economic theory himself, which eventually led to his pursuit of an M.A. in society with a specialization in economic ethics. As Gushee comments on *Rich Christians*, Sider's "striking, biblically based attack on Christian complacency in a world with 'a billion hungry neighbors' won him both plaudits and enemies and launched his career with a flourish." Apparently, it also launched the career of the major evangelical critic of the creation care movement more than ten years before Sider decided to establish the EEN as a ministry of his ESA.[33]

Before his graduation from International College in 1983, Beisner received a grant to work on economic ethics under the tutelage of the late Russell Kirk in 1982. Among others, the "grandfather of American conservative thought" was a "very important thinker in shaping [Beisner's] way of approaching issues." In addition, Austrian economist F. A. Hayek's *Road to Serfdom* (1944) would profoundly influence Beisner's anti-statist embrace of the free market. It is important to note, though, that Beisner's previous interest in the defense of the Christian faith and doctrine was not simply superseded by a newfound passion for economics incited by the reading of Sider's book. Rather, the two became inextricably linked.[34]

Still at International College, Beisner had a "theologian friend," Jay Grimstead, who was forming a new organization at the time. The idea behind the Coalition on Revival (COR) was to "bring together Christian scholars from a variety of different fields," such as law, government, education, media, arts, and economics, in order "to flesh out how the Christian worldview affected [their] understanding of those fields." Grimstead wanted Beisner to chair the COR's economics committee for the very reason that Beisner was newly acquainted with economics and would thus bring "a fresh mind to this." Also on the COR's economics committee, among others, was Marvin Olasky, later editor-in-chief of *World* magazine and at the time editor of Crossway's Turning Point Christian Worldview Series, out of which Beisner's *Prospects for Growth* would be published.[35]

The COR is "a network of evangelical leaders from every major denominational and theological perspective" dedicated to biblical obedience and holiness. Using the Christian reconstructionist language of kingdom or dominion theology, the COR asserts that "wherever God's people, His willingly obedient subjects, are obeying Him in every aspect of their lives, there is where the King's Kingdom is being brought forth in this world in time and space to implement His Biblical worldview." Living out the biblical worldview thus implies that Christians bring the totality of their lives "under the King's dominion," so that in turn "the Kingdom of God increases, advances, and becomes measurable in this space-time world in every sphere of life."[36]

Obviously influenced by Francis Schaeffer and other neo-Calvinists, the COR has developed a series of seventeen "worldview documents" designed to set forth what the COR "believe[s] are the fundamental and essential points of the total Christian world and life view." Their intended function is to "unify" pastors and help them summon "their people to 'Get God's will done in their city as it is in heaven' to whatever degree that is possible before the return of Christ." If enough people participated in this "Kingdom effort," so the idea behind the coalition went, "America [could] be turned around and once again function as a Christian nation as it did in its earlier years." In addition, "any city in the world" could thus become "'a city set upon a hill' and be 'a place where righteousness dwells.'"[37]

Among the signatories of the COR's initial declaration and covenant, "A Manifesto for the Christian Church" (1986), were D. James Kennedy; former *CT* Editor-in-Chief Harold Lindsell; Ted McAteer of the Religious Roundtable, one of the first Religious Right movement organizations; Francis Schaeffer's wife, Edith; and affiliates with the Institute for Creation Research, the Home School Legal Defense Association, Family Research Council, American Family Association, and other Religious Right movement organizations. Making the association with Christian reconstructionism even more obvious and compelling, among the signatories were John Rousas Rushdoony and Gary North, as well.[38]

---

The COR's sphere document "The Christian World View of Economics" was written by Beisner and his economics committee cochairman, Daryl S. Borgquist. It starts with an exploration of what economics is—a former branch of moral philosophy turned modern science detached from ethics and spiritual reality—and what "Biblical economics" should be instead—"a description of man and society based on Biblical truth." The purpose of economics, according to the COR, is therefore not the prescription of certain tactics in order to alleviate poverty or (re)distribute wealth more evenly. Rather, "the function of Biblical economics" is "to offer principles and truths that, when implemented as policies, programs, and individual behavior, will conform the economic conduct and condition of men and society to the norms of Scripture."[39]

While the document does not mention a link between economics and environmental degradation, it condemns the "idea of planetary 'overpopulation' [as] a myth" in one of its forty-two "Statements of Affirmation and Denial" that follow. It also views humankind's fall as the "root cause of all poverty," and thus, historically speaking, poverty as "the ordinary condition of fallen mankind." Poverty can be overcome on an individual and societal level but ultimately only by having a consistently applied biblical worldview.

Furthermore, the authors strongly defend private property as "so inextricably intertwined [with personal liberty (civil and religious)] that destruction of the one must either require or cause destruction of the other." Although the document would certainly deserve a deeper analysis than this cursory overview, it should be clear that its intended purpose is to deeply anchor the sphere of economics within a literalist biblical framework—and not to present a conservative or libertarian economic ideology supported by biblical references here and there in order to appeal to Christian believers.[40]

Similarly, *Prospects for Growth*, which was republished in 2019, proceeds from a truth defined by Beisner's understanding of God as revealed in Scripture. As the author emphasizes, economic growth and property rights are paramount when dealing with the issue of poverty, in particular as it intersects with environmental matters. Caring "about our neighbors near and far, present and future" thus means first and foremost caring "about the future of economic growth." Referring not only to Hayek but also to Max Weber's thesis that Judeo-Christianity was essential in fostering a worldview free from nonrational magic forces—and thus for the development of scientific, technological, and economic life—according to Beisner the biblical worldview and free market capitalism are inseparable: due to the biblical "ethic of property and liberty," which forms "the foundation of the free market," the biblical worldview "provides the best philosophical basis for rapid economic growth."[41]

Analyzing current CA materials that display the same economically and ecologically optimistic understanding of the link between Christianity and capitalism, Kearns notes, "Beisner, like many evangelicals, views capitalism as the economic expression of Christianity." By implication, any potential threat to capitalism, as for instance "'socialist' environmentalism," can therefore be regarded as "a threat to Christianity and America."[42]

**Christianity and Science**

Political scientists convincingly argue that environmental skepticism is about (global) politics instead of science. As Jacques emphasizes, "Environmental skepticism is not, unlike its name might suggest, a disposition to withhold judgment until more compelling evidence is provided. Instead, environmental skepticism is a project that is skeptical of mainstream environmental claims and values but very faithful (i.e., *not* skeptical) to contemporary conservative values and issues." In the realm of evangelical environmentalism and the countermovement it has triggered from within its own community, politics certainly plays a role as well. If we look at the creation care movement from an evolutionary perspective, however, it seems hardly inconsequential that the very first evangelical environmental organization, the Au Sable Institute, was established with the aim to bridge the divide between evangelical faith and (environmental) science by means of education, and not for political purposes.[43]

While science and religion are not necessarily in a constant state of "epistemological warfare" anymore, in particular the creationism versus evolution debate is still a source of actual social conflict in the United States. In addition, battles over evolution seem to be increasingly tied to battles over the Big Bang and climate change. To Lawrence Krauss of the Origins Institute at Arizona State University, these battles are "all about casting doubt on the veracity of science—to say it is just one view of the world, just another story, no better or more valid than fundamentalism." Creation care pioneer Calvin DeWitt is thus not alone in his conviction that evangelical environmental skepticism is not only motivated by politics but also by a severe apprehension toward science.[44]

According to former NAE lobbyist and ECI supporter Richard Cizik, the evangelical reasoning behind climate change goes like this: "Scientists believe in evolution. Scientists say climate change is real. I don't trust scientists. So I don't buy climate change." Likewise, the EEN's Jim Ball notices a cultural dislike for scientists that supposedly compels believers to be skeptical: "This group already feels like scientists are attacking their faith and calling them idiots, so they are likely to be skeptical about global warming." More importantly to Ball, however, many evangelicals consider it "hubris to think that human beings could disrupt something that God created." As conservative radio host Rush Limbaugh put it, "You must be either agnostic or atheistic to believe that man controls something that he can't create. The vanity!"[45]

When we discussed the proposition that global warming denialism was an offshoot of creationism, Calvin Beisner was frank about being a young-Earth creationist and how his belief made him appear like a "fool" to people who did not agree with him. Unlike Krauss, however, Beisner does not see a "correlation" between creationism and climate change denial, counting himself and other young-Earth creationists among a tiny minority of the environmental skeptics. That he sees some young-Earth creationists in the non-skeptic camp and some "old-Earth Darwinist evolutionists who are on our side" leads Beisner to conclude that creationism "is not determinative" when it comes to certain positions on climate change. According to him, the linkage of the two seems to be strategically motivated instead: "There has been a very clear attempt on the part of some of the climate activists to just paint all critics of it as creationists. Because we all know that creationists are inherently stupid people, you know?"[46]

While there is evidently room in America for "creationists" who are neither evangelicals nor climate change deniers, we also need to acknowledge that evangelical environmentalists do not consider different theological positions regarding the age of the earth relevant to creation care activism.

Rather, as Illyn put it, "If you are a creationist of ANY kind, young-Earth, old-Earth, theistic, deistic, I don't care, the only consistent position is to also be an environmentalist." It is therefore important to emphasize that Beisner does not discredit scientists and science per se. Many of the scientists that he, by his own account, corresponds with are not young-Earth creationists; some are not even Christians but atheists instead.[47]

Nonetheless, creation care leaders and evangelical environmental skeptics trust different authorities and epistemic communities when it comes to the scientific bases for environmental problems. DeWitt, Ball, and other creation care leaders have thus readily cooperated with environmentally concerned non-evangelical mainstream scientists like E. O. Wilson, James E. Hansen, and James Gustave Speth through "An Urgent Call to Action: Evangelicals and Scientists Unite to Protect Creation" (2007). Beisner and the CA, on the other hand, have relied on the work of scientists the mainstream scientific community defines as contrarian, such as Siegfried Frederick Singer and Roy Spencer. Moreover, Beisner and the CA seem to espouse a rather dualistic view of science itself and reject any science that runs counter to their rigid biblical worldview. The following should illustrate this more clearly.[48]

In 1967, leading Christian reconstructionist Rousas Rushdoony argued in *The Mythology of Science* that Christianity and modern science were two rival faiths. Published the same year as Lynn White's thesis about the ecological culpability of Christianity, the purpose of Rushdoony's book was "to point out the fraud of the empirical claims of much modern science since Charles Darwin." Whereas to Lynn White Judeo-Christianity had become exploitative toward nature because of its linkage with the forces of progress unleashed by the scientific revolution, to Rushdoony, humankind, essentially by a similar development and linkage of forces, had become disobedient to God with the help of Darwin's *On the Origin of Species*. Since then science had been religiously devoted to the "myth of evolution" because Darwinian theory had allowed humankind to abandon God and to view themselves as the highest expression of intelligence and reason.[49]

But Rushdoony was not opposed to science; on the contrary, he viewed science as a tool to help humankind exercise dominion over the earth under God's control. Science and Christianity could thus coexist and complement each other—but only as long as the former proceeded from the presuppositions of the latter. As Mark R. Rushdoony explains in the foreword to a 2001 reprint of his father's book, both Christianity and Darwinian science depend on "circular reasoning" and are only compatible as long as they share the same "starting point." When it comes to origins, though, the said starting point is ultimately a matter of history—and thus faith—because "origins of matter and life cannot be subject to the empirical method."[50]

Similar to Beisner's understanding of economics, science is thus a matter of one's starting point. As the COR's sphere document on science and technology puts it, "In order to understand the created universe truly and to use the knowledge gained from scientific research properly, man must pursue science and technology in the light of the Word of God." To Christian reconstructionists like Rushdoony and evangelical environmental skeptics like Beisner, science is good and helpful as long as it starts from the truth of Scripture. But a "false starting point"—like human reason unconstrained by God's word or any another worldview not proceeding from the truth of Scripture (such as environmentalism)—inevitably "produces skewed conclusions regarding ultimate meaning" and should thus be resisted and rejected.[51]

As Beisner wrote in a personal letter to Dean Ohlman on January 5, 1994, the intention behind his *World* magazine critique of the EDCC had not been "to polarize but to prompt careful, critical thinking." The issue of environmentalism and the evangelical response to it demanded such scrutiny in Beisner's view because evangelicals like Calvin DeWitt and Ronald Sider were "uncritically and unwittingly embracing the worldview and empirical claims of a movement that is increasingly anti-Christian and whose use of science is increasingly politicized."[52]

More than fifteen years later, Beisner strongly echoed his concern about environmentalism's politicization of science. In particular the CA's Resisting the Green Dragon campaign (RGD) announced the week of Earth Day 2010 that "one of the greatest threats to society and the church today is the multifaceted environmentalist movement." Designed as an educational campaign that includes a book, a twelve-part DVD series, discussion guides, and other resources for small group projects, the stated aim of RGD has been to help "churches, schools, and other ministries to understand the difference between a Biblical definition of creation stewardship and both the secular environmental movement and its pagan religious counterpart." Such a definition of creation stewardship is expedient to the CA because both secular and pagan environmentalism are supposedly "making inroads into the evangelical community" by infiltrating churches with a false worldview, harmful policy proposals, and false claims of crisis not well supported by science. As RGD's press release quotes Beisner, "Environmentalism has become a new religion. . . . Its policies are devastating to the world's poor. It threatens the sanctity of human life. It targets our youth. And its vision is global."[53]

Although Beisner displayed a more modified position in person, according to the CA the alleged infiltration of Evangelicalism with a false environmentalist worldview is a "concerted, well-funded effort." Taking "its cue from James 4:7, 'Submit therefore to God. Resist the devil and he will flee from you,'" the RGD suggests that the spread of "green dragon environmentalism" is devil's work and is therefore to be exposed and resisted.[54]

Considering this division into "good" and "evil" environmentalism, science, economics, etc., as well as the rigid commitment to the total implementation of the biblical worldview, two observations should not come as a surprise. First, to Christian reconstructionists and environmental skeptics like Beisner, fidelity to Christ and Scripture is much more important than any environmental problem could ever be. As Beisner put it while we were discussing the meaning of the term "evangelical" (which he thinks has become "empty" for systematic theological purposes over the course of the twentieth century), "I am first and foremost a theologian committed to defending and perpetuating . . . the faith once for all delivered to the saints. My interest in environmental matters is absolutely a secondary issue for me. Maintaining the biblical faith is far and away my highest priority." Second, since the guarding of their faith is their overriding mission, Christian reconstructionists and environmental skeptics like Beisner seem to be equipped with very strict "cognitive defenses." Those allow them to condemn whatever challenges the "truth" of their worldview as an opportunistic and ultimately satanic rival to biblical Christianity.[55]

------

When we paraphrase Matthew 7:24-25 and accept the premise that a fixed and unquestionable starting point is like the rock upon which to build everything else, I cannot help but notice a similarity to what economist F. A. Hayek said regarding the intellectual system of National Socialism: "Once one accepts the premises from which it starts, there is no escape from its logic." Every time two or more such rigid systems and their followers clash with each other, a mediating middle path of mutual transformation and synthesis seems neither plausible nor possible.[56]

Speaking of National Socialism specifically, after our conversation Beisner gave me a book by Gene Edward Veith titled *Fascism: Modern and Postmodern* (2000). To Veith, and arguably by extension to Beisner as well, fascism is not constricted by the corset of European history; it is first and foremost a sin problem intricately and globally tied to the fallen human condition. As Veith puts it in the conclusion of his book, "Fascism is the modern world's nostalgia for paganism. It is a sophisticated culture's revolt against God." Even though Beisner and other evangelical environmental skeptics have also repeatedly linked German National Socialism with environmentalism to further discredit the latter, neither fascism nor paganism in and of themselves appear to be the opposed other to them. Rather, they seem to understand their fight to be against Satan and humankind's rebellious nature toward God, which led to paganism and fascism in the first place.[57]

In a similar vein, climate change does not seem to be the real issue to Beisner and the CA, just as the environmental and creation care movements do not appear to be the real enemies. Apart from the fact that Beisner still seems to view (some?) creation care advocates as fellow parts within the "body of Christ" (see 1 Corinthians 12), for him the biggest problem of the twenty-first century is the "in practice divinization of the state, that is not recognizing any higher authority than the state." Since the overriding authority of everything ought to be God and his word, however, the ultimate enemy remains a world corrupted by Satan. This world is thus revolting against the absolute authority and truth of Christianity and its biblical worldview in various social institutions and cultural spaces. Specifically at the intersection of Evangelicalism and environmentalism, paganism and totalitarianism are assumed to be forming a satanic alliance threatening the integrity of the Christian faith. It is therefore in this part of the marketplace of ideas where Beisner and the CA are trying to restore the truth of Christianity. This truth affirms the Christian responsibility of biblically based environmental stewardship but nevertheless has a fixed and theologically rigid starting point. This starting point is, according to evangelical environmental skeptics' understanding, most congruent with free market (biblical) economics, God-guided human reason, caution, prudence, and scientific data that does not undermine it.[58]

According to politically active green evangelicals like Jim Ball, global warming is not only a scientifically sound and serious environmental problem that demands a response from every segment of American society (including the evangelical community); global warming is also "the great cause of freedom in the twenty-first century" and thus a chance for evangelicals to be "on the right side of history" considering their lack of participation in the civil rights movement.[59]

Evangelical environmental skeptics like Beisner, on the other hand, also seem to view their advocacy efforts along a historical continuum of evangelical public witness and social action. Note, however, that their engagement aims to right an even earlier perceived wrong of American Christianity. As one of the CA's electronic newsletters states, "Today, the Christian church stands with regard to environmentalism where it stood a century ago with regard to Darwinism." The "response to environmentalism," according to the CA, "must be better than our forebears' response to Darwinism. To restore the teaching and reclaim the blessings of Genesis 1:28, we must respond both critically and constructively." If Jim Ball and the EEN have an elective affinity to the politically active freedom- and justice-oriented Evangelicalism of Martin Luther King Jr., Beisner and the CA's relation is much closer to the fundamentalists of the early twentieth century. The difference, of course, is that they actively and openly participate in social and political advocacy efforts with the aim to reconstruct American society and culture instead of retreating from it like the early fundamentalists did after the Scopes Trial.[60]

# 6
# APOLITICAL CREATION CARE ORGANIZATIONS

I stay out of [politics] primarily because I don't need to do it because they [i.e. the EEN] are there. But there is also a conviction in my own mind that . . . Washington is the tip of the iceberg, but the rest of it is underneath. And there are not nearly as many people working in the heartland, church by church by church.

Edward R. Brown, Care of Creation[1]

[We] are not taking a public stand on climate change . . . because the heated rhetoric about global warming and disagreements on the role of government have paralyzed the church's consideration of deeper responsibilities to care for God's creation.

Jim Jewell, Creation Care, Inc.[2]

At the beginning of the new millennium, global warming had turned into the most pressing ecological problem. Running against Al Gore, "who had done more than almost any other politician to speak for the urgency of addressing climate change," Republican presidential candidate George W. Bush was certainly aware of polls indicating that "concern about global warming [had reached] a historic high." Once Bush was in office, however, environmental issues were soon, and for obvious reasons, overshadowed by those pertaining to foreign policy and national security. In the aftermath of 9/11, political polarization and the culture war/s then further intensified, and the scientifically complex issue of climate change was usurped as a simple binary marker of cultural and political identity warfare.[3]

By the mid-2000s the mainstream environmental advocacy community thus began to prepare for a broader, bipartisan, and more values-based national campaign to advocate for the reduction of carbon emissions. The strategists behind this effort aimed for support from some unlikely allies too, such as Republican business leaders and evangelical Christians, the latter of whom had turned out to be "the largest single demographic group among Bush voters" in the 2004 election. This strategy seemed promising between 2004 and 2008, when America experienced a heightened sense of environmental awareness again, and the ECI caused national and international headlines. Shortly thereafter, however, it became obvious that the ECI may have demonstrated "convening power" on the part of the EEN but not "mobilized power." In addition, some ECI signatories seemed lackadaisical when it came to their commitment to limit greenhouse gas emissions, not to mention their willingness "to defend climate action from [the increasing] Christian right attacks."[4]

It is significant that at the height of the EEN's climate change activism and the CA's countermobilization against it, the three new creation care organizations founded between 2005 and 2009 moved their advocacy foci away from not only the contentious issue of global warming but also from political action. With this conscious bracketing of politics, the younger creation care organizations have to some extent tried to circumvent the countermobilization and guilt-by-association that the EEN in particular has faced due to grants from politically progressive donors, association with secular environmentalism, and engagement with climate change. Whereas the EEN and CES/RE have, at least until 2009, attempted to witness and win primarily in Washington, D.C., and on the West Coast, the newer organizations have tried to spread their depoliticized and broader creation care message in order to witness and win in the individual evangelical heart and the American heartland. It would be unwarranted, however, to deem the apolitical approaches of Care of Creation, Inc. (2005), Blessed Earth (2006), and temporarily dormant Creation Care, Inc. (2009) purely strategic. As we shall see, their "no politics, no agendas" stance does not only accommodate a changing opportunity structure. It is also more compatible with those organizations' self-understanding as bridge-builders, visionary educators, grassroots mobilizers, and sustainable lifestyle-changers rather than catalysts for political action.

## MOBILIZING THE CHURCH TO CARE FOR CREATION: EDWARD R. BROWN AND CARE OF CREATION, INC. (2005–)

CoC was founded in April 2005 in Madison, Wisconsin, by Edward (Ed) R. Brown (1953–), a pastor trained at Gordon-Conwell Theological Seminary and a former missionary to Pakistan. With Brown's background in traditional evangelical ministry and missions, the incentive for the organization's establishment was to "bring together three concepts—'evangelical,' 'environmental,' and 'missions'—in a way that had never been done before." Although this idea was not entirely novel if we recall Scott Sabin's PWP, CoC's activism has been more globally visionary than locally hands-on. Convinced that creation care needs to become a permanent fixture within the value system and practice of the worldwide evangelical church, Brown's goal has thus been nothing less than that of a "second reformation."[5]

After spending several years as pastor of the Protestant International Church in Islamabad, Pakistan, where he had grown up as the child of American missionaries, Brown moved to Madison, Wisconsin in 1996. In 2000 he joined the Au Sable Institute as Calvin DeWitt's chief operating officer. Until then Brown had mostly been involved in evangelical missions and student ministry. Although he always thought that recycling might not be a bad idea, for most of his adult life, Brown thought he had a "higher calling" and "more important things to be involved in" than taking part in environmental activism. In addition, Brown used to be rather suspicious of the environmental movement. Not only did he see an environmentalist "tendency to put spotted owls and other creatures ahead of the needs of human beings"—a violation of the God-created hierarchy in creation—but also because the movement "seemed to have more than its share of New Age crackpots" among its supporters.[6]

Brown's perspective on environmentalism and the importance of creation care would change once he began working at Au Sable. Though DeWitt had hired him for his organizational skills and not for his environmentalist credentials, Brown started "listening and talking and asking questions," which eventually inspired him to "go back and look at [his] own religious convictions in the light of this environmental situation." What he found during this reexamination of his faith was similar to what Dean Ohlman and other creation care evangelicals had discovered more than a decade earlier: "If I understand from my reading that God and Jesus is concerned about His creation and I'm following Him, how can I not be concerned about His creation? And how can that not then affect how I live and the decisions I make?"[7]

Becoming aware of the biblical call to care for creation, however, does not necessarily imply actively engaging in environmental efforts, as we have seen in the previous chapter. Additionally, whether evangelical or not, attitude and belief do not always transpire into concrete social or political action, let alone the founding of an environmental nonprofit organization during a financially insecure transitional phase late in a person's professional career. In Brown's case his experiences at Au Sable did eventually turn him into a creation care activist and the founder of CoC, but that took not only a reexamination of his faith and vocation but also the acceptance of the reality and problematics of eco-crisis *and* "God's guidance." On top of that, it also took the vision of—and a "Macedonian call" from—Craig Sorley, an acquaintance of Brown's based in Kenya, who had been attempting to establish an environmental missions project near Nairobi since 2003.[8]

While Brown came to creation care through his work at Au Sable, "Craig Sorley's conversion to environmentalism came after doctors removed a tumor from his brain" in 1989. A life-changing experience, his illness prompted Sorley to pursue an academic career more in line with his experiences as the son of medical missionaries, who had seen firsthand the environmental degradation in third world countries. Like medical missionaries attempting to show Christ's love by moving to developing countries to heal those in need, environmental missionaries—according to the idea Sorley developed after his cancer treatment—would demonstrate their love to people "by helping them to heal their parts of God's creation." Hence Sorley pursued degrees in resource management and forestry at the University of Minnesota after his recovery.[9]

When Sorley and his family finally moved to Kenya in 2002 to turn his long-held vision of environmental missions into reality, they had no organization at hand that would support their efforts. In December 2004 Sorley thus asked Brown—whom he had previously met in person during the first "God and Creation" conference the Sorleys had organized in Nairobi—to start a new evangelical environmental organization in the United States, which would raise funds for Sorley's project in Kenya and of which Brown would then be the U.S.-based director.[10]

Sorley's "message, 'We want to transform people and the land they live on,' went to [Brown's] heart." But financially the founding of a new creation care organization did not seem like a good idea. For one, Brown was facing unemployment because his job at Au Sable was ending due to DeWitt's retirement and some organizational restructuring based on financial difficulties. Additionally, there were Brown's college-age children to take care of. Reminisces Brown, "Unemployment when you're over fifty, with three college-age children and no money in the bank, is not a pleasant prospect, but starting a brand-new organization that's both evangelical and environmental is just crazy—sort of like walking on the water. It would take that much faith and more."[11]

Despite his initial refusal to get involved, however, Brown agreed to help complete and edit Sorley's half-written proposal. Eventually convinced that not only was God guiding his and his family's life toward creation care but that he and Sorley had also discovered "a new perspective in [their] response to the environmental crisis that others needed to be aware of," Brown finally decided to found CoC despite the reasons against it. As we have seen in the case of Dean Ohlman as well, faith can indeed be a very potent motivator and resource.[12]

Unlike the EEN or the Au Sable Institute, CoC is an organization truly built from scratch and initially upon not much else but the vision, faith, and the organizational talent of its founders. Reflecting the originally intended purpose to provide funds for Sorley's environmental missions project in Kenya, Brown has concentrated on "vision work" and fundraising in the United States. Sorley, on the other hand, runs CoC's sister organization, Care of Creation Kenya (CCK), which was separately incorporated in 2007 as a local nongovernmental organization that focuses on missions work and practical environmental restoration programs. In addition to CCK, CoC also supports the environmental missions efforts of other evangelical families, such as Erik and Rachel Ness, who are based in Tanzania and launched Care of Creation Tanzania (CCT) in June 2012.[13]

Even though he was initially reluctant to become an environmentalist, to Brown both "evangelical" and "environmental" are two terms that are now inextricably connected: "If you are truly evangelical, you must be environmental." Considering his and Sorley's background in the mission field, creation care and missionary efforts are likewise inextricably linked. It was during Brown's cautious turn toward environmentalism when he "realized that the missionary task in its most complete sense could not be carried out without including environmental issues as part of a strategic agenda." Despite decades—or, in some cases, even centuries—of missionary presence, developing countries like Kenya, Tanzania, Uganda, and the Philippines "are approaching environmental and ecological tipping points" and are therefore, at least regarding their environmental health, "a great deal worse off than before the gospel arrived." Success in fulfilling the Great Commission in those countries should therefore not be measured by numbers of converts and church attendances alone, because those numbers only display the success of the "lightweight gospel of personal salvation." Rather, the new model of environmental missions that Sorley and Brown espouse is much more holistic as it includes not only the healing of the people by sharing the gospel with them but also the healing of their land by teaching them how to care for their part of God's creation.[14]

CoC and CCK's organizational philosophy is inspired by the vision to see a worldwide environmental response of the evangelical church, which is seen as "the best and perhaps the only hope for a true solution to the global environmental crisis." While Brown is not "involved in any practical stuff" in the United States, CCK directly addresses local issues of deforestation, water scarcity, and agriculture. Those measures are directed at farmers, schools, and residents, and are geared toward the improvement of local living standards and sustainable food production. According to the organization, they are expressions of a sound (creation care) "theology in action," which places the "responsibility for God's creation where it belongs—on the shoulders of each local church body." "Farming God's Way," the name for CCK's biblically inspired conservation agriculture training, is thus not merely a snappy slogan of an environmental advocacy organization catering to the jargon of evangelical Christians. Rather, it is a serious reminder of the fact that everything evangelical environmentalists do "is related to God and his original creative designs for this earth."[15]

As for Brown's work in the United States, CoC attempts to "mobilize the world-wide church to respond to the environmental crisis and embrace environmental stewardship." Though the term "mobilization" is crucial for the organization and used forcefully by Brown, it does not have a political dimension in the sense that CoC attempts to influence the voting behavior and (environmental) policy preferences of evangelical Christians. Rather, the term "carries a certain military aspect that conveys urgency. It also suggests a deployment of resources that already exist." Those resources include "beliefs," "people," and "programs [already] in place." Hence Brown's thesis that "the church needs to change little to be effective in the environmental crisis." The "equipment" to tackle ecological problems is certainly there; the "warehouse doors," however, need to be opened and said equipment moved out and finally used.[16]

To fulfill its mission, along with providing consulting services on environmental missions, CoC has developed preaching and teaching tools to be provided upon request during conferences and trainings in the United States and abroad. Moreover, networking and connecting its mission to more traditional and global evangelical efforts has been a crucial aspect of CoC's advocacy work. As Brown repeatedly emphasized in the past, a "deliberate focus on the church" and its various arms of social and global missionary engagement make CoC unique among creation care organizations. This strategic approach is largely based on accepting the fact that "this [i.e., the environmental crisis] is too big for us." Like his former boss and initiator of creation care, Calvin DeWitt, Brown believes that caring for creation must be a team effort. Mutual support instead of competition are thus crucial for Brown, who generally promotes evangelical environmental engagement as a whole and not only CoC. After all, his wish and calling are to turn creation care into an "acceptable value" within the evangelical church and not simply to maintain a viable nonprofit organization.[17]

Though self-identified as one of the more politically progressive creation care leaders within the movement, Brown concurs with the politically conservative Dean Ohlman regarding his emphasis on changing hearts and minds rather than legislation. This does not mean that both men deem politics and public policy irrelevant. To Ohlman the idea behind "teaching [creation care] principles" has been tied to the conviction that once internalized, those principles are eventually going to affect people's lifestyles, voting behaviors, legislation, and thus society at large. Approaching the matter from a similar vantage point albeit with a stronger focus on inspiring churches and parachurch institutions, Brown also believes that change has to "percolate upward." Rather than focusing on influencing political decisions in the nation's capital, as important as he deems them, Brown is convinced that effective and lasting change can only happen through team-work efforts at the grassroots level, in the heartland of America, within each and every individual church. That actions focused on the grasstops, such as EEN's ECI, have not created a more lasting impact has therefore not been surprising to Brown.[18]

In addition, Brown deems the environmental crisis simply unsolvable by governments and political action alone, because it is a "sin crisis" and thus in need of a more encompassing spiritual solution. Like other creation care evangelicals who signed the EDCC, Brown believes that Adam and Eve's disobedience in the Garden of Eden has disturbed *shalom*, and that all rela-tionships with God and among his creatures have thus fallen like a series of dominoes knocking each other down. Creation care is therefore not a means to an end. Rather, it is but one part of the more encompassing effort of "putting the dominoes back in place," albeit a very integral one.[19]

As a result of Brown's broad-based engagement with the evangelical (para-)church, in the summer of 2012 he took on the additional role of the first senior associate for creation care of the Lausanne Movement. Initiated by Billy Graham in the 1970s, the international organization for "world evan-gelization" formally declared creation care a "gospel issue within the Lord-ship of Christ" in 2010. Since his involvement with Lausanne, Brown has attended several international conferences on "creation care and the gos-pel" around the globe. His role within the Lausanne Creation Care Network and his work for CoC have thus more or less merged in recent years. As he put it, "The mission statement of Care of Creation is to mobilize the church throughout the world for creation. My job description within Lausanne is to mobilize the church. . . . Two masters, but the same job."[20]

Although Brown has never seemed afraid to talk about ideologically con-troversial environmental topics like population growth, especially as they intersect with issues of poverty and prosperity, CoC was initially very cau-tious in its approach to climate change. For one, to Brown creation care is much more encompassing than the single issue of global warming. While the latter is a "long-term problem" that "makes everything else worse," there still are plenty of other problematic environmental conditions that need to be addressed as well, such as water scarcity for instance. Secondly, and more importantly considering the widening green gap in the aftermath of EEN's ECI, Brown was purposely very cautious not to lose potential supporters of creation care simply because of this one contentious issue.[21]

This cautious patience and his willingness to bracket the issue of climate change to fruitfully engage more skeptical evangelicals toward an openness to environmental missions has arguably enabled Brown's organization to grow "quietly" by building bridges within segments of the evangelical community that may have been unresponsive to an explicitly climate-centered creation care agenda. Moreover, this apolitical, small-steps approach has allowed Brown to gradually become more outspoken on climate change, especially since his involvement with Lausanne. Unlike the creation care organizations in the United States—which are perceived as "fringe" within the national evangelical community according to Brown—Lausanne holds very strong symbolic capital as it evokes Billy Graham and thus provides "theological protection" for organizations compelled to engage with climate change and other environmental problems. Creation care advocates may thus have very well lost the climate change policy battle inside America. Beyond the nation's borders, however, a transnational creation care "reformation" seems to be making progress indeed, enabling leaders like Brown to speak out on pressing global environmental threats while remaining deeply anchored within the core tenets of the evangelical faith.[22]

## SERVE GOD, SAVE THE PLANET: THE SLEETH FAMILY AND BLESSED EARTH (2006–)

Although not less evangelical in its self-described religious identity, Blessed Earth (BE), the second apolitical creation care group to emerge at the height of the EEN's climate change activism, occupies a special niche within the creation care movement for reasons beyond motives, strategy, and tactics. For one, BE is a family-run, educational nonprofit that has steadily grown from a "mom-and-pop-operation" based in Kentucky to a national creation care organization delivering its message to audiences as diverse as the viewers of Pat Robertson's television programs and the board members of the Sierra Club. Moreover, BE founders, J. Matthew and Nancy Sleeth, were environmentally concerned non-evangelicals before they turned to the world's sacred texts in search of spiritual guidance, becoming green followers of Christ. Not only is their biography untypical compared to other creation care leaders, it also makes for a rather anachronistic portrait considering that we live in times when losing one's Christian religion is more likely than finding it. Hence, by their own example the Sleeths prove what creation care veterans have believed since the early days of their movement: caring for creation is not only the obedient thing to do for evangelical Christians, but it can likewise be an excellent "on-ramp" to biblical Christianity for environmentally concerned non-evangelicals.[23]

The Sleeths have told their ecological and religious conversion story many times as it is an integral part of who they are, what they do, and why they do what they do. One February early in the new millennium, the couple spent their family vacation together with their two children on a barrier island off the coast of Florida. At the time Matthew Sleeth, M.D., held a post as emergency room director and chief of staff in a New England hospital. He would never have reached this position without the relentless support of his wife, Nancy, who holds a master's degree in journalism and whose own résumé includes the position of communications director for a Fortune 500 company.[24]

As Nancy recalls the apex of her husband's career, "We were living out the American dream, enjoying the affluence and status of a successful physician's family." Consequently, the vacation setting in Florida that would trigger the couple's conversion was equally fantastic and dreamlike, if not to say paradisiac. One night after their kids had played in the ocean all day and gone to bed early, the couple relaxed on the balcony, "enjoying a peaceful breeze beneath silent stars," discussing the little and big questions of life. It was during that night when Nancy, from a narrative perspective similar to the biblical Eve, disturbed the peacefulness of the moment by asking her husband "two questions that would change [their] lives forever": what was the biggest problem facing the world today, and what were they going to do about it?[25]

It may seem odd to ask such questions in a moment and setting like the one described. Apart from their socioeconomic success, however, the Sleeths had not been spared their personal share of tragedy. Around the same time she asked her husband those critical, life-changing questions, "horrible" things had been happening to the couple, such as Nancy's brother drowning in front of their children. Personal sorrow and the medical suffering her husband was witnessing at work on a daily basis showed Nancy that she was missing "a moral anchor or a spiritual compass . . . when things go wrong in life"—thus the reason for her contemplative and disturbing questions in a setting that could otherwise easily evoke Eden.[26]

Her husband's answer to question number one was prompt and simple, namely that the world was "dying." Not only were his patients dying at alarming rates of breast cancer and other environmentally related health conditions, but nature and the biodiversity of the planet were also negatively affected, as there were "no chestnuts on Chestnut Lane, no elms on Elm Street, no caribou in Caribou, Maine, and no buffalo in Buffalo, New York" anymore. What to do about the dying planet, however, was a question that would take more contemplation.[27]

Upon their return from Florida, Matthew started going through the world's major sacred texts in order to find answers to his wife's second question. Nancy had grown up in a conservative Jewish home and Matthew came from a Protestant family in the rural Midwest, but especially in his case religion "hadn't taken," and they both "threw [it] out" when they got married, which their respective parents disapproved of. As Sleeth, who considered himself a "secular humanist" at the time, turned to the world's religious traditions as a middle-aged adult, he would find much wisdom for sure. But neither the Bhagavad-Gita, the Qur'an, nor the Ramayana would provide the answer he sought. Finally, however, a Gideon Bible placed in the emergency room of his hospital "changed everything."[28]

In particular Matthew 7:1-2 turned out to be crucial in Sleeth's transition from emergency room doctor to evangelical creation care activist: "Do not judge, so that you may not be judged. For with the judgment you make you will be judged, and the measure you give will be the measure you get." As Sleeth details, he did not like what he found when he applied these words of Christ to himself. On the one hand he was "concerned about pollution and the death of the world." On the other, however, he had never reflected on his family's contribution to environmental destruction until then—even though he had considered himself an "enlightened environmentalist."[29]

Thus prompted by the piece of Scripture that also inspired civil rights leader Mohandas Gandhi to be the change he wanted to see, the Sleeth family "took an accounting" and thoroughly measured their ecological footprint. This practice, combined with reading the Bible from an environmental perspective and feeling a call from God, finally led Matthew to take a rather unusual "downward[ly] mobile" step: "I told [Nancy] that I would quit my job and start working full time in a job with no title: green doctor? creation-care minister? ecoevangelist? I didn't even know how to describe my new calling, but I felt certain that the call was from God."[30]

Although reluctant at first, eventually the rest of his family converted to green Evangelicalism as well. To live up to their newfound calling, the Sleeths sold or gave away most of what they owned in New England and moved into "a house the size of their former garage" in rural Kentucky. While their children attended nearby Asbury College (now Asbury University), a nondenominational Christian liberal arts institution, Sleeth published his first book, *Serve God, Save the Planet: A Christian Call to Action* (2006). This book gave birth to BE, which the Sleeths founded in 2006 to "help with the flood of speaking invitations and requests for additional creation care resources" that resulted from Sleeth's publication.[31]

---

BE's mission is to inspire "faithful stewardship of all creation" through various venues and tools of education. Initially established with the help of the organization Trust for the Future, BE quickly grew beyond its midwife's umbrella and received independent nonprofit status in 2010. The organization largely focuses on individual evangelical churchgoers and students. To reach their audience the Sleeths have written several books on creation care, and in particular Matthew has spoken in hundreds of evangelical churches and colleges across the United States since the publication of *Serve God, Save the Planet*.[32]

Because of the globally encompassing eco-crisis, Sleeth compares the earth to "a sinking ship with billions of passengers aboard." In order to deal with this moral and spiritual crisis, Sleeth attempts to lead by example and advocates individual action rather than institutional change. Deeply influenced by—and true to—his family's own environmental and spiritual conversion experience, his goal is "to elicit personal accountability." Faith and works, according to Sleeth, clearly are inseparable. Therefore, "humble anonymous acts like turning off the lights, hanging clothing on the line, bicycling to work, and planting trees" are expressions of an ecologically sensible life dedicated to God and his commandments.[33]

While Sleeth gave up his former career to reorient his family's life toward God and creation care full time, he still claims to be involved in healthcare, albeit on a "global scale" now. Given his professional background, he also seems more conscious of the detrimental effects of environmental degradation on human health than some of the other creation care leaders. At times we can even see parallels to the environmental health discourse initiated by Rachel Carson's *Silent Spring*, especially when Sleeth laments that "we live in a sea of chemicals" with hundreds of toxins building up in our tissue and are therefore forced to participate in an uncontrolled "experiment in just how much we, and the planet, can withstand."[34]

Note, however, that Sleeth looks at eco-crisis as a multifaceted problem requiring holistic solutions. Inasmuch as he transcends the environmental health discourse by taking spiritual, economic, and justice aspects into account, Sleeth is eager to point out the multifaceted advantages of individual acts of creation care, too. The countercultural act of drying clothes on an old-fashioned line rather than using an electric dryer is thus not only advocated as a way to downscale one's greenhouse gas emissions and electricity bill. It also becomes a healthful practice and a "spiritual event" during which family members can spend time with each other and with God.[35]

Conversely, watching television or divorcing one's spouse become issues with environmental dimensions as well. Not only are televisions "the third largest user of electricity in homes nationwide" but also very difficult to dispose of or recycle. Moreover, they represent a cultural space devoid of God and filled instead with morally questionable tales, characters, and deceptive advertising. Hence, "Television separates us from our Creator while killing his creation." Likewise, Sleeth expands on the religio-conservative view of marriage by adding an environmental dimension to the (in evangelical circles) lauded societal and spiritual ones: "Nothing is worse for the environment than a broken family. Where once one house and one kitchen table might have sufficed, two homes, two kitchens, and two living room sofas become a necessity."[36]

Similar to her husband, Nancy Sleeth does not separate environmental activism from spiritual growth. As she claims in her first book, *Go Green, $ave Green* (2009)—which provides more explicit guidelines for creation-friendlier lifestyles and is interspersed with numerous calculations aimed at establishing the business case for environmentalism—the bottom line of all creation care endeavors should be determined by two questions: "Does this bring me closer to God? And, does this help me love my neighbor?" Both questions are derived from the two "greatest" commandments enunciated by Jesus

Christ in the gospels of the New Testament: "'Love the Lord your God with all your heart and with all your soul and with all your mind.' This is the first and greatest commandment. And the second is like it: 'Love your neighbor as yourself.' All the Law and the Prophets hang on these two commandments." The answers to the two creation care benchmarking questions will "always lead [believers] down the right path." In particular pertaining to consumerism and its negative ecological implications, these two questions help balance the individual's materialistic wants and needs, as Matthew details in *Serve God, Save the Planet* as well.[37]

The Sleeths' written works, including their daughter Emma's book, *It's Easy Being Green* (2008), largely complement each other and place their own family's creation care journey at the center. While doing so they follow a shared autobiographical narrative that emphasizes the importance of their family to each of its members but also the importance of the cultural institution of family in general. Inasmuch as the Sleeths celebrate the cultural, spiritual, and environmental benefits of unbroken families, they also stress the role parenting plays when it comes to raising children to be responsible stewards of creation. Additionally, in particular Matthew claims that upholding the "sanctity of life" provides the foundation for his creation care activism: "If I did not hold unborn life as sacred, why would I work to improve living conditions for future generations?" Reversely, Sleeth challenges pro-life activists who insist that being against abortion is more important than fighting for environmental protection: "If I don't work for a better tomorrow, I don't really believe in the sanctity of life."[38]

In contrast to the celebratory attitude toward economic growth exhibited by evangelical environmental skeptic Calvin Beisner, the Sleeths do not believe in the sustainability of consumer capitalism. While an evangelical critique of the "destructive unbridled consumerism of modern society"—allegedly rooted in the "narcissistic individualism and materialistic naturalism that flows from the Enlightenment"—can also be found in old editions of *Green Cross* magazine, BE's discontent with the negative consequences of consumerism appears more vocal and explicit.[39]

According to Matthew, materialism is the subject that Jesus Christ is most clear about: "A life focused on possessions is a poor and misguided life." In addition, Sleeth reminds his followers that the "wealthy-consumer demands" of the industrialized world are a profound factor contributing "to the ill health of much of the third world" and "the factory-like exploitation of resources" there. Considering the process and the effects of globalization, Lazarus, the biblical beggar who spent his life in unacknowledged physical agony and material poverty in front of a rich man's house (Luke 16:19-31), thus "sits at all of our doorsteps."[40]

Consequently, if one follows the Christian mandate to coherently align faith and life, the lifestyle of a consumer dedicated to the possessing and hoarding of "stuff"—and blindly ignoring the detrimental environmental and global justice effects of this dedication—is certainly not one to "shine as a light to the world." As Nancy further details, although Americans only make up 5 percent of the world's population, they use 26 percent of the world's energy—a rather unneighborly act considering world poverty and the global ecological crisis. Viewed in this light, not only consumerism but in particular America's exceptional role in the arena of resource consumption and environmental degradation become deeply morally troublesome.[41]

To counteract the "blind" and "hyper" consumerism of present-day America, the Sleeths propose a lifestyle "governed by simplicity and humility." Unlike some mainstream environmentalists who may share their call for simplicity, the Sleeths do not take any sociopolitical ideas from current anti-consumerist and corporate capitalism critics. Neither do they take their inspiration for simple living from Thoreau and the like. Rather, the Sleeths claim to be directly influenced by their reading of the Bible and those within the Christian tradition who have tried to emulate a simple way of life, such as desert father St. Anthony (251–356), St. Francis of Assisi, and more recently the Amish, Mennonite, and Bruderhof communities.[42]

According to Nancy, the Amish in particular "are islands of sanity in a whirlpool of change," and they are thus able to offer essential advice on how to keep "simplicity, service, and faith at the center" of the ecologically sensitive Christian life. In her second book, *Almost Amish: One Woman's Quest for a Slower, Simpler, More Sustainable Life* (2012), Sleeth defines several Amish principles in order to provide concrete guidelines. Amish start from the premise that homes are supposed to be "simple, uncluttered, and clean" and that "faith life and way of life are inseparable." Other principles include a cautious attitude toward technology, an embrace of "financial simplicity," and a preference of "small and local" over big and global. According to Nancy, living out these principles has allowed the Amish to "opt out" of mainstream American culture and its "false promise of infinite growth." The Amish have thus been able to successfully preserve "a traditional way of life centered on God, family, and neighbors" amidst everything that is "terribly wrong about our time."[43]

Despite her appreciation of the Amish as a role model for a more ecologically sensitive Christian way of being in this world but not of it, it is important to emphasize that Sleeth proposes an *almost Amish* lifestyle rather than a full conversion. As she jokes in the introduction of her book, the Sleeths travel by Prius, not by pony. Likewise, Matthew admits that not everybody can—or should—lead a socially and culturally isolated life. Nonetheless, the Sleeths insist on the Pauline command that all Christians be imitators of Christ. Hence, they praise the apostle's "formula" of loving God, loving neighbor, and being "happy with what we have" as a basis for "a pure and simple life dedicated to godly concerns, not worldly ones." The simplicity they advocate is thus much more than an ecologically sustainable alternative to consumerism; it is a way to God while consumerism "draws us to the devil."[44]

While some of the Sleeths' simple living measures could arguably pass for "political consumerism," BE's embrace of simplicity is nevertheless tied to a decidedly apolitical attitude. Although Sleeth and her husband deem the political process in America important and do exercise their right to vote, they "very deliberately stay away from politics." Moreover, they consider their faith-based advocacy work through BE purely educational and refuse to place themselves anywhere on the political spectrum, at least publicly. Congruent with the typically evangelical "personal influence strategy," to the Sleeths the change of the heart is the most important one. Following their strategy to change hearts and minds instead of environmental policies, the Sleeths are convinced that this bottom-up approach will eventually influence lawmakers as well.[45]

Along with their avoidance of politics, the Sleeths also consciously bracket the problem of global warming. While Matthew signed the EEN's ECI, BE has not taken an explicit stand on climate change. The reason for this quiescence is the divisiveness of the issue within American Evangelicalism, which, quite like the intra- and extra-evangelical controversy over creationism, is considered a hamper to the organization's ability to effectively open hearts and minds. "Ears will shut," says Nancy, "the minute you mention global warming or the age of the earth." Hence, the Sleeths deem scientific arguments largely detrimental to their attempt to build bridges to environmentally skeptical evangelicals in order to inspire them to care for creation. Unlike the EEN, who claimed with the ECI that an evangelical engagement with climate change hinged on the scientific data, the Sleeths avoid any references to climate science. If embraced by enough evangelicals, according to Nancy, BE's suggested creation care efforts "will make the air cleaner" no matter if those evangelicals who engage in them believe in the scientific arguments for climate change or not.[46]

Whereas more politically active environmentalists may be skeptical of BE's apolitical strategy, the Sleeths are convinced of its efficacy. By their own account, it has allowed them to make considerable inroads into more fundamentalist congregations in the Bible Belt. In the past, BE was also favorably featured on Pat Robertson's *The 700 Club*, while Nancy's book *Go Green, $ave Green* caught the positive attention of the late Chuck Colson as a good example of "common-sense environmentalism." To Nancy, both of these particular endorsements by Religious Right leaders were "miracles" and a sign that God was supporting BE's work.[47]

Apart from the publications of their books and their numerous speaking engagements at primarily evangelical churches, colleges, and universities, through BE the Sleeths have also established the so-called Sabbath Living

Initiative Program and the Seminary Stewardship Alliance (SSA). Referred to as "stop day" by the Sleeths, the gift of Sabbath is seen as God's prescription for a happier and healthier life with regard to spiritual, physical, and environmental matters in today's "24/7 world of constant change." In order to help individuals, small groups, and clergy reclaim and observe the Sabbath, the program provides various resources, such as stories, sermon outlines, and Sabbath plan worksheets.[48]

Established by the Sleeths in 2012, the SSA's goal is to unite seminaries throughout the United States who are committed to educating future evangelical leaders about environmental issues and creation care. The effort kicked off with a signing ceremony held during the Earth Day celebrations of 2012 at the National Cathedral in Washington, D.C. Under the directorship of Dr. A. J. Swoboda—a pastor, professor, and author as well as BE's regional liaison for the Pacific Northwest—the SSA has grown to fifty participating schools, including George Fox Evangelical Seminary (now Portland Seminary), Denver Seminary, and Asbury Seminary. In addition to Swoboda operating the SSA in the Pacific Northwest, a regional chapter of BE was started by Heather and Ryan Bennett in Tennessee. Like apolitical CoC, BE has thus been able to grow and establish itself as a fixture within the creation care movement over the past ten-plus years.[49]

REVIVING LIVES AND LANDSCAPES: LOWELL PRITCHARD, JAMES JEWELL, AND CREATION CARE, INC./FLOURISH (2009–2012/2013; ASSIMILATION OF RESTORING EDEN 2014–)

Neither the founding of BE nor CoC was intended as an explicit break with the politically unafraid strategy employed by dominant creation care organization the EEN. Upon taking an entrepreneurial leap of faith, both Brown and the Sleeths saw open niches within the creation care movement that jibed more with their own reservations about political involvement and would thus provide better suited advocacy platforms for them, respectively. BE and CoC can therefore be described as "niche seekers," whereas the third apolitical evangelical environmental organization to emerge, Creation Care, Inc., provides the slightly different case of the first "dissident organization" within the creation care movement.[50]

Mostly referred to as Flourish, after its online magazine and first creation care advocacy event, Creation Care, Inc., was founded by former EEN staff Lowell (Rusty) Pritchard and James (Jim) Jewell in Atlanta, Georgia, in March 2009. Pritchard holds a Ph.D. in natural resource economics from the University of Florida and was an assistant professor at Emory University's Department of Environmental Studies from 1999 until 2006. While Pritchard served as the national director of outreach for the EEN until February 2009, which included the editorship of *Creation Care* magazine, Jim

Jewell's public relations agency, Rooftop Media Works, was contracted in 2005 to introduce the ECI. In addition, Jewell functioned as the EEN's chief operating officer from 2006 until 2008–2009.[51]

In the past Jewell had worked for World Vision, Trinity Forum, and Prison Fellowship Ministries. Considering himself "probably the most conservative guy . . . in the Christian environmental movement," Jewell had been Chuck Colson's chief of staff for many years and describes himself as a "professional Christian" because of his deep involvement with evangelical nonprofits since the 1970s. Unlike Pritchard, he had not been concerned about environmental problems prior to his work for the EEN. In his own words, he came to creation care as a "mercenary," although the cause eventually "kind of captured [his] heart." When he and Pritchard left the EEN, they also took with them young evangelical (freelance) writer Kendra Langdon Juskus, who would take on the role of contributing and managing editor for *Flourish* magazine, and faith and culture writer Jonathan Merritt, who would function as an advisor for Flourish's planned church programs.[52]

While niche seekers consciously design their organizations to occupy previously unoccupied advocacy spaces, dissidents "might be more likely to compete with former colleagues, at least for a while, given the circumstances of their departure." Since there was a downturn in the EEN's finances in 2008, Pritchard and Jewell's departure must have meant financial relief for the network. Their subsequent founding of a potentially competitive creation care organization, however, was not looked upon benevolently by the remaining EEN staff. Moreover, loyalty and competition within the movement were a hot topic during the CCCC in August 2009, where the founding circumstances of Flourish and its inaugural conference were passionately debated by the leaders present.[53]

Flourish's "National Church Leaders' Conference on Creation Care" was held at former Southern Baptist Convention (SBC) president James Merritt's Cross Pointe Church in Duluth, Georgia, from May 13 to 15, 2009. The organizers' aim was to assemble evangelical church leaders from a wide theological and ideological spectrum and to concentrate on "three major areas . . . that organizers believe are necessary for the church to have a robust Gospel-witness in the 21st century: 1. Creation care in theology, worship, and evangelism; 2. The greening of church operations, and 3. Personal discipleship." Among others, speakers included creation care advocates Scott Sabin, Peter Illyn, and Matthew Sleeth; pastors Tri Robinson and Joel Hunter; and Larry Schweiger, who was at the time still president of the NWF. As *CT*'s David Neff (who had previously signed the ECI) noted favorably, the conference organizers intended to focus on the "church ministry and personal faithfulness elements of creation care" and would thus avoid politics and the issue of global warming.[54]

Roughly three months after the conference, Pritchard and Jewell were not present during the CCCC in Elgin, Illinois. They had sent Kendra Juskus as Flourish representative, along with a letter reporting on the significance and turnout of their conference. The fact that their conference had been "held at a Southern Baptist mega-church pastored by a former president of the SBC, and that speakers included a Southern Baptist seminarian and church planter," was, according to the organizers, "indicative of the conference's reach into new communities of evangelical Christians." The Flourish team thus regarded it as a success not only for Flourish but "for the creation care community" as a whole.[55]

What became obvious during the discussion that followed, however, was that the idea for a national pastors' conference on creation care had actually been born during previous CCCC meetings. Originally it had even been intended as a joint event. Some of the participants thus felt that Jewell and Pritchard had somewhat betrayed the CCCC by using this collectively developed idea as the starting event and name for their new organization, and this apparently without giving all CCCC participants a proper heads up. While some lamented mere "confusion" over what had happened, others felt left out and complained about a lack of "transparency." Moreover, they saw a potential internecine conflict developing, whereas Juskus made the attempt to defend Flourish's founding as a case of movement "evolution" instead.[56]

After everybody had vented their anger and frustration, though, the CCCC was quick to decide, benevolently and by consensus, that the conference would remain a creation care event implemented by the Flourish team. In addition, the leaders present made constructive use of the occasion to reflect upon the purpose of the CCCC more generally. They emphasized that they would keep supporting each other and their organizations through the CCCC, a venue for idea generation, information exchange, mutual support, motivation, and fellowship. What had started as a dispute, thus eventually ended with a "blessing" of the new organization.[57]

Looking back at Flourish's founding circumstances, Jewell seemed amused that other creation care leaders thought he and Pritchard had "hijacked the Flourish name, conference and all that" when they founded their organization. Like Juskus during the CCCC, Jewell emphasized that the founding of their organization had been driven by a community internal need. As a public relations expert, he was always looking for "gaps." Jim Ball, on the other hand, was a public policy expert, and the EEN was clearly "the leader in terms of evangelicals working on [federal] climate policy in Washington." In addition to its advocacy efforts around climate change, however, the EEN was generally seen as a more progressive voice within American Evangelicalism. Therefore, the network was unable to "make inroads in most of the church anyway," considering that only "twenty per-cent" of evangelicals could be regarded as "more progressive," while "eighty percent" would be found on the "moderate to very conservative" spectrum. As for his and Pritchard's attempt to reach the latter, Jewell deemed the founding of Creation Care, Inc., a matter of constructive sector partitioning instead of competitive rivalry.[58]

Whether founded by niche seekers or dissidents, "the creation of new organizations ultimately extends the aggregate reach of environmental advocacy into a greater number of policy and tactical niches." Though Jewell and Pritchard were equally convinced that climate change was "a huge problem" about which Christians needed to do something urgently, the ideological and cultural polarization surrounding the issue, and the paralysis that had thus ensued within the evangelical church, made it expedient for them to integrate creation care into the broader church culture by means of a more conservative and apolitical attempt. As much as this conviction resulted in some initial discord, it is imperative to note that the need to circumvent the green gap was not disputed by other creation care leaders. After all, the idea for Flourish's first advocacy event had been born collectively *within* the CCCC. As politically unafraid Peter Illyn reflected upon Flourish's founding, "The original thinking was that one of the mistakes we've made as a movement, is these conversations came so embedded in politics that we didn't do the due diligence." To Illyn, who sat on Creation Care, Inc.'s board (along with Scott Sabin from PWP), Flourish was therefore an attempt to move "a little to the right" in order to inspire a broader evangelical environmental conversation.[59]

---

When Jewell and Pritchard founded Creation Care, Inc., the facilitation of a yearly pastors' conference was just one item on their agenda. True to its encompassing mission to "inspire" and "equip" churches "to better love God by reviving human lives and the landscapes on which they depend," Flourish intended to help mission teams, church (youth) groups, and pastors integrate creation care into their projects. One such project was the intended teamwork with Christian community development organizer Leroy Barber in order to foster "green-collar jobs" and sustainable urban development in sprawling cities like Atlanta, for instance. Advocacy tools were the quarterly publication of *Flourish* magazine and an organizational website, which would provide a monthly online newsletter and other educational materials, including the online version of *Flourish*.[60]

Flourish itself was to be only one part of Creation Care, Inc., however. Convinced that there was a great need for evangelical leaders who would approach the environmental conversation from a decidedly conservative framework, Jewell and Pritchard also planned to establish the Terra Dei Institute for Environmental Policy in order to "reach out to—and develop a group of—leaders from moderate to conservative within the Christian conservative community on policy." Not a physical place but "a virtual institute on environmental policy," Terra Dei would provide a platform for "better conversations about God's earth," including the issue of climate change. The aim was "to advance prudent and effective public policies on energy and the environment—in the context of traditional conservative principles and Christian values." In order to reach this aim, "the most dramatic" part of Terra Dei's strategy was to hold private forums in the shape of weekend retreats, where about twenty leaders and their spouses would meet in a "relaxed" social setting and engage environmental matters constructively.[61]

Despite this rather hidden personal influence strategy, Pritchard and Jewell officially introduced a Terra Dei website early in 2011, through which they intended to present research, opinion briefings, and other resources and materials. They distinguished eight topics of environmental concern and policy that would be of interest to more politically conservative Christians: place, food, climate change, conservation, international development, children's environmental health, clean energy, and population. Regarding the most passionately contested environmental problem of climate change, it seems that Terra Dei attempted to deflate some of the pressure and urgency surrounding the issue by framing it as only *one* environmental problem resulting from $CO_2$ "pollution." Attempting to strike a middle ground between the scientific positions of the ECI on one hand, and those of evangelical environmental skeptics possibly supportive of the CA on the other, Terra Dei asserted that "the science that establishes the human contribution to dramatic increases in $CO_2$ in the atmosphere is *sufficiently conclusive* to make [the] effort to curb this pollution a *prudent, moral imperative*."[62]

As for how to tackle the problem, Terra Dei voiced support for "strong federal carbon pollution limits" consistent with "conservative values." Limits proposed should therefore "not endanger either the economic health of the nation or the ability of low income families to pay energy costs," nor should they "involve large subsidies for cooperating industries or funding for a variety of pet Congressional interests." While the ECI had voiced support for market-based cap-and-trade programs such as the one proposed by the Domenici-Bingaman resolution of 2005, Terra Dei provided a link to the Cantwell-Collins sponsored CLEAR Act, a cap-and-dividend bill that would have returned most of its revenue to consumers and was, at the time, favored by conservatives.[63]

Despite the intention to keep Terra Dei "separate from Flourish" in order not to "taint" the more depoliticized efforts of the latter, direct and indirect links between the two Creation Care, Inc., projects nonetheless existed. Terra Dei's population stance, for instance, could be found verbatim as the introduction to a lengthier post—entitled "The 'Other' Environmental Crisis"—written by Pritchard on Flourish's website. While in this case the type of intertextuality consisted of unmarked quotations only, Terra Dei's "conservation" rubric, on the other hand, provided an explicit hyperlink to Pritchard's text. Though not necessarily applicable vice versa, the environmental claims and positions staked out more extensively by Flourish thus seemed nonetheless suitable as discursive bases for the condensed policy considerations Terra Dei would promote.[64]

In particular, on Flourish's more extensive website—which has been inactive but not shut down since Creation Care, Inc.'s dormancy since 2012/2013—we can find several attempts to draw a distinction from secular environmentalism and to carve out a distinctly evangelical shade of green instead. In the article "The Real Earth Day," for instance, Pritchard voices his discomfort with Earth Day as a "holiday" of secular origin, "unrooted in religious tradition," and insists that "for Christians, in America at least, Thanksgiving Day is the real Earth Day." In a similar vein, *Flourish* guest contributor and "Republican tree-hugger" John Murdock draws attention to "Earth Day's Forgotten Founder" and the "Christian roots" of the "original" Earth Day, established by John McConnell on March 21, 1970.[65]

Arguably the most encompassing apolitical attempt to get more skeptical evangelicals on board, however, is Pritchard's article "The Myth of Overpopulation." It is not remarkable because of its nuanced view of population dynamics and the arguments against population control. Rather, it is the reframing of the problem itself, and Pritchard's interwoven critique of the secular environmental movement's inability to shed "the fundamental mythology" that overpopulation is a problem that can be "solved by abundant and free contraceptive technologies." Though Pritchard is fair enough to discern that most secular environmentalists are not "misanthropic" population control advocates, he nevertheless insists that "the idea of population control" remains salient within environmentalism because it keeps being "raised by population control advocates who can't find support for their policies on their own." Hence it is comparable to "a cuckoo's egg, secretly placed in another bird's nest in hopes of it being adopted by trickery." It is therefore exactly around the issue of population where family-oriented evangelicals can make a difference: they can "help push the cuckoo's egg of population control out of the nest of environmental action" and "reclaim that space" for pro-family concerns and actions instead.[66]

If some feared that Flourish was conceding too much ground to the evangelical Right with its stances on climate change, Pritchard's efforts of reframing and reclaiming ideas and spaces within the larger environmental movement to make them more attractive to politically conservative and environmentally skeptical evangelicals could be viewed similarly. Whether intentionally conceding ground or not, however, it is impossible to ignore the deeper and more complicated goal Pritchard and Jewell seemed to have pursued with this tactic, namely the intentional creation of an evangelical *culture* of environmentalism.[67]

This particular intention of green-culture-making is arguably most evident in Pritchard's article "The Danger of Derivatives," published in ESA's *Prism* magazine in 2009. Here, Pritchard harshly critiques the "evangelical penchant for wholesale cultural copying." Although he uses the Christian music industry as a prime example, his concern focuses on the creation care movement, where he detects a similar tendency to create "a derivative Christian version." Hence his warning that if unreflectively copied or consumed, environmentalism and Evangelicalism can only "reinforce each other's most destructive aspects": legalism, judgmentalism, hypocrisy, elitism, and excessive politicization. To avoid them Pritchard urges fellow believers "to cultivate the good" they can find in secular environmentalism, such as "a strong sense of place, a desire for community, a recognition of the sacred nature of creation," while also looking to "create forms of stewardship and respect for nature that extend what [they] find." Only if Christians strive toward this larger goal of creating a specifically evangelical environmental culture would they avoid reenacting "an environmentalism almost as good as what the secular world has created."[68]

---

While both apolitical CoC and BE have generally flourished since their founding in the mid-2000s, Creation Care, Inc., never organized a second Flourish conference. Moreover, concrete achievements in the realm of evangelical environmental culture making are lacking, as the organization appears to be more or less dormant since 2012/2013. Since then, Pritchard has moved on to the U.K.-based Christian charity Tearfund USA, whereas Jewell returned to public relations.[69]

It is not clear why Pritchard and Jewell's effort failed from their point of view. On May 4, 2014, however, Jewell posted a list of "7 Reasons NonProfits Flounder or Fail" on his blog, hinting at the financial difficulties a "group of friends" experienced while trying to set up a nonprofit "to reach faith-based constituencies who were not traditional supporters of environmental concerns." Although he did not explicitly refer to Creation Care, Inc., his text resonated with remarks he had previously made about a "fundraising dead zone" created by the culture war, in which ideologically bridging evangelical organizations fell. Considering his and Pritchard's intent to mediate between politically unafraid creation care evangelicals and those on the more conservative side of the political spectrum who were not concerned at all—in addition to creating a specifically evangelical green culture on top of it—it is understandable why raising sufficient funds for such a project would be challenging in the long run.[70]

Although the organization usurped Peter Illyn's RE project in 2014, and its future development thus remains unclear, in its original conception

Creation Care, Inc., signifies another failed attempt to expand the intra-evangelical reach of environmentalism. Like Ohlman's CNF, it thus serves best as a boundary marker of—and for—the creation care movement. A marker that indicates a persisting incapability on the part of the creation care movement—namely the inability "to produce groups like Prison Fellowship and Right on Crime, organizations built around bona fide conservative voices such as the late Chuck Colson and Grover Norquist"—to champion a cause still counterintuitive to most evangelicals on the political Right.[71]

# CONCLUSION

*In the Middle but Not Necessarily of It*

I'm in the middle. But some of it is "I'm here on this [issue], and I'm here on [that] one," so it's not always in the middle. It's a very strange place to be!

Ben Lowe[1]

This is not a left issue or a right issue, this is not Democrat or Republican. Everybody breathes the same air, everybody drinks the same water, it's part of our job to . . . love God and love our neighbor, particularly the disenfranchised, by caring for God's creation.

Nancy Sleeth, Blessed Earth[2]

## CREATION CARE, PARTISANSHIP, AND POLITICAL IDEOLOGY

When I met Ben Lowe in the Chicago suburb of Glen Ellyn in April 2010, the twenty-six-year-old Asian American Wheaton College graduate was in the midst of an election campaign against the Republican incumbent of his alma mater's congressional district. A "missionary kid from Singapore" who had studied environmental science at Wheaton, Lowe had become an outspoken creation care activist during his student years and at the time juggled full-time activism through involvement with several creation care movement organizations, including Au Sable, the EEN, and BE. The year prior Lowe had published his first book, *Green Revolution: Coming Together to Care for Creation* (2009), to introduce creation care to the younger generation of evangelicals. Creation care, as he echoed fellow leaders from within organized evangelical environmentalism who were mostly older than he was, was not only an integral part of Lowe's faith and vocation. It was also a great opportunity for the evangelical church "to make a real difference here and to leave a lasting legacy that will point others toward Christ."[3]

Apart from Glen Ellyn and Wheaton, Illinois' sixth congressional district includes economically prosperous and predominantly white towns like South Barrington, the location of Willow Creek Community Church, formerly led by ECI signatory Bill Hybels, and Carol Stream, the headquarters of both Christianity Today International and of evangelical publisher Tyndale House. Peter J. Roskam had only been in office since 2007, after he had defeated Democratic nominee Tammy Duckworth in a very close race following the announcement of Henry Hyde's retirement from politics in 2005. Under Hyde the district had been a suburban Republican stronghold since 1975. Like his predecessor, who was the major force behind the 1976 Hyde Amendment restricting federal funds for abortions, Roskam was strongly opposed to abortion. As Lowe critiqued, however, he also had a very poor environmental track record and did not believe in the problematics of climate change. Running against Roskam as an environmentally active, pro-life Democrat solely depending on grassroots support from people who neither rejected his being pro-life nor his campaigning as a Democrat, young and politically inexperienced Ben Lowe likened their race to the biblical battle between David and Goliath. Needless to say, in this instance Goliath would win.[4]

Lowe had never been registered with any political party prior to his pitch for Roskam's seat. In fact, like the EEN's James Ball and Alexei Laushkin, who at the time both considered themselves independents politically, Lowe suggested that until his very recent and rather pragmatic turn toward the Democratic Party he had fallen into the independent category as well. After all, there were "strengths and weaknesses to both [political parties]." Curiously enough, the person who had finally pushed Lowe into campaigning against Roskam as a pro-life Democrat was the EEN's new president and CEO Mitch Hescox, a former pastor and coal industry employee with a B.A. in geosciences who strongly identified as a Republican.[5]

While I have not encountered any outspoken supporters of the Green Party of the United States—or another third party specifically—among them, the rest of the creation care leaders do not neatly fall into one political (party) category either. Discounting the Sleeths and their definitive denial to express any political preference beyond their organization's apolitical approach to creation care, the creation care movement leadership does include Republicans, Democrats, and self-described independents.[6]

Whereas independents generally display reluctance toward party affiliation and instead make their votes dependent on issues, they are not necessarily neutral nonpartisans. In the United States they often lean toward one of the major political parties and thus, thanks to the two-party system, often come in different shades of reds and blues. To add additional hues to the dichromatic blue-and-red picture exacerbated by the culture wars, even the creation care leaders who do follow a personal voting pattern in preference of either the Democrats or the Republicans do so with a certain sense of dilemma. Similar to Facebook users updating their relationship status to account for their more ambiguous love lives, evangelical environmental leaders feel that "it's complicated" because their social and moral values are spread across the partisan divide. As Ed Brown concluded, speaking not only for himself, "And so I'm one of these guys, I need a third party. I need a third party that is, shall we say, morally conservative and socially liberal? Because I really think those go together."[7]

Evangelical environmentalists especially think being antiabortion *and* pro-creation care should not constitute a partisan conflict. Creation care *is* "a matter of life," and in particular Mitch Hescox has been very active around the link between pro-life sentiment and environmental concern, most notably through the EEN's campaign against the mercury poisoning of the unborn. "Christian Scripture," stated Hescox in his testimony before the Energy and Power Subcommittee of the U.S. House of Representatives' Energy and Commerce Committee in February 2012, "demands we protect the vulnerable, and yet we gather here today to choose in effect if protecting our unborn children and newborns from mercury pollution from the largest domestic source, coal-burning power plants, is in our national interest and in keeping with our national character." Evangelicals, of all citizens, should not be forced to make such a choice. Expressed succinctly as a more radical demand by one of RE's bumper stickers, "If you are pro-life, be anti-coal."[8]

Yet the political reality in the United States is that none of the parties reflect what evangelical environmentalists embrace as a *consistent* ethic of life. Noted historian Daniel Williams in his study on Left-leaning pro-lifers, "For the past three decades, the politics of abortion have made it difficult for even the most liberal evangelicals to support the Democratic Party." Likewise, the politics of global warming and the refusal of most of the GOP leadership to take on more ecological responsibility has made it difficult for environmentally concerned evangelicals to support the Republican Party impartially and uncritically. As Jim Ball resentfully remarked during the CCCC 2010 in Washington, D.C., how could creation care advocates deliver Republican votes in favor of a comprehensive climate legislation if there were no GOP leaders sponsoring such legislation, and if Republicans did not even believe that climate change was real?[9]

While other creation care leaders seem to agree that it is up to the EEN to deal with the especially politically divisive issue of climate change on a policy level, none of them expressed a disbelief in the reality and problematic nature of climate change. Moreover, because of the perceived severity of the problem and its intense politicization in America, there was a consensus regarding the strong need to establish common ground across national partisan lines, if only by means of a completely depoliticized creation care message. Lacking a consensual political affiliation and corresponding communal advocacy strategy, creation care leaders are united by a cautious reluctance toward a full alignment with either the Democratic or the Republican Party because neither of the two represents their core values in a holistic fashion.

———

In addition to their strained sense of partisanship, creation care leaders consciously challenge the common view of environmentalism as a liberal or progressive cause. Likewise, they display an uneasiness with contemporary American conservatism and its role in the various cultural battles of our time. Though most of them seem to largely view themselves as conservatives engaged in a moral cause that is inextricably tied to their faith and thus beyond the confines of political philosophy and partisan politics, several leaders have expressed a need for clarification regarding what it means to be "conservative." Intertwined with that, some of them have also stressed that conservation *is* conservative, and that it was Republican President Theodore Roosevelt, after all, who had championed conservationist policies in the United States.[10]

Not having to go as far back in time as to evoke Roosevelt as role model and inspiration, according to Peter Illyn even neo-conservatives like Bill Kristol had been "more thoughtful" in their ideology. Represented by culture warriors like Bill O'Reilly, the conservative movement, on the other hand, had "just become bombastic and really, I think, mean-spirited." Despite the fact that Illyn is one of the politically unafraid creation care leaders, note that his criticism does not come from a leftist political ideology. Again, the matter appears to be more complicated. Admitting that "it's really hard to label who and what we are," Illyn offered that he leaned toward libertarianism, which meant to him that "people should have a right to pursue their hearts."[11]

In addition, Illyn does not feel uncritical toward what he calls the "progressive community" in the United States either. Progressives quite often behaved like "fundamentalists" too, making mediation across divides impossible. Hence Illyn does not look at contemporary American society through the lens of the political liberal-versus-conservative paradigm anymore. Perceiving the scenario of the culture war from a more psychological point of view, Illyn has come to understand "the rift as more accurately defined as *compartmentalized* and *disconnected* versus *integrative* and *interconnected.*" People within the latter category "tend to see complex interrelationships interacting in a dynamic, constantly-in-motion world." Compartmentalized and disconnected people, however, "tend not to see the interrelationships between actions and consequences. They do not see the world as complex, ambiguous, or filled with paradox but instead see a much simpler world often framed as dualistic choices between extremes." Admitting that this model was somewhat "simplistic," Illyn nevertheless views it as a reasonable explanation for his experiences as a creation care advocate.[12]

Belying the conventional wisdom that it is usually the younger generation who is more liberal than the older, only the grandfather of the movement, Calvin DeWitt, explicitly self-identified as "progressive." But just like his fellow creation care co-laborers, DeWitt was somewhat evasive when it came to pinpointing his ideological label. Cautiously, he remarked that the meaning of the term "progressive" depended on what one understood to be "progress," of course. In his view, progress was certainly not having "to give up a beautiful world" for the sake of "increased traffic," "increased crime," "increased air pollution," "less safety for our children," and "more taxes" to be paid. That constituted "regress" instead.[13]

Similar to Illyn, DeWitt also spoke out against compartmentalization, emphasizing that the Christian worldview was much more holistic than the fundamentalist reduction of it: "We are compartmentalizing things to the point where you compartmentalize yourself away from the impacts of your activity on the rest of the world. And the Christian worldview is just absolutely opposed to that! I mean fundamentally it is, if you want to get to the fundamentals." In addition, DeWitt reflected upon the fact that during his long career as a creation care advocate, there had been times when he was accused of being "pretty radical" and of being "too conservative," respectively, even though he had always been doing the same things. "You know you are in the middle of the road," according to Brown, "when you are being shot at from both sides."[14]

Even if we distinguish strictly along the theoretical line that pits a generally conservative preference for individual responsibility against the liberal penchant for government regulation, creation care leaders emphasize both—the need to change laws *and* the need to change light bulbs. While politically unafraid creation care organizations put a stronger emphasis on systemic solutions, none of them regard the individual as powerless (unless the individual operates without God—then evangelicals perceive any human effort to be ultimately futile). Neither do evangelical environmental leaders who favor an apolitical personal responsibility approach to creation care outright deny the need for a certain degree of government regulation. Their preferred environmental policy tools may at times align more with those preferred by the political Left or the Right, respectively, but they are nonetheless united in their view of environmentalism as a moral, spiritual, and ideologically transcending issue to be tackled holistically on an individual and a collective level.[15]

Considering their view of environmentalism as beyond (partisan) politics and ideology, creation care advocates thus cannot be neatly placed on a political spectrum stripped of its finer nuances by culture war reductionism. Moreover, dismayed by the culture war and the extreme politicization of conservative religion in America, creation care leaders seem undivided in their refusal to reduce their faith and their activism to the encrusted ideological structures on which the culture warriors on the Left and the Right thrive. While the Religious Right has not had any difficulty closely aligning with the Republican Party—if only on grounds of a lesser-of-two-evils principle—a constrained suitability with the American two-party system is very obvious in the case of evangelical environmentalists, who may indeed collectively epitomize the "nomads" or "political orphans" as Jonathan Merritt portrays himself and his co-laborers in Lowe's book *Green Revolution*.[16]

## CREATION CARE, ENVIRONMENTALISM, AND EVANGELISM

In part related to their rejection of an ideologically curtailed and politically partisan Evangelicalism as non-reflective of the breadth of their religious belief and faith tradition, creation care leaders at large have also not embraced the environmentalist label without reservation. Moreover, their preferred use of the term "creation care" instead of "environmentalism" displays the need for a different linguistic code of identification. In addition, creation care advocates consider their movement to be consistently "pro-life." Although their environmentally skeptical evangelical brethren have thus charged that they are, intentionally or unintentionally, co-opting pro-life language in order to advance the "Machiavellian" agenda of the population control movement, the simple usage of this term popularized by the antiabortion movement also sets them off from mainstream environmentalists.[17]

Intertwined with the theologically grounded preference for the term "creation care" seems to be a cultural reason too, namely to mark and uphold a religio-cultural identity boundary. A boundary that is not necessarily rigid and impervious as it does allow partial identification and cooperative interaction with non-evangelical environmentalists, it nevertheless makes clear that theirs is a God-centered, "earth third" movement with the overarching aim to integrate creation care into the value-system of the evangelical church. As Mitch Hescox put it, "This movement is not about the earth; it's not even about people. It's about Jesus Christ!"[18]

While their identification with the environmentalist label and the larger environmental movement remains constricted, creation care leaders do display a strong identification with Evangelicalism. Though they come to creation care from different denominational backgrounds, they strongly adhere to the evangelical Protestant faith tradition and seem to espouse the trans-denominationalism characteristic of modern (neo-)Evangelicalism. It hardly seems inconsequential that EEN board members, for instance, "must ascribe to the National Association of Evangelicals statement of faith and be comfortable with this [i.e., evangelical] label." That said, not all creation care organizations explicitly subscribe to the NAE's statement of faith. Nonetheless, all of the creation care leaders portrayed identify as "evangelical." If some of them have expressed discomfort with the evangelical label, it has been dissatisfaction with what Evangelicalism has come to represent in culture war-ridden America but not regarding their personal belief and religious identity.[19]

The Reformed tradition of the Northeast may have been culturally more willing to react to the moral pressure of mainstream environmentalism and theologically more conducive to discursively shape the evangelical steward-ship ethic or creation care theology. Even to leaders like Dean Ohlman, however, who came to the cause from a fundamentalist Baptist background, the "lost fundamental" of creation care became an integral part of his faith after his born-again again experience and subsequent conversion to environmentalism. Moreover, the very politically and theologically conservative Ohlman was involved in the drafting and revision process of the EDCC, which is only one example that pays testimony to the remarkable cooperation that seems to have been going on *within* the creation care movement across denominational and ideological differences.[20]

Furthermore, and despite their critics' fear that an engagement for creation care could somehow make evangelicals less Christian as it brings them in cultural proximity to a theologically corrupt and ideologically manipulative "green dragon," creation care leaders view their encroachment into the spiritual marketplace of environmentalism as providing evangelistic opportunities instead. Their intent to save souls along with the planet may sound surprising to non-evangelicals, but as eminent religious history scholar Martin E. Marty clarified before, evangelicals "would not be evangelicals if they were not evangelistic." The Great Commission, writes megachurch pastor and ECI signatory Rick Warren in his bestseller, *The Purpose Driven Life,* is not called the "*Great Suggestion.*" To make disciples of all nations is Jesus Christ's mandatory task for every believer, and "to ignore it would be disobedience."[21]

Consequently, the idea that environmentalism provides a novel cultural and global space for evangelicals to share their faith can be traced from Schaeffer's *Pollution and the Death of Man* (1970) to statements of the most recent creation care leaders. Politically unafraid organizations may not actively pursue evangelism as part of their strategic agenda and, as Illyn remarked, concentrate on converting evangelicals to environmentalists rather than vice versa. Nonetheless, even the EEN has praised creation care as "one of the greatest tools for evangelism in younger generations." Beyond that, in particular PWP's activism, Sorley's concept of environmental missions, and Brown's cooperation with the Lausanne Movement do strongly testify to the creation care movement's deep and traditional anchoring within the core tenets of the evangelical faith. An anchoring that is further compounded by creation care leaders' profoundly evangelical conversions to environmentalism and the impact that their faith apparently had on the founding of their respective organizations.[22]

Granted, not all non-evangelical environmentalists may necessarily (like to) conceive of themselves as souls potentially waiting to be saved by evangelical creation care advocates. It is therefore important to emphasize that although creation care *can* be a tool for evangelism, it must not be reduced to that. As Brown passionately declared, "We don't do this in order to evangelize!" As we have seen, creation care advocates are sincerely concerned about eco-crisis and the ecotheological foundation of their activism, and thus perceive of their movement as an authentic expression of their faith. As such, however, creation care does have an evangelistic dimension as well. It has to simply because "it's part of who we are as evangelicals."[23]

As much as its evangelistic dimension does ground the creation care movement strongly within the evangelical tradition, it certainly compounds the religio-cultural boundary with non-evangelical environmentalism as well. However, it also needs to be stressed that this boundary does not connote a sectarian behavior on part of creation care advocates. Rather, it is indicative of the typical evangelical subcultural orientation of "engagement-with-distinction": creation care advocates are engaged in environmental matters, but they are so as clearly identifiable evangelicals because they hold on to their religious core. Their engagement stays true to their religious identity and faith tradition, but they are willing, to use E. O. Wilson's words, "to meet on the near side of metaphysics in order to deal with the real world we share." They trust the mainstream scientific community regarding the ecological state of the world and to some extent bracket eschatological questions in order to focus on the here and now. Yet they also insist on approaching environmental problems through an evangelical theological, spiritual, and moral framework in ways and with the help of policy tools that are negotiated within their own community and through the work of their own creation care advocacy organizations. Unlike their critics, such as Calvin Beisner, who seem to demonize most of the environmental movement, creation care advocates engage in environmentalism—but they do so in a faithfully distinct manner, which thus precludes an impartial identification with the larger environmental movement.[24]

## POPULATION, CAPITALISM, AND THE INTRA-EVANGELICAL BOUNDARY OF CREATION CARE

Predominantly those environmentally concerned religious groups associated with evangelical Protestantism, Islam, and Roman Catholicism have in the past displayed an uneasiness around the issue of population. As stated by Brown, evangelicals "want [their] babies" because the Bible simply tells them to. Being pro-life and against abortion thus constitutes a fairly straightforward matter for evangelicals, whereas the population question is much more difficult to address because the call to curb human population numbers directly conflicts with the Genesis 1:28 command "to be fruitful and increase in number."[25]

In addition, and as Jonathan Franzen vividly illustrates in his novel *Freedom* (2010), speaking about overpopulation has a very "elitist" ring to it. Even more challenging in American culture specifically is that claiming the problematic nature of increasing population numbers is often perceived as an attempt to curtail individual liberties. Moreover, it essentially entails a critique of free market capitalism since it expresses the view that there are limits to growth. Explains fictitious Richard Katz, a cynic rock musician whom environmental organizer Walter Berglund is trying to enlist in a population control advocacy event, "Capitalism can't handle talking about limits, because the whole point of capitalism is the restless growth of capital. If you want to be heard in the capitalist media, and communicate in a capitalist culture, overpopulation can't make any sense. It's literally nonsense. And that's your real problem."[26]

While the issue of (over)population is admittedly "tricky" to tackle from within a biblical framework, creation care advocates have not shied away from discussing the issue. Moreover, unlike their critics, such as Beisner, who displays a very optimistic understanding of both population growth and capitalism, creation care advocates largely agree with non-evangelical environmentalists that growing population numbers amplify environmental degradations, and that there is a carrying capacity of the earth. This agreement is reflected in the text of the EDCC as much as in the literature on creation care by apolitical leaders like Matthew Sleeth, to whom the use of "ethically designed birth control" is no less reprehensible than the manipulation of the human death rate with the help of modern medicine.[27]

According to Lowe, the issue of (over)population also intersects with questions about technology and values, and must be addressed alongside them. In addition, and seemingly more and more important to younger evangelicals, it touches upon animal welfare because it constitutes a matter of rightful cocreation: since God not only told humans to be fruitful and multiply but also the sea creatures and birds he created (see Genesis 1:22), humans "have no right" to multiply in a way as to "impede on them [i.e., other creatures] fulfilling the blessing as well." As Brown and Sleeth both note in agreement with an acknowledgment of limits, "any blessing can be overdone."[28]

That said, creation care advocates nevertheless stress that every human being is "precious," and that they "rightly abhor government policies such as forced abortion and forced sterilization." As detailed previously, in particular Rusty Pritchard has gone to lengths to advocate an evangelical environmentalism untainted by the agenda of the population control movement.

Other than awaiting the occurrence of natural self-regulation and reminding evangelicals that they have more than fulfilled the biblical command to multiply, however, creation care advocates have no policy advice to curb the actual number of people on earth. What they offer instead is a faith-based critique of consumerism and the idea of continuous economic growth.[29]

As early as 1995 the fall edition of *Green Cross* magazine was exclusively dedicated to the theme of consumerism and its connection to environmental degradation. According to editor Fred Kruger, overconsumption was "at root, an issue of Christian integrity" and not compatible with the lifestyle demanded by the gospel. Motivated by similar considerations, the Sleeths have been especially vocal in their criticism of the "American dream" vis-à-vis "God's dream." Though not as radical in calling for individual anti-consumerist lifestyle makeovers as the Sleeths, after his born-again again experience, creation care pioneer Dean Ohlman also decried "runaway consumerism" and the "debauchery of materialism." Furthermore, Ohlman explicitly condemned Calvin Beisner's "preaching [of] Julian Simon's strange combination of economic fatalism/optimism" in the aftermath of Beisner's EDCC criticism.[30]

While their critique of consumerism largely remains embedded in a biblically inspired social justice frame, note that it does not turn into a coherent critique of the industrial capitalist economic system. In the case of the Sleeths, it orients creation care practitioners toward historical and contemporary Christian exemplars of simple living instead. In the case of other creation care leaders, it mostly takes the shape of a general skepticism regarding capitalism's ability to solve environmental problems and a disbelief in the free market's capacity to function unaffected by human sinfulness.

According to Brown the "disease" of what non-evangelical activist and filmmaker John DeGraaf had termed "*affluenza*"—characterized, among other things, by an "unsustainable addiction to economic growth"—originates in the human heart and not in economic theory. Rules therefore matter. Although he largely views governmental control "as a poor substitute for personal and corporate responsibility," conservative Republican Dean Ohlman also sees a need for environmental regulation. Moreover, even Ohlman is convinced that the economy should not "grow unchecked primarily to make the rich richer. That's when growth becomes cancer."[31]

That being said, note that creation care advocates' critical view of American capitalism and consumerism is *not* indicative of an espousal of socialism or other, more radical economic and political theories often associated with environmentalism. As Ohlman wrote to Beisner on March 11, 1994, "Are you calling the appeal to government to limit abuse of the environment *socialism*? Of the concerned Christians in this arena that I am familiar with, I don't know of a single one calling for our nation to adopt socialism and reject capitalism." At some point between his 1994 and 1995 letter exchange with Beisner, Ohlman even accused Beisner and other environmentally skeptical free market champions of exhibiting a "new McCarthyism" intent on defaming "most environmentally concerned individuals [as] nature worshippers and pinkos." Though he later admitted that his criticism may have appeared too personal and his idea of a new McCarthyism "too strong," at least for publication in an editorial as he had intended to, Ohlman nevertheless insisted that it was "entirely unfair" to call "those who want to see more environmental controls 'socialists.'" According to his understanding, creation care advocates did not have an economic agenda. Rather, they only tried to come to terms with environmental degradation from within a Christian framework that obviously differed from Beisner's on some crucial points, including the latter's unquestioned belief in the free market's capacity to solve the problem.[32]

Especially in comparison to Calvin Beisner and the CA, it becomes obvious that creation care advocates do not seem to have a vested theological interest in the insistence on free market capitalism as the economic expression of Christianity. Neither are they as optimistic about economic growth in general. Hence, they do not perceive a critical view of capitalism as an attack on Christianity but rather entertain the idea of a more compassionate and environmentally aware approach to economics than that of the completely unregulated free market. Their critique of the contemporary capitalist order may thus not be as explicitly and intricately tied to a condemnation of fossil fuels and the free market as, for instance, that of anti-globalist activist Naomi Klein's. As much as they consider anthropogenic climate change to be real and problematic and ever increasing human population numbers to have a negative environmental impact, creation care leaders also believe that there are limits to growth and limits to economic theory when it comes to ameliorating environmental degradation and interrelated problems.[33]

In addition, creation care advocates do not seem to be theologically distressed by the potential metaphysical implications of anthropogenic climate change and the like. Unlike the young-Earth creationists involved in the various and ongoing cultural battles to "scientifically prove" the Bible, they seem more "epistemologically modest" in general. Hence, they bracket questions about evolutionary theory and the age of the earth for the sake of common ground. Moreover, while creation care advocates certainly are creationists in the sense that they believe God created everything, instead of being overly concerned with questions surrounding the exact when and how of creation, they are more concerned about their role in the human mistreatment of creation and what they can do better to adhere to the biblical obligation of creation care.[34]

It is certainly beyond the scope of this book to evaluate how theologically conclusive creation care advocates reconcile the epistemological tensions that have existed between Evangelicalism and science in general, and whether their reconciliation makes them, theologically speaking, more "liberal evangelicals," or not. From an anthropological point of view, however, their approach to science and pretty much everything else does seem less fundamentalist than that of Beisner, Kennedy, and others. While the intra-evangelical fault line of the green gap can be traced along several points of discrepancy, including stances on (over)population and capitalism, ultimately the friction seems to occur mostly along an axis of rigidity and certitude.[35]

In the case of creation care advocates, there seems to be more room for doubt and more room for ambiguity. There is no fear of science possibly debunking their faith and no fear of the liberal/progressive and/or unchristian "other" attempting to manipulate their belief for satanic purposes. As Ohlman writes in one of his letters to Beisner, "We are not dupes or heretics without brains or orthodoxy chasing after a bunch of wackos. Most of us are merely coming to the place Francis Schaeffer was twenty-five years ago." Schaeffer, we should not forget, accepted the reality of a global environmental crisis just as much as he was convinced that the only solution to the problem would be provided by the "Christianity of the Reformation" and a "genuine biblical worldview."[36]

Although they do embrace the biblical worldview, creation care movement leaders do not insist on upholding a rigid boundary between themselves and non-evangelicals by means of demonization and an authoritative biblicalism that makes nonnegotiable truth claims on all spheres of life. Even though creation care advocates are no relativists who subscribe to "the naturalistic faith of a secular worldview," they do insist on the reality of biblical symbolism and a certain extent of mystery surrounding God and his creation. Unlike fundamentalists, who generally "banish mystery" in order to make God "knowable and predictable," creation care advocates accept that there are certain things "beyond [human] grasp." What is clear to them, nevertheless, is that according to science, creation is in peril, and according to Scripture, creation care is imperative.[37]

Although creation care advocates since Schaeffer have insisted on establishing their own environmental organizations with missions being reflective of how they understand and intend to practically apply their biblical worldview in ecologically sensible ways, they are nevertheless eager to dialog with—and work alongside—non-evangelical environmentalists, across divides, and toward common environmental goals. They may not formally partner with the majority of non-evangelical environmental organizations for reasons already addressed, and there certainly are limits to common ground between creation care and non-evangelical environmentalism. Nonetheless, it is crucial to emphasize that the general cultural posture of creation care advocates leans toward a mediating engagement that attempts to build bridges between themselves and non-evangelical others.

Especially if we view culture as "the rules of the game" and the culture war as a struggle to define and implement those rules, creation care advocates also seem more culturally accommodating and inclusive than their critics affiliated with the CA. According to WallBuilders founder, David Barton—a signatory of the CA's "Call to Truth," who is also featured on the organization's DVD series "Resisting the Green Dragon"—America was founded as a "Godly nation" and needs to be rebuilt as such. Thus, WallBuilders' mission is to recover America's "forgotten history and heroes" from the nonprofit's special collection of rare books and handwritten documents of the Founding Fathers. The idea behind the effort is that the Christian part of American history has been muted or erased by non-righteous forces. The name of Barton's organization is taken from the Old Testament book of Nehemiah, which describes the rebuilding of the walls of Jerusalem. It was chosen "to represent allegorically the call for citizen involvement in rebuilding our nation's foundations," because, as the organization goes on to cite Psalm 11:3, "if the foundations be destroyed, what shall the righteous do?" Comparable to the aim of Beisner and other Christian reconstructionists at the COR, according to WallBuilders, the righteous must rebuild the nation according to the rules that they believe ought to define America.[38]

Unlike Barton, who has also critiqued environmentalism as anti-Christian and, consequently, anti-American together with Beisner on the *Glenn Beck Program*, creation care advocates do not labor toward rebuilding the Christian foundations of America. Neither do they seem to appreciate culture warriors like Glenn Beck. As Lowe told me, America is not a Christian society but one characterized by pluralism instead. Hence the rules of the game are not to be defined by evangelicals alone, but in a creative, faithful, and diplomatic exchange with non-evangelicals as well.[39]

As their environmental "engagement-with-distinction" thus ultimately demonstrates, creation care advocates are more willing to engage with and be influenced by non-evangelical segments of American culture than their critics affiliated with the CA. They do not regard Christianity as under constant attack by outsiders; neither do they aspire to (re)build walls and Christian empires. Instead, they intend to construct bridges. Moreover, they view their attempt to build bridges as not only necessary in order to further the Great Commission and to achieve common environmental goals, but also as a duty of the faithful in contemporary, polarized America. "If the Church won't act as a bridge for political and cultural divides," asks Mitch Hescox rhetorically, "who will?"[40]

Though creation care advocates and evangelical environmental skeptics share a theological core and a basic agreement regarding the value of creation and the biblical mandate of stewardship, Calvin Beisner and the

CA have not attempted to culturally mediate between Evangelicalism and environmentalism in order to tackle environmental degradations and foster shared ecological responsibility, neither on the individual nor on the collective level. Instead, they have been deeply suspicious of environmentalism and its evangelical shade of green on grounds that reach well beyond the realm of (partisan) politics and specific environmental and economic policies. Apart from finer theological, economic, and political/ideological discrepancies among the two camps, the green gap thus points toward the deeper, complex, and still-persisting fault zone between a more accommodating and mediating Evangelicalism on the one side, and a less flexible yet highly socially and politically engaged fundamentalism on the other.

Occupying a non-fundamentalist "in-between-but-still-within" space at the intersection of American Evangelicalism and environmentalism, creation care advocates are not only wrestling with questions of environmental degradation and engagement but also with what it means to be evangelical and live faithfully in America and the world beyond. The answers they have thus far given us place moral responsibility and mediation across boundaries above ideology and dogmatic certainty.

As Paul Hawken concurs with creation care leaders from a non-evangelical perspective, "Healing the wounds of the earth and its people does not require saintliness or a political party, only gumption and persistence. It is not a liberal or conservative activity; it is a sacred act." Engaged in such transcendentally motivated activism, creation care advocates are here to further the creation care reformation inside and outside of America, despite the backlash from the Trump administration and the rise of environmentally skeptical nationalism worldwide. As Illyn observed, using a metaphor deeply reflective of his love for the wild, in their attempt to make the evangelical church more environmentally conscious and concerned, creation care activists have to be like wolves hunting the caribou: they have to "come at it from all these different sides." Besides young evangelicals, creation care leaders' strongest ally at this point in time may very well be the global Christian mission movement.[41]

# APPENDIX



SELECTION CRITERIA FOR ORGANIZATIONS IN THE STUDY

To find other groups like the EEN in order to make the case for a creation care movement as a distinctive, organizationally localizable place at the intersection of American Evangelicalism and environmentalism, before further analyzing the religiopolitical space it occupies, I first worked from the outside (i.e., links on the EEN's website, Internet searches, secondary academic and non-academic sources) toward the inside (i.e., e-mail exchange with Janel Curry and subsequent participation in the CCCC) and formulated the following set of selection criteria for the organizations to be included in this study along the way:

1.  Like the EEN, other organizations to be included needed to roughly fit the general definition of "interest group" in the sense that they were "organized in some minimal fashion, [sought] to influence public policy, and [were] not a political party." Regarding the individual organization's attempt to influence public policy, the advocacy methods employed did not have to be overtly political and could also be mostly understood as educational.[1]

2.  The individual organization to be included needed to seek contact with the public in order to spread information about itself, its ideas, and its positions by providing an interface in the shape of a functioning website.

3.  The primary interest of the organization had to be environmental issues/creation care.

4.  The organization's mission had to be linked with the evangelical faith (i.e., the organization needed to be identifiable—or self-identify—as "evangelical" instead of generally Christian or mainline Protestant).

5. The organizations to be included had to be "parachurch organizations," which means that they consider themselves as part of "the church" and as promoting concerns of interest to "the church" but are not housed within certain ecclesiastical bodies or maintained as programs by certain denominations or congregations.[2]

6. The respective headquarters of the organizations had to be located within the United States, and their outlook had to be national or global, not regionally confined.

7. They could not be a national affiliate of an international organization. (It was primarily on the basis of this provision that A Rocha, USA, the American affiliate of the international A Rocha network, was excluded, although Executive Director Tom Rowley was present during both the CCCC meetings I attended.)

8. The organizations to be included had to be networking partners and understand themselves as part of the creation care movement or the creation care community (a requirement they fulfilled by participating in the CCCC, for instance).

9. They had to be founded before the CCCC 2009 meeting. Organizations that had not survived financially or been disbanded for other reasons before 2012/2013 were also included if their founders were still connected with the CCCC in 2009 and/or 2010, or approachable in some other way. This led to the inclusion of Dean Ohlman and the CNF, as much as to the exclusion of Gorden Aeschliman and the Christian Environmental Association/Target Earth.

## PARTICIPANT OBSERVATION AND INTERVIEWS

I attended two meetings of the CCCC, the first one at Judson University in Elgin, Illinois, from August 6 to 7, 2009, and the second one at Western Presbyterian Church in Washington, D.C., from August 2 to 3, 2010. Participating in those two meetings helped identify other creation care movement organizations besides the EEN and enabled me to make personal contact with participating leaders to discuss the possibility of subsequent interviews. Additionally, I was able to observe the way in which creation care movement leaders acted and interacted as a group; to see how they resolved in-group conflict; and to get firsthand insights into what kind of topics aroused their interest and what problems they struggled with. To keep my interference to a minimum, I refrained from recording or videotaping those meetings and stuck to taking handwritten notes. While I participated in group prayers, individual small talk, and lunches, I did not ask the group any questions, neither did I comment on any of the issues it collectively discussed.

The interviews that largely resulted from my participation in the CCCC were in many instances much more intimate. The aim was to speak with at least one representative of each respective organization represented in the CCCC. Instead of requesting a specific interviewee, I left it up to the groups to decide who would speak to me. Being flexible with regard to the duration of our meetings depending on the time interviewees would make available, and also regarding the meeting sites they suggested, some of the interviews were comparatively short (i.e., about one hour) and took place at restaurants and coffee shops, whereas others took several hours and were conducted at interviewees' homes. Since the opportunity arose to discuss the creation care movement with two sympathetic yet critical evangelical insiders, supplemental interviews were conducted with David Neff, at the time editor-in-chief of the evangelical publication *CT*, and Rand Clark, at the time senior pastor of a small Southern Baptist Convention church plant in Castle Rock, Colorado, and speaker at a national pastors' conference on creation care in 2009, organized by Creation Care, Inc. In addition, Peter Bakken and Nelson Bock offered to comment on the creation care movement from the Protestant mainline position.

With the exception of a September 2009 structured e-mail interview with Janel Curry, who was the chairwoman of the EEN's board, all my interviews were semi-structured and, excluding one follow-up interview in London, United Kingdom, in June 2016, conducted in the United States between April and August 2010 (see below).

## INTERVIEWEES IN THE STUDY

| Name | Organization and Position at the Time of Interview | Interview Date and Duration | Interview Location |
|---|---|---|---|
| Peter Bakken | Wisconsin Council of Churches; Coordinator for Public Policy | April 10, 2010; 1:08:27 | Madison, Wis. |
| E. Calvin Beisner | Cornwall Alliance for the Stewardship of Creation; National Spokesman | April 27, 2010; 4:43:10 | Pembroke Pines, Fla. |
| Nelson Bock | Colorado Interfaith Power and Light; Program Director | January 22, 2010; ca. 1.5 hours, non-recorded interview w. semi-structured questionnaire | Denver, Colo. |

| Edward R. Brown | Care of Creation, Inc.; Founder and Director | April 11, 2010; 1:14:23. June 6, 2016; 1:25:11. | Madison, Wis. London, UK |
|---|---|---|---|
| Rand Clark | Genesis Church, Castle Rock, CO; Lead Pastor | July 19, 2010; 1:30:33 | Centennial, Colo. |
| Janel Curry | Evangelical Environmental Network; Chairwoman of the Board | September 25, 2009; e-mailed questionnaire | N/A; e-mail interview |
| Calvin DeWitt | Au Sable Institute of Environmental Studies; former director. Academy of Evangelical Scientists and Ethicists; President. | April 10, 2010; 1:22:52 | Town of Dunn, Wis. |
| Peter Illyn | Christians for Environmental Stewardship/Restoring Eden; Founder and Executive Director | March 25, 2010; 1:53:23 | La Center, Wash. |
| Jim Jewell | Creation Care, Inc.; Chairman of the Board and Co-founder | April 29, 2010; 3:04:08 | Suwanee, Ga. |
| Alexei Laushkin | Evangelical Environmental Network; Senior Director of Communications and Editor of *Creation Care* | August 2, 2010; 1:28:01 | Washington, D.C. |
| Ben Lowe | Renewal; Coordinator. Evangelical Environmental Network; Director Young Adult Ministries | April 9, 2010; 1:23:42 | Glen Ellyn, Ill. |
| David Neff | *Christianity Today*; Editor-in-Chief | April 14, 2010; 57:43 | Carol Stream, Ill. |

| Dean Ohlman | Christian Nature Federation; Founder. Wonder of Creation/RBC Ministries; Writer. | April 8, 2010; 3:08:47 | Grand Rapids, Mich. |
|---|---|---|---|
| Nancy Sleeth | Blessed Earth; Program Director and Co-Founder | April 21, 2010; 1:00:55 | Altamonte Springs, Fla. |

## INTERVIEW GUIDE

This is the outline of a general questionnaire that I, based on my pre-knowledge, tailored to the respective interviewee's particular background and position. With the exception of the e-mail interview with Janel Curry and the conversations with Peter Bakken, Nelson Bock, and David Neff, the interviews were designed to be semi-structured and open-ended. Hence, I tried to be as flexible as possible without losing sight of the items that I was interested in discussing with participants. Since the sample of creation care organizations and their leaders is so small and the creation care movement characterized by a certain degree of collective organizational steering and cooperation through the CCCC, the aim was not to discuss all the questions pertaining to the larger creation care community and its relation to mainstream environmentalism with all of the interviewees, but rather to view individual answers as cumulative and collectively representative. The interview with E. Calvin Beisner focused more on the opposition toward the creation care movement.

**Introductory and Biographic Details**

1.  When were you born?

2.  What is your professional background?

3.  How did you get into creation care?

4.  If I am not mistaken, X was founded in Y. Could you tell me more about the founding history of the organization? What motivated you, who helped, who chose the name of the organization, and why?

**Religious Identity, Personal and Organizational**

1.  What is your religious background?

2.  Would you identify yourself as an "evangelical Christian"? If so, what does this mean to you?

3. Would you describe the organization you represent as an "evangelical" organization?

4. [OR Would you describe the organization you represent as an "evangelical" organization? Is this a label you personally subscribe to as well? If so, what does this mean to you?]

5. [OR (for EEN, etc.): Your organization defines itself as "evangelical." Is this a label you personally subscribe to as well? If so, what does this mean to you?]

## Political Identity, Ideological Philosophy

1. Where on the political spectrum would you place yourself?

2. Do you consider yourself a conservative, libertarian, independent, liberal, or progressive? What does this mean to you?

3. Are you registered with any of the political parties?

4. Who did you vote for in the last presidential election?

5. [Have you heard of the Manhattan Declaration? If so, do you support it?]

## Issue Positions

### *environmental*

1. What would you say is the most pressing environmental issue at this point in time?

2. How does your organization approach the issue of population growth? Would you say that human population growth is a problem or a blessing in the twenty-first century?

3. Would you—and if so, how?—refute the claim that protecting the environment hurts the economy?

4. What do you think is more important when it comes to combating environmental degradation: advocating individual responsibility or governmental regulation?

### *consumerism/capitalism*

1. According to your belief, does God provide material wealth to those he favors?

2. Would you say that prosperity without growth is a Utopian dream or a financial and ecological necessity at this point in time?

3. Is there hope for a "green capitalism" or do you think environmentalists have to be anti-capitalist at this point in time?

*abortion*

1. For quite some time, the agenda of evangelical Christians in America seems to have been mainly shaped by the issues of abortion and homosexuality. Are these issues that concern you as well? If so, where on your priorities list would you place them?

2. What is your position on abortion? (Legal in all cases? Illegal in all cases? Legal in most cases? Illegal in most cases?)

3. Is this an issue that your organization has to face in one way or the other as well? (Connection of creation care and sanctity of life; idea of seamless garment of life; abortion as a means of population control?)

*homosexuality*

1. What is your take on homosexuality? Do you support gay marriage? Civil unions?

2. Is this an issue that your organization has to face in one way or the other as well?

**Culture Wars / Religion and Politics / Public Image of Evangelicals**

1. How would you describe the space that environmentally concerned evangelicals like yourself occupy in contemporary American politics and culture?

2. What's the ideal role of religion in the public square? Do you think that Christians should retain political independence/neutrality?

3. Some would say that the image of American evangelical Christianity has suffered during the past two decades or so. Do you agree with this statement?

**Larger Creation Care Movement**

1. What is the greatest challenge to the creation care movement at this point in time?

2. The greatest opportunity/ies?

3. What would you say makes your organization unique among the groups in the creation care movement?

4. Would you say that the creation care movement has a geographical center? (How do you explain the lack of creation care groups in the Mountain West, for example?)

5. What is the role of people like Joel Hunter and Richard Cizik in the creation care movement?

6. [Do you feel like Richard Cizik speaks for you or represents you and others involved in creation care in the public square? Do you support his new organization The New Evangelical Partnership for the Common Good?] Who speaks for evangelicals at this point in time? (Who sets the agenda?)

7. Would you say that the creation care movement has triggered a new kind of Evangelicalism? Or is creation care only one aspect of something bigger that is going on in the evangelical community and American society at large?

8. Many labels have been employed in the media and blogosphere to classify supporters of creation care. They call you "progressive evangelicals," "new evangelicals," or "the evangelical Left." What do you think about these labels? Do you and others affiliated with your organization subscribe to any of them?

9. How would you describe the relationship of the creation care movement to the so-called Religious Right? (Religious Right movement as driven by organizations such as Focus on the Family, Family Research Council, Eagle Forum, Concerned Women for America)

10. It has been noted (especially before the election in 2008) that concern about the state of the environment/creation compels evangelicals to break with the Republican Party. Judging from the people you know in the creation care community, would you say that such a partisan realignment is indeed occurring/could indeed occur in the near future?

11. At this point in time, would you say that we can speak of a "green revolution" in the evangelical community at large? If so, what drives it?

**Relation to "Mainstream" Environmentalism**

1. How would you describe the relationship of the creation care movement to the mainstream environmental movement? (Mainstream environmentalism = the environmental movement as it has been driven by organizations such as the Sierra Club, NRDC, NWF, etc.)

2. Has your organization in any way been collaborating with non-faith-based environmental organizations? If so, what was the experience like? Has this collaboration led to difficulties with maintaining your integrity/keeping your biblical values intact?

3. In which issues and positions do you see the greatest potential for common ground with secular and/or non-evangelical environmentalists?

## ADDITIONAL SOURCES

Whenever I had the chance, I tried to follow political scientist Allen D. Hertzke's timelessly valuable advice to prioritize "attending church, and otherwise hanging around religious people" in order to challenge my preconceived notions about "religious America." Apart from attending services at numerous churches across the Christian spectrum, mostly in Colorado but also in New Mexico, Missouri, Florida, Tennessee, Illinois, Wisconsin, and Washington, D.C., I visited several Christian bookstores and gift shops in those areas, an antiabortion rally on the thirty-seventh birthday of *Roe v. Wade*, the Creation Museum in Kentucky, the Billy Graham Center Museum at Wheaton College, and Focus on the Family's Visitors Center in Colorado Springs. In addition, Dean Ohlman provided copies of documents in his personal file collection (Grand Rapids, Michigan), including an exchange of letters with Calvin Beisner during the mid-1990s. Furthermore, I conducted library research at evangelical Wheaton College in Illinois, which has archived early editions of *Green Cross* magazine, a creation care publication rebranded as the EEN's magazine, *Creation Care*, in 1998.[3]

# NOTES

PREFACE

[1]   For "the human hybrid known as a Green Evangelical," see Laurie Goodstein, "Living Day to Day by a Gospel of Green," *New York Times*, March 8, 2007, https://www.nytimes.com/2007/03/08/garden/08ball.html (accessed April 2, 2019).

[2]   Scholarship on evangelical environmental engagement was rare before EEN's ECI. Notable exceptions are David K. Larsen's historical account, "God's Gardeners: American Protestant Evangelicals Confront Environmentalism, 1967–2000" (Ph.D. dissertation, University of Chicago, 2001). And see sociologist Laurel Kearns' work, "Saving the Creation: Religious Environmentalism" (Ph.D. dissertation, Emory University, 1994); "Saving the Creation: Christian Environmentalism in the United States," *Sociology of Religion* 57 (1996): 55–70; and "Noah's Ark Goes to Washington: A Profile of Evangelical Environmentalism," *Social Compass* 44 (1997): 349–66. Furthermore, EEN's James G. Ball finished his dissertation under the partial supervision of Laurel Kearns in 1997: "Evangelical Protestants, the Ecological Crisis and Public Theology" (Ph.D. dissertation, Drew University, 1997). Starting with Brian McCammack's article "Hot Damned America: Evangelicalism and the Climate Change Policy Debate," *American Quarterly* 59, no. 3 (2007): 645–68, academic research on the topic has become much more frequent. With a few exceptions—such as J. Aaron Simmons, "Evangelical Environmentalism: Oxymoron or Opportunity?" *Worldviews* 13 (2009): 40–71; Sabrina Danielsen, "Fracturing Over Creation Care? Shifting Environmental Beliefs Among Evangelicals, 1984–2010," *Journal for the Scientific Study of Religion* 52 (2013): 198–215; and Laurel Kearns, "Green Evangelicals," in *The New Evangelical Social Engagement*, ed. Brian Steensland and Philip Goff (New York: Oxford University Press, 2014), 157–78—the studies that have dealt with evangelical environmental engagement since then can be divided into two categories crossing the academic disciplines from which they respectively arose. First, one rather broadly oriented strand of studies has looked at evangelical environmental concerns as intertwined with the rise of a "new evangelicalism" or a "new evangelical social engagement": see Marcia Pally, *Die Neuen Evangelikalen: Freiheitsgewinne durch fromme Politik* (Berlin: Berlin University Press, 2010); Marcia Pally, *The New Evangelicals: Expanding the Vision of the Common Good* (Grand Rapids: Eerdmans, 2011); and Brian Steensland and Philip Goff, eds., *The New Evangelical Social Engagement* (New York: Oxford University Press, 2014). And second, a

more narrowly construed strand of studies has been preoccupied with the link between Evangelicalism and climate advocacy: McCammack, "Hot Damned America," 645–68; Paul Maltby, "Fundamentalist Dominion, Postmodern Ecology," *Ethics & the Environment* 13, no. 2 (2008): 119–41; John Copeland Nagle, "The Evangelical Debate Over Climate Change," *University of St. Thomas Law Journal* 5, no. 1 (2008): 53–86; Jonathan Harrington, "Evangelicalism, Environmental Activism, and Climate Change in the U.S.," *Journal of Religion and Society* 11 (2009): 1–24; Laurel Kearns, "The Role of Religious Activism," in *The Oxford Handbook on Climate Change and Society*, ed. John S. Dryzek, Richard B. Norgaard, and David Schlosberg (Oxford: Oxford University Press, 2011), 414–28; Katharine K. Wilkinson, *Between God & Green: How Evangelicals Are Cultivating a Middle Ground on Climate Change* (Oxford: Oxford University Press, 2012); Nicholas Smith and Anthony Leiserowitz, "American Evangelicals and Global Warming," *Global Environmental Change* 23 (2013): 1009–17; Bernd Zaleha and Andrew Szasz, "Keep Christianity Brown! Climate Denial on the Christian Right in the United States," in *How the World's Religions Are Responding to Climate Change: Social Scientific Investigations*, ed. Robin G. Veldman, Andrew Szasz, and Randolph Haluza-DeLay (New York: Routledge, 2014), 209–28; and Lydia Bean and Steve Teles, "Spreading the Gospel of Climate Change: An Evangelical Battleground," *Newamerica.org*, Washington, D.C., November 2015, https://static.newamerica.org/attachments/11649-spreading-the-gospel-of-climate-change/climate_care11.9.4f0142a50aa24a2ba65020f7929f6fd7.pdf (accessed May 12, 2018). While some have favored political perspectives and explanations, McCammack and others have identified additional differences regarding theology, science, and economics as intertwined with those political discrepancies. Recently, in particular Robin Globus Veldman has urged scholars to pay more attention to the evangelical "meaning of greening." Robin Globus Veldman, "What Is the Meaning of Greening? Cultural Analysis of a Southern Baptist Environmental Text," *Journal of Contemporary Religion* 31, no. 2 (2016): 199–222.

<sup>3</sup> Regarding "critical empathy," see R. Marie Griffith, *God's Daughters: Evangelical Women and the Power of Submission* (Berkeley: University of California Press, 1997). As Lindsay describes his application of Griffith's approach: "I try to recount both the content and the spirit of what people told me, but I also reserve the right to comment on what they are not saying in these accounts and to point to inconsistencies and unintended consequences that flow from their actions. In the end, they may not agree with all of my conclusions, but I hope they will sense my earnest desire to present a full, balanced perspective with all of the subtlety and complexity of the lives they lead and the worlds they inhabit." D. Michael Lindsay, *Faith in the Halls of Power: How Evangelicals Joined the American Elite* (Oxford: Oxford University Press, 2007), xiii.

## INTRODUCTION

<sup>1</sup> For "oil and water," see Brian Palmer, "God's EPA Administrator," *Slate*, June 8, 2018, https://slate.com/technology/2018/06/evangelicals-lack-of-environmentalism-explains-scott-pruitt.html (accessed March 26, 2019). Regarding Pruitt's faith and politics, cf. Tom Dreisbach and Joe Wertz, "'On Fire for God's Work': How Scott Pruitt's Faith Drives His Politics," *NPR*, May 1, 2018, https://www.npr.org/2018/05/01/607181437/on-fire-for-gods-work-how-scott-pruitts-faith-drives-his-politics?t=1554641208545 (accessed April 7, 2019).

²     For the details of the WWJD? campaign, see James Ball, "WWJDrive in the Bible Belt," *Creation Care*, Summer 2003; Roger S. Gottlieb, *A Greener Faith: Religious Environmentalism and Our Planet's Future* (Oxford: Oxford University Press, 2006), 129–30; and Danny Hakim, "The Media Business: Advertising; A Group Links Fuel Economy to Religion," *The New York Times*, November 19, 2002.

³     The estimate of WWJD?'s media attention is from Fenton Communications, the firm that had served as public relations consultant of the campaign at the time. "Environmentalists with a Higher Purpose: Getting the Best Mileage for 'What Would Jesus Drive?,'" Fenton Communications, http://www.fenton.com/pages/3 _ourwork/4_casestudies/environment/wwjd.htm (accessed August 23, 2008). While this link is outdated now, the connection between Fenton and the EEN with regard to WWJD? can still be traced via Discover the Networks: A Guide to the Political Left, "David Fenton," *Discoverthenetworks.org*, http://discoverthenetworks.com/individualProfile.asp?indid= 814 (accessed April 10, 2019). For references to WWJD? in Crichton's anti-global warming thriller, see Michael Crichton, *State of Fear* (2004; repr., New York: HarperCollins, 2013), 72; 457. For Becker's assessment, see Markus Becker, "A Greener US One Year After Katrina: 'What Would Jesus Drive?'" *Spiegel Online*, August 29, 2006, http://www.spiegel.de/ international/a-greener-us-one-year-after-katrina-what-would-jesus-drive-a-434191 .html (accessed June 17, 2013). Noting that America was finally taking more environmental responsibility, *The Economist* also mentioned the campaign favorably in "Waking Up and Catching Up: Belatedly, and for Many Reasons, America Is Embracing Environmentalism," January 27, 2007, 22–24.

⁴     ECI's "Call to Action" and the names of its initial signatories can be found in David P. Gushee, *The Future of Faith in American Politics: The Public Witness of the Evangelical Center* (Waco, Tex.: Baylor University Press, 2008), 275–81. For Warren praying with George W. Bush and speculations about the meaning of his ECI support, see: "Klimapolitik; Was würde Jesus fahren?" *Frankfurter Rundschau*, February 17, 2006. Compared to other religious groups in America, white evangelical Protestants are the least likely to believe in the reality of anthropogenic climate change: 33 percent say that the earth is warming due to natural reasons, and 37 percent say that there is "no solid evidence" that climate change is occurring at all: Pew Research Center, "Religion and Science: Highly religious Americans are less likely than others to see conflict between religion and science," Pew Research Center, October 22, 2015, http://assets.pewresearch.org/wp-content/uploads/sites/14/ 2015/10/PI_2015-10-22_religion-and-science_FINAL.pdf (accessed August 21, 2017). Evangelicals thus sharply contradict the 97 percent of the world's scientists who share the consensus position that humans have induced and are rapidly accelerating the problem. For the consensus among scientists, see John Cook et al., "Quantifying the Consensus on Anthropocentric Global Warming in the Scientific Literature," *Environmental Research Letters* 8, no. 2 (2013): 024024. Whereas 66 percent of Democrats worry "a great deal" about global warming, only 18 percent of Republicans are concerned. As pollster Jim Norman notes, the current partisan gap on global warming is wider than on other contentious issues such as race relations and illegal immigration: Jim Norman, "Democrats Drive Rise in Concern About Global Warming," Gallup, March 17, 2017, http://www.gallup .com/poll/206513/democrats-drive-rise-concern-global-warming.aspx (accessed August 25, 2017). Regarding the "war on science," see Chris Mooney, *The Republican War on Science* (New York: Basic Books, 2005). The ECI was immediately countered by the CA's "A Call to Truth, Prudence, and Protection of the Poor: An Evangelical Response

to Global Warming," Cornwall Alliance, 2006, http://www.cornwallalliance.org/2006/
07/25/a-call-to-truth-prudence-and-protection-of-the-poor-an-evangelical-response-to
-global-warming/ (accessed October 21, 2019). I use the term "Religious Right" as shorthand for the social movement that attempts to mobilize evangelical Protestants and other
orthodox Christians and Jews into conservative political action. This movement has been
driven by national groups such as Focus on the Family, Family Research Council, and
Concerned Women for America. Chapter 1 provides more details on the Religious Right,
and chapter 5 deals extensively with the CA specifically.

⁵ "Evangelicals Go 'Green' With Caution," Barna Group Inc., September 22,
2008, https://www.barna.com/research/evangelicals-go-green-with-caution/ (accessed
March 26, 2019). On the trend toward a more progressive evangelical youth movement at
the time, see David R. Swartz, *Moral Minority: The Evangelical Left in an Age of Conservatism*
(Philadelphia: University of Pennsylvania Press, 2012), 261. Regarding ECI signatories'
criticism of the Religious Right, see Richard Cizik, foreword to *The Future of Faith in
American Politics: The Public Witness of the Evangelical Center*, by David P. Gushee (Waco,
Tex.: Baylor University Press, 2008), xi-xiii; Joel C. Hunter, *A New Kind of Conservative*
(Ventura, Calif.: Regal, 2008); and Joel C. Hunter, *Right Wing, Wrong Bird: Why the Tactics
of the Religious Right Won't Fly With Most Conservative Christians* (Longwood, Fla.: Distributed
Church Press, 2006). According to *Time* magazine, the "birth of the new evangelicalism"
was attested to by the fact that "powerful pastors" like Warren and Hunter were finally
voicing their concern about economic inequality, international aid, and environmental
degradation, thereby joining the ranks of Jim Wallis, Tony Campolo, and Ronald Sider;
David Van Biema, "Top 10 Religion Stories," *Time*, December 22, 2008, 41.

⁶ Gregory Warner, "What Would Jesus Drive?" NPR, Rough Translation,
July 24, 2019, https://www.npr.org/transcripts/743118522?storyId=743118522
&t=1570716107445&t=1575188070330?storyId=743118522&t=1570716107445
&t=1575188070330 (accessed November 29, 2019). Although they initially seemed at
odds with each other regarding their preference for the Republican presidential contend-
er during the 2016 election, 81 percent of white evangelicals voted for Donald Trump:
"The most they have voted for a Republican presidential candidate since 2004, when they
overwhelmingly chose President George W. Bush by a margin of 78–21 percent." Sarah
Pulliam Bailey, "White evangelicals voted overwhelmingly for Donald Trump, exit polls
show," *The Washington Post*, November 9, 2016, https://www.washingtonpost.com/news/
acts-of-faith/wp/2016/11/09/exit-polls-show-white-evangelicals-voted-overwhelmingly
-for-donald-trump/?utm_term=.cdbf0026cc2f (accessed August 21, 2017). For Republican anti-environmentalism and deregulation efforts since Reagan, see James Morton
Turner and Andrew C. Isenberg, *The Republican Reversal: Conservatives and the Environment
from Nixon to Trump* (Cambridge, Mass.: Harvard University Press, 2018). Like Reagan,
the Trump administration has appointed officials keen on environmental deregulation,
such as Scott Pruitt and current EPA Administrator Andrew R. Wheeler. Especially EPA's
criminal enforcement has hit a "30-year low," illustrating the diminishing influence and
size of the agency under Trump; Sarah Gibbons, "15 Ways the Trump Administration
Has Changed Environmental Policies," *National Geographic*, February 1, 2019, https://
www.nationalgeographic.com/environment/2019/02/15-ways-trump-administration
-impacted-environment/ (accessed May 20, 2019). The president has also approved further construction of the Keystone XL pipeline and the opening of the Arctic National
Wildlife Refuge to oil and gas drilling. Furthermore, Trump announced the U.S. with-

drawal from the Paris Climate Accord on June 1, 2017, a decision that "moves the country toward isolation on a global stage": Michael Greshko, "Map Shows How Paris Reversal Isolates U.S. From World," *National Geographic*, https://news.nationalgeographic.com/2017/06/climate-change-paris-agreement-map/ (accessed May 25, 2019).

[7]  The intense politicization of conservative religion starting in the late 1970s has triggered a countermovement into a more nonreligious, or decidedly politicized anti-religious, direction since the 1990s and early 2000s: Robert D. Putnam and David E. Campbell, *American Grace: How Religion Divides and Unites Us* (New York: Simon & Schuster, 2010). Religiosity and partisanship have thus become so tightly interwoven that this linkage seems to have produced a two-party religious system divided by a "God gap" running through the American electorate and political system. In particular, evangelicals, who have made up the majority of the Religious Right movement, have become the "religious centerpiece" of the Republican Party: Lyman Kellstedt et al., "Faith Transformed: Religion and American Politics from FDR to George W. Bush," in *Religion and American Politics: From the Colonial Period to the Present*, 2nd ed., ed. Mark A. Noll and Luke E. Harlow (Oxford: Oxford University Press, 2007), 272. The Democratic Party, on the other hand, has largely turned into the party of secularists, anti-fundamentalists, and the less religiously committed and theologically rigid: Louis Bolce and Gerald De Maio, "Secularists, Antifundamentalists, and the New Religious Divide in the American Electorate," in *From Pews to Polling Places: Faith and Politics in the American Religious Mosaic*, ed. J. Matthew Wilson (Washington, D.C.: Georgetown University Press, 2007), 251–85. As George W. Bush's former speechwriter put it, "Through active Democratic alienation of conservative Christians, and active Republican courting, America has moved toward the development of one secular political party, and one religious political party. And this is a true danger to democracy, because it turns nearly every political disagreement into a culture-war battle." Michael J. Gerson, *Heroic Conservatism: Why Republicans Need to Embrace America's Ideals (And Why They Deserve to Fail If They Don't)* (New York: HarperOne, 2007), 117. To explain the intra-evangelical conflict over climate change, previous studies have identified differences regarding theology, science, and economics as intertwined with ideological and political discrepancies: see McCammack, "Hot Damned America"; Kearns, "The Role of Religious Activism"; Wilkinson, *Between God & Green*; Zaleha and Szasz, "Keep Christianity Brown"; and Bean and Teles, "Spreading the Gospel." In particular Veldman has pointed toward the necessity of also considering social context and cultural identity as factors that shape evangelical attitudes toward climate change: "What Is the Meaning."

[8]  The phrase "culture war(s)" has become shorthand to describe any kind of conservative/progressive, religious/nonreligious, Left/Right, red state/blue state, etc. dispute among civil actors in the United States, and it is difficult to assess when it is more apt to speak of one macro-societal "culture war" and when to speak of "culture wars" in the sense of several ideological battles simultaneously being fought over individual issues. Regarding the initial formulations of the culture wars thesis (or the "Wuthnow-Hunter hypothesis") as a macro-theoretical approach in the field of American religion and politics, see Robert Wuthnow, *The Restructuring of American Religion: Society and Faith since World War II* (Princeton, N.J.: Princeton University Press, 1988); and James Davison Hunter, *Culture Wars: The Struggle to Define America* (New York: Basic Books, 1991). Whereas the twentieth-century culture war battles used to largely revolve around policy issues pertaining to faith and sexuality (i.e., religious freedom, abortion, marriage, and homosexuality), considerable segments of the American citizenry today seem to get easily

divided over almost anything, including the truth of scientific findings on climate change and presidential inauguration day crowd sizes. In the press release announcing the series "Divided America," intended to explore the tensions underlying the presidential race in 2016 through individual stories of American citizens, Associated Press noted, "It's more than just Democrat vs. Republican, liberal vs. conservative . . . It's the 1 percent vs. the 99 percent and rural vs. urban. Climate doubters clash with believers. Bathrooms have become battlefields, borders are battle lines. Sex and race, faith and ethnicity, and the melting pot is boiling over." See "'Divided America' series to explore tensions underlying campaign," Associated Press, June 6, 2016, https://www.ap.org/press-releases/2016/divided-america-series-to-explore-tensions-underlying-campaign (accessed April 12, 2017).

[9] Bean and Teles ("Spreading the Gospel") use the climate-centered "strange bedfellows coalition" of evangelicals and environmentalists between 2006 and 2009 as an example of a failed attempt at transpartisan coalition building. See also Heather Hurlburt with Chayenne Polimedio, "Can Transpartisan Coalitions Overcome Polarization? Lessons from Four Case Studies," *Newamerica.org* (Washington, D.C.: New America, 2016), https://www.newamerica.org/political-reform/policy-papers/can-transpartisan-coalitions-overcome-polarization/ (accessed May 26, 2019). The more voters adhered to a Christian nationalist ideology, the more likely they were to vote for Donald Trump in 2016: Andrew L. Whitehead, Samuel L. Perry, and Joseph O. Baker, "Make America Christian Again: Christian Nationalism and Voting for Donald Trump in the 2016 Presidential Election," *Sociology of Religion* 79, no. 2 (2018): 147–71.

[10] Regarding social movements arising at the "cracks of culture," see Hank Johnston and Bert Klandermans, "The Cultural Analysis of Social Movements," in *Social Movements and Culture*, ed. Hank Johnston and Bert Klandermans (Minneapolis: University of Minnesota Press, 1995), 3–24. For movements as "prophets,"see Alberto Melucci, *Challenging Codes: Collective Action in the Information Age* (Cambridge: Cambridge University Press, 1996). According to Steve Bruce, movements are created and held together by "a reasonably coherent story about why what is wrong is wrong and what can be done about it": *The Rise and Fall of the New Christian Right: Conservative Protestant Politics in America, 1978–1988* (Oxford: Oxford University Press, 1988), 76–77. For "embryos of a new society," see Manuel Castells quoted in Verta Taylor, "Mobilizing for Change in a Social Movement Society," *Contemporary Sociology* 29, no. 1 (2000): 227. See also Andrew McFarland, "Public Interest Lobbies vs. Minority Faction," in *The American Polity Reader*, 2nd ed., ed. Ann G. Serow, W. Wayne Shannon, and Everett C. Ladd (New York: W. W. Norton, 1993), 418. For social movements as a "regular part of the political process," see Andrew McFarland, *Neopluralism: The Evolution of Political Process Theory* (Lawrence: University Press of Kansas, 2004), 63–65. For the historic variability of the academic definition of social movements, see John S. Dryzek et al, *Green States and Social Movements: Environmentalism in the United States, United Kingdom, Germany, & Norway* (Oxford: Oxford University Press, 2003), 2.

[11] I use terms such as "social movement organizations" (often referred to as "SMOs" by social movement scholars) and what political scientists prefer to call "interest groups" interchangeably because they ultimately designate the same thing: Jeffrey M. Berry, *The New Liberalism: The Rising Power of Citizen Groups* (Washington, D.C.: Brookings Institution Press, 1999), 142. Other terms that are often used to describe similar groups, albeit with a slightly different meaning depending on the context, are public interest organizations, advocacy organizations, citizen groups, nonprofit organizations (NPOs), or, on the broader international stage, nongovernmental organizations (NGOs). What they have in common

is that they "organize, educate, and lobby" in order to bring about social (or global) change: Berry, *The New Liberalism*, 142; 49. While some interest group politics scholars reserve the term "group" for membership organizations, I use "group" and "organization" interchangeably and refer to "membership organizations" as membership organizations. In addition, I use the term "lobbying" neutrally as a designation for advocacy attempts aimed at influencing others (i.e., legislators, the public, etc.). In one of their groundbreaking studies, Benford and Snow view social movement actors as "signifying agents actively engaged in the production and maintenance of meaning for constituents, antagonists, and bystanders or observers," and thus also actively engaged in what Hall had termed "the politics of signification": Robert D. Benford and David A. Snow, "Framing Processes and Social Movements: An Overview and Assessment," *Annual Review of Sociology* 26 (2000): 613. Although he was wrong with his prediction about the future of the Religious Right, my understanding of social movements has also been shaped by Steve Bruce's account of the New Christian Right, where Bruce explains his choice of methodology as follows: "Ideologies require embodiment. Ideas do not fall from heaven like the Holy Spirit of Pentecost. *They are developed, preserved and transmitted by social groups*": Bruce, *The Rise and Fall*, 1–2 (emphasis added). According to Eyerman and Jamison, social movements are "best conceived of as temporary public spaces, as moments of collective creation that provide societies with ideas, identities, and even ideals": Ron Eyerman and Andrew Jamison, *Social Movements: A Cognitive Approach* (University Park: Penn State University Press, 1991), 4. According to Bruce, movement actors do "social construction work": *The Rise and Fall*, 187. Regarding the importance of resource mobilization, see John D. McCarthy and Mayer N. Zald, "Resource Mobilization and Social Movements: A Partial Theory," *American Journal of Sociology* 82, no. 6 (1977): 1212–41; and Mayer N. Zald and John D. McCarthy, *The Dynamics of Social Movements: Resource Mobilization, Social Control, and Tactics* (Cambridge, Mass.: Winthrop, 1979). For the role of organizations with regard to embedding (environmental) values into society, see Christopher J. Bosso, *Environment, Inc.: From Grassroots to Beltway* (Lawrence: University Press of Kansas, 2005). According to Wuthnow, the nonprofit or "third sector is of interest primarily as a locus of public discourse about the collective values of the society" as it provides an arena in which both fundamental political and nonpolitical values "can be discussed, experimented with, symbolized, and ritually enacted": Robert Wuthnow, *The Struggle for America's Soul: Evangelicals, Liberals, and Secularism* (Grand Rapids: Eerdmans, 1989), 11. In particular for nonprofit organizations the Internet offers a financially feasible way to bring their supporters together and to communicate their messages to multiple publics: Seok Kang and Hanna E. Norton, "Nonprofit Organizations' Use of the World Wide Web: Are They Sufficiently Fulfilling Organizational Goals?" *Public Relations Review* 30 (2004): 279–84. 501(c)(3) organizations, or "public charities," are tax-exempt and donations to them are tax-deductible. They are restricted in their lobbying expenditures. The database of the information service Guide-Star USA, Inc. makes available information on IRS-registered nonprofits in the United States (guidestar.org). Another good source is ProPublica's nonprofit explorer (projects .propublica.org/nonprofits/). For more information on their IRS filing requirements, visit irs.gov/charities-non-profits/charitable-organizations (accessed December 1, 2019).

[12]   Brulle defines "environmental organization" as "an identifiable association of citizens, primarily concerned with improvement of the natural environment, that takes action to attempt to realize some public or general good": Robert J. Brulle, *Agency, Democracy, and Nature: The U.S. Environmental Movement from a Critical Theory Perspective* (Cambridge,

Mass.: MIT Press, 2000), 283. According to his dated estimate, the total number of environmental organizations in the United States is about ten thousand: Brulle, *Agency, Democracy, and Nature*, 114. A more recent GuideStar search (February 2, 2019) for organizations dedicated to the broad cause of environmental quality protection and beautification lists 35,541 results nationwide. These include botanical gardens, landscape services, horticultural programs, and organizations dedicated to other environmental sub-causes, however. For movements being "quintessentially changeful" and in "continuous flux," see Johnston and Klandermans, "Cultural Analysis," 4. Regarding movement analysis as an act of construction, see Alberto Melucci, "The Process of Collective Identity," in *Social Movements and Culture*, ed. Hank Johnston and Bert Klandermans (London: Routledge, 1995), 41–63.

[13]    The description of the CCCC is taken from Ed Brown's invitation reminder for the meeting in Washington, D.C., sent by e-mail to participants on July 15, 2010.

[14]    Examples of new additions to the movement since my participation in the CCCC 2010 would be the Seminary Stewardship Alliance and Blessed Earth Tennessee (see chapter 6). Regarding the difficulty of establishing new organizations, see Bosso, *Environment*, 85–86. The mainline Protestant eco-justice ethic "combines an already present Christian social justice framework with environmental concerns" and is "firmly located in the mainline denominations and denomination-specific special purpose groups": Kearns, "Saving the Creation: Christian Environmentalism," 57. More on the different Christian ecotheologies that developed in the United States in the 1980s follows in chapter 2. In particular the NWF should have been attractive for evangelicals because of its former president Larry Schweiger, an evangelical Christian himself. See for instance Schweiger's article in the ecumenical environmental magazine *Green Cross*, "On the Healing Edge: One Christian's Response to a Polluted Planet," *Green Cross*, Summer 1995.

[15]    Allen Johnson, a member of the steering committee of the Appalachia-based anti-mountaintop removal network Christians for the Mountains, also participated in the CCCC 2009. While Johnson may personally identify as an evangelical Christian, apart from its more regionally confined focus, Christians for the Mountains does not explicitly subscribe to an evangelical identity and was therefore not included.

[16]    There is a large body of literature on religious environmentalism in general. Apart from Gottlieb's groundbreaking *A Greener Faith* (2006), see also: Stephen Ellingson, *To Care for Creation: The Emergence of the Religious Environmental Movement* (Chicago: University of Chicago Press, 2016); and Mallory McDuff, *Natural Saints: How People of Faith Are Working to Save God's Earth* (New York: Oxford University Press, 2010).

[17]    Self-identification is one important marker of (religious) identity: Christian Smith et al., *American Evangelicalism: Embattled and Thriving* (Chicago: University of Chicago Press, 1998), 233. However, not only are religious identities fluid and complex; they also "must be understood as political constructions . . . [which] have been created by political operatives and the media as much as by church leaders themselves: Robert Wuthnow, "Quid Obscurum: The Changing Terrain of Church-State Relations," in *Religion and American Politics: From the Colonial Period to the Present*, 2nd ed., ed. Mark A. Noll and Luke E. Harlow (Oxford: Oxford University Press, 2007), 457. Denominational affiliation is another method commonly employed by social scientists to measure evangelicals: see Conrad Hackett and D. Michael Lindsay, "Measuring Evangelicalism: Consequences of Different Operationalization Strategies," *Journal for the Scientific Study of Religion* 47, no. 3 (2008): 500. Scholars recognize in particular four evangelical sub-traditions among the

American Protestant denominations: Baptist (Southern Baptist Convention, Seventh Day Adventists, restorationist churches, etc.); Reformed-Confessional (Presbyterian Church in America, Christian Reformed Church, Lutheran denominations within the evangelical tradition, etc.); Pentecostal-Holiness (Church of the Nazarene, Salvation Army, Assemblies of God, International Church of the Foursquare Gospel, etc.); and Anabaptist (the Amish, Mennonites, and other "peace churches"). See Robert Wuthnow, ed., *The Encyclopedia of Politics and Religion* (Washington, D.C.: CQ Press, 1998). As explored during qualitative interviews, among the denominational affiliations of creation care advocates are Calvinist/Reformed; Congregationalist (i.e., Evangelical Free Church); Baptist, Anglican, Methodist, and non-denominational (all in the evangelical tradition); Southern Baptist Convention; and Anabaptist. For Bebbington's standard definition of core evangelical beliefs and practices, see David W. Bebbington, *Evangelicalism in Modern Britain: A History from the 1730s to the 1980s* (London: Unwin Hyman, 1989), 2–3. In particular historian George Marsden has popularized a more complex definitional approach to American Evangelicalism, distinguishing three overlapping senses—two broad and one narrow—of the evangelical "mosaic" or "kaleidoscope." First, there is a "conceptual unity" of shared beliefs and practices among Protestant Christians. Second, there are "common heritages, common tendencies, an identity, and an organic character," which trace their roots to the sixteenth-century Reformation but have also since shaped and been shaped by specific cultural factors and trends within different countries and subcultures. And third, there is an identity marker that signifies belonging to "a more narrow, consciously 'evangelical' transdenominational community with complicated infrastructures of institutions and persons who identify with 'evangelicalism'" in America. George M. Marsden, "The Evangelical Denomination," introduction to *Evangelicalism and Modern America*, ed. George M. Marsden (Grand Rapids: Eerdmans, 1984), vii–xix. More recently, Molly Worthen has argued that "history—rather than theology or politics—is the most useful tool for pinning down today's evangelicals": *Apostles of Reason: The Crisis of Authority in American Evangelicalism* (New York: Oxford University Press, 2013), 4. The fundamentalist sub-movement within the larger evangelical tradition in the United States and the (neo-)evangelical departure from it are discussed in more detail in chapter 1.

[18]  For a critique of the validity of Bebbington's quadrilateral as a definitional approach to American Evangelicalism, see Seth Dowland, "American Evangelicalism and the Politics of Whiteness," *Christian Century* (June 19, 2018), https://www.christiancentury.org/article/critical-essay/american-evangelicalism-and-politics-whiteness (accessed February 25, 2019). Both Marsden and Bebbington are concerned with the history of Evangelicalism in their respective countries, hence the titles of their works are similar: *Evangelicalism and Modern America* (1984) and *Evangelicalism in Modern Britain: A History from the 1730s to the 1980s* (1989). The fact that their definitions of Evangelicalism are at the core identical underscores that Evangelicalism in the sense of a certain set of shared beliefs and practices is not tied to a particular country or region. Moreover, given its focus on missionary work and transnational outreach, these basic tenets of the evangelical faith have spread around the globe and been applied in various cultural settings that are quite different from the Anglo-American context. For a comprehensive account of Evangelicalism and race in the United States, see Michael O. Emerson and Christian Smith, *Divided by Faith: Evangelical Religion and the Problem of Race in America* (New York: Oxford University Press, 2000). That the politicization of American Evangelicalism has had an impact on the meaning and usage of the term "evangelical" is attested to by the Evangelical

Manifesto (2008) as well. This nineteen-page document seeks to clarify the evangelical faith and identity from within a theological framework, all while it criticizes the politicization of conservative Protestantism in the United States. The document's intention is to explain the term "Evangelical" to outsiders and to challenge insiders of the movement to represent their faith more accurately. For more information, see "Evangelical Manifesto: A Declaration of Evangelical Identity and Public Commitment," The Evangelical Manifesto Steering Committee, Washington, D.C., May 7, 2008, http://evangelicalmanifesto .com/wp-content/uploads/2016/03/Evangelical_Manifesto.pdf (accessed July 22, 2019). Regarding "a significant number," see Dowland, "American Evangelicalism." For the conception of "myths" as politically effective second order semiological systems, see Roland Barthes, *Mythologies*, trans. Annette Lavers (New York: Hill and Wang, 1972).

[19] For the usage of the term "environment" and "as a synonym," see Jean-Guy Vaillancourt, "Environment," in *Conservation and Environmentalism: An Encyclopedia*, ed. Robert Paehlke (London: Fitzroy Dearborn, 1995). As the EEN's Jim Ball explained, unlike the term "environment," the word "creation" does "impl[y] a creator" and not "not just some environment that popped up out of nowhere, [with] no meaning to its existence": quoted in Leah Fabel, "Credo: The Rev. Jim Ball," *Washington Examiner*, July 12, 2009, http://www.washingtonexaminer.com/local/people/50481552.html (accessed October 10, 2009).

[20] Regarding the more strategic use of "creation care" over "environmentalism," see Ball quoted in Fabel, "Credo." For environmentalism as a science-based ideology that is neither inherently Left nor Right, see Robert C. Paehlke, *Environmentalism and the Future of Progressive Politics* (New Haven, Conn.: Yale University Press, 1989). Regarding the numbers of Americans who identify with environmentalism and the growing partisan split among them, see Jeffrey M. Jones, "Americans Identification as 'Environmentalists' Down to 42%," Gallup, April 22, 2016, http://www.gallup.com/poll/190916/americans -identification-environmentalists-down.aspx (accessed August 22, 2017). For the political polarization of movement support, see Riley E. Dunlap and Aaron M. McCright, "Social Movement Identity: Validating a Measure of Identification with the Environmental Movement," *Social Science Quarterly* 89, no. 5 (2008): 1045–65. For an encompassing account of the "Republican Reversal" on environmental protection and legislation since the Reagan Revolution, see Turner and Isenberg, *Republican Reversal*.

[21] The terms "liberal" and "progressive" are not synonymous but in the context of lived American political ideology sometimes used interchangeably. A poll from 2010 revealed uncertainty about the meaning of "progressive" among conservatives, moderates, and liberals alike. The latter, however, were "more likely to embrace than reject the label (26% vs. 17%), while conservatives [were] more likely to reject than embrace it (48% vs. 7%)." Lydia Saad, "Americans Unsure About 'Progressive' Political Label," Gallup, July 12, 2010, https://news.gallup.com/poll/141218/americans-unsure -progressive-political-label.aspx (accessed February 28, 2020). Roger Gottlieb poses that there is "a near universal tendency of religious environmentalism to move religions to the left"; see "The Case of Religious Environmentalism," *The Immanent Frame* blog, entry posted on November 17, 2008, https://tif.ssrc.org/2008/11/17/the-case-of-religious -environmentalism/ (accessed May 31, 2019). For environmentalism as "neither left nor right," see Paehlke, *Environmentalism*, 274. Wilkinson (*Between God & Green*) has employed a Left-Center-Right trichotomy in order to locate ECI signatories vis-à-vis CA supporters on the political spectrum. Likewise, Pally (*Die Neuen Evangelikalen* and *The New Evangelicals*)

has used it in order to describe the "new evangelicals" located within the "evangelical center." Both derive this trichotomy from Gushee's rather prescriptive framework presented in *The Future of Faith in American Politics*. But as Gushee (*The Future*, 87–88) acknowledges here, the "centrist" label is not one that is shared by many evangelicals—a fact that he has been trying to change with the publication of his book. While *The Future of Faith in American Politics* may thus serve well as an academic insider's guide to three broad ideological currents or political camps within the evangelical leadership community, it must also be seen, arguably and at least in part, as an involved activist's attempt at identity politics. Moreover, even Gushee (*The Future*, 221) admits in his conclusion that "these categories are provisional and in many ways unsatisfactory" for followers of Christ because "Jesus . . . was not and could never be confined within our ideological categories or political loyalties." If proposed by a few involved insiders only and then applied by academic outsiders to a broader group who may not self-identify as such, the "evangelical center" is an unreliable marker of identification. Moreover, the political center may generally be "the most comfortable place in American politics," but it is nevertheless a rather "strange and wild place because many who fall into it have vastly different combinations of beliefs." E. J. Dionne, "Misunderstood progressive," *Pittsburgh Post-Gazette*, July 19, 2010, http://www.post-gazette.com/opinion/Op-Ed/2010/07/19/E-J-Dionne-Jr-Misunderstood progressive/stories/201007190190 (accessed September 30, 2017). It is therefore more apt to accept historian David Swartz' proposal of a "politically diverse and fluid evangelicalism" between the outer limits of the political Right and Left (*Moral Minority*, 7), and to explore this in-between diversity and fluidity more carefully case by case instead of masking it by forcing a simplistic binary into an artificial trichotomy.

[22]    Regarding the population ecology approach to interest representation, see Bosso, *Environment*; and Virginia Gray and David Lowery, *The Population Ecology of Interest Representation: Lobbying Communities in the American States* (Ann Arbor: University of Michigan Press, 1996).

[23]    At its most common denominator, social movement theory emphasizes the following three factors for the emergence and development of social movements: shifting political opportunities, indigenous social networks, and the formation of a collective identity. See Taylor, "Mobilizing for Change," 221. Social movement theory has gone through several paradigm shifts over the past decades. Whereas older approaches focused on either the importance of resources (resource mobilization theory) or political opportunity structures and contentious politics, "new social movements" theorists emphasized the importance of collective identity construction and culture. According to Wald, Silverman, and Fridy, the different approaches from within the social movement theory family—cultural identity theory (including frame analysis), resource mobilization theory, and political opportunity theory—provide a complementary framework. "Like homicide detectives," state Wald, Silverman, and Fridy, "scholars of religion and politics need to understand motives, means, and opportunity: the motives that draw religious groups into political action, the means that enable the religious to participate effectively, and the opportunities that facilitate their entry into the political system." Kenneth D. Wald, Adam L. Silverman, and Kevin S. Fridy, "Making Sense of Religion in Political Life," *Annual Review of Political Science* 8 (2005): 124. The question about motives is crucial not only regarding organizational founding but also regarding the underlying factors that may help explain individual concern for the environment—or, as in the case of evangelicals like Calvin Beisner, skepticism toward environmentalism and the creation care movement. Furthermore, if

asked individually it also sheds light on the biographic dimension of social/political activism, which is an often neglected variable in theories about social movements, although the complex biographies, personalities, and idiosyncrasies of individuals "matter enormously to protest, especially when they found new groups or make key strategic decisions." James M. Jasper, *The Art of Moral Protest: Culture, Biography, and Creativity in Social Movements* (Chicago: University of Chicago Press, 1997), xi. Explains Jasper: "Humans hold a dizzying array of sensibilities and sensitivities, inchoate assumptions, utopian fantasies, ego defenses, and explicit beliefs, any of which can be threatened or shocked by new knowledge, requests, and activities. We pursue a variety of pleasures; we try to do what we consider the right thing; but we also tend to fall into routines because they are easy. Our choices and actions are, finally, shaped by an infinite number of personality quirks and character traits. Most protesters are compelled by a combination of motivations, compulsions, and desires, some of them conscious and others not. Simple models of human motivation, whether rationalist or crowd-based, miss the lion's share of reality. So do theories that look for the motivations of entire protest movements rather than those of the individuals who compose them. The biographical dimension of protest cries out for exploration" (*The Art of Moral Protest*, 214). Regarding religiously motivated social activism specifically, see Christian Smith, "Correcting a Curious Neglect, or Bringing Religion Back In," in *Disruptive Religion: The Force of Faith in Social Movement Activism*, ed. Christian Smith (London: Routledge, 1996), 1–25.

## 1 EVANGELICALISM AND ENVIRONMENTALISM

[1]    Brulle, *Agency*, 267.

[2]    Evangelical Manifesto Steering Committee, "An Evangelical Manifesto."

[3]    For "the most significant social movement in America," see Joshua S. Reichert, quoted in Philip Shabecoff, *American Environmentalism in the 21st Century* (Washington, D.C.: Island Press, 2000), 10. According to the Pew Research Center, the number of evangelical Protestants in the United States has remained relatively stable, "ticking downward slightly from 26.3% to 25.4% of the population" between 2007 and 2014: "Evangelicals now constitute a clear majority (55%) of all U.S. Protestants." Seventy-six percent of evangelicals are white. The percentage of evangelical women is higher than that of evangelical men (55 percent vis-à-vis 45 percent). Pew Research Center, "America's Changing Religious Landscape," Pew Research Center, May 12, 2015, http://assets.pewresearch .org/wp-content/uploads/sites/11/2015/05/RLS-08-26-full-report.pdf (accessed July 2, 2019). While there is a higher percentage of evangelical women than men in America, not many women play leadership roles in the evangelical parachurch sector: Lindsay, *Faith in the Halls*, 223–26. As early as 1971, Richard John Neuhaus, who would later become the notorious critic of *The Naked Public Square: Religion and Democracy in America* (Grand Rapids: Eerdmans, 1984), viewed environmentalism as an elitist white movement out of sync with common Americans and the economic and social realities of the time, in particular the reality of African Americans and the poor. Richard John Neuhaus, *In Defense of People: Ecology and the Seduction of Radicalism* (New York: Macmillan, 1971). Responding to more recent critiques of elitism and heterogeneity, the initiative Green 2.0 was launched in 2013 to increase racial diversity within the environmental movement. A follow-up survey in 2018 found that the number of people of color in senior staff positions had further declined: see Justine Calma, "The Green Movement Has a Diversity Problem. And It Is

Getting Worse," *Grist*, January 11, 2019, https://grist.org/article/the-green-movement -has-a-diversity-problem-and-it-is-getting-worse/ (accessed July 2, 2019). Regarding the understanding of environmentalism as a religion, see for example Bron Taylor, *Dark Green Religion: Nature Spirituality and the Planetary Future* (Berkeley: University of California Press, 2010.) On the politicization of religion in America, see for instance Andrew Kohut, John C. Green, Scott Keeter, and Robert C. Toth, *The Diminishing Divide: Religion's Changing Role in American Politics* (Washington, D.C.: Brookings Institution, 2000).

4    For the "three P's" and "the marks of those initial influences," see Randall H. Balmer, *Thy Kingdom Come: How the Religious Right Distorts the Faith and Threatens America. An Evangelical's Lament* (New York: Basic Books, 2006), xiv. Regarding "true religion of the heart," see Mark A. Noll, *American Evangelical Christianity: An Introduction* (Malden, Mass.: Blackwell, 2001), 10. Further information on the First Great Awakening, in particular the conversion numbers cited, can be found in George Brown Tindall and David E. Shi, *America: A Narrative History* (New York: W. W. Norton, 1993), 66–70. For "'colonized' the frontier regions of the South," see Balmer, *Thy Kingdom Come*, xiv-xv. As William Martin emphasizes, "It is difficult to overstate the impact of the Great Revival on the development of Southern culture. Southern religion, which thoroughly permeated and informed Southern culture, was characterized by its absolute and unquestioning confidence in the Bible, its emphasis on piety and purity, and its unswerving dedication to the primary task of the revivals: the winning of lost souls." In the North, on the other hand, Evangelicalism was most closely associated with the progressive and "pious power elite" of the time. William Martin, *With God on Our Side: The Rise of the Religious Right in America*, rev. ed., (New York: Broadway Books, 2005), 4–5.

5    Brulle equates "discourse" with "worldview" and utilizes the method of frame analysis to study the different discursive frames of the environmental movement: "One way to understand the complexity of the U.S. environmental movement is to see it as a series of historically developed networks of communicative action based on multiple discursive frames . . . These discursive frames form the basis for the many different forms of action, organization, and objectives within the current movement" (Brulle, *Agency*, 96). For "Promethean" or "cornucopian discourse," see John S. Dryzek, *The Politics of the Earth: Environmental Discourses*, 2nd ed. (Oxford: Oxford University Press, 2005), 51. The different environmental discourses are not absolute and rigid categories; some organizations and individual environmentalists might subscribe to more than one discursive frame or combinations thereof. Also, depending on the theoretical framework they use and whether they analyze global or national environmentalism, scholars slightly differ in the way they categorize environmental discourses (see Dryzek, *The Politics of the Earth* vis-à-vis Brulle, *Agency*). According to Opie, "American triumphalism depends on environmental imperialism," a reckless commodification of nature and the world. Opie uses this terminology to express a more encompassing critique of America. To him the tenets of triumphalism "are very hypnotizing: The power of science and technology is unlimited, nature is to be tamed to serve humanity, material progress is inevitable, and enlightened humans like Americans represent the pinnacle of all creation." John Opie, *Nature's Nation: An Environmental History of the United States* (Orlando, Fla.: Harcourt Brace, 1998), 2.

6    Regarding environmentalism as protest against the discourse of Manifest Destiny, see Brulle, *Agency*. For more information on the history of environmentalism as a global phenomenon, see Ramachandra Guha, *Environmentalism: A Global History* (Oxford: Oxford University Press, 2000). As Taylor (*Dark Green Religion*, 45) notes, "Most historiographies

suggest that attitudes in North America did not shift toward nature appreciation until this had first occurred in Europe," beginning with the writings of Jean Jacques Rousseau, Edmund Burke, and Immanuel Kant in the mid-eighteenth century. For "the first comprehensive description," see Roderick Frazier Nash, *The Rights of Nature: A History of Environmental Ethics*, History of American Thought and Culture, ed. Paul S. Boyer (Madison: University of Wisconsin Press, 1989), 38.

7    Brulle, *Agency*, 134–41.

8    Brulle, *Agency*, 133–72. Yellowstone National Park was created by Grant in 1872, and Harrison established the National Forests in 1891: Turner and Isenberg, *Republican Reversal*, 22. To illustrate the often subtle differences between Preservation and Conservation and the early victory of the latter, the battle over the Hetch Hetchy Reservoir in Yosemite National Park is often used as an example: see Samuel P. Hays, *Beauty, Health, and Permanence: Environmental Politics in the United States, 1955–1985* (Cambridge: Cambridge University Press, 1987); and Daniel G. Payne, *Voices in the Wilderness: American Nature Writing and Environmental Politics* (Hanover, N.H.: University Press of New England, 1996).

9    Guha, *Environmentalism*, 3–4.

10   German biologist and philosopher Ernst Heinrich Philipp August Haeckel (1834–1919) coined the term "ecology" ("oecologie") to designate the holistic interrelationships of organisms with each other and their environment in 1866: Nash, *Rights of Nature*, 55. For comprehensive historical information on Evangelicalism's dominance within American Protestantism, see Nathan O. Hatch, *The Democratization of American Christianity* (New Haven, Conn.: Yale University Press, 1989); and Christine Leigh Heyrman, *Southern Cross: The Beginnings of the Bible Belt* (Chapel Hill: University of North Carolina Press, 1997). For a detailed account of the "Great Reversal," see David O. Moberg, *The Great Reversal: Evangelism and Social Concern* (Philadelphia: Lippincott, 1977).

11   Protestantism in America never was a unified whole, but until the late nineteenth century it did display a certain degree of coherence: "After the turn of the century, [however], it became increasingly clear that [it] was more a very rough category for non-Catholic Christians than a cohesive religious force." Mark A. Noll, *The Old Religion in a New World: The History of North American Christianity* (Grand Rapids: Eerdmans, 1984), 142–49. The twelve volumes of the magazine *The Fundamentals: A Testimony to the Truth* (circulation about three million) were published between 1910 and 1915 by an affiliate of Moody Bible Institute in Chicago and financed by California oil magnates Lyman and Milton Stewart (Martin, *With God*, 10). On the history of fundamentalism as a type of "militant antimodernism," see George M. Marsden, *Fundamentalism and American Culture: The Shaping of Twentieth Century Evangelicalism, 1870–1925* (New York: Oxford University Press, 1980). For further information on dispensational eschatology and end times prophecy, see for example Paul S. Boyer, *When Time Shall Be No More: Prophecy Belief in Modern American Culture* (Cambridge, Mass.: Harvard University Press, 1992).

12   Quotations are from Edward J. Larson, *Summer for the Gods: The Scopes Trial and America's Continuing Debate Over Science and Religion* (1997; new afterword, New York: Basic Books, 2006), 268. A detailed account of the Scopes Trial can be found in this source as well.

13   Quotations are from Balmer, *Thy Kingdom Come*, 113–14.

14   Nancy Tatom Ammerman, *Bible Believers: Fundamentalists in the Modern World* (New Brunswick, N.J.: Rutgers University Press, 1987). Joel A. Carpenter, *Revive Us Again: The Reawakening of American Fundamentalism* (New York: Oxford University Press, 1997). About

fundamentalists' detachment having been reinforced by biblical principles and prophesies, see John C. Green, "Seeking a Place: Evangelical Protestants and Public Engagement in the Twentieth Century," in *Toward an Evangelical Public Policy: Political Strategies for the Health of the Nation*, ed. Ronald J. Sider and Diane Knippers (Grand Rapids: Baker, 2005), 19. For conservative Protestants' feeling of cultural alienation, see D. G. Hart, *That Old-time Religion in Modern America: Evangelical Protestantism in the Twentieth Century*, The American Ways Series (Chicago: Ivan R. Dee, 2002). John H. Evans and Michael S. Evans, "Religion and Science: Beyond the Epistemological Conflict Narrative," *Annual Review of Sociology* 34 (2008): 87–105.

[15]  See Smith, *American Evangelicalism*, 9. For "true outsiders" versus "wounded lovers," see Carpenter, *Revive Us Again*, 5–6. About the fundamentalist resentment after Scopes, see also Frances FitzGerald, *The Evangelicals: The Struggle to Shape America* (New York: Simon & Schuster, 2017), 176.

[16]  Regarding a "more intellectually respectable . . . alternative," see Smith, *American Evangelicalism*, 14. For a comprehensive account of the neo-evangelical movement, see Carpenter, *Revive Us Again*. For "to present a positive testimony" and "to pull together," see National Association of Evangelicals, "History," National Association of Evangelicals, https://www.nae.net/about-nae/history/ (accessed May 10, 2019). Pentecostalism has its origin in a series of "Spirit baptism" experiences among revivalist and Holiness groups in the early twentieth century. Adherents of the movement believe in the gifts of the Holy Spirit, such as speaking in tongues and spiritual healing, that Christians supposedly receive as described on the day of Pentecost (Acts 2:1-4). The charismatic movement developed out of Pentecostalism, and the Assemblies of God is the largest Pentecostal body in the United States. See E. A. Livingstone, *The Concise Oxford Dictionary of the Christian Church*, s.v. "Pentecostalism," rev. 2nd ed. (Oxford: Oxford University Press, 2006). Martin (*With God*, 279) describes Pentecostalism as "high-intensity religion" because it stresses spontaneity during worship. The Anabaptist and Mennonite traditions developed as an early sixteenth-century alternative to the Reformed and Lutheran wing of the Reformation. Anabaptists view the world as fallen and practice an ethic of nonconformity, which includes a radical distinction between church and state, as well as Christ and culture, and a commitment to pacifism (they belong to the so-called "peace Protestants"). See Christopher J. Soper, "Differing Perspectives on Politics among Religious Traditions," in *In God We Trust? Religion and American Political Life*, ed. Corwin E. Schmidt (Grand Rapids: Baker Academic, 2001), 13–34.

[17]  See Smith, *American Evangelicalism*, 12–13. For "standard bearer," see National Association of Evangelicals, "History." A concise listing of the most important neo-evangelical institutions and organizations can be found here. For a detailed account of *CT*'s ideological mission and how the magazine has shaped modern American Evangelicalism, see Phyllis Elaine Alsdurf, "*Christianity Today* Magazine and Late Twentieth-Century Evangelicalism" (Ph.D. dissertation, University of Minnesota, 2005).

[18]  Carl F. H. Henry as cited in Richard Cizik, "A History of the Public Policy Resolutions of the National Association of Evangelicals," in *Toward an Evangelical Public Policy: Political Strategies for the Health of the Nation*, ed. Ronald J. Sider and Diane Knippers (Grand Rapids: Baker, 2005), 38. Lindsell became editor-in-chief at *CT* in 1968. Upholding biblical inerrancy—the belief in the literal truth of the Bible—as the defining criterion of an evangelical was a core concern of Lindsell's, and in 1976 he published his book: Harold

Lindsell, *The Battle for the Bible* (Grand Rapids: Zondervan, 1976). Other evangelicals in the neo-evangelical fold, however, were not as adamant about this doctrine (Lindsay, *Faith*, 258n21). For "service in one's occupational calling," see Robert Booth Fowler, *A New Engagement: Evangelical Political Thought, 1966–1976* (Grand Rapids: Eerdmans, 1982), 26. Smith (*American Evangelicalism*, 10–11) describes evangelicals' "engaged orthodoxy" as follows: "In keeping with their nineteenth-century Protestant heritage, they were fully committed to maintaining and promoting confidently traditional, orthodox Protestant theology and belief, *while at the same time* becoming confidently and proactively engaged in the intellectual, cultural, social, and political life of the nation. Their commitment to orthodoxy and engagement, respectively, distinguished these incipient 'neo-evangelicals'— as they began to call themselves—from their liberal Protestant cousins, on the one hand, and from their fundamentalist siblings, on the other" (emphasis original). For an overview of the different variations of civic engagement within the evangelical movement, see Michael Cromartie, ed., *A Public Faith: Evangelicals and Civic Engagement* (Lanham, Md.: Rowman and Littlefield, 2003), in particular the chapter by John C. Green, "Evangelical Protestants and Civic Engagement: An Overview," 11–29.

[19]     For fundamentalist separatism and "militant anti-modernism," see James Davison Hunter, *American Evangelicalism: Conservative Religion and the Quandary of Modernity* (New Brunswick, N.J.: Rutgers University Press, 1995). Other quotations in this paragraph are taken from Ammerman, *Bible Believers*, 5. Despite differences in mentality and attitude, in addition to nuances among shared beliefs and practices, a clear-cut distinction between evangelicals and fundamentalists has never been easy to draw. For one, both (neo-) Evangelicalism and fundamentalism are movements within the larger, much older, and internally diverse evangelical tradition that hearkens back to the Protestant Reformation of sixteenth-century Europe. Both can therefore be subsumed under the broader label of evangelical Protestants. However, while "all fundamentalists are evangelicals . . . not all evangelicals are fundamentalists": James A. Reichley, quoted in Daniel J. B. Hofrenning, *In Washington But Not of It: The Prophetic Politics of Religious Lobbyists* (Philadelphia: Temple University Press, 1995), 78. If Evangelicalism were clearly definable, the contours of the fundamentalist current within might be more pronounced as well. George M. Marsden, *Understanding Fundamentalism and Evangelicalism* (Grand Rapids: Eerdmans, 1991), 1–2.

[20]     Regarding "restless" fundamentalist leaders, see Smith, *American Evangelicalism*, 14. For environmentalism during the interwar period, see Bosso, *Environment*, 27–33. Further quotations in this paragraph are taken from Bosso, *Environment*, 27–33.

[21]     For the importance of the interwar period regarding the evolution of organized environmental advocacy, see Bosso, *Environment*, 27. For "erected upon the legal platform of the New Deal" and the conservative resistance toward the New Deal, see Turner and Isenberg, *Republican Reversal*, 32.

[22]     For a broadening agenda of environmental concerns during the interwar period, see Bosso, *Environment*, 27–34.

[23]     For the surge of religiosity after World War II, specific polls, and "churchgoing [as] the thing to do," see Putnam and Campbell, *American Grace*, 84–87. It is also important to keep in mind, however, that historical trends cannot be interpreted by singular causes because "too many things are going on in modern society for any simple story to be explanatory" (Putnam and Campbell, *American Grace*, 82). Regarding civil religion, see Robert N. Bellah, "Civil Religion in America," in *American Civil Religion*,

ed. Donald G. Jones and Russell E. Richey (1974; repr., San Francisco: Mellen Research University Press, 1990), 21–44.

24    Richard V. Pierard and Robert D. Linder, *Civil Religion & the Presidency* (Grand Rapids: Academie Books, 1988), 63. Will Herberg posed that in the 1950s, the larger denominations in the United States (i.e., Jews, Protestants, and Catholics) formed a "tripartite system" that clearly demarcated and defined their respective religiopolitical identities: *Protestant-Catholic-Jew* (Garden City, N.Y.: Doubleday-Anchor, 1955). This pattern was eventually replaced by a "two-party system," splitting the "culturescape of American religion" into "religious conservatives" and "religious liberals" (Wuthnow, *The Struggle*, 21; 31–32). Regarding the agreement between Eisenhower and Graham, see FitzGerald, *The Evangelicals*, 185–86.

25    For "era of," "represented a perfect storm," and "death of God," see Putnam and Campbell, *American Grace*, 91–97. See also Leonard I. Sweet, "The 1960s: The Crises of Liberal Christianity and the Public Emergence of Evangelicalism," in *Evangelicalism and Modern America*, ed. George Marsden (Grand Rapids: Eerdmans, 1984), 29–45.

26    For "Jane Fonda and Malcolm X," see Lindsay, *Faith in the Halls*, 7. Regarding the distinction of two waves of environmentalism in the historiography of the environmental movement and "more reformist," see Bosso, *Environment*, 39. Guha (*Environmentalism*, 3–5) also speaks about two waves of environmentalism on a global scale.

27    Rachel L. Carson, *Silent Spring* (Boston: Houghton Mifflin, 1962). According to McNeill, Carson was the most important catalyst for the environmental movement because she was such a great communicator. J. R. McNeill, *Something New Under the Sun: An Environmental History of the Twentieth-Century World* (London: Penguin, 2000), 337. Regarding Carson's crucial role within modern environmentalism, see also Opie, *Nature's Nation*, among many others. The Carson quotes are taken from "Rachel Carson Warns of a Silent Spring, 1962," in *Major Problems in American Environmental History: Documents and Essays*, 2nd ed., ed. Carolyn Merchant (Boston: Wadsworth Publishing, 2006), 439. For more information on Carson's life, see Linda Lear, "The Life and Legacy of Rachel Carson," Linda Lear, http://rachelcarson.org (accessed July 3, 2019).

28    Brulle, *Agency*, 98; 173–93. Regarding second wave environmentalism as a certain type of "antimodernism," see Frank Zelko, "Challenging Modernity: The Origins of Postwar Environmental Protest in the United States," in *Shades of Green: Environmental Activism Around the Globe*, ed. Christof Mauch, Nathan Stoltzfus, and Douglas R. Weiner, German Historical Institute Studies in International Environmental History (Lanham, Md.: Rowman & Littlefield, 2006), 13–14. For "failed to connect," see Brulle, *Agency*, 181.

29    For Ehrlich's and Carson's books as apocalyptic narratives, see M. Jimmie Killingsworth and Jaqueline S. Palmer, "Millennial Ecology: The Apocalyptic Narrative from *Silent Spring* to *Global Warming*," in *Green Culture: Environmental Rhetoric in Contemporary America*, ed. Carl G. Herndl and Stuart C. Brown (Madison: University of Wisconsin Press, 1996), 21–45. As Ehrlich begins the prologue of his book, "The battle to feed all of humanity is over. In the 1970s the world will undergo famines—hundreds of millions of people are going to starve to death in spite of any crash programs embarked upon now." Paul R. Ehrlich, *The Population Bomb* (New York: Ballantine Books, 1968), xi. The sales number of *The Population Bomb* is taken from Killingsworth and Palmer, "Millennial Ecology," 32.

30    Ehrlich, *Population Bomb*, 66–67 (emphasis in original). In his *An Essay on the Principle of Population*, first published in 1798, Thomas Robert Malthus posed that while population numbers grew exponentially during times of abundance, food production could only be

increased arithmetically in order to keep up with population growth. Thus continued population increases lead to famines and poverty. T. R. Malthus, *An Essay on the Principle of Population*, ed. with introduction and notes by Geoffrey Gilbert (New York: Oxford University Press, 2008).

31    Ehrlich, *Population Bomb*, 135.

32    Ehrlich, *Population Bomb*, 136–141; 88; 138.

33    According to economist Julian Simon, natural resources were either abundant or, if threatened by scarcity, easily replaceable due to the entrepreneurial spirit of the free market (see Turner and Isenberg, *Republican Reversal*, 44–45). Disagreeing with Ehrlich's view of resource scarcity, in 1980 Julian Simon dared Ehrlich to bet on the price development of nongovernment-controlled raw materials over the next ten years (i.e., the Simon-Ehrlich wager), a bet Ehrlich lost. For a short summary of Commoner's critique, see Killingsworth and Palmer, "Millennial Ecology," 34–35. For the book's influence on the establishment of the UNFPA, see for instance Natalia Kanem, "Foreword: Make Rights and Choices a Reality for All," in *UNFPA State of World Population 2019*, 2019, https://www.unfpa.org/sites/default/files/pub-pdf/UNFPA_PUB_2019_EN _State_of_World_Population.pdf (accessed July 8, 2019); and Donella H. Meadows, Dennis L. Meadows, Jørgen Randers, and William W. Behrens, *The Limits to Growth. A Report for the Club of Rome's Project on the Predicament of Mankind* (New York: Universe Books, 1972). Regarding "economic growth fetish," see McNeill, *Something New*, 336. As Ehrlich (*Population Bomb*, 149) charges, "The idea of an ever-expanding economy fueled by population growth seems tightly entrenched in the minds of businessmen, if not in the minds of economists. Each new baby is viewed as a consumer to stimulate an ever-growing economy."

34    For "melancholy hue," see Malthus, *An Essay*, 4. A display of Paul Ehrlich's self-confident pessimism as the only ecologically and rationally sensible attitude can be found in chapter 6 of *The Population Bomb*, entitled "What If I'm Wrong?" 197–98.

35    For "rare political alignment," see Earth Day Network, "Earth Day: The History of a Movement," Earth Day Network, http://www.earthday.org/earth-day-history -movement (accessed August 24, 2012). For more information on the first and subsequent Earth Days, see also the documentary *Earth Days*, directed by Robert Stone, Zeitgeist Films, 2009. Regarding Nixon as "no 'green' radical," see Shabecoff, *American Environmentalism*, 5–6.

36    Regarding "billions of dollars," see Turner and Isenberg, *Republican Reversal*, 13. For Ford's disavowal of the EPA, see Turner and Isenberg, *Republican Reversal*, 46.

37    Berry, *New Liberalism*. Bosso, *Environment*, 39. Andrew McFarland, *Public Interest Lobbies: Decision Making on Energy* (Washington, D.C.: American Enterprise Institute, 1978), 4–5.

38    Putnam and Campbell, *American Grace*, 3, 91ff.

39    Putnam and Campbell, *American Grace*, 100ff. Write Putnam and Campbell (*American Grace*, 119): "We can say that many Americans became deeply concerned about public and private morality in the Long Sixties, and that a disproportionate number of those people ended up in evangelical pews in the 1970s and 1980s." The number of adherents to evangelical churches grew during the 1970s and 1980s in absolute numbers but especially in comparison to the mainline Protestant churches. As Sweet ("The 1960s," 32) also argues, "The rise of evangelicalism . . . must be seen against the backdrop of a dispirited and ailing conventional Protestantism that had little to declare theologically

and was seldom able to answer even the simplest questions about the faith, to say nothing of answering them with a distinctive or strong voice." There are several other reasons for the evangelical expansion, among them demography, theological conversion, and the innovative marketing skills of evangelical faith leaders who have understood very well to accommodate the spiritual and logistical needs of the modern believer. However, as Putnam and Campbell, among others, view it, the main attraction of Evangelicalism at the time was its moral certainty, the strong conviction of its beliefs, and its sense of embattlement due to the values it espoused and saw threatened by the liberalizing and secularizing trends of the sixties. For the "embattled and thriving-thesis" regarding the expansion of the evangelical movement, see Smith, *American Evangelicalism.*

[40]   For the evangelical reactions to environmentalism and "moral pollution" in the 1960s, see Larsen, "God's Gardeners," 73–75.

[41]   Putnam and Campbell, *American Grace,* 82; 114–17. For pluralism but dominance of conservative ideas, see Fowler, *A New Engagement,* 191. For the "political aims" and "domestic issues" see Hart, *That Old-time Religion,* 154–55.

[42]   On the evangelical involvement in politics and the rise of the New Christian or Religious Right, see for example Robert C. Liebman and Robert Wuthnow, *The New Christian Right: Mobilization and Legitimation* (New York: Aldine, 1983); Bruce, *The Rise and Fall;* Clyde Wilcox, *God's Warriors? The Christian Right in Twentieth-Century America* (Baltimore, Md.: Johns Hopkins University Press, 1992); Lisa McGirr, *Suburban Warriors: The Origins of the New American Right* (Princeton, N.J.: Princeton University Press, 2001); William Martin, *With God;* and Clyde Wilcox and Carin Larson, *Onward Christian Soldiers?: The Religious Right in American Politics,* 3rd ed. (Boulder, Colo.: Westview, 2006). For a useful guide to the voluminous literature on conservative Christian activism that covers accounts dealing with older incarnations of the Christian Right, see Richard V. Pierard, "The New Religious Right in American Politics," in *Evangelicalism and Modern America,* ed. George Marsden (Grand Rapids: Eerdmans, 1984), 161–74. Regarding "on the American cultural and political map," see Christian Smith, *Christian America? What Evangelicals Really Want* (Berkeley: University of California Press, 2000), 1.

[43]   Randall Balmer, *Redeemer: The Life of Jimmy Carter* (New York: Basic Books, 2014), 56. Regarding the sales number for Colson's *Born Again,* see Hart, *That Old-time Religion,* 144. For Gallup's polling and "the year of the evangelical," see "Born Again! The Year of the Evangelicals," *Newsweek,* October 25, 1976. For "evangelicals began to feel," see Martin, *With God,* 156–57.

[44]   For abortion "suddenly surfaced," see Balmer, *Redeemer,* 65. "Committed adultery" and other information in this paragraph is taken from Martin, *With God,* 157–58.

[45]   Regarding "inject some morality," see Lindsay, *Faith in the Halls,* 16–17. Billy Graham explains his reluctance to take sides in the 1976 election as follows: "The injection of the religious issue in the 1976 campaign concerned me. On the one hand, I was delighted to hear a presidential candidate speak so openly . . . about his personal faith. On the other hand, I knew Gerald Ford to be a man of deep conviction also, even if his own religious background was much different and less public. Religious conviction alone was not the most reliable guide as to who would be the best or most effective leader." Billy Graham, *Just As I Am: The Autobiography of Billy Graham* (New York: Harper Collins, 1997), 493. Explained Ohlman: "I really thought quite favorably toward Carter at that point, but we are from Grand Rapids and Jerry Ford was, you know, he was our man. And Jerry Ford was a very honest, hard-working, conservative Republican, and so it was natural for us

to vote for him instead of Carter." Dean Ohlman, interview by author, Grand Rapids, April 8, 2010. For Jim Jewell's support of Carter, see Jim Jewell, "50 Leaders of the Evangelical Generation: #5 Jimmy Carter. Born Again President," *The Rooftop Blog*, April 9, 2010, https://therooftopblog.wordpress.com/2010/04/09/50-leaders-of-the-evangelical-generation-5-jimmy-carter-born-again-president/ (accessed July 12, 2019).

[46]   For the evangelical percentages of the Nixon and Carter elections, see Kellstedt et al., "Faith Transformed," 272f. Regarding "born-again liberal," see Peter L. Berger, *Adventures of an Accidental Sociologist: How to Explain the World Without Becoming a Bore* (Amherst, N.Y.: Prometheus, 2011), 137. For Carter's alienating stances, see for example Lindsay, *Faith in the Halls*, 18. Other points of disagreement concerned the Equal Rights Amendment (ERA) and the *Roe v. Wade* Supreme Court decision from 1973 (see Martin, *With God*, 173–90). For the significance of the IRS plan, see Martin, *With God*, 173–90 and Bruce, *The Rise and Fall*, among others.

[47]   Regarding the evangelical fear of government intrusion and their understanding of the increasing spread of secularism in the public school system, see for instance FitzGerald, *The Evangelicals*, 303–304; and Martin, *With God*, 168–69. The quote "they were never simply refuges" is from FitzGerald, *The Evangelicals*, 303. For "secular humanism," see Hart, *That Old-time Religion*, 160–61. As Steve Bruce succinctly summarizes, "Secular humanists believe in the removal of religion from the public arena, in the tolerance of alternative lifestyles, and in the extension of choice." Despite the publication of diverse humanist manifestos, Bruce (*The Rise and Fall*, 185) stresses that the secular humanist position is not espoused and propagated by a small group of secular humanists in a quasi-conspiracy, as some conservative Christians seem to assume, but rather one of the "*unintended* consequences of modernity" (emphasis original). For Jimmy Carter's role in the proposed IRS ruling and his unwarranted blame, see Balmer, *Redeemer*, 104; and FitzGerald, *The Evangelicals*, 303.

[48]   For "secular humanism" as ideological enemy, see Hart, *That Old-time Religion*, 160–61. Regarding L'Abri as "shelter" and for a short historical overview of the study center, see L'Abri Fellowship, "History," *Swisslabri.org*, https://swisslabri.org/history/ (accessed July 14, 2019). For "almost singlehandedly," see Hart, *That Old-time Religion*, 160. Regarding the Religious Right's thinkers, see FitzGerald, *The Evangelicals*, 337. For more information about Rousas J. Rushdoony, the movement's other systematic thinker and cross-denominational authority, see chapter 5.

[49]   Regarding "specifically targeted," see Hart, *That Old-time Religion*, 160. For a short but detailed analysis of Schaeffer's publications and ideas, see for instance FitzGerald, *The Evangelicals*, 347–63. For "co-belligerency," see Martin, *With God*, 204. As Paul Weyrich explained, "Suddenly it dawned on them that they were not going to be able to be left alone to teach their children as they pleased. It was at that moment that conservatives made the linkage between their opposition to government interference and the interests of the evangelical movement, which now saw itself on the defensive and under attack by the government. That was what brought those people in the political process. It was not the other things" (Martin, *With God*, 173). Due to the increasing publicly expressed agitation of conservative Christians, the IRS gave up the plan to regulate private schools in 1978. As Randall Balmer (*Thy Kingdom Come*, 11–16) charges, in the 1980s the leaders of the Religious Right "constructed an *abortion myth*" in order to claim that their movement started as a response to the Supreme Court's *Roe v. Wade* (1973)

decision, whereas it started, like Weyrich explained, as a response to the IRS threat against segregated schools (emphasis original).

50 For "rise of the environmental regulatory state" and its conservative discontent, see Turner and Isenberg, *Republican Reversal*, 41. Regarding specific conservative "visions of abundance," see Turner and Isenberg, *Republican Reversal*, 54–97. For Carter's positions on energy, see for example Jimmy Carter, "Report to the American People on Energy," February 2, 1977, accessible via C-SPAN, https://www.c-span.org/video/?153913-1/president-carters-fireside-chat-energy (accessed July 15, 2019). Carter's "crisis of confidence" speech can be found at "Energy and National Goals: Address to the Nation," July 15, 1979, accessible via Jimmy Carter Presidential Library & Museum, https://www.jimmycarterlibrary.gov/assets/documents/speeches/energy-crisis.phtml (accessed July 15, 2019).

51 For the sociological concept of "moral shock," see Jasper, *The Art of Moral Protest*, 106. Agitated by the success of the New Left and inspired by the Barry Goldwater nomination in 1964, political activism on the Right increased in the 1960s and the 1970s. Some of the leading figures within this wave of conservative activism, such as Weyrich, Richard Viguerie, and others, referred to themselves as the "New Right." According to Martin (*With God*, 192), Weyrich was "perhaps the most important figure in the small constellation of leaders who were consciously referring to themselves as the New Right." The conservative religiopolitical activism that had started in southern California (Orange County) in the late 1960s anticipated and inspired much of the later Religious Right activism on the national level; see McGirr, *Suburban Warriors*. See also Anton K. Jacobs, "The New Right, Fundamentalism, and Nationalism in Postmodern America: A Marriage of Heat and Passion," *Social Compass* 53, no. 3 (2006): 357–66.

52 Richard A. Viguerie, *The New Right: We're Ready to Lead* (Falls Church, Va.: Viguerie, 1980), 55. Jo Freeman, "On the Origins of Social Movements," in *Waves of Protest: Social Movements Since the Sixties*, ed. Jo Freeman and Victoria Johnson (Lanham, Md.: Rowman and Littlefield, 1999), 8.

53 Falwell's quotations in this paragraph are taken from Jerry Falwell, "Introduction by Jerry Falwell," in *The New Right: We're Ready to Lead*, by Richard A. Viguerie (Falls Church, Va.: Viguerie, 1980). Paul Weyrich coined the name for the Moral Majority during a talk with Falwell (Martin, *With God*, 200). While he still claimed to be "a separatist" in the sense that he refused "to conform to the standards of a sinful society," eventually Falwell deemed it "irresponsible" for Christian citizens to completely avoid the political process and the social life of America. See Jerry Falwell, "An Agenda for the 1980s," in *Piety and Politics: Evangelicals and Fundamentalists Confront the World*, ed. Richard John Neuhaus and Michael Cromartie (Washington, D.C.: Ethics and Public Policy Center, 1987), 119–20.

54 For New Right support in the founding of Religious Right organizations, see for instance Martin, *With God*, 170–73; and Wilcox and Larson, *Onward Christian Soldiers?* 40–41. Writes Hart (*That Old-time Religion*, 164) about the Moral Majority: "This organization was not simply a consequence of cultural analysis or theological nuance. It was also the product of secular conservative political strategists who saw morality as an opening for the Republican party to recapture the White House." A concise example of Jerry Falwell's mediating effort between fundamentalists and evangelicals can be found in his "An Agenda for the 1980s": "We Fundamentalists appeal to our Evangelical brethren to stand with us for the truth of the gospel in this hour when America needs us most. Stop looking down your theological and ecclesiastical noses at your Fundamentalist brethren. As the

English theologian James Barr has already pointed out, non-Evangelicals already view Evangelicals and Fundamentalists alike. We have so much in common. Only the radicals among us (to the Left and to the Right) divide us. I say it is time we denied the 'lunatic fringe' of our movements and worked for a great conservative crusade to turn America back to God" (122–23). For Falwell shocking other fundamentalists with his espousal of an evangelical and fundamentalist "co-belligerency" requiring concerted social and political action, see Martin, *With God*, 204. In 1982, Hunter argued that the division of conservative Protestants into fundamentalists and evangelicals, which had been valid in the past and may again be valid in the future, could no longer be upheld in the form of two distinct sociological categories. See James Davison Hunter, "Operationalizing Evangelicalism: A Review, Critique, and Proposal," *Sociological Analysis* 42 (1982): 363–72.

[55]   For the Religious Right as a movement of "cultural defence," see Bruce, *The Rise and Fall*, 168. In particular Paul Weyrich's culture war rallying call ("It may not be with bullets . . . and it may not be with rockets and missiles, but it is a war nevertheless. It is a war of ideology, a war of ideas, it is a war about our way of life.") and Pat Buchanan's often cited culture war speech during the Republican National Convention in 1992 illustrate that, by proxy, the Religious Right must be understood as defender of a particular ideology and lifestyle. Paul Weyrich as quoted in Viguerie, *The New Right*, 55. Patrick Joseph Buchanan, "Culture War Speech: Address to the Republican National Convention" (17 August 1992), *Voices of Democracy: The U.S. Oratory Project*, http://voicesofdemocracy .umd.edu/buchanan-culture-war-speech-speech-text/ (accessed July 20, 2019). For "coalition of *most* of the religious," see Putnam and Campbell, *American Grace*, 376 (emphasis original). Regarding abortion and homosexuality as the glue that has held this coalition together, see Putnam and Campbell, *American Grace*, 384–88. Opposition to abortion was the dominant issue of the Religious Right throughout the 1980s, whereas the movement's condemnation of homosexuality was formulated in the 1990s.

[56]   See David Biello, "Where Did the Carter White House's Solar Panels Go?" *Scientific American*, August 6, 2010, https://www.scientificamerican.com/article/carter-white -house-solar-panel-array/ (accessed July 19, 2019); and John Wihbey, "Jimmy Carter's Solar Panels: A History That Haunts Today," Yale Climate Connections, November 11, 2008, http://www.yaleclimateconnections.org/2008/11/jimmy-carters-solar-panels/ (accessed July 22, 2019). *A Road Not Taken*, directed by Christina Hemauer and Ronald Keller, Atelier Christina Hemauer & Ronald Keller, Switzerland, 2010.

[57]   For "year of evangelical politics," see Hart, *That Old-Time Religion*, 144. For "polarizing figure," see Pierard and Linder, *Civil Religion*, 258. Regarding the distinction of a "third wave" of environmentalism, see Mark Dowie, *Losing Ground: American Environmentalism at the Close of the Twentieth Century* (Cambridge, Mass.: MIT Press, 1995).

[58]   As Turner and Isenberg (*Republican Reversal*, 52) observe, "Reagan's ascendancy marked a turning point in environmental politics: it was the beginning of the Republican reversal and the party's gradual disavowal of the laws and institutions of environmental protection it had helped to craft." For Reagan's antienvironmental positions as governor, his derision of environmentalists as "doom-cryers," and for "blithe ignorance," see Turner and Isenberg, *Republican Reversal*, 50–52. Regarding Reagan's openness about his antienvironmental sentiments and his selection of officials for leadership roles in environmentally crucial positions, see Hays, *Beauty*, 492–94.

[59]   Information on the Group of Ten is taken from Dowie, *Losing Ground*, 70. For "opening chapter," see Turner and Isenberg, *Republican Reversal*, 100. It was Richard Nixon who

had referred to the 1970s as the "Environmental Decade" (Turner and Isenberg, *Republican Reversal*, 100).

[60]    For "synonymous with," see Dowie, *Losing Ground*, 70. Bosso (*Environment*, 87; 89) describes the membership surge of environmental organizations during the Reagan presidency, as much as their professionalization due to a shift toward insider lobbying strategies. Regarding corporate alliances of the Group of Ten, see Carolyn Merchant, *American Environmental History: An Introduction* (New York: Columbia University Press, 2007), 200–201.

[61]    For discursive frames of the environmental movement, see Brulle, *Agency*. For a better understanding of deep ecology's arguments, see Arne Naess, "The Shallow and the Deep, Long-Range Ecology Movement: A Summary," in *Debating the Earth: The Environmental Politics Reader*, ed. John S. Dryzek and David Schlosberg, 2nd ed. (Oxford: Oxford University Press, 2005), 343–47. Regarding deep ecology's radically biocentric goal, see Merchant, *American Environmental History*, 206. For Earth First! as "nonhierarchical 'anti-organization,'" see Bosso, *Environment*, 60. The term "monkeywrenching" as a specific type of environmental sabotage is derived from Edward Abbey's novel *The Monkey Wrench Gang*, first published in 1975. Edward Abbey, *The Monkey Wrench Gang*. Harper Perennial Modern Classics. 1975. (Reissue, New York: Harper Collins, 2006). Earth First! describes "monkeywrenching" as "the unlawful sabotage of industrial extraction and development equipment, as a means of striking at the Earth's destroyers where they commit their crimes and hitting them where they feel it most—in their profit margins." The organization "officially neither advocates nor condemns" the practice. See Earth First!, "Monkeywrenching," *Earth First! Journal*, https://earthfirstjournal .org/monkeywrenching/ (accessed July 20, 2019).

[62]    See Brulle, *Agency*, 207–21. Environmental justice proponents have been more grassroots and locally oriented than mainstream environmentalists. An example of an organization steeped in the environmental justice discourse would be Lois Gibbs' Center for Health, Environment, and Justice (1989). For more information on the environmental justice movement, see Robert D. Bullard, *Dumping in Dixie: Race, Class and Environmental Quality*, 3rd ed. (Boulder, Colo.: Westview Press, 2000).

[63]    For the discursive specifics of Ecofeminism, see Dryzek, *Politics of the Earth*, 185–86. For more detailed information on the movement, see Carolyn Merchant, *Radical Ecology: The Search for a Livable World* (New York: Routledge, 1992).

[64]    For "master frame," see Brulle, *Agency*, 267. Regarding the population ecology of interest representation and its application to American (establishment) environmentalism, see Bosso, *Environment*, 157. For the remaining quotations in this paragraph, see Bosso, *Environment*, 157. Jeffrey Berry (*The New Liberalism*) also argues that citizen groups concerned with quality of life and postmaterialist issues have been more politically effective than often assumed by their activists and others sympathetic to their cause.


## 2 THEOLOGY FIRST!

[1]    Steven Bouma-Prediger, *For the Beauty of the Earth: A Christian Vision for Creation Care* (Grand Rapids: Baker, 2001), 88.

[2]    Russell Kirk, "Common Reader for Everyday Ecologists," *New Orleans Times-Picayune*, September 20, 1971.

3     Lynn White Jr., "The Historical Roots of Our Ecologic Crisis," in *The Environmental Handbook*, ed. Garrett De Bell (New York: Ballantine/Friends of the Earth, 1970), 12–26. White's essay, which is based on his 1966 address to the American Academy of Arts and Sciences, first appeared in *Science* magazine in 1967. See Lynn White Jr., "The Historical Roots of Our Ecologic Crisis," *Science* 155, no. 3767 (1967): 1203–7. Quotations in this book are taken from Lynn White Jr., "The Historical Roots of Our Ecologic Crisis," in *Machina Ex Deo: Essays in the Dynamism of Western Culture*, ed. Lynn White Jr. (Cambridge, Mass.: MIT Press, 1968), 75–94.

4     Regarding White's thesis as an "update" of Max Weber's linkage between capitalism and Protestantism, see Elspeth Whitney, "Christianity and Changing Concepts of Nature: An Historical Perspective," in *Religion and the New Ecology: Environmental Responsibility in a World in Flux*, ed. David M. Lodge and Christopher Hamlin (Notre Dame, Ind.: University of Notre Dame, 2006), 26–52. Other quotations in this paragraph are from White, "The Historical Roots," 75–94.

5     For White not being alone in his criticism, see Mokhtar Ben Barka, "Religion and Environmental Concern in the United States," in *"Nature's Nation" Revisited: American Concepts of Nature from Wonder to Ecological Crisis*, ed. Hans Bak and Walter W. Hölbling, European Contributions to American Studies (Amsterdam: VU University Press, 2003), 282–83. As Nash (*Rights of Nature*, 97) emphasizes as well, an earlier critique of Christian anthropocentrism was also uttered by Thoreau and Muir. For a similar critique in the German context of the early modern environmental movement, see for example Green Party cofounder Carl Amery's critique *Das Ende der Vorsehung: Die gnadenlosen Folgen des Christentums* (Reinbek bei Hamburg: Rowohlt, 1972). Barka ("Religion and Environmental Concern," 283) asserts that literary critic Leo Marx, ecologist Paul R. Ehrlich, historian Arnold J. Toynbee, and theologian Paul H. Santmire were among the ones who readily accepted White's line of argument. Fowler adds the examples of environmental ethicist Roderick F. Nash and Australian philosopher John Passmore specifically: Robert Booth Fowler, *The Greening of Protestant Thought* (Chapel Hill: University of North Carolina Press, 1995). In his history of the environmental movement, Kline writes, "Although it is true that many non-Western societies abused their environments to various degrees, White's argument provides some explanation for the West's energetic exploitation of nature." Benjamin Kline, *First Along the River: A Brief History of the Environmental Movement*, 3rd ed. (Lanham, Md.: Rowman & Littlefield), 3. Citing White frequently, in the first chapter of his book, Kline explains that Western European culture developed a philosophy toward nature on biblical grounds, and that the early European settlers brought this attitude to the New World where they applied it to tame the new environment. Consequently, Kline does not acknowledge the existence of faith-based environmental activism in his book. For empirical verifications of the White thesis, see for example Douglas Lee Eckberg and T. J. Blocker, "Varieties of Religious Involvement and Environmental Concern," *Journal for the Scientific Study of Religion* 28 (1989): 509–17; and Carl M. Hand and Kent D. Van Liere, "Religion, Mastery-Over-Nature, and Environmental Concern," *Social Forces* 63 (1984): 555–70. Although they assert that "White's mastery thesis is far too simplistic to explain the religion-environmental nexus," James L. Guth et al. find a connection between low concern with the environment, dispensational theology, and evangelical self-identification: "Faith and the Environment: Religious Beliefs and Attitudes on Environmental Policy," *American Journal of Political Science* 39 (1995): 377. For a comprehensive review of the environmental sociology studies that have explored the Judeo-Christian

and ecology nexus since 1977, see Gregory E. Hitzhusen, "Judeo-Christian Theology and the Environment: Moving Beyond Scepticism to New Sources for Environmental Education in the United States," *Environmental Education Research* 13, no. 1 (2007): 55–74. For "pervasive otherworldliness" and the "traditional Christian view of wilderness as a cursed land," see Nash, *Rights of Nature*, 91–92. Regarding social-scientific studies critiquing White, see Hitzhusen, "Judeo-Christian Theology." Contrary to Guth et al., Wolkomir et al. found that demographic characteristics of members are more likely to impact members' environmental attitudes and behaviors than denominational predispositions toward dominion belief. Michelle Wolkomir et al., "Denominational Subcultures of Environmentalism," *Review of Religious Research* 38 (1997): 339. For additional research that finds a positive religion-environment correlation, see Conrad L. Kanagy and Hart M. Nelsen, "Religion and Environmental Concern: Challenging the Dominant Assumptions," *Review of Religious Research* 37, no. 1 (1995): 33–45. Elspeth Whitney claims the opposite of White, namely that the Judeo-Christian tradition has instilled environmental attitudes in its followers: "Lynn White, Ecotheology, and History," *Environmental Ethics* 15 (1993): 151–69. See also Whitney, "Christianity and Changing Concepts." For a claim based on similar grounds, see Arne Naess, *Ecology, Community, and Lifestyle: An Outline of Ecosophy* (Cambridge: Cambridge University Press, 1989). With regard to the dominance of the White paradigm in academia, environmental historians Christopher Hamlin and John T. McGreevy stated as recently as 2006 that it had finally "become possible to shake off Lynn White" and to look at religiously motivated American environmentalism from a less biased perspective. Christopher Hamlin and John T. McGreevy, "The Greening of America, Catholic Style, 1930–1950," *Environmental History* 11 (2006): 487. For more on White's impact, see also Hitzhusen, "Judeo-Christian Theology."

6    White, "The Historical Roots," 90–93 (emphasis added). In general, Ecotheology is "an attempt to come to grips with [the environmental crisis] from the standpoint of faith, the divine, and spiritual truth" (Gottlieb, *A Greener Faith*, 19). It is a discourse that deals with the environmental crisis and the human response to it *from within the framework of a religion*. While environmentalism at large may be a movement with a moral or ethical dimension, and while many environmentally active individuals may have religious backgrounds, Ecotheology is more than environmentalism done by religious people. Regarding White as the initiator of the discourse of Ecotheology, see Gottlieb, *A Greener Faith*, 22. That said, however, it must be stressed that White cannot be seen as the sole initiator of faith-based environmental activism. There were some early conservation advocates that foreshadowed the discourse of ecotheology in the beginning of the twentieth century, such as the Conservation Committee of the American Unitarian Association; botanist Liberty Hyde Bailey; and Assistant Chief of the U.S. Soil Conservation Service Walter Lowdermilk (Brulle, *Agency*, 230–31). Additionally, the National Catholic Rural Life Conference tried to bring about a "green revolution" as early as the 1930s (Hamlin and McGreevy, "Greening of America"). Moreover, the study of religious awakenings or revitalization movements shows that religions react to troubling times with increased activism (Kearns, "Saving the Creation: Christian Environmentalism," 65). Thus, considering the increase in environmental problems over the course of the twentieth century, the rise of general environmental concern toward the late 1960s, and the "values vacuum" that developed with the bureaucratization of the environmental movement after the 1970s, Ecotheology and religious environmentalism may have developed in a similar way even if White had not directly challenged Judeo-Christianity.

7    For quotes from White, see "The Historical Roots," 85–91 (emphasis added). Reagan said the following before the Western Wood Products Association: "We've got to recognize that where the preservation of a natural resource like the redwoods is concerned, that there is a common sense limit. I mean, if you've looked at a hundred thousand acres or so of trees—you know, a tree is a tree, how many more do you need to look at?" Incumbent Pat Brown, his opponent in the gubernatorial race, mocked Reagan and turned this comment into the often-quoted, "If you've seen one redwood, you've seen them all" (quoted from Turner and Isenberg, *Republican Reversal*, 50).

8    Regarding St. Francis as the "patron saint for ecologists," see White, "The Historical Roots," 91. For the three different ecotheological ethics or modes within American Christianity, see Kearns, "Saving the Creation: Christian Environmentalism."

9    According to Larsen ("God's Gardeners"), evangelical thinking about environmental issues was largely prompted by the "White thesis." See also Ball, "Evangelical Protestants," 63. Fowler (*The Greening*, 19) notes a general "defensiveness surrounding much of Protestant environmentalism."

10    Larsen, "God's Gardeners," 43–52. For more information on ASA and its founding in order "to integrate," see American Scientific Affiliation, "About ASA," American Scientific Affiliation, http://network.asa3.org/?page=ASAAbout#And%20why (accessed August 11, 2019).

11    For "God-ordained balance" and "sin against," see Cizik, "A History," 48. Regarding "cooperation to any responsible effort," see National Association of Evangelicals, "Resolution on Environment and Ecology," 1971, https://www.nae.net/environment-and-ecology/ (accessed August 11, 2019). Richard Cizik was asked to resign—or, as he claims, he was fired—from his long-held NAE job after expressing support for climate policy, homosexual civil unions, and Barack Obama in an interview with Terry Gross on NPR in December 2008. See "Rev. Richard Cizik on God and Global Warming," interview by Terry Gross, *Fresh Air*, National Public Radio, December 2, 2008; and also Cizik's article "My Journey Toward the 'New Evangelicalism'," *Religionandpolitics.org*, September 13, 2012, http://religionandpolitics.org/2012/09/13/my-journey-toward-the-new-evangelicalism/?utm_source=R%26P+Master+List&utm_campaign=52c4572015-MC_RSS_EMAIL_CAMPAIGN_20120917&utm_medium=email (accessed August 11, 2019). Even prior to his interview with Gross, however, Cizik's activism with regard to environmental policy and what he understood to be a "new evangelicalism" had caused unease among the ranks of religious rightists like James Dobson (Focus on the Family) and Tony Perkins (Family Research Council). Wrote Perkins in a blog post for the Family Research Council shortly after Cizik's NPR interview: "This is the risk of walking through the green door of environmentalism and global warming—you risk being blinded by the green light and losing your sense of direction. How else can you explain enthusiastic support for what will probably be the nation's most pro-abortion, anti-family president in our nation's 232 year history?" Tony Perkins, "If Rich Cizik Doesn't Speak for Them, Who Does He Speak For?" *FRCBlog*, December 10, 2008, http://www.frcblog.com/2008/12/if-naes-rich-cizik-doesnt-speak-for-them-who-does-he-speak-for/ (accessed August 11, 2019).

12    See Larsen, "God's Gardeners," 55–56. The fact that Earth Day is celebrated on April 22, which coincides with Lenin's birthday, helped stereotype environmentalists as communists (Larsen, "God's Gardeners," 135).

[13] Dean Ohlman, "The Evangelical Creation Care Movement: A Brief History," Sustainlane, entry posted June 16, 2009, http://www.sustainlane.com/review/the-evangelical-creation-care-movement-a-brief-history/NADJNPTDJU2U9SW7CQCJVTWPYAMD (accessed July 17, 2009).

[14] Francis A. Schaeffer, *Pollution and the Death of Man: The Christian View of Ecology* (London: Hodder and Stoughton, 1970). Quotations in this paragraph are taken from Schaeffer, *Pollution*. For "men do what they think," see Schaeffer, *Pollution*, 10 (emphasis original).

[15] Schaeffer, *Pollution*, 32–33.

[16] Schaeffer, *Pollution*, 29–69.

[17] For "do justice to the testimony of Scripture," see Bouma-Prediger, *For the Beauty*, 120. In addition to his acknowledgment that Christians had "missed the opportunity to help man save the earth," Schaeffer lamented that "in our generation *we are losing an evangelistic opportunity*, because when modern young people . . . have a real sensitivity to nature, they turn to the hippy communities or mentality, where there is at least a genuine sense of nature (even if a wrong one), because they have seen that most Christians simply do not care about the beauty of nature, or nature as such. So we have not only missed our opportunity to save the earth for man but this also partly accounts for the fact that *we have largely missed an opportunity for reaching the twentieth century*," *Pollution*, 62 (emphasis added).

[18] See Larsen, "God's Gardeners," 97–129. For "neglected" and followed "the conservative and business-friendly orthodoxy," see Balmer, *Thy Kingdom Come*, 143–4.

[19] Larsen, "God's Gardeners," 114–28. For "creation-care theology" as a need that had to be fulfilled before more concrete environmental actions, see Calvin B. DeWitt, "The Scientist and the Shepherd: The Emergence of Evangelical Environmentalism," in *The Oxford Handbook of Religion and Ecology*, ed. Roger S. Gottlieb (Oxford: Oxford University Press, 2006), 569. Regarding DeWitt as the "grandfather" of creation care, see Janel Curry, e-mail interview by author, September 25, 2009.

[20] DeWitt, "The Scientist," 578–79.

[21] Loren E. Wilkinson, ed., *Earthkeeping: Christian Stewardship of Natural Resources* (Grand Rapids: Eerdmans, 1980). For "human-subduing-which-is-service," see Loren E. Wilkinson, ed., *Earthkeeping in the '90s: Stewardship of Creation*, rev. ed. (Grand Rapids: Eerdmans, 1991), 226. Regarding "most clearly defined," see Larsen, "God's Gardeners," 249.

[22] Regarding Au Sable as "the first evangelical environmental organization," see Larsen, "God's Gardeners," 226. Au Sable Trails Camp for Youth was founded by Dr. Harold Snyder, a professor at Taylor University (Upland, Indiana), and three of his colleagues in 1961. For more detailed information on Au Sable, see "Our Story," Au Sable Institute of Environmental Studies, https://www.ausable.org/our-story (accessed August 25, 2019).

[23] Larsen, "God's Gardeners," 181–204.

[24] The leading study of the main frames of Christian Ecotheology is Kearns, "Saving the Creation: Christian Environmentalism." See also Brulle, *Agency*, 228–35. For reflects "the differences," see Kearns, "Saving the Creation: Christian Environmentalism," 57. Like Brulle (*Agency, Democracy, and Nature*) and Fowler (*The Greening of Protestant Thought*), Kearns ponders that Ecofeminism might be a fourth ecotheological ethic, considering that many ecofeminists are Christians and that Ecofeminism has influenced all three emerging modes of Christian Ecotheology. However, since many ecofeminists also oppose Christianity and other systems of belief, Kearns argues convincingly that Ecofeminism does not qualify as a fourth category of Christian Ecotheology. Regarding creation spirituality's

orientation "to a possible new religion" and the evangelical ecotheological adherence to a theologically conservative framework, see also Kearns, "Saving the Creation: Christian Environmentalism," 60–62.

[25]  Quotations and explanations in this and the following two paragraphs are taken from Kearns, "Saving the Creation: Christian Environmentalism."

[26]  For "work from parachurch groups" and "firmly located," see Kearns, "Saving the Creation: Christian Environmentalism," 57. The United Church of Christ's Social Justice Committee played a key role in getting the environmental justice movement off the ground as it was deeply involved in the 1984 toxic waste struggles in Warren County, North Carolina, and subsequently commissioned and helped facilitate a nationwide study on toxic waste in the United States. This 1987 study showed that African Americans, Latinos, and Native Americans were more likely to be exposed to toxic waste than white Americans and propagated the concepts of "environmental racism" and "environmental justice" (Gottlieb, *A Greener Faith*, 134–38). For eco-justice as a variety of the Environmental Justice frame, see also Gottlieb, *A Greener Faith*, 45 and Brulle, *Agency*, 230. For potential limits in compatibility between the two, see Kearns, "Saving the Creation: Christian Environmentalism," 64.

[27]  Fowler (*The Greening*, 76) notes that "stewardship has been the environmentalist path most often proposed by Protestant Christians seeking to serve God and God's creation" since 1970, yet there has been no generally agreed upon definition. During our interview, DeWitt emphasized that one of the major purposes of Au Sable under his directorship until 2005 was "to manage the meaning of 'stewardship,' nationally and internationally" out of fear that economic interests would usurp the term and use it in a misleading way. Although Au Sable's board never accepted this task as the primary mission of the institute, DeWitt personally did what he could in this respect and regards Au Sable as "instrumental in reintroducing the word into Western culture." Calvin DeWitt, interview by author, Town of Dunn, Wis., April 10, 2010. For stewardship as "earthkeeping" and "caring," see DeWitt, "The Scientist," 569. Chapter 5 deals with the CA extensively. Due to the countermobilization efforts of the CA, especially with regard to climate change, Kearns no longer uses the label "Christian stewards" for green evangelicals involved with the creation care movement; see Kearns, "Role of," 420; and Kearns, "Green Evangelicals," 158. Reserving the stewardship label strictly for affiliates of the CA, however, is in my opinion also misleading because creation care movement leaders often use "creation care" and "stewardship of creation" interchangeably. Regarding mainline Protestant's more celebratory attitude toward nature, see Fowler, *The Greening*, 87.

[28]  See Larsen, "God's Gardeners"; and Ball, "Evangelical Protestants," 85. For detailed information on the evangelical Left during the 1970s and 1980s, see Swartz, *Moral Minority*. Billy Graham, *Approaching Hoofbeats: The Four Horseman of the Apocalypse* (Minneapolis, Minn.: Grason, 1983). Carl F. H. Henry as quoted in Larsen, "God's Gardeners," 217.

[29]  Watt quoted in Larsen, "God's Gardeners," 162. For a detailed account of Watt's positions and the controversy that erupted over his nomination among environmentalists and evangelicals, see Larsen, "God's Gardeners," 160–74. See also Turner and Isenberg, *Republican Reversal*, 55–71. Regarding "divine destruction," see Stephenie Hendricks, *Divine Destruction: Wise Use, Dominion Theology, and the Making of American Environmental Policy*, Melville Manifestos (Hoboken, N.J.: Melville House Publishing, 2005).

[30]    For more information on the wise use movement, see Brulle, *Agency*, 115–31. Regarding wise use rhetoric drawing "on private militia," see Opie, *Nature's Nation*, 431. Both Opie and Hendricks note that the term "wise use" was coined in 1907 by Gifford Pinchot and espoused by Theodore Roosevelt. It was thus a term of the early conservation movement before it became the designation of its more radical and libertarian spin-off movement in the 1980s. For the "perversion of wise use" and the wise use movement's reinvocation of Manifest Destiny, see Hendricks, *Divine Destruction*, 27–58. Environmental journalist Mark Dowie (*Losing Ground*, 11) described Watt as a "self-described apocalyptic." Regarding "Watt was able to," see Larsen, "God's Gardeners," 173.

[31]    Although Larsen mentions one older example of an ecotheology written from a distinctly premillennial dispensationalist perspective (see "God's Gardeners," 252), a recent study by political scientists seems to confirm that end-times thinking causes indifference toward environmental problems, at least when it comes to the problem of climate change: David C. Barker and David H. Bearce, "End-Times Theology, the Shadow of the Future, and Public Resistance to Addressing Global Climate Change," *Political Research Quarterly* 66, no. 2 (2013): 267–79. Veldman, however, critiques the Barker and Bearce study for several methodological flaws and poses that end-times thinking and climate change apathy do not correlate in such a straightforward manner: "Does End-Times Belief Really Cause Climate Change Apathy?" *Religion Dispatches*, August 20, 2013, http://religiondispatches.org/does-end-time-belief-really-cause-climate-change -apathy/ (accessed May 16, 2016). Pike notes that starting with the first emergence of the New Age in the 1970s, Christian concerns about the movement were voiced, in particular regarding its potentially negative influence on children and adolescents. Many Christians thus began to view their opposition to these new religions as being part of the "spiritual war" of good against evil raging on the earth. Sarah M. Pike, *New Age and Neopagan Religions in America* (New York: Columbia University Press, 2004), 161–63. For "the new pagans," see Ron Arnold, quoted in Opie, *Nature's Nation*, 431. Arnold has been influential within the wise use movement since its inception.

[32]    For an extensive sociological account of the history of the New Age and neo-pagan movements in America, see for example Pike, *New Age*. See also Paul Heelas, *The New Age Movement: The Celebration of the Self and the Sacralization of Modernity* (Oxford: Blackwell, 1996). Regarding "version of American nature religion," see Catherine L. Albanese, "Fisher Kings and Public Places: The Old New Age in the 1990s," *Annals of the American Academy of Political and Social Science* 527 (1993): 131–43.

[33]    For New Agers "had also aligned themselves," see Albanese, "Fisher Kings and Public Places," 142. For the New Age movement as a threat and/or challenge to evangelical Christianity, see Ball, "Evangelical Protestants," 71–73; Larsen, "God's Gardeners," 209; and John P. Newport, *The New Age Movement and the Biblical Worldview: Conflict and Dialogue* (Grand Rapids: Eerdmans, 1998).

[34]    Constance E. Cumbey, *Hidden Dangers of the Rainbow: The New Age Movement and Our Coming Age of Barbarism* (Shreveport, La.: Huntington House, 1983). Berit Kjos, *Your Kid and the New Age* (Wheaton, Ill.: Victor Books, 1990). Berit Kjos, *Under the Spell of Mother Earth* (Wheaton, Ill.: Victor Books, 1992). Kjos' quotations are from *Under the Spell*, 187–90. According to Randall Balmer (*Thy Kingdom Come*, 145), Cumbey's book "gave political conservatives the excuse they needed to shy away from an issue more commonly associated with the Democratic Party."

35   For "an almost unavoidable, irresistible cultural pressure," see Loren Wilkinson, quoted in Larsen, "God's Gardeners," 209. David Oates was writing for the now non-evangelical magazine *The Other Side* in 1983 and is quoted in Larsen, "God's Gardeners," 212. H. Richard Niebuhr, *Christ & Culture*, expand. ed. (San Francisco: HarperSanFrancisco, 2001).

## 3 PIONEER CREATION CARE ORGANIZATIONS

1   DeWitt, "The Scientist," 569.

2   Regarding green Protestants' initial strategies to tackle environmental issues and "a choice permeated with ambivalence," see Fowler, *The Greening*, 160; 168–70. For mainstream environmental movement organizations' professionalization and shift of focus to lobby Washington after the election of Ronald Reagan, see Bosso, *Environment*, 86–95.

3   DeWitt quotations in this paragraph are taken from DeWitt, interview. For DeWitt's being "born this way," see Edward R. Brown, attending the Calvin B. DeWitt interview by author, Town of Dunn, Wis., April 10, 2010.

4   According to Evans and Evans, the Western academic understanding of the relationship between science and religion has traditionally been limited by the framework of an "epistemological warfare narrative." Social-institutional studies that examine actual public conflicts between religion and science tell a different story, however. Thus, Evans and Evans ("Religion and Science," 87–105) suggest that "the best empirical work comes from treating religion and science not as predetermined categories but as the words and actions of institutionally embedded persons." DeWitt quotations in this paragraph are taken from Calvin B. DeWitt, "Science, Scripture, and Con-serving Creation," in *Holy Ground: A Gathering of Voices on Caring for Creation*, ed. Lyndsay Moseley (San Francisco: Sierra Club Books, 2008), 75–76. Here, DeWitt cites the first and second article of "The Confession of Faith." For "most elegant book" and "creatures great and small," see DeWitt, "Science, Scripture," 75–76.

5   Mark Stoll argues that the Protestant theology and doctrine regarding nature is complex and ambiguous, and that both capitalism and environmentalism in America have Calvinist roots. The "book of nature" was important not only to the early transcendentalists and the first environmentalists like Muir; it was also important long before to Cotton Mather and Jonathan Edwards, and later on to prominent modern environmentalists like Rachel Carson and David Brower. Mark Stoll, *Protestantism, Capitalism, and Nature in North America* (Albuquerque: University of New Mexico Press, 1997). Larsen critiques that Muir's theism was much closer to Emerson and Thoreau's transcendentalism than to nineteenth-century American Evangelicalism. David K. Larsen, "God's Wilds: John Muir's Vision of Nature by Dennis C. Williams," *The Journal of Religion* 83, no. 2 (2003): 284–85. Quotations in this paragraph are taken from DeWitt, "Science, Scripture," 79; 77.

6   DeWitt, "The Scientist," 585.

7   DeWitt, "The Scientist," 576. For an earlier text exemplifying DeWitt's understanding of the science-ethics-praxis triad, see Calvin B. DeWitt, "Knowing and Doing: The Science-Ethics-Praxis Triad and the Human Predicament," *Green Cross* (Winter 1997): 10–11.

8   For "a reasonably coherent story," see Bruce, *The Rise and Fall*, 76–77. Regarding DeWitt's understanding of "two great divides," see Calvin B. DeWitt, "The Place of

Creation in Today's Missionary Discourse: Evangelical Environmentalism in America," in *Missiology and the Environment*, ed. Lukas Vischer (Geneva, Switzerland: John Knox Center, 2007), 176–78.

9    DeWitt, "The Place of Creation," 176–78.

10    DeWitt, "The Place of Creation," 176–78. For Schaeffer's understanding of the "covenant of creation," see *Pollution*, 29–51.

11    DeWitt, "The Place of Creation," 176–78. DeWitt, interview.

12    Regarding "Babies or Birds?" see for instance D. James Kennedy and Jerry Newcombe, *How Would Jesus Vote? A Christian Perspective on the Issues* (Colorado Springs, Colo.: WaterBrook Press, 2008), 139. For "trees have souls," see image seen on *Liberal Logic 101*, a Religious Right blog designed to help "those of us with brains understand how 'Liberal Logic' works," at http://LiberalLogic101.com (accessed May 4, 2014).

13    DeWitt, interview. As DeWitt put it, "But the Christian Reformed and generally the Reformed tradition . . . has a much stronger academic component . . . and scholarly . . . and justice. Hunger. Creation. So, Princeton Theological Seminary, in those early days, was pretty key here, nationally, probably even internationally, but it was key in my education at Calvin College because the idea there . . . was that you had to have a real liberal arts education. You had to understand the society, you had to understand nature, you had to understand astronomy, and you had to know art and music. And what the Bible colleges were doing, [was] saying no, you just need to know the Bible." Although evangelical environmental thinking was largely triggered by pressure from the surrounding non-evangelical culture, the Christian Reformed tradition, to which DeWitt belongs, seems to have been much more open and conducive to ecological considerations than what DeWitt calls "the Bible colleges." DeWitt, interview. While leaders within the creation care movement have different denominational backgrounds, adherents to the Christian Reformed tradition seem to have played an outstanding role among early academic creation care proponents. In addition, Calvin College in Grand Rapids, Michigan, seems to have played a supportive role within the movement. Since its founding in 1876, Calvin College has been shaped by several Dutch Calvinist thinkers, most notably among them theologian and politician Abraham Kuyper (1837–1920). As sociologist Alan Wolfe notes, unlike American fundamentalists, those Dutch Calvinist thinkers "took very seriously the life of the mind in ways that set them apart from anti-intellectualism;" "The Evangelical Mind Revisited," *Change: The Magazine of Higher Learning* 38, no. 2 (2006): 9–13. In particular, Kuyper, who founded the Free University in Amsterdam in 1880, left a lasting description of (Neo-)Calvinism as a way of life with his six Stone Lectures at Princeton in 1898 (published in England under the title *Calvinism* in 1932) and profoundly influenced the Reformed community in North America. Kuyper's understanding that ideas have consequences and that there is a significant difference with real world impacts between the Christian worldview, on the one hand, and non-Christian worldviews on the other, also influenced Francis Schaeffer's social and political activism (Hart, *That Old-Time Religion*, 138–40). That said, it does not seem justified to claim that a background in the Christian Reformed tradition is generally more conducive to environmental concern and engagement, especially since key evangelical environmental skeptics engaged in countermobilization efforts are apparently also influenced by Reformed theology and Schaeffer's understanding of worldviews (see chapter 5). Regarding the decline of denominationalism in America, see Wuthnow, *The Restructuring*. For "trivialization of creation," see DeWitt, interview.

14    DeWitt, interview.

15    DeWitt, interview. DeWitt was a founding member of the North American Conference on Christianity and Ecology, now Network Alliance of Congregations Caring for the Earth (NACCE), which no longer identifies as evangelical. During the first NACCE conference in 1987, a group of religiously disenfranchised and spiritually/theologically more progressive NACCE members split off and founded the North American Coalition on Religion and Ecology (NACRE), which embraced the ecotheology of creation spirituality described in the previous chapter. During the interview, DeWitt also mentioned the organizational difficulties he encountered through NACCE and his more strongly pronounced conviction to work within the evangelical church. For more details regarding creation spirituality and the NACCE/NACRE split, see Kearns, "Saving the Creation: Christian Environmentalism," 60–62.

16    See Au Sable Institute, "Our Story," *Ausable.org*, https://www.ausable.org/our-story (accessed September 25, 2019). For the organization's mission, see *Ausable.org*, https://www.ausable.org/ (accessed September 25, 2019).

17    For "bridge-building and 'defragmentation,'" see DeWitt, "Science, Scripture," 86–87. DeWitt, interview; and DeWitt, statements made during the CCCC in Judson, Illinois, August 6–7, 2009. Regarding the IEEN soon being "overshadowed" by EEN, see Larsen, "God's Gardeners," 243. The UK-based "educational charity" called John Ray Initiative was founded in 1997 and promotes "responsible environmental stewardship in accordance with Christian principles and the wise use of science and technology." Patrons of the initiative include the Archbishop of Canterbury, Calvin DeWitt, Sir Ghillean Prance, and the former Rev. John Stott. See "The John Ray Initiative," in *The Care of Creation: Focusing Concern and Action*, ed. R. J. Berry (Downers Grove, Ill.: InterVarsity, 2000), 205–6. Sir John Houghton, chairman of the initiative, was also chairman (since 1992 co-chairman) of the Science Working Group of the Intergovernmental Panel on Climate Change (IPCC) between 1988 and 2002.

18    Plant With Purpose, "History," Internet Archive: Wayback Machine, captured on June 1, 2013, https://web.archive.org/web/20130601222055/http://www.plantwithpurpose.org/history (accessed September 27, 2019). For "address the environmental, economic, and spiritual needs," cf. "Bylaws of Floresta USA," included in *Form 990: Return of Organization Exempt From Income Tax: Floresta USA Incorporated* (Internal Revenue Service, 2006; retrieved from GuideStar USA, Inc.). PWP's mission statement is quoted from Plant With Purpose, "Annual Report 2009" (San Diego, CA: Plant With Purpose, July 2008–June 2009), 2.

19    See Scott C. Sabin, *Tending to Eden: Environmental Stewardship for God's People*, ed. Kathy Ide (Valley Forge, Pa.: Judson Press, 2010), 50–51.

20    Sabin, *Tending to Eden*, 50–51.

21    Plant With Purpose, "Did You Know Planting Trees Is One Of The Most Effective Ways Of Fighting Poverty?" (San Diego, CA: Plant With Purpose). This PWP information brochure exemplifies the contrast between "a village without purpose" and "a village that plants with purpose" by graphically depicting the former with the help of the colors beige, brown, and black as barren and hopeless, and by contrasting it with a lush and green village with an intact infrastructure, including a school and a Christian church. For PWP's tree count as of 2018, see Philippe Lazaro, "The 2018 Annual Report is Here," *Plantwithpurpose.org*, https://plantwithpurpose.org/2019annualreport/ (accessed September 27, 2019).

22    Plant With Purpose, "Did You Know."

23    "Pat Robertson says Haiti paying for 'pact to the devil'," Haiti Earthquake, *CNN*, January 13, 2010, http://edition.cnn.com/2010/US/01/13/haiti.pat.robertson/index .html (accessed September 27, 2019). For PWP's response and other quotations in this paragraph, see Plant With Purpose, "Five Years After the Haiti Earthquake: Reflecting on Impact," January 15, 2015, https://www.plantwithpurpose.org/blog/five-years-after -the-haiti-earthquake/ (accessed June 13, 2015).

24    Sabin, *Tending to Eden*, 104–5. For "landmark legislation," see Deann Alford, "Trees of Life: How Floresta integrates development discipleship, and creation care overseas," *Christianity Today*, November 20, 2009, http://www.christianitytoday.com/ct/2009/ november/32.54.html (accessed April 6, 2015). Regarding "unlikely environmentalist," see Wilkinson, *Between God & Green*, 111.

25    Sabin, *Tending to Eden*, 1.

26    Sabin, *Tending to Eden*, 1–4.

27    Regarding "was the Christian" and "planting trees for Jesus," see Sabin, *Tending to Eden*, 10. For "no intention" and "foundational," see Sabin, *Tending to Eden*, xv. Sabin describes one of the last steps in his gradual conversion to creation care in the introduction to his book: "As I observed these mountains [due to charcoal production, the depleted hills of southern Haiti], I realized how fundamental the work of reforestation and restoration is to the needs of the poor. And somehow I knew God was calling me to this ministry. At the time I didn't realize how strongly the Bible encourages us to be good stewards of God's creation. I didn't understand that caring for the environment is good and necessary because it shows respect and love for the Creator. I just knew people needed trees." Sabin, *Tending to Eden*, xvi.

28    Sabin, *Tending to Eden*, 114; xvi-xvii; 66. For "broken quality of life," see Donald Miller, *Blue Like Jazz: Nonreligious Thoughts on Christian Spirituality* (Nashville, Tenn.: Thomas Nelson, 2003), 14. In another part of the book, Miller (*Blue Like Jazz*, 77) describes the human experience as "living in the wreckage of the fall." See also Dean Ohlman, "The Evangelical Christian's Relationship to Governments and to Individuals that Influence Economic Policy," Dean Ohlman Private Papers, Grand Rapids, Mich. (courtesy of Dean Ohlman, April 2010); Schaeffer, *Pollution*, 48–49; and creation care advocate Scott R. Rodin's book-length exposition on the topic, *Stewards in the Kingdom* (Downers Grove, Ill.: InterVarsity, 2000). Regarding the biblical vision of *shalom*, see for instance Bouma-Prediger, *For the Beauty*, 96–98.

29    Sabin, *Tending to Eden*, xvii. For more details, see Sabin's second chapter, "A Vicious Cycle," 10–21.

30    Sabin, *Tending to Eden*, xviii.

31    Sabin, *Tending to Eden*, 60–72. As Deann Alford reported from the Dominican Republic for *CT*: "Floresta also promotes the gospel as central to any lasting cultural change. It believes that hope in Christ brings a shift in worldview and empowers the poor who subsist outside the globalized economy. It has been Floresta's experience that without Christian discipleship, some farmers are tempted to squander their new-found profits instead of investing in their communities, farms, or families. With Floresta's encouragement, 61 churches in 40 Dominican communities launched 288 Bible studies for Floresta's program participants in 2008. About 2,000 farmers attended the Floresta Bible studies, and about 500 embraced Christ as their Savior." Alford, "Trees of Life."

32   Sabin, *Tending to Eden*, 86; 67.

33   Sabin, *Tending to Eden*, 63–66.

34   According to a GuideStar search on May 12, 2018, the budget of PWP amounted to $4,343,000, thus by far exceeding the budgets of the other creation care organizations. Sabin, *Tending to Eden*, 114.

35   Sabin, *Tending to Eden*, 89–92; 96. Sabin explains that on his journey toward environmentalism he has met "many Christian biologists and ecologists who have helped [him] to rediscover awe and wonder in creation and to see the signature of the Creator in unexpected places" (*Tending to Eden*, 109).

36   Regarding "'safe' alternative," see Larsen, "God's Gardeners," 230. Other quotations in this paragraph are from Ohlman, interview; and Dean Ohlman, "Finding the Lost Fundamental," Dean Ohlman Private Papers, Grand Rapids, Mich. (courtesy of Dean Ohlman, April 2010). According to Larsen, a (possibly shorter) version of "Finding the Lost Fundamental" was published as Dean Ohlman, "Finding the Lost Fundamental: A Personal Reflection," *Target Earth* 1, no. 4 (1997): 7. See "God's Gardeners," 231. Throughout this book, quotes are taken from the version I personally received from Ohlman in April 2010.

37   Writes Larsen ("God's Gardeners," 210): "It is impossible to gauge the extent to which the association of environmentalism with the New Age made evangelicals hesitant to identify with environmentalism." Ohlman, interview.

38   Ohlman, interview. Dean Ohlman, "This Is Our Father's World—a Christian View of Ecology," in *Under the Spell of Mother Earth*, by Berit Kjos (Wheaton, Ill.: Victor Books, 1992), 161.

39   Mike Samuels and Hal Zina Bennett, *Well Body, Well Earth: The Sierra Club Environmental Health Sourcebook* (San Francisco: Sierra Club Books, 1983). For "I was stunned" and a Christian alternative "that relates," see Ohlman, "Finding the Lost Fundamental." For "the granddaddy of environmental action agencies," see Ohlman, "This Is Our Father's World," 161.

40   During our interview, DeWitt noted that Ohlman was "a long-standing friend" of his who "goes way back before that time" (i.e., back before Ohlman founded the CNF in 1989). Although less publicly visible than DeWitt, Ohlman has been a key figure of evangelical creation care since the movement's early days, enjoying grandfather status within the creation care community as well.

41   Ohlman's brother was a land developer, and he and his wife had a charitable trust, out of which they provided the start-up money for the organization and Ohlman's salary for the duration of eighteen months; Ohlman, interview. Regarding his "dream to develop a sort of Audubon Society for Christians" and "even address," see Ohlman, "Finding the Lost Fundamental," 4.

42   Christian Nature Federation, brochure, Dean Ohlman Private Papers, Grand Rapids, Mich. (courtesy of Dean Ohlman, April 2010).

43   For "right up front," see Ohlman, interview. The "Member's Understanding" on the back of CNF membership cards reads as follows: "I believe a personal, caring God created the heavens and the earth, and that He created mankind in His own image. I understand that human beings are unique in all of creation. Endowed alone with the ability to reason and to make moral choices, mankind has a superior position to the rest of creation which involves a God-given authority and responsibility to care for it as a good steward. While recognizing that the finite human mind cannot fully comprehend the

'why' nor the 'how' of the creation process, I nonetheless thank God for the natural world that sustains life and humbly submit myself to the earthkeeping responsibilities handed down to me as a descendant of the caretakers of Eden." Christian Nature Federation, membership card, Dean Ohlman Private Papers, Grand Rapids, Mich. (courtesy of Dean Ohlman, April 2010).

[44]    Ohlman, interview. Christian Nature Federation, bumper sticker, Dean Ohlman Private Papers, Grand Rapids, Mich. (courtesy of Dean Ohlman, April 2010).

[45]    Ohlman, interview.

[46]    Ohlman, interview. Information on the McColl Superfund site was derived from United States Environmental Protection Agency, "Pacific Southwest, Region 9: Superfund: McColl," http://yosemite.epa.gov/r9/sfund/r9sfdocw.nsf/BySite/McColl? (accessed May 12, 2015). For "confession," "the reality," and "began suggesting," see Ohlman, "Finding the Lost Fundamental," 5.

[47]    Ohlman, interview. Dannemeyer served as U.S. Representative for the 39th Congressional District of California from 1979 until 1993. Comments Ohlman on his public criticism of Dannemeyer's positions: "And so I began to write some editorials for the *Orange County Register* in opposition to Will Dannemeyer and his callous approach to, you know, 'Forget the dumb bird . . . build! People have the right to build whether or not' . . . and I was all of a sudden becoming an environmentalist! And it shocked me, and it shocked everybody else." Ohlman, interview.

[48]    Ohlman, interview. For "after three thrilling," see Ohlman, "Finding the Lost Fundamental," 5. World Vision is the largest humanitarian organization in the world and was, as of 2005, one of Evangelicalism's largest nonprofits (Lindsay, *Faith in the Halls*, 214). The next chapter provides more details on the organization's connection to the creation care movement.

[49]    Regarding the difficulties of organizational survival, see Bosso, *Environment*, 102. For "have a harder time," see Bosso, *Environment*, 101. For "challenged to repent," see Larsen, "God's Gardeners," 234.

[50]    Ohlman, interview.

[51]    Dean Ohlman, unrecorded conversation with author while touring RBC Ministries on April 8, 2010. For "empire," see DeWitt, interview. Further information on RBC Ministries was derived from info materials picked up while touring the organization on April 8, 2010, and from Ann Byle, "RBC Shuffles Leadership Roles," *Mlive.com*, October 15, 2011, https://www.mlive.com/living/grand-rapids/2011/10/rbc_ministries _shuffles_leader.html (accessed October 3, 2019).

[52]    Dean Ohlman, *Celebrating the Wonder of Creation*, Discovery Series, ed. David Sper (Grand Rapids: RBC Ministries, 1998; 2004); *Celebrating the Wonder of a Tree*, Discovery Series, ed. David Sper (Grand Rapids: RBC Ministries, 2002); *Celebrating the Wonder of Water*, Discovery Series, ed. David Sper (Grand Rapids: RBC Ministries, 2003); *Celebrating the Wonder of Soil*, Discovery Series, ed. David Sper (Grand Rapids: RBC Ministries, 2006); *Celebrating the Wonder of the Wilderness*, Discovery Series, ed. David Sper (Grand Rapids: RBC Ministries, 2007). For "wrong attitude" and "stimulate," see Ohlman, *Celebrating the Wonder of Creation*, 32. Originally, Thomas Aquinas is accredited with stating, "Any error about creation also leads to an error about God" (quoted in Bouma-Prediger, *For the Beauty*, 13). In an article published a year before *Celebrating the Wonder of Creation*, Ohlman also referred to love and obedience as the primary reasons why Christians should care about the earth. In this context he spoke of the biblical creation care mandate as the "forgotten

mandate" of the evangelical church: Dean Ohlman, "Green Cross Bible Study," *Green Cross* (Fall 1997): 17.

[53] Ohlman, interview. Dean Ohlman, *The Genesis Account of Creation: Diffusing the Controversy*, Discovery Series, ed. David Sper (Grand Rapids: RBC Ministries, 2008).

[54] Ohlman, interview. Regarding "advocate for property rights," see Sabin, *Tending to Eden*, 108–9. For "robust free markets" and "the practice of 'compassionate capitalism,'" see Ohlman, "The Evangelical Christian's Relationship." For "hard, cold, and unloving" and "with compassion," see Francis Schaeffer, quoted in Ohlman, "The Evangelical Christian's Relationship."

[55] For "governments have," see Ohlman, "The Evangelical Christian's Relationship." Regarding "negative witnesses," see Dean Ohlman, "The Lion, the Curse, and the Evangelical," July 10, 2008, Dean Ohlman Private Papers, Grand Rapids, Mich. (courtesy of Dean Ohlman, February 2012).

## 4 POLITICALLY UNAFRAID EVANGELICAL ENVIRONMENTAL ORGANIZATIONS

[1] Alexei Laushkin, interview by author, Washington, D.C., August 2, 2010.

[2] For "united more people," see Robert Cahn and Patricia Cahn, "Did Earth Day Change the World?" *Environment* 32, no. 7 (1990): 17. Despite the Reagan administration's "antagonism to environmental regulations at home," in 1988 Reagan signed the Montreal Protocol, an international treaty to phase out CFCs held responsible for the ozone hole over the Antarctic. See Turner and Isenberg, *Republican Reversal*, 145–47.

[3] Larsen, "God's Gardeners," 225–27.

[4] Although the NAE had passed resolutions on the importance of ecological issues and environmental stewardship in 1970–1971 and again in 1990, note that the organization and its former lobbyist Richard Cizik were also concerned about environmentalists' positions on abortion and pantheism. For more details on Cizik's and the NAE's unease regarding the abortion/population-control link prior to Cizik's conversion to environmentalism and climate change activism, see Larsen, "God's Gardeners," 227–30. For climate change had not become "a deeply partisan issue" yet, see Turner and Isenberg, *Republican Reversal*, 157. But nonetheless, between 1970 and 1990, environmentalism and Evangelicalism experienced a gradual politicization along opposing partisan lines. Political polarization intensified over the course of the 1990s despite President Bill Clinton's centrist leanings, which narrowed mainstream environmentalists' tactical options because they were forced to keep depending on the Democratic Party in order to remain involved in the policymaking process (Bosso, *Environment*, 127).

[5] According to Larsen ("God's Gardeners," 132) it was the evangelical social and political activism connected to the Religious Right that ensured that those evangelicals who were concerned about ecological issues would eventually overcome their hesitation to get involved in politics as well. For "giving up," see Dean Ohlman, letter to Cliff Benzel, November 4, 1993, Dean Ohlman Private Papers, Grand Rapids, Mich. (courtesy of Dean Ohlman, April 2010).

[6] Target Earth's roots go back to a Christian retreat center called Hidden Lakes, which was created by Roy and D'Aun Goble in 1986, in the Sierra mountains near San Francisco. In 1993 Hidden Lakes was renamed Christian Environmental Association, and the board hired Gordon D. Aeschliman (1957–) to turn the organization into an evangelical environmental group with the motto, "Serving the earth, Serving the poor." Apart

from its strong eco-justice orientation, Target Earth has promoted direct creation care efforts, operated a nature conservancy in Belize (i.e., the Eden Conservancy Project), published a bimonthly magazine, and catered mainly to evangelical students. Aeschliman was an avid promoter of creation care throughout the 1990s and early 2000s. He copublished various books with Tony Campolo and served as editor for *Prism* magazine, a publication of Ronald Sider's ESA. For more information on the founding history and initial activities of the organization, see Larsen, "God's Gardeners," 281–87.

[7] Quite similar to the second provision of Lynn White's thesis thirty years prior, after the end of the Cold War, there developed an understanding among scientists and (secular) environmentalists that recruiting the major religious traditions as allies was crucial in order to tackle the global eco-crisis. Explains Tucker: "Religions were acknowledged by scientists in the early 1990s as having an important role to play in revisioning a sustainable future. They recognized the importance of religion as key repositories of deep civilizational values and indispensable motivators in moral transformation around consumption, energy use, and environmental protection." Mary Evelyn Tucker, "Religion and Ecology: Survey of the Field," in *The Oxford Handbook of Religion and Ecology*, ed. Roger S. Gottlieb (Oxford: Oxford University Press, 2006), 402.

[8] See for example Lyndsay Moseley, "Editors' Preface," in *Holy Ground: A Gathering of Voices on Caring for Creation*, ed. Lyndsay Moseley and the staff of Sierra Club Books (San Francisco: Sierra Club Books, 2008), 9.

[9] In his book *Earth in the Balance*, Gore dedicates one chapter to the "Environmentalism of the Spirit," which attempts to reconcile the religious, scientific, and philosophical understanding of nature. Here, Gore also mentions his efforts to organize the series of dialogs between religious leaders and scientists at Saint John together with Morton, Carl Sagan, and then Senator Tim Wirth (D-CO). Al Gore, *Earth in the Balance: Forging a New Common Purpose* (London: Earthscan, 1992), 238–65.

[10] For Sider's and ESA's association with the evangelical Left, see for instance Joel Fetzer and Gretchen S. Carnes, "Dr. Ron Sider: Mennonite Environmentalist on the Evangelical Left," in *Religious Leaders and Faith-Based Politics: Ten Profiles*, ed. Jo Renee Formicola and Hubert Morken (Lanham, Md.: Rowman & Littlefield, 2001), 159–73; Laura R. Olson, "The Religious Left in Contemporary American Politics," *Politics, Religion & Ideology* 12, no. 3 (2011): 271–94; and Swartz, *Moral Minority*. For Sider's classification as a centrist, see Gushee, *The Future*, 92–94. According to Lindsay, Sider has not endorsed a presidential candidate since George McGovern in 1972. He voted for George W. Bush in 2000 "because he was drawn to the president's agenda for compassionate conservatism" but was later disappointed with Bush. Additionally, Lindsay (*Faith in the Halls*, 68) notes that Sider was mentioned favorably by many of Lindsay's evangelical interviewees for his "bridging ability" across the political divide. Writes Larsen ("God's Gardeners," 238): "Although Evangelicals for Social Action (ESA) tended toward the political left on most issues, it shied away from the radical politics typical of the Sojourners Community and *The Other Side* magazine while resolutely remaining within the mainstream of evangelical opinion on issues like abortion and homosexuality." Regarding the fact that Sider had never heard of Gorman and "mainline Protestant friend," see Ronald Sider, "ESA's History: A Reflection," *Evangelicalsforsocialaction.org*, http://www.evangelicalsforsocialaction .org/about/history/ (accessed October 7, 2019).

[11] According to Gushee (*The Future*, 94), Sider was influenced "by the example of Senator Mark Hatfield (R-OR) and by Catholic thought in the 1970s and 1980s" and

had thus "long embraced a 'consistent pro-life agenda.'" The concept of a consistent life ethic "was first publicly introduced through Cardinal Joseph Bernardin's Gannon Lecture at Fordham University" in the early 1980s and has entered the public lexicon and gained some scholarly attention since then: James D. Unnever, John P. Bartowski, and Francis T. Cullen, "God Imagery and Opposition to Abortion and Capital Punishment: A Partial Test of Religious Support for the Consistent Life Ethic," *Sociology of Religion* 71, no. 3 (2010): 308–9. For a detailed formulation, see Joseph Bernardin, *The Seamless Garment* (Kansas City, Mo.: National Catholic Reporter, 1984). Although there used to be a sharp cultural boundary dividing American evangelicals and Catholics, scholars of the new evangelical engagement note an "evangelical-Catholic rapprochement" long in the making: R. Stephen Warner, "Evangelicals of the 1970s and 2010s: What's the Same, What's Different, and What's Urgent," in *The New Evangelical Social Engagement*, ed. Brian Steensland and Philip Goff (New York: Oxford University Press, 2014), 286. On the influence of Catholic social thinking on various evangelical leaders and institutions, such as Sider, Gushee, and the NAE, see also Omri Elisha, "All Catholics Now? Specters of Catholicism in Evangelical Social Engagement," in *The New Evangelical Social Engagement*, ed. Brian Steensland and Philip Goff (New York: Oxford University Press, 2014), 73–93. Regarding a "biblically informed pro-life agenda," see Ronald J. Sider, *Completely Pro-Life* (Downers Grove, Ill.: InterVarsity, 1987), 189. For other quotations in this paragraph, see Sider, *Completely Pro-Life*, 189.

12    Regarding Sider's affirmation that "dominion [was] not devastation" and the other quotations in this sentence, see Sider, *Completely Pro-Life*, 14. For "life-and-death-issue" and "vigorous political action," see Sider, *Completely Pro-Life*, 194–96.

13    See Ronald J. Sider, "Biblical Foundations for Creation Care," in *The Care of Creation: Focusing Concern and Action*, ed. R. J. Berry (Downers Grove, Ill.: InterVarsity, 2000), 43–44. Sider, *Completely Pro-Life*, 14.

14    For "wise choice" and "was sufficiently liberal," see Larsen, "God's Gardeners," 238. Robert Seiple was World Vision's former CEO. Seiple stepped down to assume the post of the State Department's first ambassador-at-large for religious freedom under President Clinton in 1998 (Lindsay, *Faith in the Halls*, 214).

15    Larsen, "God's Gardeners," 240–42; 257. Most of the information Larsen provides about the founding of the EEN is derived from phone interviews he conducted with Sider, Seiple, and James Ball in April and May 2001.

16    Au Sable Institute, "Evangelical Christianity and the Environment," Summarizing Committee Report, Au Sable Forum, August 1992, http://www.ausable.org/or.fora.1992 .summary.cfm (accessed August 7, 2008). DeWitt, "The Scientist," 580. Evangelical Environmental Network, "EEN Board Retreat Materials," Board Strategic Planning Retreat, June 13–14, 2008 (courtesy of Janel Curry, 2011).

17    Regarding "catalyst for a new outpouring," see Larsen, "God's Gardeners," 258. NRPE's other partners are the U.S. Conference of Catholic Bishops (USCCB), participating through its Environmental Justice Program (and more recently Catholic Climate Covenant); the ecumenical National Council of Churches of Christ (NCC), which participates through its affiliate Creation Justice Ministries; and the Coalition on Environment and Jewish Life (COEJL), an affiliate of the Jewish Council of Public Affairs. Dedicated to cooperation across theological differences, NRPE partners do not collaborate in a strained fashion. Rather, NRPE leaves it up to each of its partners to implement and communicate common messages and priorities in their own way and to their own audiences, a laissez-

faire approach that was praised early on as rather untypical for interfaith coalitions: "The National Religious Partnership for the Environment (NRPE)," *Green Cross*, Fall 1995, 26. With the establishment of the NRPE, Gorman became the organization's director and the Joint Appeal was dissolved. Currently NRPE is headed by Executive Director Cassandra Carmichael. For more information, see National Religious Partnership for the Environment, *Nrpe.org* (accessed October 7, 2019).

[18]    NCC was officially founded in 1950 and played a crucial role in the civil rights movement of the 1960s, whereas the USCCB was formed in 1966 to represent all active and retired members of the Catholic hierarchy in the United States. Similar to the EEN, NRPE's Jewish partner COEJL was exclusively founded "to create a specifically Jewish response to the environmental crisis" (Gottlieb, *A Greener Faith*, 114).

[19]    Loren E. Wilkinson, "The Making of the Declaration," in *The Care of Creation: Focusing Concern and Action*, ed. R. J. Berry (Downers Grove, Ill.: InterVarsity, 2000), 50–59. Susan (Drake) Emmerich is a longtime evangelical creation care advocate and was also among the few women to attend the CCCC at Judson University in August 2009. A draft was also sent to Dean Ohlman by Ronald Sider; see Ronald Sider, letter to Dean Ohlman, October 12, 1993, Dean Ohlman Private Papers, Grand Rapids, Mich. (courtesy of Dean Ohlman, April 2010). According to Wilkinson ("Making of the Declaration," 51) the EDCC session after the symposium in Chicago was only a reviewing session, which included Sider, DeWitt, Emmerich, former *CT* editor Kenneth Kantzer, and "one or two people from the editorial staff of *Christianity Today*." Regarding signatories from the "mainstream evangelical establishment" and the lack of signatories affiliated with the Religious Right, see Larsen, "God's Gardeners," 271. For information on the "Let the Earth be Glad" kit, see Larsen, "God's Gardeners," 321. Regarding NAE's role as representative of American Evangelicalism, see Robert Booth Fowler et al., *Religion and Politics in America: Faith, Culture, and Strategic Choices*, 3rd ed. (Boulder, Colo.: Westview, 2004), 132. Swartz cautions, however, not to equate the NAE with American Evangelicalism at large because "the National Association of Evangelicals proper consists of only 43 member denominations, [while] scholars consider at least a thousand more of the nearly 4,000 Protestant denominations in the United States to be evangelical." David R. Swartz, "Left Behind: The Evangelical Left and the Limits of Evangelical Politics, 1965–1988, Volume One" (Ph.D. dissertation, University of Notre Dame, 2008), 616. As Lindsay notes, leading evangelicals are "the 'hidden hand' of evangelicalism" and thus important agents when it comes to the legitimation of organizations and initiatives "as their support can secure critical institutional backing." D. Michael Lindsay, "Elite Power: Social Networks within American Evangelicalism," *Sociology of Religion* 67, no. 3 (2006), 215. Public declarations such as the EDCC or the "Chicago Declaration," the founding creed of Sider's ESA, are common within the evangelical community and certainly not uniquely declared by evangelicals associated with EEN and ESA. On its website, the EEN refers to the EDCC as "the foundational statement for those engaged in the ministry of creation care." See Evangelical Environmental Network, "Resources," *Creationcare.org*, https://www.creationcare.org/resources (accessed October 9, 2019).

[20]    Unless otherwise indicated, the following quotes are directly taken from the EDCC. The text of the EDCC can be accessed via EEN's website at Evangelical Environmental Network, "An Evangelical Declaration on the Care of Creation," *Creationcare.org*, https://www.creationcare.org/evangelical_declaration_on_the_care_of_creation (accessed October 9,

2019). For an anthology of contextual and theological commentary on the EDCC, see Berry, *The Care of Creation*.

21   Larsen, "God's Gardeners," 277–78. For "leadership committee," see Larsen, "God's Gardeners," 290. During the CCCC in Elgin, Illinois, in 2009, Dean Ohlman referred to the group as the original "advisory council" for the EEN. According to Ohlman, the CCCC meeting felt like a "reunion" of the CEC. Regarding the names of the attendees listed, see Dean Ohlman, informal conversation with author, Grand Rapids, Mich., April 7, 2010. Several comments Jim Ball made during the CCCC in Washington, D.C., August 2, 2010, support the assumption that the CEC reemerged as the CCCC. See also Ben Lowe, *Green Revolution: Coming Together to Care for Creation* (Downers Grove, Ill.: InterVarsity, 2009), 149.

22   For the text of EEN's resolution and a petition to support it, see Calvin DeWitt and Susan Drake, "Resolution on the Care and Keeping of Creation and Its Living Species," *Green Cross* (Winter 1996): 16–17.

23   See Bruce Barcott, "For God So Loved the World," *Outside Online* (March 2001) https://www.outsideonline.com/1888006/god-so-loved-world (accessed October 10, 2019); Fetzer and Carnes, "Dr. Ron Sider," 166; Kearns, "Noah's Ark," 356–57; and Larsen, "God's Gardeners," 292. For "because God" and "blew away," see Sider, "ESA's History."

24   Barcott, "For God." Jim Ball, comment made during the CCCC in Washington, D.C., August 2, 2010.

25   According to David Gushee (*The Future*, 176), who has been involved with ESA/EEN since 1993 and led the drafting process of the ECI, the growing evangelical impossibility to ignore climate change as an overarching issue of creation care has been due to two developments specifically, which have both occurred in concordance with the growing national attention to the phenomenon: (1) Richard Cizik's decision "to take up the climate change issue" while he was still vice president for governmental affairs at the NAE; (2) Jim Ball's "skillful work" to "engage a widening circle of evangelical leaders in addressing climate change along with other issues." Although Cizik was extremely important for this development because of his NAE position and influence, we need to keep in mind that his turn toward climate change only occurred after Jim Ball had been able to "drag" him to a Global Climate Change conference in Oxford, England, in 2002. It was here where Cizik experienced his "conversion" to the cause; see Richard Cizik quoted in The Great Warming, "Interview," *Thegreatwarming.com*, August 23, 2008, http://www.thegreatwarming.com/revrichardcizik.html (accessed September 10, 2008).

26   For "in a moderate," see Ball, "Evangelical Protestants," 22. Regarding "accepted Jesus" and "Baptist Christian," see James G. Ball, interview by Fabel, "Credo." Regarding Ball's participation in the CEC, see James G. Ball, "Jesus Christ, Creation and the Protection of God's Creatures," *Green Cross* (Winter 1996): 8. For his work with the Union of Concerned Scientists and "understand," see James G. Ball, "Walk the walk . . . and drive the talk," *Creation Care* 19 (Fall 2002), 10.

27   As Ball describes his creation care awakening: "As a child I loved being in the forest surrounded by trees. Unfortunately, at that time no one actively nurtured my love for God's creation. But at Drew, which is described as a 'university in the forest,' another first year graduate student and now close friend began speaking to me about her love for God's creation. At first I just thought that this was simply a charming eccentricity of hers, to put it delicately. Now I know that when Bonnie Gisel began to share her love for God's

creation with me, it changed the direction of my life. When we met I had a deep concern for peace and justice issues; Bonnie slowly and gently showed me that my Christian faith also called me to protect the rest of creation as well. In this sense, Bonnie gave me 'new eyes' through which to see the world—as all great teachers do." James G. Ball, "A Word from EEN's new director: When did your creation-care awakening begin?" *Creation Care* (Winter 2000) http://www.creationcare.org/magazine/winter00.php (accessed August 10, 2008). In his book *Global Warming and the Risen Lord*, Ball describes his turn to creation care in a more unemotional and sober way, diminishing Gisel's role to someone who merely suggested he read the Bible in light of the question why anyone would study the Christian approach to nature. James G. Ball, *Global Warming and the Risen Lord: Christian Discipleship and Climate Change* (Washington, D.C.: Evangelical Environmental Network, 2010), 21.

28    Ball, "A Word." Regarding "that Christ's reconciliation," see Jim Ball, "A Personal Greeting from the President & CEO," *Creationcare.org*, http://www.creationcare.org/welcome.php (accessed March 18, 2009). For the influence of Gore's *Earth in the Balance* and Ball's "calling," see Wilkinson, *Between God & Green*, 21–22. Regarding "touches on many other concerns," see Ball, *Global Warming*, 21.

29    See Ball, "Evangelical Protestants," 400–401. Regarding the importance of climate policy especially, including the acknowledgment that "we should not become myopic in thinking that it all revolves around Washington," see Jim Ball, "From the Publisher's Desk," Creation Care (Summer 2005), http://creationcare.org/magazine/summer05 .php (accessed August 10, 2008). Evangelical Environmental Network, "EEN Board Retreat Materials."

30    Eric Roston, "The Evangelical Activist Preaching for the Planet," *Time*, March 26, 2006, http://content.time.com/time/magazine/article/0,9171,1176991-3,00.html (accessed October 15, 2019). Regarding EEN's participation in the Clinton Global Initiative, see Jim Jewell, interview by author, Suwanee, Ga., April 29, 2010.

31    For "PR coup" and John Stott's role in getting Rick Warren on board of the ECI, see Jewell, interview. Regarding NAE's support of the EEN, see Wilkinson, *Between God & Green*. A creation care conference organized by the EEN and cosponsored by *CT* and the NAE, which took place at the Sandy Cove Christian Conference Center in Maryland in June 2004, "mark[ed] a new phase in the history of evangelical creation-care efforts" (Wilkinson, *Between God & Green*, 25). In James Ball's words, "Simply having the cosponsorship of *CT* and NAE made the event significant. But it was the level of participation from senior leadership that helped to mark the event as historic. . . . What made it what I believe a kairos moment, however, was the work of the Holy Spirit. Ted Haggard, President of the NAE, described this experience as 'an epiphany.' Others stated how they had been 'converted' to the cause. You could hear the ice breaking at the center of evangelical life on our cause. Evangelical creation-care is no longer a fringe movement. It now lives at the center." Ball, "From the Publisher's Desk," *Creation Care* (Fall 2004), http://www.creationcare.org/magazine/fall04.php (accessed August 17, 2008). As an internal EEN document states, "Simply put: without Sandy Cove—no ECI." See Evangelical Environmental Network, "EEN Board Retreat Materials," 8. For the funding of the ECI, see Sheryl Henderson Blunt, "The New Climate Coalition: Evangelical leaders bolster the fight against global warming," *Christianity Today*, February 8, 2006, http://www.christianitytoday.com/ct/2006/februaryweb-only/106-34.0.html (accessed December 4, 2017); and Kevin Kovaleski, "Warming Up to Environmentalism: A Changing

Climate in the Politics of Evangelicals," *Responsive Philanthropy* 3 (2006): 4. As the tax returns of the NRPE show, EEN and NRPE's other partners received allocations from the partnership on a regular basis at least until 2013: EEN obtained $200,000 in 2004/05, $457,000 in 2005/06, and $425,000 in the tax year of 2006/07. It has to be noted, though, that the money that NRPE itself received in public support, such as gifts, grants, contributions, and membership fees, changed drastically between 2009 ($1,300,000) and 2013 ($67,594). This is reflected in the changing sums made available to the organization's partners throughout that time. Whereas the EEN received $902,408 in 2011, a peek year during which NRPE itself received a total of $1,484,050 in public support, EEN received only $164,967 from the NRPE in 2012. Also, in 2011, NCC received $121,000, COEJL $7,000, and USCCB $51,000, whereas in 2012 only EEN and USCCB received grants. In 2013, NRPE was only able to allocate two grants totaling $75,000 to recipients not specified. Unlike Paul Gorman, who retired from NRPE in April 2010, and Matthew Anderson, who filled in between 2010 and 2013, the organization's new executive director Cassandra Carmichael, however, did not receive a compensation from NRPE in 2013. For further information, see NRPE's tax returns available through GuideStar.

32    Evangelical Environmental Network, "EEN Board Retreat Materials," 9. Regarding EEN's employment of the services of Russ Reid Co., see the data provided by The Center for Responsive Politics on the EEN. Note, however, that data is only available for the years 2007 and 2008. The Center for Responsive Politics, "Evangelical Environmental Network," *Opensecrets.org*, http://www.opensecrets.org/lobby/clientsum.php?id=F6634& year=2008 (accessed October 26, 2015).

33    For "past year" and "the EEN," see Rusty Pritchard, "From the Editor," *Creation Care* (Winter 2007), http://www.creationcare.org/magazine/winter07.php (accessed August 17), 2008. Apart from its major campaigns, EEN's *Creation Care* magazine was an important advocacy tool until the network announced the end of its publication in November 2013. In the past, *Creation Care* provided updates on EEN's activities and important environmental policy issues; discussed proposed bills; announced senators' and representatives' positions on certain issues; and advised readers to contact public officials to either get them involved in the environmental debate or thank them for their efforts to address ecological problems. In addition, the magazine assembled articles on ecotheological questions by creation care leaders such as DeWitt, Ohlman, Sider, and many others; gave practical creation care tips; made announcements regarding creation care events and initiatives; and provided book reviews. Alexei Laushkin was one of EEN's full-time staff from 2006 until November 2016. Quotations are taken from Laushkin, interview.

34    For the resonance of the ECI within evangelical churches, see Wilkinson, *Between God & Green*, 85–110.

35    Regarding "unexpected voice," see Kearns, "Noah's Ark," 349. EEN's endangered species campaign was supported by a larger one-million-dollar budget campaign initiated by the Environmental Information Center (EIC); see Larsen, "God's Gardeners," 291; and Kearns, "Noah's Ark," 362 n14. The EIC was formed in 1994 "to work on environmental issues with religious, scientific, consumer and health groups that are not primarily part of the environmental movement;" Peter Steinfels, "Evangelical Group Defends Law Protecting Endangered Species Act as a Modern 'Noah's Ark,'" *The New York Times*, January 31, 1996. As Larsen ("God's Gardeners," 291) comments, "The EIC saw the strategic potential of having a group of evangelicals mount a campaign against conservative Republicans," hence the support. To cover the advertisement

costs of the What Would Jesus Drive? campaign in 2002, $65,000 came from The Energy Foundation—a partnership of major donors including The Pew Charitable Trusts and the MacArthur Foundation—which is interested in finding solutions for the world's energy problems; see Katherine Ellison, "Going for a Sunday Drive: Evangelical Campaign Focuses on Environmental Awareness," *The Washington Post*, November 8, 2002, https://www.washingtonpost.com/archive/politics/2002/11/08/going-for-a-sunday-drive/2b9ae05c-2cac-412a-b57c-4fb8850e8538/?utm_term=.161cc8256cfe (accessed December 4, 2017).

[36]    Quotations are taken from EEN's announcement of the position. The job description was posted on the server of Calvin College in Grand Rapids, Michigan. See Calvin College, "EEN's Strategic Transition," Calvin College, http://www.calvin.edu/~drc5/EEN/ (accessed June 3, 2009). Hescox has been particularly outspoken on the matter of mercury pollution. In February 2012, he testified before the Energy and Power Subcommittee of the U.S. House of Representatives' Energy and Commerce Committee, after the EEN, the NAE, and the USCCB had joined together in 2011 to support a federal mercury standard regulated by the EPA. For Hescox's testimony, see Mitchell C. Hescox, "Witness Testimony," accessed via The Energy and Commerce Committee, "The American Energy Initiative: What EPA's Utility MACT Rule Will Cost U.S. Consumers," February 8, 2012, https://energycommerce.house.gov/sites/republicans.energycommerce.house.gov/files/Hearings/EP/20120208/HHRG-112-IF03-WState-MHescox-20120208.pdf (accessed August 4, 2016).

[37]    "Good News for God's Creation: Green Cross Hires Northwest Director," *Green Cross* (Winter 1997): 5. For "ninety percent," see Peter Illyn, interview by author, March 25, 2010, La Center, Washington.

[38]    Regarding "down the street" and "kind of got in trouble," see Illyn, interview. Tracy Ross, "Hike. Pray. Protest," *Backpacker Magazine* (March 9, 2011) https://www.backpacker.com/stories/hike-pray-protest (accessed October 14, 2019).

[39]    Illyn, interview.

[40]    Peter Illyn, "Belly-Button Christianity," *Notre Dame Journal of Law, Ethics & Public Policy* 23, no. 2 (2009): 615. Quotations in this paragraph are from Ross, "Hike."

[41]    Illyn, "Belly-Button Christianity," 615–17.

[42]    Illyn, "Belly-Button Christianity," 615–17.

[43]    For "site of carnage" and "the words," see Illyn, "Belly-Button Christianity," 617. Regarding "the greatest devastation," "shocked," and "this sense of unnecessary destruction," see Ross, "Hike."

[44]    *Sierra Club v. Morton*, 404 U.S. 727 (1972).

[45]    Illyn, "Belly-Button Christianity," 617.

[46]    Illyn, "Belly-Button Christianity," 618. In the early 1990s, ESA not only became the mother organization of the EEN but also of The Christian Society of the Green Cross, a financially struggling Christian environmental group that catered to a broader evangelical, mainline Protestant, Eastern Orthodox, and Roman Catholic audience with the publication of a creation care magazine called *Green Cross*. The executives of both Green Cross and EEN were housed in the same office space provided by ESA, hence *Green Cross* editor Fred Kruger, a member of the Russian Orthodox Church, also participated in activities of the EEN, and affiliates with the EEN frequently published articles in *Green Cross*, a process that eventually "blurred" the distinction between the two ministries. In the fall of 1997, and in an attempt to lend

the magazine more evangelical credibility, Michael Crook, an evangelical Quaker, was hired to replace Kruger. In the spring of 1998, *Green Cross* was renamed *Creation Care* and became fully integrated as an outreach and education tool of the EEN until the network decided to cease its publication in 2013. For more details surrounding the founding history of The Christian Society of the Green Cross and the merger with the EEN, see Larsen, "God's Gardeners," 267–70; 299–301. Regarding Illyn's position as first regional director in the Pacific Northwest for Green Cross, see Green Cross, "Good News," 5. For "became Restoring Eden in 2001," see Restoring Eden, "History: In the beginning . . ." *Restoringeden.org*, http://restoringeden.org/about/history (accessed June 18, 2014).

[47] CES DBA Creation Care Study Program (CCSP), "Return of Organization Exempt from Income Tax," (IRS 990), 2002–2007. For "three programs," see Illyn, interview. Illyn's description of the CES in 2010 was in line with CES's tax returns at the time. As of July 1, 2014, CES "transferred all assets, liabilities and equities associated with the Restoring Eden program to the Georgia-based non-profit Creation Care, Inc." See Christians for Environmental Stewardship, "Supplemental Information to Form 990 or 990-EZ," 2014. Neither Illyn nor Elisara participated in the CCCC 2009 and 2010. CES representatives present in 2009 were Gretchen Peck and Ben Lowe, both of Renewal at the time. In 2010, only Peck was present while Lowe was running an election campaign against the Republican incumbent of Illinois' 6th congressional district. Lowe functioned as Y.E.C.A.'s first national spokesperson upon the group's founding in 2012; see Ben Lowe, "The Audacity of Faithfulness," *Relevant*, July 17, 2012, http://www.relevantmagazine.com/current/politics/audacity-faithfulness?utm (accessed July 23, 2012).

[48] Restoring Eden, "Mission Statement," *Restoringeden.org*, http://restoringeden.org/about (accessed June 18, 2014).

[49] Illyn, interview.

[50] *Restoringeden.org* (accessed June 18, 2014).

[51] *Restoringeden.org* (accessed June 18, 2014). For "you don't individually stop," see Illyn, interview.

[52] For "just power" and "climate justice," see Restoring Eden, "More on JUST-power," *Restoringeden.org*, http://www.restoringeden.org/campaigns/justpower/more/view (accessed June 18, 2014).

[53] Regarding RE's excursion to Haines and "apologize," see "Peter Illyn, Restoring Eden," *Grist*, March 10, 2003, http://grist.org/article/illyn-restoringeden/full/ (accessed February 10, 2020). When I interviewed Illyn in Washington state in 2010, he had just returned from Washington, D.C. He had visited the capitol with an indigenous Christian friend from Papua New Guinea and a coalition of seventy evangelical college students. Among other lobbying activities, the group had had talks about climate policy and greenhouse gas pollution with then senator John Kerry. For RE's activism in Appalachia specifically, see Ross, "Hike."

[54] Said Illyn (interview) about RE, "We are not focusing that much on angry fundamentalists; we're not as successful down South as we are in the Northwest." Gretchen Peck of CES's Renewal said RE was more "edgy" than other creation care organizations during the CCCC 2010. For Illyn's background in the Jesus Movement, see Illyn, interview. Regarding "lose collection" and "more relaxed brand of evangelicalism," see Hart, *That Old Time Religion*, 191–92. As sociologist Stephen R. Warner ("Evangelicals of the 1970s and 2010s," 181–82) observes: "[The] self-designated Jesus freaks and hippie

Christians . . . and others like them brought the long hair and beards, country dress and folk-rock music, and verbal demonstrativeness of the counterculture into the previously straitlaced world of conservative white American Protestantism, along with their personal histories of interrupted college educations, protest politics, drug use, and sexual experimentation." CES received donations through the Grateful Dead's Rex Foundation and Further Foundation; Illyn, interview. RE, bumper sticker (courtesy of Peter Illyn, March 25, 2010).

55    For "theology of wild," see "Peter Illyn, Restoring Eden." During our interview, Illyn said that he considered himself an evangelical Christian but that he was "not a biblical literalist." Regarding "the wall between," see also Illyn, interview. Illyn's tribal friends from Papua New Guinea consider themselves "belly-button Christians," because despite their adoption of the Christian faith, they view their umbilical cords still connected to their mother, the earth. To Illyn, calling the earth "mother" is not "a slippery slope leading to paganism and earth worship." Rather, citing Romans 8:22, Illyn ("Belly-Button Christianity," 605–7) points out that "even [the Apostle] Paul refers to the earth as mother."

56    Illyn, interview. The Emerging Church and the related New Monasticism may share some similarities with each other but are both social movements of younger Christians in their own right: Brian Steensland and Philip Goff, "Introduction: The New Evangelical Social Engagement," in *The New Evangelical Social Engagement*, ed. Brian Steensland and Philip Goff (New York: Oxford University Press, 2014), 13. Illyn (interview) acknowledges that there are differences between those movements and the creation care movement, but he nevertheless sees them espousing a common missional and relational theology. The case can be made that there is some overlap, especially if we consider a "concern with the evangelical identity and what it has come to represent"—a connecting thread between them. For "concern with," see Steensland and Goff, "Introduction," 14.

57    Illyn, interview. RE partnered with the Wilderness Society and the National Wildlife Federation, for instance, but would not work with "anarchist" groups such as People for the Ethical Treatment of Animals (PETA); Illyn, interview.

58    See Illyn, "Belly-Button Christianity" and Illyn, interview. Illyn has worked closely with younger Christians such as Gretchen Peck and Ben Lowe but also with older and more traditional evangelical leaders within the creation care movement. Among the latter, he has collaborated even with those who have theologically and culturally rather conservative backgrounds, such as Dean Ohlman, who has contributed various articles to RE's website and newsletter. Upon its founding in 2009, Illyn also sat on the board of Creation Care, Inc., which would absorb RE in 2014.

59    See Illyn, "Belly-Button Christianity," and Illyn, interview.


## 5 ORGANIZED EVANGELICAL ENVIRONMENTAL SKEPTICISM

1    Kennedy and Newcombe, *How Would Jesus Vote?*, 135.

2    E. Calvin Beisner, interview by author, Pembroke Pines, Florida, April 27, 2010.

3    Kearns ("Green Evangelicals," 158) uses the term "wise use stewards" for evangelical environmental skeptics affiliated with the CA. Other observers primarily engaged in the study of environmental skepticism and denialism usually distinguish between "free market environmentalism," "environmental skepticism/denialism," and the "wise use movement" briefly described in chapter 1. According to Peter Jacques, free market

environmentalism "questions the legitimate role of government in environmental problems but does not argue that environmental problems are imagined or politically fabricated," as environmental skeptics (and especially climate change denialists) do. Yet environmental skepticism "is also distinct, if sympathetic with, the US counter-environmental Wise Use movement for local industrial access to public lands, though Wise Use leaders such as Ron Arnold and Alan Gottlieb are also environmental skeptics." Peter J. Jacques, "The Rearguard of Modernity: Environmental Skepticism as a Struggle of Citizenship," *Global Environmental Politics* 6, no. 1 (2006): 76–77. Unlike Kearns, I prefer to use the term "evangelical environmental skeptics" for Beisner and other affiliates with the CA because they are deeply (and admittedly) skeptical of the environmental movement, as succinctly exemplified by Kennedy and Beisner's quotes in the beginning of this chapter. As we shall see, however, Beisner and other supporters of the CA are not skeptical about environmental problems across the board and do prefer a free market approach to tackle the environmental issues they recognize as problematic.

[4]    D. James Kennedy, "To Tend the Earth: Our Christian Responsibility," *The Coral Ridge Encounter* 3 (May 1990).

[5]    Kennedy is the founder of Coral Ridge Ministries and Coral Ridge Presbyterian Church, a member of the theologically conservative Presbyterian Church in America (PCA). He was "a close colleague of the Rev. Pat Robertson, the Rev. Jerry Falwell and other religious broadcasters and was an early board member of the Moral Majority, which Falwell formed in 1979. But Kennedy wasn't nearly as well-known as other conservative Christian activists, preferring a behind-the-scenes role that helped maintain his independence." See "Megachurch Pioneer D. James Kennedy dies at 76," *USA Today*, September 6, 2007, http://usatoday30.usatoday.com/news/religion/2007-09-05-kennedy_N .htm (accessed August 10, 2014). Regarding "evangelical Christianity's best kept secret," see Robert Lanham, *The Sinner's Guide to the Evangelical Right* (New York: New American Library, 2006), 104. Lanham (*The Sinner's Guide*, 172) refers to Coral Ridge Ministries as the "most underestimated grassroots propaganda machine in America." For "God's junior partners" and "to care for," see Kennedy, "To Tend the Earth," 6. Regarding Kennedy's reaffirmation of a politically and practically unspecified but biblically mandated responsibility for the earth, see Kennedy and Newcombe, *How Would Jesus Vote?*, 143. For "the Lord has," see Kennedy, "To Tend the Earth," 7.

[6]    James B. Jordan, "Making a Difference," *The Coral Ridge Encounter* 3 (May 1990), 24.

[7]    For "primary opponent," see Wilkinson, *Between God & Green*, 64. Writes Gushee (*The Future*, 177): "Beisner's niche has become his role as *the* anti-EEN, anti-ECI spokesman" (emphasis in original). Right Wing Watch, a group that monitors people and organizations on the political Right, operates as a separate file on Beisner in its "people" category and calls him "the Religious Right's favorite climate change-denying 'expert.'" See Right Wing Watch, http://www.rightwingwatch.org/content/fischer-beisner-say -not-using-fossil-fuels-insult-god and http://www.rightwingwatch.org/category/people/ calvin-beisner (both accessed July 14, 2014). E. Calvin Beisner, *Prospects for Growth: A Biblical View of Population, Resources, and the Future*, Turning Point Christian Worldview Series, ed. Marvin Olasky (Westchester, Ill.: Crossway Books, 1990).

[8]    Jordan, "Making a Difference," 25.

[9]    Jordan, "Making a Difference," 25–26.

[10]    Regarding "that all was not well," see Ohlman, "The Lost Fundamental."

[11]    *World* magazine was modeled after *Time* magazine and launched in 1986 by Joel Belz. Marvin Olasky, the magazine's editor-in-chief, has been connected with Beisner through his editorship of the Turning Point series, among others, in which *Prospects for Growth* was published. The book was endorsed by D. James Kennedy, Michael Novak of the American Enterprise Institute, and by libertarian economist Julian L. Simon. Due to the reputation he had gained with *Prospects for Growth*, Beisner began to establish connections to other leaders and organizations who shared his views, such as the Ethics and Public Policy Center in Washington, D.C (Beisner, interview). Quotations in this paragraph are from "Are God's Resources Finite? A Group of Christian Leaders Claim They Are, but Does the Claim Square with the Evidence?" *World*, November 27, 1993, 10–13.

[12]    "Are God's Resources Finite?", 10–13.

[13]    See "Another View: ESA's Sider Takes Issue with *World* Critique," *World*, January 8, 1994, 22–24. Note that Beisner's rejoinder did not have a separate headline.

[14]    "Another View," 22–24.

[15]    "Another View," 24.

[16]    E. Calvin Beisner, *Where Garden Meets Wilderness: Evangelical Entry into the Environmental Debate* (Grand Rapids, Mich.: Acton Institute for the Study of Religion and Liberty, 1997). Writes Larsen ("God's Gardeners," 312) about Beisner's ecotheology displayed in *Where Garden Meets Wilderness*: "Although Christian moral principles were supposed to guide the exercise of stewardship, these principles spoke almost entirely to individual choices and had nothing to say about policy at a societal or global level. With regards to public policy, one simply had to have faith that a largely unregulated free market and a growing population would create a 'wealthier and environmentally cleaner' future." As exemplified in more detail later, Beisner and Kennedy had been connected through the COR, for instance.

[17]    For "a distillation" and "free-market-friendly," see Larsen, "God's Gardeners," 312; 314. As both Kearns and Wilkinson point out, the opposition to the EEN from within Evangelicalism is a reaction to the "significant inroads" creation care has made within the evangelical community over the course of the evolution of evangelical environmentalism; see Kearns, "Green Evangelicals," 163; and Wilkinson, *Between God & Green*. After all, countermobilization only occurs when the opposed movements and organizations reach a critical mass of supporters and a certain degree of establishment in the respective communities they attempt to represent and mobilize. According to social movement theory, "countermovements" are defined as organized efforts of individuals and organizations that are opposed to the objectives of social movements with whom they share some concerns but to whose desire to change the status quo they are largely opposed. See David S. Meyer and Suzanne Staggenbord, "Movements, Countermovements, and the Structure of Political Opportunity," *American Journal of Sociology* 101, no. 6 (1996): 1628–60; and Robert J. Brulle, "Institutionalizing Delay: Foundation Funding and the Creation of U.S. Climate Change Counter-movement Organizations," *Climatic Change* 122 (2014): 683.

[18]    According to Beisner, ICES "never did anything" but "post the [Cornwall] Declaration on the web"; Beisner, interview. Quotations in this paragraph are taken from "The Cornwall Declaration on Environmental Stewardship," *Cornwallalliance.org*, https://cornwallalliance.org/landmark-documents/the-cornwall-declaration-on-environmental-stewardship/ (accessed October 20, 2019).

[19]    For a list of the Cornwall Declaration's early signatories, see E. Calvin Beisner, "Early and Notable Signers of the Cornwall Declaration," *Cornwallalliance.org*,

October 29, 1999, https://cornwallalliance.org/1999/10/notable-signers-of-the
-cornwall-declaration/ (accessed October 21, 2019). Regarding "virtually no overlap," see Larsen, "God's Gardeners?" 339–40.

20    Despite his skepticism and the reservations he has had about creation care since the
movement's early days, Beisner did not pay much attention to the creation care movement
between 2000 and 2005 because he was busy finishing his Ph.D. in Scottish history through
the University of St. Andrews in Scotland, and teaching at Knox Theological Seminary
in Ft. Lauderdale, Florida, the latter of which was founded by D. James Kennedy in
1989. When climate change was becoming the dominant concern of the environmental
movement and an increasingly politically divisive issue, Beisner was prompted by the libertarian environmental think tank CFACT to reengage in the evangelical environmental
debate (Beisner, interview). Regarding the CA's statement of faith, see Cornwall Alliance,
"Cornwall Alliance Statement of Faith," *Cornwallalliance.org*, https://cornwallalliance
.org/about/cornwall-alliance-statement-of-faith/ (accessed October 20, 2019). From
1984 until 2007, Beisner was a member of the Presbyterian Church of America (PCA).
In 2007 he became involved with Holy Trinity Presbyterian Church, which is part of the
Orthodox Presbyterian Church (OPC), a more conservative branch of Presbyterianism
(Beisner, interview).

21    In February 2019, Beisner informed subscribers to CA's electronic newsletter about
the organization's separation from TJP as of March 1, 2019, and its application process
with the IRS. E. Calvin Beisner, "Awesome Changes Coming to the Cornwall Alliance!,"
Cornwall Alliance electronic newsletter, February 8, 2019. Regarding "project" and Beisner's compensation through TJP, see The James Partnership, "Return of Organization
Exempt From Income Tax" (IRS 990), 2010 until 2017. For "Republican operative"
and CDR's clients, see Wilkinson, *Between God & Green*, 71. On November 7, 2019, CA's
newsletter announced: "Cornwall Alliance for the Stewardship of Creation is a project
of a Committee for a Constructive Tomorrow until we become an independent 501(c)
(3). CFACT is a 501(c)(3) organization. All gifts are tax deductible to the full extent of
the law." See E. Calvin Beisner, "26 Days until #Giving Tuesday!," Cornwall Alliance
electronic newsletter, November 7, 2019. For more information on CFACT, see "About,"
*Cfact.org*, https://www.cfact.org/about/ (accessed November 18, 2019).

22    For CA's mission statement, see Cornwall Alliance, "What Drives Us," *Cornwal-
lalliance.org*, https://cornwallalliance.org/about/what-drives-us/ (accessed October 20,
2019). Cornwall Alliance, "An Open Letter to the Signers of 'Climate Change: An
Evangelical Call to Action' and Others Concerned About Global Warming," Cornwall
Alliance, June 2006, http://www.cornwallalliance.org/wp-content/uploads/2006/07/
Open-Letter-Final-Document-4-16-15.pdf (accessed October 21, 2019). Cornwall Alli-
ance, "A Call to Truth." Regarding Beisner's appearance on the *Glenn Beck Program*, see
"Glenn Beck: Dangers of Environmental Extremism," *Fox News*, October 15, 2010.

23    Beisner, interview. For a current listing of CA's key staff, advisory board, and affiliated scholars, see Cornwall Alliance, "Who We Are," *Cornwallalliance.org*, https://
cornwallalliance.org/about/who-we-are/ (accessed October 20, 2019).

24    For "climate change denial machine," see Riley E. Dunlap and Aaron M. Mc-
Cright, "Organized Climate Change Denial," in *The Oxford Handbook on Climate Change and
Society*, ed. John S. Dryzek, Richard B. Norgaard, and David Schlosberg (Oxford: Oxford
University Press, 2011), 149. Regarding "extensive evidence" and "effectively protect,"
see Cornwall Alliance, "An Open Letter." Endorsers of CA's subsequent "Call to Truth"

include "non-evangelicals with special expertise in climatology or related sciences, economics, environmental studies, theology, or ethics," among them well-known contrarian Siegfried Frederick Singer, who believes that variations in solar activity are the primary cause of climate change. For more information on Singer and the climate change "Denialosphere," see Eric Pooley, *The Climate War: True Believers, Power Brokers, and the Fight to Save the Earth* (New York: Hyperion, 2010), 33–44.

[25]    According to Brulle ("Institutionalizing Delay," 688), the climate change countermovement is a "subsidiary movement of the larger conservative movement." See also Aaron M. McCright and Riley E. Dunlap, "Challenging Global Warming as a Social Problem: An Analysis of the Conservative Movement's Counterclaims," *Social Problems* 47, no. 4 (2000): 499–522; Dunlap and McCright, "Organized Climate Change Denial," 144–60; and Peter J. Jacques, Riley E. Dunlap, and Mark Freeman, "The Organisation of Denial: Conservative Think Tanks and Environmental Scepticism," *Environmental Politics* 17, no. 3 (2008): 349–85.

[26]    Right Wing Watch, "The 'Green Dragon' Slayers: How the Religious Right and the Corporate Right are Joining Forces to Fight Environmental Protection," Right Wing Watch (Washington, D.C.: People for the American Way, 2011), 2–3. Corporations like ExxonMobil and Koch Industries were known for extensively and openly funding climate change skepticism and denial until 2007, when they changed their strategy due to pressure from environmental movement organizations. Since then they have been funding the Climate Change Counter-Movement (CCCM) with concealed donations—or what Brulle calls "dark money"—through foundations such as Donors Trust and Donors Capital; see Brulle, "Institutionalizing Delay," 692–93. For "the most obvious objection" and "wellcredentialed," see Jacques Berlinerblau, *Thumpin' It: The Use and Abuse of the Bible in Today's Presidential Politics* (Louisville, Ky.: Westminster John Knox), 40–41. For a full description of the "web of deception and subterfuge" into which Beisner and the CA are entangled according to Balmer, see *Thy Kingdom Come*, 152–53.

[27]    For CFACT and the "climate change denial machine," see Dunlap and McCright, "Organized Climate Change Denial," 149. Regarding the CFACT/CA connection, see Beisner, interview; and Beisner, "26 Days." The number of lobbyists hired to influence climate change policy increased by about 300 percent between 2003 and 2008. In 2008, 2,340 climate change lobbyists were hired by 770 interest groups and organizations, and their lobbying expenditures were about ninety million dollars. There were more than four climate lobbyists for every member of Congress in 2008. During the same time span the number of environment and health lobbyists grew only to about 185, which means they were outnumbered by climate lobbyists by more than 8:1 in 2008. By 2008 "virtually every segment of the economy" was seeking to influence climate change policy. See Marianne Lavelle, "The Climate Change Lobby," Center for Public Integrity, February 25, 2009, http://www.publicintegrity.org/2009/02/25/4593/climate-change -lobby-explosion-0 (accessed August 2, 2014). Environmental organizations and other citizens groups "depend almost entirely on voluntary donations for their financial lifeblood" (Bosso, *Environment*, 96). Those groups confront the free rider problem while they need money on an ongoing basis to maintain themselves: Jeffrey M. Berry and Clyde Wilcox, *The Interest Group Society*, 4th ed. (New York: Pearson Longman, 2007), 47. Whether conservative or progressive, the financial support provided by private foundations and individual patrons considerably influences the capabilities of nonprofit organizations: Jack

L. Walker, *Mobilizing Interest Groups in America: Patrons, Professions, and Social Movements* (Ann Arbor: University of Michigan Press, 1991).

[28]   For the Acton Institute and IRD's joint paper, see "Evangelical Leaders Exploited by Global Warming—Population Control Lobby," *Christian Newswire*, September 29, 2009, http://www.christiannewswire.com/news/429601108.html (accessed September 24, 2019). Regarding Beisner's association with Acton and the IRD, see Beisner's résumé, which he sent me upon my interviewing him in April 2010, "E. Calvin Beisner, Ph.D.: Professor, Author, and Lecturer" (courtesy of E. Calvin Beisner). Regarding Acton's "smear," see Jewell, interview.

[29]   Beisner, interview. Jim Ball cited in Wilkinson, *Between God & Green*, 78.

[30]   Cornwall Alliance, "A Renewed Call to Truth, Prudence, and the Protection of the Poor," *Cornwallalliance.org*, May 1, 2009, https://cornwallalliance.org/2009/05/a-renewed-call-to-truth-prudence-and-protection-of-the-poor/ (accessed October 26, 2019). Although climate change denial is heavily funded by fossil fuel interests, Pooley cautions not to simply dismiss deniers as "liar-for-hire," because "fossil fuel money alone didn't explain their position any more than grant money explained why most climatologists embraced the consensus" (Pooley, *The Climate War*, 38).

[31]   The Heartland Institute questions the scientific consensus on global warming and sponsors international conferences on climate change. Beisner was among the speakers in 2008 and in 2010, and the CA is a cosponsor of some of the conferences. For "many of them" and for additional information on Heartland's first "deniers' convention," see Pooley, *Climate War*, 33–51. Regarding "fact-checker-type," see Beisner, interview. Beisner told me that once he had embraced Evangelicalism as a teenager, he was very outspoken about his faith. He mentioned a particular instance when a Jehovah's Witness was "trying to witness to [him]." Since "[he]'d never liked to lose an argument," he started reading up on "Christian apologetics, reasons for Christian faith, and defenses of doctrine" after the incident. Note that Beisner also wrote an apologetics book in 1985: *Answers for Atheists, Agnostics, and Other Thoughtful Skeptics: Dialogs About Christian Life and Faith*, rev. ed. (Wheaton, Ill.: Crossway Books, 1993). As he clarifies in the preface to the revised edition of 1993, emphasizing his interest in debate, he is not the type of Christian who shies away from "the seriousness of intellectual objections to faith" (Beisner, *Answers for Atheists*, xv-xvii).

[32]   Beisner, interview. Ronald Sider, *Rich Christians in an Age of Hunger* (Downers Grove, Ill.: InterVarsity, 1977).

[33]   Beisner, interview. Gushee, *The Future*, 93.

[34]   Regarding "grandfather," "very important thinker," Beisner's connection to Kirk, and the importance of *The Road to Serfdom* to him, see Beisner, interview. As Turner and Isenberg (*Republican Reversal*, 25) note, Hayek's *Road to Serfdom* was the "foundational text of American conservatism." As Beisner writes in *Prospects for Growth* (186–87): "Friedrich Hayek warned forty-five years ago of the dangers of allowing the state to become increasingly involved in planning people's lives. The dangers rise, he warned in the title of his book *The Road to Serfdom*, because state planning is the road to a society in which civil government is the master and citizens are slaves. When control of property is placed in the hands of the state, a new and dangerous power is created: the power to coerce everyone to do whatever the state chooses."

[35]   Beisner, interview. As Beisner states in his résumé, he became involved in the founding of the COR in 1984 and has served on COR's board of directors and "its executive, steering, central editing, and theological review committees" (see "E. Calvin Beisner").

36    Quotations in this paragraph are from COR, *Reformation.net*, http://www .reformation.net (accessed November 21, 2019). According to Wilcox and Larson (*Onward Christian Soldiers?*, 155), Christian reconstructionists "are postmillennialists who believe that Christians must work to recover control of America from the forces of Satan in order to establish the millennium and allow Christ to come again. To do this requires that society be reconstructed from the ground up, generally in keeping with Mosaic law . . . as detailed in the first five books of the Bible." Note, however, that COR portrays itself as much more inclusive. States COR's website: "People of Anabaptist, Arminian, Lutheran, Calvinist, and Wesleyan denominational backgrounds are represented among COR's leaders. Pre-, a-, and post-millennialists are cooperating with each other, sharing the exciting task of getting God's will done on earth as it is in heaven insofar as that is possible between now and whenever Christ comes back to Earth. Charismatics and non-charismatics, covenant and dispensationalist theologians, have joined arm in arm in prayer and hard work to develop and implement the Biblical worldview through revival, renewal, and reformation in the Christian Church and the American culture." Denominational background, preferred style of worship, and eschatology thus appear to be secondary, whereas the primary and overriding concern uniting the group's members is the aim to implement the biblical worldview in every aspect of sphere of life. For a recent and comprehensive account on Christian reconstructionism, see Julie J. Ingersoll, *Building God's Dominion: Inside the World of Christian Reconstructionism* (New York: Oxford University Press, 2015). See also Sara Diamond, *Spiritual Warfare: The Politics of the Christian Right* (Boston: South End Press, 1989); and *Roads to Dominion: Right-Wing Movements and Political Power in the United States* (New York: Guilford Press, 1995).

37    See Jay Grimstead and E. Calvin Beisner, "42 Articles of the Essentials of a Christian World View," The Coalition on Revival, Inc., 1989 and 1999, http://theapologeticsgroup .com/wp-content/uploads/2012/06/42_Articles_Christian_Worldview.pdf (accessed November 21, 2019). Grimstead functioned as general editor of the documents, Beisner as his assistant.

38    See Jay Grimstead and Calvin Beisner, "A Manifesto for the Christian Church," Coalition on Revival, July 4, 1986, https://www.reformation.net/uploads/1/1/7/6/ 117618790/a_manifesto_for_the_christian_church.pdf (accessed November 21, 2019). FitzGerald (*The Evangelicals*, 337) poses that the Religious Right had only two "systematic thinkers" or "intellectual authorities" of "cross-denominational importance, R. J. Rushdoony and Francis Schaeffer." Rushdoony (b. 1916) died in 2001; Gary North was his son-in-law. For more on Rushdoony and the movement he inspired, see Molly Worthen, "The Chalcedon Problem: John Rousas Rushdoony and the Origins of Christian Reconstructionism," *Church History* 77, no. 2 (2008): 399–437.

39    E. Calvin Beisner and Daryl S. Borgquist, "The Christian World View of Economics," Coalition on Revival, https://www.reformation.net/uploads/1/1/7/6/117618790/ the_christian_world_view_of_economics.pdf (accessed November 22, 2019).

40    Beisner and Borgquist, "Christian World View." Regarding the issue of overpopulation, note that the authors admit that "local overcrowding strains the limits of some local economies."

41    Beisner, *Prospects for Growth*, 171; 172–73.

42    Kearns, "Green Evangelicals," 168. Note that COR's worldview document on economics also lists several concrete steps to be taken toward the achievement of its goals, such as step thirteen: "making special, focused efforts to diminish the influence

of so-called 'Christian socialism,' the 'simple life style,' the 'Evangelical Left,' and other such ideas, movements, and their representatives among evangelicals, other Christians, and non-Christians" (Beisner and Borgquist, "The Christian World View").

43    Jacques, "The Rearguard of Modernity," 78 (emphasis original).

44    A good starting point and introduction into the creationism/evolution controversy in the United States is Eugenie C. Scott, *Evolution vs. Creationism: An Introduction*, 2nd ed. (Berkeley: University of California Press, 2009). According to Scott (*Evolution vs. Creationism*, 57), "creationism" has a broad definition in the sense that it "refers to the idea of creation by supernatural force"; in its more narrow sense, however, it "reflects a literalist view of the Bible." The relationship between creationism and evolution in Christianity is a continuum that "reflects the degree to which the Bible is interpreted as literally true," thus the progression of position ranges from "flat earthism" to "materialist evolutionism" at the opposite ends of the continuum (Scott, *Evolution vs. Creationism*, 63–73). For "epistemological warfare" and actual social conflict surrounding the creationism/evolution controversy in the United States, see Evans and Evans, "Religion and Science." Regarding "all about casting doubt," see Lawrence M. Krauss, cited in Leslie Kaufman, "Darwin Foes Add Warming to Target," *New York Times*, March 3, 2010, https://www.nytimes.com/2010/03/04/science/earth/04climate.html (accessed November 23, 2019). Says Krauss: "Wherever there is a battle over evolution now, there is a secondary battle to diminish other hot-button issues like Big Bang and increasingly climate change."

45    Richard Cizik, cited in Ben Szobody, "Young conservatives seek fixes for climate change," *Greenville Online*, July 18, 2012, http://www.greenvilleonline.com/article/20120718/NEWS/307180020/Young-conservatives-seek-fixes-climate-change (accessed July 20, 2012). Jim Ball, cited in "Darwin Foes." Rush Limbaugh, cited in David Edwards, "Limbaugh: Christians 'cannot believe in manmade global warming'," *Rawstory*, August 12, 2013, http://www.rawstory.com/rs/2013/08/12/limbaugh-christians-cannot-believe-in-manmade-global-warming/ (accessed March 10, 2016). Before he started graduate studies in environmental science in 2016, Ben Lowe (Renewal and EEN) spoke on behalf of creation care regularly at Christian colleges and universities. During these speaking engagements the age of the earth either came up or hung in the air frequently. To get a discussion started even among the most conservative, quietly dismissive student audiences, all Lowe had to write on the board after his presentation was "Al Gore" and "evolution." Ben Lowe, interview by author, Wheaton, Illinois, April 9, 2010. To address the evangelical suspicion of climate change specifically from a perspective of faith, Katharine Hayhoe, an evangelical atmospheric scientist and scientific advisor of the EEN, has coauthored a book with her pastor husband, Andrew Farley, *A Climate for Change: Global Warming Facts for Faith-Based Decisions* (New York: FaithWords, 2009).

46    All quotations in this paragraph are from Beisner, interview. Says Beisner: "If I were to, say, look down a list of all the speakers at The Heartland Institute's International Conference on Climate Change, I'd be hard-pressed to identify more than three or four who might be young-Earth creationists. The correlation just isn't there" (Beisner, interview). According to Scott, young-Earth creationists consider the earth to be between six thousand and ten thousand years old. They "accept heliocentrism but reject the conclusions of modern physics, astronomy, chemistry, and geology concerning the age of Earth, and they deny biological descent with modification. . . . They reject the Big Bang theory and postulate catastrophic mechanisms as the cause of most of the world's geological features" (Scott, *Evolution vs. Creationism*, 66–68).

[47] A Pew Research Center analysis conducted in spring 2013 found that about one-third (33 percent) of Americans reject evolution, whereas 60 percent believe that "humans and other living things have evolved over time." Twenty-four percent of the latter group, however, take the view that the process of evolution was guided by a supreme being. See "Public's Views on Human Evolution," Pew Research Center, December 30, 2013, http://www.pewforum.org/2013/12/30/publics-views-on-human-evolution/ (accessed September 12, 2014). So according to this study at least 40 percent of Americans could generally be labeled "creationists." For one, this number was higher than the percentage of American evangelicals at around that time (i.e., 26.3 percent of the U.S. adult population). The Pew Forum on Religion & Public Life/ U.S. Religious Landscape Survey, "Religious Beliefs and Practices: Diverse and Politically Relevant" (Pew Research Center, Washington, D.C.: June 2008), 110. It was also more than five times higher than the number of Americans who "are very sure [global warming] is not happening and are actively involved as opponents of a national effort to reduce greenhouse gas emissions," which amounted to 7 percent as of 2009. See The Yale Project on Climate Change and the George Mason University Center for Climate Change Communication, "Global Warming's Six Americas 2009: An Audience Segmentation Analysis," May 20, 2009, http://environment.yale.edu/climate-communication/files/Six-Americas-September-2012.pdf (accessed May 3, 2013). Crudely judging by these numbers, there apparently are many creationists in America who are neither evangelicals nor climate change denialists. For "if you are," see Illyn, interview. Regarding Beisner's correspondence with non-creationist scientists, see Beisner, interview.

[48] For "An Urgent Call to Action: Evangelicals and Scientists Unite to Protect Creation" (2007), see Gushee, *The Future*, 283–85. Regarding the scientific consensus on global warming, see Cook et al., "Quantifying," 024024.

[49] Rousas John Rushdoony, *The Mythology of Science* (1967; repr., Vallecito, Calif.: Ross House Books, 2001). For "to point out," see Mark R. Rushdoony, foreword to *The Mythology of Science*, by Rousas John Rushdoony (1967; repr., Vallecito, Calif.: Ross House Books, 2001), 1.

[50] Mark R. Rushdoony, *The Mythology of Science*, 3–4.

[51] Duane T. Gish and Arthur C. Cunningham, "The Christian World View of Science and Technology," Coalition on Revival, https://www.reformation.net/uploads/1/1/7/6/117618790/the_christian_world_view_of_science_and_technology.pdf (accessed November 25, 2019). For "false starting point" and "produces skewed," see Peter Jones, "The Antithesis: Ephesians 4:17–20," in *On Global Wizardry: Techniques of Pagan Spirituality and a Christian Response*, ed. Peter Jones (Escondido, Calif.: Main Entry Editions, 2010), 260–61. Jones is a contributor to the CA, and his book contains an article by E. Calvin Beisner as well. E. Calvin Beisner, "Deep Ecology, Neopaganism & Global Warming," in *On Global Wizardry: Techniques of Pagan Spirituality and a Christian Response*, ed. Peter Jones (Escondido, Calif.: Main Entry Editions, 2010), 171–85. Beisner gave me this book after our interview. The crucial importance of the right starting point is also something that the Creation Museum in Petersburg, Kentucky, emphasizes. Operated by the young-Earth creationist organization Answers in Genesis–USA (AiG), among the exponents designed to question the mainstream science on many issues, including the creation/ evolution of the Grand Canyon, the museum displays a poster that points out how "human reason" and "God's word" are two "different starting points," which inevitably

lead to "different views." Observations made at the Creation Museum, Petersburg, Kentucky, April 15, 2010.

52   E. Calvin Beisner, letter to Dean Ohlman, January 5, 1994 (courtesy of Dean Ohlman, April 2010; used with permission from E. Calvin Beisner).

53   Quotations in this paragraph are from Cornwall Alliance, "America's Leading Voice of Faith on Stewardship Issues Announces New Initiative to Expose Serious Dangers of 'Green Dragon' Environmentalism; Says 'The Time is Now to Stand and Resist,'" press release (Burke, Va.: Cornwall Alliance, April 20, 2010). Particularly reprehensible to Beisner is the so-called "post-normal science" that consciously breaks with Karl Popper's philosophy and is used as an "instrument" for policy decisions (Beisner, interview). The term "normal science" was first introduced by Kuhn to designate "research firmly based upon one or more past scientific achievements, achievements that some particular scientific community acknowledges for a time as supplying the foundation for its further practice." Kuhn viewed scientific advancement as progressing from normal science (i.e., tradition-bound "puzzle-solving"; to "revolutionary science," where paradigms shift; to new normal science). Thomas S. Kuhn, *The Structure of Scientific Revolutions*, 4th ed. (Chicago: University of Chicago Press, 2012), 10. As scientific knowledge came to play a bigger role in policy considerations pertaining to risk assessment and environmental impacts of postmodern society, philosophers of science Silvio O. Funtowicz and Jerome R. Ravetz proposed the concept of post-normal science. Explains Ravetz: "The insight leading to Post-Normal Science is that in the sorts of issue-driven science relating to environmental debates, typically facts are uncertain, values in dispute, stakes high, and decisions urgent. Some might say that such problems should not be called 'science'; but the answer could be that such problems are everywhere, and when science is (as it must be) applied to them, the conditions are anything but 'normal.' For the previous distinction between 'hard,' objective scientific facts and 'soft,' subjective value-judgements is now inverted. All too often, we must make hard policy decisions where our only scientific inputs are irremediably soft." Jerome R. Ravetz, "What Is Post-Normal Science," *Futures* 31, no. 7 (1999): 649. According to Ravetz ("What Is Post-Normal Science," 653), post-normal science should not be regarded as a rival to normal science, however, but as "an assistance" with which to assure and improve (environmental) quality because the "maintenance and enhancement of quality, rather than the establishment of truth, is the key problem for science in the post-normal age." Beisner believes that "post-normal" science has affected the research on abortions as well, and that there are many "bogus studies" suppressing data on the long-term negative health effects of abortion on women (Beisner, interview).

54   Says the RGD press release: "Since 2005, the Cornwall Alliance has warned evangelicals of this concerted, well-funded effort to infiltrate churches. The *Resisting the Green Dragon* initiative provides evangelical churches with Biblically accurate resources on creation stewardship. The mask needs to be taken off of groups that call themselves Christian but spread a false environmental world view." Cornwall Alliance, "America's Leading Voice." The organization's newsletter from December 29, 2010, specifically refers to the activities of EEN and BE. It states that the CA's is "a big job given that the Green Left has spent at least $16 million over the past decade to subvert our churches and lure the faithful to the Green Dragon." CA's budget, on the other hand, "is extremely modest." E. Calvin Beisner, "Newsletter," Cornwall Alliance, December 29, 2010. As Beisner had put it during our interview, though, "I think there is SOME of that [political manipulation] going on. . . . How to quantify? I mean, is 30 percent of the impetus behind that from

manipulation by people who frankly don't share their evangelical convictions but do want them on the political bandwagon? Or is it 60 percent, or is it 80 percent? I have no idea how to quantify that. But I do know that when you have the formation of the NRPE back in '93, pushed by Carl Sagan, who was an absolute atheist materialist, as well as a self-professed Marxist, I cannot imagine how he can have had as definitive a role in starting the NRPE as he did have, and the NRPE not reflect that" (Beisner, interview).

55    Beisner, interview. During our interview Beisner also emphasized that he was a member of the Evangelical Theological Society, whose doctrinal basis is that "the Bible alone, and the Bible in its entirety, is the word of God written, and is therefore—and that word therefore is very important—therefore inerrant in the autographs. Not in any translation, not in necessarily any manuscript copy, but as it was first written down in Hebrew or in Greek it was without error, and it was so because it was the word of God." For "cognitive defenses," see Berger, *Adventures*, 37: "Any epistemological elite, religious or secular, must develop a system of cognitive defenses to defend its claims against outside criticisms, but also, very importantly, to assuage the doubts harbored by insiders." Experiments conducted through "The Cultural Cognition Project" at Yale University found that people in general "tend to conform their factual beliefs to ones that are consistent with their cultural outlook, their world view." Information that threatens one's beliefs and values is generally processed with a closed mind. But people tend to believe persons who are perceived to be more like themselves. See Christopher Joyce, "Belief In Climate Change Hinges On Worldview," NPR, February 23, 2010, http://www.npr.org/templates/story/story.php?storyId=124008307 (accessed February 27, 2010).

56    See Matthew 7:24-25 (NIV): "Therefore everyone who hears these words of mine and puts them into practice is like a wise man who built his house on the rock. The rain came down, the streams rose, and the winds blew and beat against that house; yet it did not fall, because it had its foundation on the rock." F. A. Hayek, *The Road to Serfdom*, vol. 2 of *The Collected Works of F. A. Hayek*, ed. Bruce Caldwell (New York: Routledge, 2008), 181.

57    Gene Edward Veith Jr., *Fascism: Modern and Postmodern* (Mussoorie, U.P., India: Nivedit Good Books Distributors: 2000), 194. According to Mark Musser, an evangelical pastor and contributing writer to the CA, modern environmentalism is linked to Nazi Germany; see "Hitler and Environmentalism," In the Market with Janet Parshall, Moody Radio, June 4, 2012, http://www.moodyradio.org/radioplayer.aspx?episode=89376&hour=2 (accessed June 20, 2012). Dean Ohlman responded with a critical letter to Musser's interview on Moody Radio, who in turn insisted that "at its root, I do believe that environmentalism IS fascism." See "Point/CounterPoint: Is the creation care movement rooted in Nazi history as some Christian leaders claim?" Restoring Eden, July 2012, http://restoringeden.org/connect/CreationVoice/2012/july-2012/point-counterpoint-is-the-creation-care-movement-rooted-in-nazi-history-as-some-christian-leaders-claim (accessed May 2, 2014). During our interview, Beisner recommended Karla Poewe's work on the connection between German folk religion and the Nazi movement: *New Religions and the Nazis* (New York: Routledge, 2005).

58    Writes Beisner in his January 5, 1994, letter to Ohlman regarding his EDCC criticism as well: "Where I have fallen short of the Biblical norm of graciousness in my criticisms of those with whom I disagree, I have been wrong, and I can only ask my brothers' and sisters' patience and forgiveness. But I will never apologize for speaking up—or writing—when I disagree about something." If one reads other letters infrequently exchanged between Beisner and Ohlman after the founding of the EEN and the publication of the EDCC,

the understanding that the actors on both sides of the evangelical environmental debate are family members in the larger body of Christ who could learn from each other through their disagreements persists. Though the two men eventually decided that their differences regarding creation care were not reconcilable, during our interview Beisner reiterated that the body of Christ included "fact-checker-type[s]" like himself and "lead-with-the-emotions-type[s]" like Matthew Sleeth of BE (see chapter 6). The point was that each part had to fulfill his or her duty according to his or her calling. According to his self-understanding, Beisner's duty was not to judge the creation care movement but to point out its empirical and theological weaknesses and alert other evangelicals to them (Beisner, interview). For "in practice divinization," see Beisner, interview. In this latter context Beisner also remarked that it was "interesting how one define[d] theocracy" and went on to explain, "Do I want an ecclesiocracy, where the church rules the state? Absolutely not. Neither do I want the state ruling the church. Do I want a state that recognizes that there is a creator who has set forth laws that are binding on all people everywhere in all times, and are as binding on the state as they are on individuals? Yes. And if you want to call that a theocracy, well, you know, fine, go ahead, I don't care."

[59]   See Ball, *Global Warming*, 137–39. As Wilkinson (*Between God & Green*, 81–83) notes, the signatories of the ECI periodically mentioned Martin Luther King Jr. during her interviews with them: "Sharing King's critique of the white church during that era [the era of the civil rights movement] and hoping to forge another course, climate care leaders are also reevaluating sacrophobic versus sacrophilic sensibilities and resisting spirit-flesh dualism—a reevaluation that resonates with their views on justice, eschatology, and social sin. . . . In this sense, then, leaders are engaged as much in a hermeneutical struggle—a battle of interpretation to set out a biblically based evangelical social ethic—as they are in a struggle to ameliorate climate change."

[60]   E. Calvin Beisner, "Cornwall Alliance: Who We Are, What We Do, Why We Do It–Tell Your Friends!," Cornwall Alliance, electronic newsletter, January 16, 2013.

## 6 APOLITICAL CREATION CARE ORGANIZATIONS

[1]   Brown, interview, 2010.

[2]   Jim Jewell, quoted in David Neff, "Can We Separate Creation Care from Political Action? Flourish Conference hopes to equip churches, not create 'prophetic single-issue advocates'," *Christianity Today* Blog, entry posted April 24, 2009, http://blog.christianitytoday.com/ctliveblog/archives/2009/04/can_we_separate.html (accessed March 6, 2011).

[3]   For "who had done more," and "concern about global warming," see Turner and Isenberg, *Republican Reversal*, 168. Writes Bryan Walsh for *Time* magazine: "Over time, belief in climate science has become less about the science than about establishing a cultural identity—you're a denier or a believer depending on whether you're a Republican or a Democrat, just like you're a Yankees or a Red Sox fan depending on whether you're from New York City or Boston"; "Who's Bankrolling the Climate Change Deniers?" *Time*, October 4, 2011, http://content.time.com/time/health/article/0,8599,2096055,00.html#ixzz1sey0Jzef (accessed February 26, 2017). See also Michael J. Gerson in a *Washington Post* opinion piece on climate and the culture war: "Among some groups, skepticism about global warming has become a symbol of social identity—the cultural equivalent of a gun rack or an ichthus"; "Climate and the Culture War," *Washington Post*, January 17, 2012.

The extent of political polarization and the validity of the culture war thesis have been debated, most notably by Morris P. Fiorina, with Samuel J. Abrams and Jeremy C. Pope, *Culture War? The Myth of a Polarized America*, 3rd ed. (New York: Pearson Longman, 2010). Nonetheless, most observers would probably agree that it has spread beyond the elite level and even turned "bloody" in some instances, like in the case of the fatal shooting of late-term abortion provider Dr. George Tiller on May 31, 2009, in Wichita, Kansas. Or the more recent congressional baseball shooting on June 14, 2017, in Alexandria, Virginia, when an allegedly disgruntled Bernie Sanders supporter aimed his weapons at Republican members of Congress, wounding four before he was fatally shot by the police. Write Bafumi and Shapiro: "At the elite level, we know that political polarization has led to a high level of visible political conflict, one that has reached high levels of incivility, as we saw in the debate over Clinton's impeachment, the 2000 election results, and the Iraq war, as well as in the 2004 and 2006 elections." Beyond the level of elites, Bafumi and Shapiro observe the rise of a "new partisan voter," whose attitudes and opinions are so rigid that her approach to any new information is dangerously selective and biased to the point of unsubstantiated denial. Joseph Bafumi and Robert Y. Shapiro, "A New Partisan Voter," *The Journal of Politics* 71, no. 1 (2009): 21.

[4] Lydia Bean and Steve Teles, "God and Climate," *Democracy* 36, no. 40 (2016) http://democracyjournal.org/magazine/40/god-and-climate/ (accessed March 1, 2017). For "the largest single demographic," see Scott Keeter, "Will White Evangelicals Desert the GOP? So Far, This Most Republican of Groups is Staying Loyal," Publications, Pew Research Center For The People & The Press, May 2, 2006, http://pewresearch.org/pubs/22/will-white-evangelicals-desert-the-gop/ (accessed August 26, 2008). Explain Bean and Teles ("God and Climate"): "The Evangelical Climate Initiative . . . lacked *mobilized power*—a base of supporters with intense policy demands willing to engage in conflict with organized opposition. Instead, the Creation Care movement had built only *convening power*—the ability to bring disparate people together through identity and networks." In particular, ECI signatories like Rick Warren and Bill Hybels, who have reached thousands of people with their sermons, were regarded as crucial multipliers of creation care messages. In addition, their church buildings of the "mega" variety consume considerable amounts of resources and are important sites of community, where creation care can be taught and learned but also practically implemented. I observed Willow Creek Community Church's campus in South Barrington, Illinois, on August 8 and 9, 2009, in order to possibly notice any outward signs that would reveal a heightened concern for environmental issues and the reduction of greenhouse gas emissions. Granted, this was my first visit to a mega-church, but it reminded me of a mall rather than a "creation awareness center." There were no obvious outward signs of a particular green culture being cultivated at Willow Creek, or any explicit indications that Hybels' commitment to reducing greenhouse gas emissions went beyond lending his signature to EEN's ECI. For Calvin DeWitt's vision of churches as a "creation awareness center" and their features, see Calvin B. DeWitt, "You Can Make Your Church a Creation Awareness Center," *Green Cross*, Winter 1995, 12–14. The ability of the ECI to be more than a PR coup and inspire lasting change was questioned by former EEN staff Jim Jewell during our interview in 2010. For two concrete examples of ECI signatories only paying lip service to the EEN, see Wilkinson, *Between God & Green*, 50–51. Regarding "to defend climate action," see Bean and Teles, "God and Climate."

⁵    For "bring together," see Ed Brown, "A Letter From the Director," in *Celebrating Ten Years: Our First Decade 2005–2015*, Care of Creation, Decadal Report, 2016, PDF retrievable at http://www.careofcreation.net/about/ourfirstdecade/ (accessed August 2, 2017). Regarding "second reformation," see Brown, interview, 2010.

⁶    Although he spent his childhood in Pakistan and would return to the country as a missionary pastor later, Brown went to high school in the United States. For "higher calling" and "more important things," see Ed Brown, "Missions and Creation-Care: Two Themes that Belong Together," Care of Creation, http://www.careofcreation.net/resources/papers/two-themes/ (accessed November 1, 2019). Regarding "tendency" and "seemed to have," see Ed Brown, "Missions and the Environment: Confessions of a 'Reluctant Environmentalist,'" Care of Creation, http://www.careofcreation.net/resources/papers/confessions-of-a-reluctant-environmentalist/ (accessed November 1, 2019).

⁷    Brown, interview, 2010.

⁸    As Brown describes his "conversion" to environmentalism: "So what convinced me? Well, to start with, God did. It was a question of guidance—'I'll go where you want me to go, Dear Lord.' He guided me from missions to work with an environmental organization very clearly. But beyond experiencing God's guidance, I found myself being convinced by several other things. My eyes were opened in ways they had not been before. . . . Thus I find myself compelled by my beliefs and convinced by practical realities. I reluctantly admit that I am an environmentalist" ("Missions and the Environment"). For Sorley's role in the founding of CoC and "Macedonian call," see Edward R. Brown, *Our Father's World: Mobilizing the Church to Care for Creation*, 2nd ed. (Downers Grove, Ill.: IVP Books, 2008), 13–14.

⁹    For "Craig Sorley's conversion," see Stephan Faris, "Heroes of the Environment 2008: Craig Sorley," *Time*, September 24, 2008, http://content.time.com/time/specials/packages/article/0,28804,1841778_1841781_1841810,00.html (accessed July 5, 2017). Regarding "by helping them," see Brown, *Our Father's World*, 156.

¹⁰    Brown, interview, 2010.

¹¹    For Soreley's "message," see Brown, interview, 2010. Regarding "unemployment when you are over fifty," see Brown, *Our Father's World*, 14.

¹²    For "a new perspective," see Brown, interview, 2010.

¹³    Brown, interview, 2010. CCK operates out of Moffat Bible College in Kijabe, an evangelical training institute for evangelists and pastors established in 1929 by the Africa Inland Mission.

¹⁴    Writes Brown: "I've been dragged into the environmental camp, not exactly kicking and screaming, but certainly with a little hesitation" ("Missions and the Environment"). For "realized that the missionary task," see Brown, "Missions and the Environment." Regarding "if you are truly," see Brown, interview, 2010. As Brown (*Our Father's World*, 156) describes the link between creation care and evangelism: "Caring for God's creation has everything to do with that final command that Jesus gave his disciples: 'Go and make disciples of all nations' (Matthew 28:19)." For "are approaching," "a great deal," and "lightweight gospel," see Brown, *Our Father's World*, 157–59. Despite this provocative observation, however, Brown admits that the situations in developing countries are "complicated" and that "there are a lot of factors at work, including the failure or absence of economic, government and environmental policies." For a more detailed explanation of the link between creation care and global evangelism, see Craig Sorley, "Creation Care

and the Great Commission," in *Creation Care and the Gospel: Reconsidering the Mission of the Church*, ed. Colin Bell and Robert S. White (Peabody, Mass.: Hendrickson, 2016), 71–83.

[15] Regarding "the best," see Brown, *Our Father's World*, 16. For "not involved in," see Brown, interview, 2010. The quote "theology in action," as much as "responsibility for God's creation" and "is related to God," are from Brown, *Our Father's World*, 161. In particular with its "Farming God's Way" project—which involves the avoidance of damage to top soil by not using plows, keeping the soil covered and thus protected from erosion, and "doing everything in a timely and diligent manner"—CCK has, in partnership with local church leaders and Moffat Bible College, researched and, according to its own understanding, demonstrated the effectiveness and sustainability of its biblically based approach to agriculture. See Ed Brown, "Bearing Much Fruit," CoC newsletter sent on May 4, 2016. For more information on CCK's training programs, see "Training Topics Offered by CCK," *Careofcreationkenya.org*, http://www.careofcreationkenya.org/index .php/#training-topics (accessed November 2, 2019). Apart from CCK's practical conservation efforts, the organization also facilitates creation care conferences and trainings for national and international leaders.

[16] For "mobilize the world-wide church," see for instance Care of Creation, Inc., "Return of Organization Exempt from Income Tax," 2005, retrieved through GuideStar. Note also the subtitle of Brown's first book on creation care, *Our Father's World: Mobilizing the Church to Care for Creation*. Regarding other quotations in this paragraph, see Brown, *Our Father's World*, 22.

[17] Brown, interview, 2010; and Ed Brown, interview by author, London, UK, June 6, 2016. Brown has also repeatedly spoken about creation care at his home church in Madison, Wisconsin (nondenominational Blackhawk Church). When I was visiting Brown in 2010, I attended his presentation "Why Creation Care Matters for Missions" at Blackhawk, which has an average Sunday attendance of 3,461 adults (as of 2015) and three locations in and around Madison. Brown has attended Blackhawk since 2003; in turn, the church has been one of the financial supporters of CoC; see Care of Creation, *Celebrating Ten Years*. On the particular morning of my attendance on April 11, 2010, Brown's presentation was scheduled after the first service as part of the church's Sunday School Classes program. It attracted about thirty-two people, most of them belonging to the younger and middle-aged generations and thus reflecting Blackhawk's overall demographic very well. For more information on Blackhawk Church, see *Blackhawkchurch.org*, http://www .blackhawkchurch.org/ (accessed September 2, 2016). Over the years of his activism, Brown has been particularly supportive of fellow evangelical Lowell Bliss and the environmental missions initiative Eden Vigil, established in 2009 as a project under the umbrella of the international evangelical mission organization Christar. The latter was founded as "The India Mission" in Richardson, Texas, in 1930. Bliss established Eden Vigil in close collaboration with Brown (Brown, interview, 2010). The stated purpose of Eden Vigil is "to identify opportunities for ministry in least-reached communities that combine church planting and care for creation, as well as recruit students and professionals with a passion for environmental ministry." Christar, "Eden Vigil," https://www.christar.org/ give/projects/church-planting-and-evangelism/eden-vigil/ (accessed August 20, 2016). A former missionary himself as well, Bliss has published on the concept of environmental missions. See Lowell Bliss, *Environmental Missions: Planting Churches and Trees* (Pasadena, Calif.: William Carey Library, 2013); and Lowell Bliss, "Environmental Missions: An

Introduction," in *Creation Care and the Gospel: Reconsidering the Mission of the Church*, ed. Colin Bell and Robert S. White (Peabody, Mass.: Hendrickson, 2016), 53–70.

[18]    Brown, interview, 2010. For "teaching principles," see Ohlman, interview. According to Smith (*American Evangelicalism*, 187) evangelicals generally tend to favor what he calls a "personal influence strategy" in their approach to seek social change. The first step toward an improvement of societal conditions is the conversion of the individual; the more people are following Christ, the better society will be. Regarding "percolate upward," see Brown, interview, 2016. Brown also mentioned that he thought the EEN had not kept pushing the ECI enough, and that the signatories of the call had not felt any obligations beyond their signatures (Brown, interview, 2016).

[19]    Brown, *Our Father's World*, 18; 63–71; 74–75. In "Missions and Creation Care," Brown writes, "At its root, environmental problems, like all others, are sin problems. We abuse creation because of our sin, and the only complete solution will be found in the life-changing, sin-conquering power of knowing Jesus Christ and in living out that knowledge through the new life he brings."

[20]    Originally called the Lausanne Committee for World Evangelization (LCWA), the Lausanne Movement is dedicated to fulfilling Christ's "Great Commission" on a global scale. First convened in Lausanne, Switzerland, in the summer of 1974 mostly under the leadership of Billy Graham, the purpose of the first congress, "Lausanne '74," was to develop evangelistic strategies for a new generation of evangelical leaders united by their determination to further the evangelization of the whole world. The gathering in Lausanne was attended by 2,473 official delegates from 150 countries; 1,300 observers, guests, and consultants; and several hundred journalists. It culminated with the issuance of a proclamation on evangelism under the primary leadership of John Stott, "The Lausanne Covenant," and the "formation of a permanent committee to carry on the vision and the work of Lausanne" (i.e., the LCWE); Graham, *Just As I Am*, 567–73. Since then, three world congresses have convened, which all resulted in public declarations. See also Lausanne Movement, "The Lausanne Covenant, 1974," https://www.lausanne.org/content/covenant/lausanne-covenant (accessed August 2, 2016). "The Lausanne Covenant" makes no explicit mention of environmental stewardship or creation care. "The Manila Manifesto," on the other hand, states in rather general terms that "sin also frequently erupts in anti-social behavior, in violent exploitation of others, and in a depletion of the earth's resources of which God has made men and women his stewards." In addition, it lists several "evils" to be deplored by Christians, among them "all forms of exploitation of people and of the earth"; Lausanne Movement, "The Manila Manifesto, 1989," https://www.lausanne.org/content/manifesto/the-manila-manifesto (accessed August 2, 2016). Similar to EEN's ECI, "The Cape Town Commitment," on the other hand, proclaims that climate change is "probably the most serious and urgent challenge faced by the physical world now," especially as it "will disproportionately affect those in poorer countries." Therefore, evangelical Christians worldwide are urged to address the issue. See Lausanne Movement, "The Cape Town Commitment: A Confession of Faith and a Call to Action, 2010," *Lausanne.org*, https://www.lausanne.org/content/ctc/ctcommitment (accessed August 2, 2016). For "gospel issue within," see "Cape Town Commitment." Brown's quote is from Brown, interview, 2016.

[21]    Brown, interview, 2010. Drawing an analogy to fishing, Brown explained: "When you go fishing the line is weighted by pounds. So, I'm fishing with a thirty pound line, and I hook a forty pound fish. Now the line is supposed to break, but it doesn't have to break.

If you are very careful you can still get that fish, right? The line is like my relationship to the people I'm talking to, okay? So, it's like the relationship will hold thirty pounds and this climate change thing makes it forty pounds, and so I can bring them [i.e., more skeptical, more conservative evangelicals] along as long as I don't break the relationships. So, if I'm too strong, you know, too dogmatic or whatever, then the relationship is gone, so is the fish" (Brown, interview, 2010).

22    Regarding CoC's growth, see Brown, interview, 2016. During our interview in 2010, Brown explained that the Sorleys in particular came from a "relatively conservative church" in Minneapolis (i.e., John Piper's Bethlehem Baptist Church) and that CoC's "natural constituency" at this point in time was "even on the more conservative side of the evangelical spectrum." When we talked again in June 2016 and I asked Brown whether his constituency was still on the more conservative side of the ideological spectrum than he personally was, he answered: "I think we've moved a little more to the middle of the road, and for my organization itself, we no longer hesitate to put posts up about climate change." During this occasion, Brown also mentioned local cooperation with the secular nonprofit Citizens' Climate Lobby, a bipartisan grassroots organization lobbying for a carbon fee and dividend solution to climate change. Furthermore, Brown talked about the "Jamaica Consultation," a subsequent meeting cosponsored by the World Evangelical Alliance (WEA) in October/November 2012, in St. Ann, Jamaica, during which the creation care portions of "The Cape Town Commitment" were further discussed and detailed. It was attended by fifty-seven "theologians, church leaders, scientists and creation care practitioners" from twenty-six countries, among them Brown and Peter Illyn. Colin Bell, Robert S. White, and Edward R. Brown, "Introduction," in *Creation Care and the Gospel: Reconsidering the Mission of the Church*, ed. Colin Bell and Robert S. White, Lausanne Library (Peabody, Mass.: Hendrickson, 2016), 1. It resulted in a strong affirmation of creation care as a "gospel issue" and "The Jamaica Call to Action," which, among other things, called for "radical action to confront climate change." Different from the ECI, however, the drafters outlined said action as an act of radical belief and Christ-like self-denial rather than a call for political engagement and specific measures to reduce greenhouse gas emissions. See Lausanne/WEA Creation Care Network, "The Jamaica Call to Action," in *Creation Care and the Gospel: Reconsidering the Mission of the Church*, ed. Colin Bell and Robert S. White, Lausanne Library (Peabody, Mass.: Hendrickson, 2016), 7–10. According to Brown, both "The Cape Town Commitment" and "The Jamaica Call to Action" have been crucial in the expansion of creation care on to the agenda of globally oriented missions organizations precisely because they emanated from within the Lausanne Movement and not from specific environmental agencies such as EEN (interview, 2016). Remaining quotations in this paragraph are from the same source.

23    For "mom-and-pop-operation," see Matthew Sleeth, *24/6: A Description for a Healthier, Happier Life* (Carol Stream, Ill.: Tyndale, 2012), 138. Regarding "on-ramp," see Nancy Sleeth, interview by author, Altamonte Springs, Florida, April 21, 2010. For more information on the rise of religious "nones" in America, see for instance Pew Research Center, "In U.S., Decline of Christianity Continues at Rapid Pace," Pew Research Center, Religion & Public Life, October 17, 2019, https://www.pewforum.org/2019/10/17/in-u-s-decline-of-christianity-continues-at-rapid-pace/ (accessed November 16, 2019).

24    See Nancy Sleeth, *Almost Amish: One Woman's Quest for a Slower, Simpler, More Sustainable Life* (Carol Stream, Ill.: Tyndale House Publishers, 2012), x.

25    Sleeth, *Almost Amish*, x–xii.

26    Sleeth, interview.

27    Regarding "dying," see Sleeth, *Almost Amish*, xii. For "no chestnuts," see Matthew Sleeth, "Introduction: The Power of a Green God," in *The Green Bible* (San Francisco: HarperOne, 2008), I-18.

28    See Matthew Sleeth, *The Gospel According to the Earth: Why the Good Book Is a Green Book* (New York: HarperOne, 2010). For the Sleeths' respective religious upbringings, "hadn't taken," and "threw [it] out," see Nancy Sleeth, interview. Regarding Matthew Sleeth's previous self-identification as "secular humanist," see Sleeth, *The Gospel*, xiii; and Blessed Earth, "Story," *Blessedearth.org*, http://www.blessedearth.org/about/ (accessed November 28, 2016). For "changed everything," see Matthew Sleeth, "Introduction," I-19.

29    Matthew Sleeth, "Introduction," I-19. For "enlightened environmentalist," see Matthew Sleeth, *Serve God, Save the Planet: A Christian Call to Action* (Grand Rapids: Zondervan, 2006), 23.

30    The Sleeths have both pointed out on different occasions that Matthew 7:1-2 inspired Gandhi's activism; see David Roberts, "An Interview with J. Matthew Sleeth, Evangelical Environmentalist and Author," *Grist*, October 6, 2006, http://grist.org/article/sleeth/ (accessed August 4, 2017); and Nancy Sleeth, interview. For "took an accounting," see Matthew Sleeth, "Introduction," I-19. Regarding "downward[ly] mobile" and "I told," see Matthew Sleeth, *The Gospel*, xii–xiii.

31    For "a house the size," see Matthew Sleeth, *The Gospel*, xiii. Regarding "help with the flood," see Blessed Earth, "Story."

32    For BE's mission, see Blessed Earth, "Mission and Beliefs," Blessed Earth, http://www.blessedearth.org/about/mission-and-beliefs/ (accessed November 28, 2016). Nancy Sleeth, interview.

33    Matthew Sleeth, *Serve God*, 16; 21; 24.

34    Writes Matthew Sleeth (*The Gospel*, xiii): "Although I was leaving the safety of a paycheck, I was not leaving healthcare. I was simply shifting to healthcare on a global scale." Regarding "we live in a sea," see Matthew Sleeth, *Serve God*, 28.

35    Matthew Sleeth, *Serve God*, 93; 230. In the past, drying clothes on an old-fashioned clothesline has resulted in lawsuits in some of the states, sparking a "right-to-dry movement"; see Ian Urbina, "Debate Follows Bills to Remove Clotheslines Bans," *The New York Times*, October 10, 2009, http://www.nytimes.com/2009/10/11/us/11clothesline.html (accessed December 9, 2016). The debate about the advantages of not using electric dryers is ongoing; see Cassandra Profita, "Solar Advocates Launch 'Hang Dry Your Clothes For Climate Change' Week," *OPB*, August 4, 2019, https://www.opb.org/news/article/solar-advocates-oregon-hang-dry-clothes-climate-change-energy/ (accessed November 10, 2019).

36    For "the third largest user" and "television separates us," see Matthew Sleeth, *Serve God*, 226–29; 113. Regarding "nothing is worse," see Matthew Sleeth, *Serve God*, 115.

37    Nancy Sleeth, *Go Green, $ave Green: A Simple Guide to Saving Time, Money, and GOD'S Green Earth* (Carol Stream, Ill.: Tyndale House, 2009), xix. While her husband also provides energy audit sheets in "Appendix A" of *Serve God, Save the Planet*, Nancy lists more details regarding environmentally sound actions that can lead to monetary savings—less is more is even more, so to speak—in each of her chapters, which are organized around the different areas of a person's or family's life, such as home, work, transportation, food, church, etc. For Jesus Christ's two "greatest" commandments, see Matthew 22:36-40

(NIV). See also Mark 12:28-31 and Luke 10:27. Regarding "always lead," see Nancy Sleeth, *Go Green*, xix. Matthew Sleeth, *Serve God*, 76–87.

[38]  Emma Sleeth, *It's Easy Being Green: One Student's Guide to Serving God and Saving the Planet* (Grand Rapids: Zondervan, 2008). Matthew Sleeth, *Serve God*, 114–26; 186.

[39]  Quotations are from Ronald Sider, "The Place of Humans in the Garden of God," *Green Cross*, Summer 1995, 18. See also the 1995 fall edition of *Green Cross* magazine, which was exclusively dedicated to the theme of overconsumption and its connection to environmental degradation.

[40]  Matthew Sleeth, *Serve God*, 82; 179.

[41]  Regarding "stuff" and "shine as a light," see Matthew Sleeth, *Serve God*, 82–86. Nancy Sleeth, *Go Green*, 8.

[42]  For "blind," "governed," and "hyperconsumerism," see Matthew Sleeth, *The Gospel*, 170. While not the only creation care activists advocating what evangelical eco-theologian Steven Bouma-Prediger calls "joyful simplicity," the Sleeths' outstanding condemnation of American "hyperconsumerism" is inseparable from the family's faith and lifestyle. Regarding Bouma-Prediger's concept of "joyful simplicity," see *For the Beauty*, 166–68. For Ronald Sider's embrace of simple living, see Swartz, *Moral Minority*, 153–69.

[43]  Nancy Sleeth, *Almost Amish*, xx; xviii–xix; xxi, 214, 95; 26 27.

[44]  Nancy Sleeth, *Almost Amish*, ix. Direct quotations are from Matthew Sleeth, *The Gospel*, 178; 176; 170.

[45]  When actors in a market society take into account the political impact of their consumption and make conscious decisions of what to buy and what not based on it, we can speak of "political consumerism." For more information, see Michele Micheletti, Andreas Follesdal, and Dietlind Stolle, *Politics, Products, and Markets. Exploring Political Consumerism Past and Present* (Rutgers, N.J.: Transaction Publishers, 2003). For "very deliberately," see Nancy Sleeth, interview. Nancy Sleeth was the only creation care leader who declined to share, even as a personal remark off the record, which of the political parties she preferred. When asked more generally about her political identity, she insisted that she and her husband did not place themselves anywhere on the political spectrum. Regarding "personal influence strategy" and the evangelical preference of it, see Smith, *American Evangelicalism*, 187. Both Matthew and Nancy emphasize that the change of heart is more important than policy changes; see Matthew Sleeth, *Serve God*, 193; and Nancy Sleeth, interview. As Matthew thoroughly explained in an interview with the secular environmental magazine *Grist*: "The moment you start practicing democracy at home by turning off the light switch, you become an activist saying one thing and doing the same thing. When you change the heart of people, when you get to that 5 percent that sociologists say can change a population by doing a particular behavior . . . if you've got 5 percent of Americans insisting on hanging up their laundry, then you're going to have presidential hopefuls next election primary in New Hampshire, I guarantee you, hanging up laundry with somebody." Roberts, "An Interview with J. Matthew Sleeth."

[46]  Nancy Sleeth, interview.

[47]  Blessed Earth, "Blessed Earth on 'The 700 Club,'" Blessed Earth News, http:// www.blessedearth.org/blogs/news/blessed-earth-on-%E2%80%98the-700-club %E2%80%99/ (accessed March 28, 2017). To watch one of the videos, see Christian Broadcasting Network, "Saving Your 'Green' By Going Green," CBN, http://www1 .cbn.com/cbn-search?search_term=sleeth&site=tv (accessed March 28, 2017). Blessed Earth, "Chuck Colson: Common-Sense Environmentalism," Blessed Earth News,

http://www.blessedearth.org/blogs/news/chuck-colson-%E2%80%98common-sense -environmentalism%E2%80%99/ (accessed March 28, 2017). Unfortunately, Colson's original blog post is not available online anymore. Regarding "miracles," see Nancy Sleeth, interview.

48    BE's website provides a listing of places and events where the organization has shared its message since 2006. As I counted the individual events during each year, I found a peak in 2007 with seventy-eight speaking engagements and a low point in the years 2010 until 2012, with the number of events at twenty-six (2010) and twenty-three (2011 and 2012), respectively. Since then the numbers have not sunken below thirty again. Another high point of speaking engagements since 2012 occurred in the year 2017 with fifty events in eighteen states, a combined twenty events taking place in North Carolina (eight), Kentucky (six), and Tennessee (six). The speaking engagements of 2007 took place in eighteen states and Canada (two). Among the most frequented states were Tennessee (thirteen), Kentucky (eleven), Maryland (ten), and California (nine). See Blessed Earth, "Past Events," Blessed Earth, http://www.blessedearth.org/about/past-events/ (accessed November 11, 2019). For "stop day" and "24/7 world of constant change," see Matthew Sleeth, *24/6*, 84. As Sleeth (*Serve God*, 100) muses in his first book: "It may not happen for a time, but imagine if once again everything came to rest on Sundays. We could use 10 percent less of foreign oil. The skies would be cleaner and quieter." More information on BE's Sabbath Living Program can be found at *Sabbathliving.org* (accessed November 11, 2019).

49    For more on the SSA, see Blessed Earth, "Seminary Stewardship Alliance," Blessed Earth, http://www.blessedearth.org/featured-one/seminary-stewardship-alliance/ (accessed November 11, 2019). More information on BE Tennessee can be found at *Blessedearthtn.com* (accessed November 11, 2019).

50    According to Bosso (*Environment*, 49), "dissident organizations" within specific advocacy communities are "those created primarily because a leader or group of leaders left an existing organization over fundamental differences in priorities, tactics, or management style."

51    Jewell, interview. Information on Pritchard's background is taken from his blog at https://rustypritchard.com/ and his LinkedIn page at https://www.linkedin.com/in/rustypritchard/ (both accessed on June 19, 2017). According to tax returns of the EEN, Jewell received a compensation of $25,518 for the tax year April 2007 to March 2008, and $102,000 for the tax year April 2008 to March 2009 for his work as EEN's COO. For the same two tax years, contractor Rooftop Media Works received compensations of $125,297 and $84,384, respectively. See Evangelical Environmental Network, "Return of Organization Exempt from Income Tax," 2007, retrieved through GuideStar; and "Return of Organization Exempt from Income Tax," 2008, retrieved through GuideStar.

52    Jewell, interview. Juskus had started to do contract work for EEN in May 2008. Before she joined EEN, Juskus had interned for the Mennonite Central Committee, a global relief, development, and peace organization. She worked as contributing and managing editor for *Flourish* magazine until March 2012; see Rusty Pritchard, "Inside Flourish Magazine, Spring 2012," *Flourish*, March 2, 2012, http://www.flourishonline.org/2012/03/ inside-flourish-magazine-spring-2012/ (accessed July 10, 2017). Merritt had previously supported the EEN through church outreach. See Flourish, "About: Team," *Flourishonline. org*, http://www.flourishonline.org/about/team/ (accessed June 26, 2017). For Merritt's "green awakening," see Jonathan Merritt, *Green Like God: Unlocking the Divine Plan for Our Planet* (New York: FaithWords, 2010), 1–3.

[53] For "might be more likely," see Bosso, *Environment*, 49. Regarding the downturn in EEN's finances and the remaining staff's suspicion, see Jewell, interview.

[54] On March 10, 2008, Jonathan Merritt launched the Southern Baptist Environment and Climate Initiative (SBECI) and the corresponding "A Southern Baptist Declaration on the Environment and Climate Change." Although Merritt's effort was faced with significant resistance from within the Southern Baptist Convention (SBC), he nevertheless got the support of some influential SBC leaders, including his father, James, who had served as president of the SBC from 2000 to 2002. Based in the greater Atlanta area, like Pritchard and Jewell at the time, Cross Pointe Church thus seemed like a natural choice for the upcoming Flourish conference, especially considering the younger Merritt's involvement with Flourish. Regarding the goal of Flourish's conference, "three major areas," and cast of speakers, see Jim Jewell, "Release: Surprising Cast of Christian Speakers at Flourish," *Flourish*, March 23, 2009, http://www.flourishonline.org/2009/03/release -surprising-cast-of-christian-speakers-at-flourish/ (accessed June 13, 2017). Regarding "church ministry," see David Neff, "Can We Separate Creation Care from Political Action? Flourish Conference hopes to equip churches, not create 'prophetic single-issue advocates'," *Christianity Today* Blog, April 24, 2009, http://blog.christianitytoday.com/ ctliveblog/archives/2009/04/can_we_separate.html (accessed March 6, 2011).

[55] See Flourish, letter "To the Creation Care Consultation," August 2009. Received from Kendra Juskus during the CCCC at Judson University, August 7, 2009. The Southern Baptist seminarian referred to in the letter was Mark Liederbach of Southeastern Baptist Theological Seminary; the church planter was Rand Clark of Genesis Church in Castle Rock, Colorado. As Juskus detailed in person while passing out copies of the letter along with *Flourish* magazine's first (conference) issue, the conference had yielded 131 participants and 21 sponsors. According to a Flourish survey measuring the satisfaction of conference attendees, Juskus emphasized that 86 percent said they would participate again, while 91 percent would recommend the event to others.

[56] Observations made as a participant observer during the CCCC 2009.

[57] Observations made as a participant observer during the CCCC 2009. As CCCC 2009 facilitator and chair of EEN's board, Janel Curry exclaimed before the group moved on to the next item on its agenda, "So the Flourish is blessed!"

[58] Jewell, interview. Jewell ascribes the "progressive DNA" of EEN as largely due to the organization's cofounder Ronald Sider and its initial organizational belonging to ESA. Despite the fact that Sider attempts to be an ideologically bridging evangelical who is, according to Jewell, respected by the evangelical establishment, Jewell nevertheless insists that within the evangelical community, Sider is largely associated with the political left of center. Jewell, interview. In January 2009, Jewell also explained the founding motives of Flourish in detail to the readers of his blog. After presenting a list of ten reasons why "American Christians should make environmental stewardship a primary concern," Jewell cites a Barna poll indicating "that 90 percent of evangelicals in America would like to see Christians do more to care for God's creation." Despite this overwhelming openness toward more action in the realm of creation care on part of the evangelical community at large, inspiring leadership in this area was largely missing since environmental concerns had predominantly been voiced by either "secular," "liberal messengers" on the one side, or by "evangelical brethren" who had "made it appear that Christian response [sic] to the problems facing us have to be political and must begin with controversial government action on climate change," on the other. Put off by both, some

leaders within the evangelical community had made it acceptable to ignore environmental problems altogether, hence Jewell and Pritchard's founding of Flourish in order "to stand astride the unhealthy chasm between those who prescribe only political solutions and those who would do nothing." Jim Jewell, "Christian Environmentalism That Can Flourish," Stones Cry Out blog, entry posted January 23, 2009, http://stonescryout .org/?p=1338 (accessed November 15, 2019).

59   For "the creation of new organizations," see Bosso, *Environment*, 61. Regarding climate change as a "huge problem," see Jewell, interview. Illyn's quotations are taken from Illyn, interview. Both Wilkinson and Kearns interpret Flourish's founding as signifying a "fissure" within the creation care movement: Wilkinson, *Between God & Green*, 114–22; and Kearns, "Green Evangelicals," 170. The term "fissure" is linguistically located in the semantic field of disagreement, division, and dissent as well, and it cannot be disputed that the founding of dissident Creation Care, Inc. marks a conscious departure from the strategy and issue-focus of the EEN by former staff. Nonetheless, Pritchard and Jewell's intent had not been to potentially "weaken the movement's efforts" (Wilkinson, *Between God & Green*, 122) but rather to find a mediating position between politically unafraid creation care advocates and more politically conservative environmentally skeptical evangelicals in order to advance the movement's reach—a strategic necessity that other CCCC affiliates deemed important at the time as well.

60   For Flourish's mission, see Flourish, "About," *Flourishonline.org*, http://www .flourishonline.org/about/ (accessed July 3, 2017). Regarding the collaboration with Barber and "green collar jobs," see Flourish, "Join Flourish and Help Care for Creation and the People who Depend on it," Flourish Newsletter, April 16, 2009.

61   Jewell, interview. For "a virtual institute," "better conversations," and "to advance prudent," see Terra Dei Institute for Environmental Policy, "About Us," Internet Archive: Wayback Machine, captured on September 14, 2010, http://web.archive.org/web/ 20100914021428/http://terradei.org:80/about (accessed July 4, 2017). Note that Terra Dei's website is not active anymore and only accessible through Internet archive services, such as Wayback Machine. While no private retreat had happened yet when I talked to Jewell in April 2010, the organization's IRS 990 form for the calendar year shows that one was conducted in the remainder of 2010. Additionally, Terra Dei facilitated "50 individual meetings with Christian leaders" in 2010. Both the private forum and the individual meetings resulted in Terra Dei expenses in the amount of $74,000, while Flourish costs amounted to $88,000 in 2010. See Creation Care, Inc., "Return of Organization Exempt from Income Tax," 2010, retrieved through GuideStar. Note that as of November 2019 there are only two IRS 990 forms of Creation Care, Inc. available (for the calendar years of 2009 and 2010, respectively). In 2009 the organization did not spend any funds on the Terra Dei project but concentrated on the Flourish conference (expenses $120,000) and the Flourish website, newsletter, and magazine (expenses $59,432); see Creation Care, Inc., "Return of Organization Exempt from Income Tax," 2009, retrieved through GuideStar. Both 990 forms state that Creation Care, Inc. is "doing business as" Flourish and Terra Dei Institute for Environmental Policy.

62   Terra Dei Institute for Environmental Policy, "Who We Are," Internet Archive: Wayback Machine, captured on September 14, 2010, http://web.archive.org/web/ 20100914015829/http://terradei.org:80/who-we-are (accessed July 3, 2017). See also "About Us." As Jewell explained, the intention of Terra Dei was not to appeal to "diehard skeptics" or "denialists" but rather to more open-minded skeptics; Jewell, interview.

For Terra Dei's positions on climate change specifically, see Terra Dei Institute for Environmental Policy, "Climate Change," Internet Archive: Wayback Machine, captured on September 9, 2010, http://web.archive.org/web/20100909230320/http://terradei.org:80/topics/climate-change (accessed July 4, 2017). Emphasis added.

63    Terra Dei Institute for Environmental Policy, "Climate Change," Internet Archive: Wayback Machine, captured on September 9, 2010, http://web.archive.org/web/20100909230320/http://terradei.org:80/topics/climate-change (accessed July 4, 2017). States the ECI: "On June 22, 2005, the Senate passed the Domenici-Bingaman resolution affirming this approach [i.e., a market-based cap-and-trade program], and a number of major energy companies now acknowledge that this method is best both for business and the environment" (Gushee, *The Future*, 278). For more on the Cantwell-Collins sponsored Carbon Limits and Energy for America's Renewal (CLEAR) Act, see Christa Marshall, "Cantwell-Collins Bill Creates Lobbying Frenzy," *New York Times*, February 16, 2010, http://www.nytimes.com/cwire/2010/02/15/15climatewire-cantwell-collins-bill-generates-lobbying-fre-54450.html?pagewanted=all (accessed July 6, 2017).

64    For "separate" and "taint," see Jewell, interview. While Jonathan Merritt was also a team member of Terra Dei, Juskus' role seems to have been confined to the Flourish team. For Flourish's position on (over)population, see Rusty Pritchard, "The Other Environmental Crisis," *Flourish: Deep Down Things* (June 16, 2010), http://www.flourishonline.org/2010/06/the-other-environmental-crisis/ (accessed July 10, 2017); and Rusty Pritchard, "The Myth of Overpopulation," *Flourish* (Winter 2011), http://www.flourishonline.org/2011/01/the-myth-of-overpopulation/ (accessed July 11, 2017). Regarding Terra Dei's stance on the population issue, see Terra Dei Institute for Environmental Policy, "Population," Internet Archive: Wayback Machine, http://web.archive.org/web/20100914021448/http://terradei.org:80/topics/population (accessed July 7, 2017).

65    Rusty Pritchard, "The Real Earth Day," *Flourish* (November 24, 2011), http://www.flourishonline. org/2010/11/the-real-earth-day/ (accessed July 25, 2017). John A. Murdock, "Earth Day's Forgotten Founder," *Flourish*, Spring 2012, http://www.flourishonline.org/2012/03/earth-day-forgotten-founder/ (accessed July 25, 2017). Murdock was present during the CCCC 2010. He is an environmental lawyer and stylizes himself as "your typical tree-hugging conservative Christian"; see *Johnmurdock.org* (accessed November 16, 2019).

66    Pritchard, "The Myth of Overpopulation."

67    Regarding the fear of some that Flourish was "conceding ground to the evangelical Right's resistance to address climate change," see Wilkinson, *Between God & Green*, 124–25.

68    Rusty Pritchard, "The Danger of Derivatives," *Prism*, 2009: 5. Explicitly referring to former *CT* editor and Flourish conference participant Andy Crouch's book *Culture Making* (2008), Pritchard reminds his readers that there are other postures toward culture besides copying, namely condemning, critiquing, consuming, cultivating, and creating. While so far the evangelical responses to environmentalism had largely been condemnation and critique on the one hand, or consumption and imitation on the other, Pritchard contends to be most concerned about the latter two since they often adopted certain stances on issues such as population and capitalism without thoroughly reflecting their deeper theological and ideological ramifications. Similar to Crouch, who believes that after their loss of cultural power, American evangelicals have developed a dysfunctional relationship with the surrounding, non-evangelical culture (see the culture wars), Pritchard

argues that the only way to bring about substantial cultural change for the better is "to cultivate the good and true things" (Crouch) and make more of them. See Andy Crouch, *Culture Making: Recovering Our Creative Calling* (Downers Grove, Ill.: IVP Books, 2008).

[69] Pritchard worked as a strategy advisor for the U.K.-based organization from 2014 until 2018. In December 2018 he became vice president of the newly established U.S. chapter. See Pritchard's LinkedIn page at https://www.linkedin.com/in/rustypritchard/de (accessed November 16, 2019). For more information on Tearfund USA, see *Tearfundusa.org*, https://www.tearfundusa.org/ (accessed November 16, 2019). After almost six years at a strategic marketing consulting firm called the Valcourt Group, in November 2018 Jewell transitioned into the position of director for brand communications at Tyndale House Publishers; see Jewell's LinkedIn page at https://www.linkedin.com/in/jim-jewell-793ab86?trk=people-guest_profile-result-card_result-card_full-click (accessed November 16, 2019).

[70] Unfortunately, I was not able to get either Pritchard or Jewell to explicitly comment on their organization's dormancy/demise. For Jewell's blog entry, see Jim Jewell, "7 Reasons NonProfits Flounder or Fail," The Rooftop Blog, entry posted on May 4, 2014, https://therooftopblog.wordpress.com/2014/05/04/7-reasons-nonprofits-flounder-or-fail/ (accessed July 25, 2017). As he went on to explain: "They had the plan worked out on paper, and even had a foundation to underwrite the effort for a couple of years. But although there were many who cheered from the sidelines, very few people were committed enough to provide significant financial support. When the grant money ran out, the charity all but disappeared." For "fundraising dead zone," see Jewell, interview. It is certainly important to consider additional potential factors that may have led to the organization's dormancy, though, such as Jewell's comparatively weak transcendent motivation; the further political polarization in the United States; Creation Care, Inc.'s inability to connect with more traditional evangelical causes, such as global missions, relief, and development work, etc.

[71] There are no current tax returns available for Creation Care, Inc. Over the past years, however, the organization has received a few donations, such as the $27,905 from Massachusetts-based Agape Foundation in the tax year 2016/17, allocated "to support the organization's Birmingham Alabama Health Participatory Research Project to assess the health consequences of pollution." See Agape Foundation, "Return of Private Foundation," 2016, retrieved through GuideStar. Regarding RE/Illyn's involvement in environmental health and justice issues in Alabama, see Katherine Webb-Hehn, "In Birmingham, Activists Work to Protect Family and Environment," *Equal Voice News*, Marguerite Casey Foundation, August 14, 2019, https://caseygrants.org/evn/in-birmingham-activists-work-to-protect-families-and-environment/ (accessed November 17, 2019). For "to produce groups like," see John A. Murdock, "Creation Careless: Looking for a Green Path in the Age of Trump," *First Things*, March 10, 2017, https://www.firstthings.com/web-exclusives/2017/03/creation-careless (accessed June 2, 2017).


## CONCLUSION

[1] Lowe, interview.

[2] Nancy Sleeth, interview.

[3] Lowe, interview. Regarding "to make a real difference," see Lowe, *Green Revolution*, 19. Lowe was also the national organizer for Y.E.C.A. from 2012 until 2016. Established

under the auspices of the EEN, the group's first public action was a prayer rally at Hofstra University (N.Y.) during the second presidential debate in 2012. For more information on Y.E.C.A, see *Yecaction.org*, https://www.yecaction.org/ (accessed November 27, 2019).

4    Lowe, interview.

5    Lowe, interview. During a casual exchange while attending the CCCC 2009, I asked Jim Ball about his political identity, and he said that he considered himself an independent. Laushkin identified as an independent during our interview. For "strengths and weaknesses," see Lowe, interview. For Hescox prompting Lowe's involvement in politics, see Lowe, interview. Regarding Hescox's biographical background, see Mitch Hescox and Paul Douglas, *Caring for Creation: The Evangelical's Guide to Climate Change and a Healthy Environment* (Bloomington, Minn.: Bethany House Publishers, 2016), 14–15. In an "Open Letter to Rush Limbaugh" from 2013, Hescox describes himself as "a life-long Republican"; Mitchell C. Hescox, "An Open Letter To Rush Limbaugh," retrieved from *Belovedplanet.com*, http://belovedplanet.com/2013/08/15/an-open-letter-to-rush -limbaugh/ (accessed January 26, 2018). During the White House Prayer Breakfast in 2014, Hescox introduced himself to President Obama as: "I'm your friendly Republi-can environmentalist." Mitch Hescox, "Reflections from the White House Easter Prayer Breakfast," The Creation Care Blog, entry posted April 16, 2014, accessible through In-ternet Archive: Wayback Machine, captured on May 27, 2014, https://web.archive.org/ web/20140527012623/http://creationcare.org:80/archive.php?blog=1&year=2014& month=04 (accessed March 13, 2018).

6    When I initially asked Janel Curry whether the creation care movement signified a partisan realignment and potential break with the Republican Party on part of the evangelicals involved, Curry also emphasized that the movement was not partisan. Curry, interview.

7    In the United States more voters self-identify as independents than as Democrats or Republicans. According to Jones, however, "Many Americans who initially identify as independents reveal a 'leaning' toward one of the major parties when probed." Jeffrey M. Jones, "Independent Political ID in U.S. Lowest in Six Years," Gallup, January 6, 2017, http://news.gallup.com/poll/201638/independent-political-lowest-six-years.aspx (accessed January 16, 2018). As Ed Brown explained in more detail, "I'm like some of the other people you've talked to. In some areas I would have very conservative convictions about what we call family values. I'm very uncomfortable with the idea of gay marriage for personal reasons. I'm very uncomfortable with abortion for moral reasons, although I wouldn't put that in a box because I understand how things can . . . you know, any moral conviction, when it confronts real life, there is are always difficulties in figuring out how you apply it. But I'm also very, very concerned about the poor, about social issues, about how policies effect employment. And so I'm one of these guys, I need a third party. I need a third party that is, shall we say, morally conservative and socially liberal? Because I really think those go together." Brown, interview, 2010.

8    Hescox, "Witness Testimony." RE, bumper sticker (courtesy of Peter Illyn, March 2010).

9    Daniel K. Williams, "Prolifers on the Left: Progressive Evangelicals' Campaign Against Abortion," in *The New Evangelical Social Engagement*, ed. Brian Steensland and Philip Goff (New York: Oxford University Press, 2014), 216. Ball's displeasure with the Republican Party leadership was observed during the CCCC 2010.

¹⁰   See Brown, interview, 2010: "If you go back to the roots, now what does it mean to be conservative? It usually means to be concerned about taking care of things for the future. Not wasting. And that's what conservation is. Teddy Roosevelt, our greatest president, he was a Republican, he was a conservative. So, in a lot of ways these guys, the current batch of conservatives, have lost their roots in this area." On the opposing side regarding their personal voting patterns but nevertheless echoing Brown's sentiment, Dean Ohlman stated: "I belong at the beginning of the last century, with Teddy Roosevelt. So I would consider myself probably a Teddy Roosevelt conservative Republican." Ohlman, interview. Like Ohlman specifically referring to Roosevelt as conservative protector of America's national forests, Janel Curry suggested that creation care activism signified a move back toward a more "traditional" Republican ideology "prior to the rise of the far Right" instead of a new step into a more liberal/progressive political direction. Curry, interview. Remarked EEN's Alexei Laushkin: "We are not traditional environmentalists. We are probably a little bit more pragmatic, a little bit more conservative." Laushkin, interview.

¹¹   Illyn, interview. Illyn used an example of religious freedom to emphasize his libertarian leanings. Lowe also expressed that he leaned toward libertarianism, in his case mainly regarding the question of homosexuality and gay marriage; Lowe, interview. With regard to gay marriage specifically, Illyn invoked what Putnam and Campbell have termed the "My Friend Al Principle" accounting for the "spillover" effect friendship networks can have on the perception of certain social or religious groups: though evangelicals must consider homosexuality to be "unbiblical," in particular younger evangelicals had gay friends they loved, and so how could they deny them "the right to have a meaningful relationship"? Illyn, interview. For "My Friend Al Principle" and "spillover," see Putnam and Campbell, *American Grace*, 531–34.

¹²   Illyn, interview. For "the rift as more accurately defined" and the following quotations, see Illyn, "Belly-Button Christianity," 607–8 (emphases original). As he goes on to explain his view of disconnected, compartmentalized people: "They use phrases like a battle between good versus evil; darkness versus light; us versus them; right versus wrong. In the environmental debates, these compartmentalized people espouse false dichotomies like 'jobs versus the environment' or 'man versus nature' or, as Woody Allen says, 'I am two with nature.'" Illyn, "Belly-Button Christianity," 607–8.

¹³   DeWitt, interview.

¹⁴   DeWitt, interview. Brown, interview, 2010.

¹⁵   Understood as such, environmental problems can be approached from within a progressive political framework as much as from within a conservative one. As Laushkin put it, "You can have an authentically conservative frame of mind and still be very active on the environment"; there is no need to be "a Democratic atheist" in order to advocate creation care. Laushkin, interview. Likewise states Lowe (*Green Revolution*, 158–59): "Our common concern for this planet may have political implications, but it is inherently nonpartisan and urgently needs to go beyond partisan politics."

¹⁶   Jonathan Merritt, "Uplink," in *Green Revolution: Coming Together to Care for Creation*, by Ben Lowe (Downers Grove, Ill.: IVP Books, 2009), 164.

¹⁷   For "Machiavellian," see E. Calvin Beisner, "EEN's Machiavellian Mercury Campaign Threatens Pro-Life Movement," Cornwall Alliance, December 21, 2011, http://cornwallalliance.org/2011/12/eens-machiavellian-mercury-campaign-threatens-pro-life-movement/ (accessed January 26, 2018).

[18]     For "earth third," see Illyn, interview. Hescox's remark was noted during the CCCC in 2009.

[19]     Curry, interview. For NAE's statement of faith, see National Association of Evangelicals, "Statement of Faith," *Nae.org*, http://www.nae.net/statement-of-faith/ (accessed January 22, 2018).

[20]     See chapter 2 and chapter 3.

[21]     For "green dragon," see CA's RGD initiative described in chapter 5. Martin E. Marty, "The Years of the Evangelicals," *The Christian Century* (February 15, 1989), 171–74. Rick Warren, *The Purpose Driven Life: What on Earth Am I Here For?* (Grand Rapids: Zondervan, 2002), 283 (emphasis original).

[22]     See Schaeffer, *Pollution*, 61–62. Thirty years after Schaeffer, EEN cofounder Ronald Sider ("Biblical Foundations," 43) reiterated in a strikingly similar way that evangelical ignorance or denouncement of environmental problems "would be a tragic mistake—for at least three reasons. . . . And third, because if we do not offer biblical foundations for environmental action, we will have only ourselves to blame if environmental activists turn to other, finally inadequate worldviews and religions." When asked, after another ten years had passed, whether he agreed with Sider and his perception that creation care activism provided evangelistic opportunities, Alexei Laushkin reacted enthusiastically: "It does! . . . Yeah, it's part of who we are as evangelicals, so we've had opportunities to minister, to witness." Laushkin, interview. Diagnosing the larger environmental movement with what she perceived to be "burn-out" after decades of activism, Nancy Sleeth reported on similar experiences and emphasized that of the two directions BE attempted to build bridges to, one was "for people who do love creation but perhaps don't know the Creator." Sleeth, interview. On December 28, 2011, EEN's electronic newsletter declared: "We are sharing the gospel and have seen how creation care remains one of the greatest tools for evangelism in younger generations." Mitch Hescox, "End of Year Ministry Partnership," Evangelical Environmental Network, electronic newsletter, December 28, 2011. Similar statements have been made by Brown, interview, 2010; and Ohlman, interview.

[23]     Brown, interview, 2010. See also Sabin quoted in chapter 3. For "it's part," see Laushkin, interview.

[24]     For "engagement with distinction" as the typical subcultural orientation of American Evangelicalism, see Smith, *American Evangelicalism*, 178. In *The Creation*, E. O. Wilson addresses a fictitious Southern Baptist pastor with the following words: "Let us see, then, if we can, and you are willing, to meet on the near side of metaphysics in order to deal with the real world we share." See E. O. Wilson, *The Creation: An Appeal to Save Life on Earth* (New York: W. W. Norton, 2006), 4. Says Brown, explicitly referring to E. O. Wilson's appeal to foster cooperation between scientists and religious leaders in the realm of biological conservation: "I think that the common ground is that we have a genuine threat facing all of us as human beings, and so that's like the flood coming. And at that level it doesn't matter what I believe. My grandchildren are being threatened, so let's work together. And that's where I agree with E. O. Wilson. Let's set aside our disagreements, fix the problem, and we can argue later." Brown, interview, 2010.

[25]     In particular evangelical Christians, Muslims, and Catholics have displayed an uneasiness toward the discussion of certain birth control methods at U.N. population conferences, thus provoking the conclusion that "there are limits, then, to what religions may contribute to environmental problems." Tucker, "Religion and Ecology," 412. Brown, interview, 2010.

26  Jonathan Franzen, *Freedom* (New York: Farrar, Straus and Giroux, 2010), 360–61.

27  For "tricky," see Lowe, interview. For Matthew Sleeth's more extensive treatment of the population issue, see the chapter "Population Fallout" in *Serve God*, 180–89.

28  Lowe, interview. See also former *Flourish* magazine editor Kendra Langdon Juskus' article on animal welfare, which won an award from the Humane Society of the United States: "A Call to Compassion from Our Brothers the Animals" (2012). The article was first published in ESA's *Prism* magazine and can be accessed via *Flourishonline.org*, http://www.flourishonline.org/2012/03/a-call-to-compassion-from-our-brothers-the-animals/ (accessed November 29, 2019). More recently, Sarah Withrow King has also argued that animal welfare is/should be an integral component of creation care: *Vegangelical: How Caring for Animals Can Shape Your Faith* (Grand Rapids: Zodervan, 2016). Matthew Sleeth, *Serve God*, 185. Brown made a similar remark during our interview in 2010.

29  For "precious" and "rightly abhor," see Brown, *Our Father's World*, 32. Pritchard, "The Myth of Overpopulation." Brown, interview, 2010.

30  "From Fred Krueger," *Green Cross*, Fall 1995, 1. For "runaway consumerism" and "debauchery of materialism," see Ohlman, "Finding the Lost Fundamental," 5. Regarding "preaching Julian Simon's," see Dean Ohlman, letter to E. Calvin Beisner, January 12, 1994, Dean Ohlman Private Papers, Grand Rapids, Mich. (courtesy of Dean Ohlman).

31  Brown, *Our Father's World*, 65–69. Dean Ohlman, letter to E. Calvin Beisner, March 11, 1994, Dean Ohlman Private Papers, Grand Rapids (courtesy of Dean Ohlman).

32  Ohlman, letter to Beisner, March 11, 1994 (emphasis original). For "new McCarthyism" and "most environmentally concerned," see Dean Ohlman, letter to E. Calvin Beisner, April 12, 1994, Dean Ohlman Private Papers, Grand Rapids, Mich. (courtesy of Dean Ohlman). Regarding Ohlman's apology, "entirely unfair," and "those who want," see Dean Ohlman, letter to E. Calvin Beisner, April 22, 1994, Dean Ohlman Private Papers, Grand Rapids, Mich. (courtesy of Dean Ohlman). As Ohlman concluded in his last letter to Beisner, after the two men had agreed that their differences regarding environmentalism were not reconcilable: "I think where the rub comes in our discussions is that I perceive your giving too much 'faith' to the efficacy of American capitalism to solve our environmental problems and that you perceive that I give too much credibility to environmental scientists and their conclusions about the state of the environment." Dean Ohlman, letter to E. Calvin Beisner, September 8, 1995, Dean Ohlman Private Papers, Grand Rapids, Mich. (courtesy of Dean Ohlman).

33  For Klein's critique, see Naomi Klein, *This Changes Everything: Capitalism vs. the Climate* (New York: Simon and Schuster, 2014).

34  As D. James Kennedy put it with regard to global warming, contrasting his starting point with that of environmentalists' by alluding to the propositions regarding the fragility of ecosystems made in Al Gore's *Earth in the Balance*: "Those committed to a biblical worldview understand that God made the world, and it does not hang in the balance. The world He made goes through warming and cooling periods that have nothing to do with human activities. It is simply human hubris when we declare that we are the cause of global warming (or cooling). . . . If there is a villain in this scenario, it is the sun, not the SUV." Kennedy and Newcombe, *How Would Jesus Vote?* 133. A similar attitude transpires through parts of the material subculture of Evangelicalism in the United States, where I found T-shirts in Christian gift shops in Arkansas and Colorado with the following prints: "Global Warming Is Nothing Next To Eternal Burning"; seen at a Christian bookstore

in Eureka Springs, Arkansas, September 2009. And "Global Warming: Don't Be Here When Things Really Heat Up!—2 Peter 3:10"; bought at the gift shop of Focus on the Family, Colorado Springs, August 2010. Regarding its design and message, the latter shirt is particularly impressive as it is black and displays the sphere of the earth surrounded by a ring of fire, across which the statement on global warming is printed in white letters. The back of the T-shirt shows the earth completely reddened and consumed by flames, with the Bible verse from 2 Peter 3:10 printed across in white letters: "But the day of the Lord will come like a thief. The heavens will disappear with a roar; the elements will be destroyed by fire, & the earth & everything in it will be laid bare." God's judgment and biblical apocalypse, according to these messages, are what ought to be feared, and not something mundane and, if real at all, "natural" as climate change. (Note that the T-shirt bought at Focus on the Family is distributed by the Christian company Kerusso, whose mission it is to change the world with messages displayed on T-shirts. As it says on its tag: "Did you know that the average Christian T-shirt is read as many as 3,000 times before it goes to the yard sale? You can impact your world for Jesus Christ simply by Changing Your Shirt! So what are you waiting for?" For more information, see *Karusso.com*.) For evangelicals' attempts to read the Bible scientifically, see for example Ronald L. Numbers, *The Creationists: From Scientific Creationism to Intelligent Design* (1992; exp. ed., Cambridge, Mass.: Harvard University Press, 2006). According to Peter Berger, who claims to have adopted the term from his colleague Adam Seligman, "Epistemological modesty means that you believe certain things, but you're modest about these claims. You can be a believer and yet say, I'm not really sure." Note that Berger understands epistemological modesty to define a fault line between fanaticism and relativism and is "inclined to define theological liberalism in terms of being on one side of this fault line rather than in terms of any specific beliefs." The Christian Century Foundation, "Epistemological Modesty: An Interview with Peter Berger," *The Christian Century*, October 29, 1997, 972–78. Available via *Religion-online.org*, https://www.religion-online.org/article/epistemological-modesty-an-interview-with-peter-berger/ (accessed January 13, 2018).

[35] From an anthropological viewpoint, the core symptoms of the "fundamentalist syndrome" are a quest for certainty, a preoccupation with unambiguous theological and sociological boundaries, and an insular thinking of true believers versus the enemy other/s. Judith Nagata, "Beyond Theology: Toward an Anthropology of 'Fundamentalism,'" *American Anthropologist* 103, no. 2 (2001): 481–98.

[36] Ohlman, letter to Beisner, March 11, 1994. Schaeffer, *Pollution*.

[37] When I talked to Ohlman about the Creation Museum in Kentucky, which teaches that the Bible provides the starting point for science (i.e., creation science), Ohlman sadly shook his head and said that this museum "idolize[d] science" and "belittle[d] Scripture"; Ohlman, interview. For relativists and "the naturalistic faith," see Wuthnow, *The Struggle*, 186. Regarding fundamentalists "banish" and make God "knowable," see Chris Hedges, *American Fascists: The Christian Right and the War on America* (New York: Free Press, 2006), 81.

[38] Regarding culture as "the rules of the game," see Martin E. Marty, "H. Richard Niebuhr, A Centennial Appreciation" (lecture, Elmhurst College, Elmhurst, Ill., March 6, 2012). The information on WallBuilders is from WallBuilders, "About Us," *Wallbuilders.com*, https://wallbuilders.com/about-us/ (accessed March 17, 2018).

[39] See "Glenn Beck: Dangers of Environmental Extremism." During our interview, Lowe did not express much sympathy for Beck and emphasized the importance of pluralism; Lowe, interview.

40    For "engagement-with-distinction," see Smith, *American Evangelicalism*, 178. Hescox, "Reflections."

41    Paul Hawken, *Blessed Unrest: How the Largest Social Movement in History Is Restoring Grace, Justice, and Beauty to the World* (New York: Penguin, 2007). Illyn, interview. As Brown mentioned in our follow-up interview, between 2010 and 2016 "five or six major Christian mission organizations," including international Overseas Missionary Fellowship (OMF) and Chicago-based TEAM (The Evangelical Alliance Mission), had "very quietly assigned staff people to do creation care work, and [that] usually in a central position where they are guiding the whole organization." Hence, two people within TEAM were now "working with the whole organization to recruit young people to come into TEAM to do creation care projects in different parts of the world," according to Brown, which, considering the millions of dollars the organization is able to spend each year, is a rather positive development for the creation care movement indeed. Said Brown: "Instead of having to tear down the cathedrals and build new ones, we [now] have people in those cathedrals who are quietly preaching the creation care gospel." Brown, interview, 2016. According to the organization's annual report, TEAM spent more than 30 million dollars on "church planting and related ministries" in 2016; in 2015 the number was above 28 million. See TEAM, "Annual Report 2015–2016," available for download at http://learn.team.org/annual-report (accessed on March 10, 2018). A look at the website of TEAM, an organization founded as early as 1890, confirms that creation care is one of the nine official areas in which the organization serves to fulfill its mission. As the organization explains, "TEAM missionaries establish churches by seeking to make followers of Jesus Christ who learn and obey all that he has commanded. Creation care endeavors fulfill this purpose within the context of managing and caring for the environment." Concrete "gospel-centered" creation care efforts of TEAM missionaries therefore include recycling projects in Ukraine, sustainable farming in Zimbabwe, eco-ranching in Mexico, and other reforestation, urban gardening, well drilling, and aquaponics initiatives worldwide. See TEAM, "Creation Care," https://team.org/static/uploads/HowWeServe-CreationCare1.pdf (accessed April 28, 2018).

## APPENDIX

1    For "organized in," see Lowery and Brasher, *Organized Interest*, 10–11. According to Griffith and McAlister, religious actors in America "are engaged in a variety of activities that can (and, we think, should) be construed as political: they lay claims on particular public spaces as necessarily religious; make movies and write books to forward their views; deal directly with the power of the state to define and delimit religion; and work outside the state to enact religious ideals on a global scale." R. Marie Griffith and Melani McAlister, "Is the Public Square Still Naked?" *American Quarterly* 59, no. 3 (2007), 554.

2    Parachurch organizations are organizations that are "intimately connected with and supported by a religious tradition, yet have no ties to a specific religious denomination." See Robert Booth Fowler et al., *Religion and Politics in America: Faith, Culture, and Strategic Choices*, 33.

3    Allen D. Hertzke, "American Religion and Politics: A Review Essay," *The Western Political Quarterly* 41, no. 4 (1988), 835.

Abbey, Edward. *The Monkey Wrench Gang.* Harper Perennial Modern Classics. 1975. Reissue, New York: Harper Collins, 2006.

Albanese, Catherine L. "Fisher Kings and Public Places: The Old New Age in the 1990s." *Annals of the American Academy of Political and Social Science* 527 (1993): 131–43.

Alsdurf, Phyllis Elaine. "*Christianity Today* Magazine and Late Twentieth-Century Evangelicalism." Ph.D. diss., University of Minnesota, 2005.

Amery, Carl. *Das Ende der Vorsehung: Die gnadenlosen Folgen des Christentums.* Reinbek bei Hamburg: Rowohlt, 1972.

Ammerman, Nancy Tatom. *Bible Believers: Fundamentalists in the Modern World.* New Brunswick, N.J.: Rutgers University Press, 1987.

"Another View: ESA's Sider Takes Issue with *World* Critique." *World.* January 8, 1994.

"Are God's Resources Finite? A Group of Christian Leaders Claim They Are, but Does the Claim Square with the Evidence?" *World.* November 27, 1993.

Bafumi, Joseph, and Robert Y. Shapiro. "A New Partisan Voter." *The Journal of Politics* 71, no. 1 (2009): 1–24.

Ball, James G. "Evangelical Protestants, the Ecological Crisis and Public Theology." Ph.D. diss., Drew University, 1997.

———. *Global Warming and the Risen Lord: Christian Discipleship and Climate Change.* Washington, D.C.: Evangelical Environmental Network, 2010.

———. "Jesus Christ, Creation and the Protection of God's Creatures." *Green Cross.* Winter 1996.

———. "Walk the walk . . . and drive the talk." *Creation Care* 19 (Fall 2002).

———. "A Word from EEN's new director: When did your creation-care awakening begin?" *Creation Care* (Winter 2000). http://www.creationcare.org/magazine/winter00.php (accessed August 10, 2008).

Balmer, Randall H. *Thy Kingdom Come: How the Religious Right Distorts the Faith and Threatens America. An Evangelical's Lament.* New York: Basic Books, 2006.

———. *Redeemer: The Life of Jimmy Carter.* New York: Basic Books, 2014.

Barcott, Bruce. "For God So Loved the World." *Outside Online* (March 2001). https://www.outsideonline.com/1888006/god-so-loved-world (accessed October 10, 2019).

Barka, Mokhtar Ben. "Religion and Environmental Concern in the United States." In *"Nature's Nation" Revisited: American Concepts of Nature from Wonder to Ecological Crisis,* edited by Hans Bak and Walter W. Hölbling, 281–93. European Contributions to American Studies. Amsterdam: VU University Press, 2003.

Barker, David C., and David H. Bearce. "End-Times Theology, the Shadow of the Future, and Public Resistance to Addressing Global Climate Change." *Political Research Quarterly* 66, no. 2 (2013): 267–79.

Barthes, Roland. *Mythologies.* Translated by Annette Lavers. New York: Hill and Wang, 1972.

Bean, Lydia, and Steve Teles. "God and Climate." *Democracy* 36, no. 40 (2016). http://democracyjournal.org/magazine/40/god-and-climate/ (accessed March 1, 2017).

———. "Spreading the Gospel of Climate Change: An Evangelical Battleground." *Newamerica.org.* Washington, D.C., November 2015. https://static.newamerica .org/attachments/11649-spreading-the-gospel-of-climate-change/climate _care11.9.4f0142a50aa24a2ba65020f7929f6fd7.pdf (accessed May 12, 2018).

Bebbington, David W. *Evangelicalism in Modern Britain: A History from the 1730s to the 1980s.* London: Unwin Hyman, 1989.

Beisner, E. Calvin. *Answers for Atheists, Agnostics, and Other Thoughtful Skeptics: Dialogs About Christian Life and Faith.* Revised edition, Wheaton, Ill.: Crossway Books, 1993.

———. "Deep Ecology, Neopaganism & Global Warming." In *On Global Wizardry: Techniques of Pagan Spirituality and a Christian Response,* edited by Peter Jones, 171–85. Escondido, Calif.: Main Entry Editions, 2010.

———. *Prospects for Growth: A Biblical View of Population, Resources, and the Future.* Turning Point Christian Worldview Series, edited by Marvin Olasky. Westchester, Ill.: Crossway Books, 1990.

———. *Where Garden Meets Wilderness: Evangelical Entry into the Environmental Debate.* Grand Rapids: Acton Institute for the Study of Religion and Liberty, 1997.

Bell, Colin, Robert S. White, and Edward R. Brown. "Introduction." In *Creation Care and the Gospel: Reconsidering the Mission of the Church,* edited by Colin Bell and Robert S. White, 1–6. Peabody, Mass.: Hendrickson, 2016.

Bellah, Robert N. "Civil Religion in America." In *American Civil Religion,* edited by Donald G. Jones and Russell E. Richey, 21–44. 1974. Reprint, San Francisco: Mellen Research University Press, 1990.

Benford, Robert D., and David A. Snow. "Framing Processes and Social Movements: An Overview and Assessment." *Annual Review of Sociology* 26 (2000): 611–39.

Berger, Peter L. *Adventures of an Accidental Sociologist: How to Explain the World Without Becoming a Bore.* Amherst, N.Y.: Prometheus, 2011.

Berlinerblau, Jacques. *Thumpin' It: The Use and Abuse of the Bible in Today's Presidential Politics.* Louisville, Ky.: Westminster John Knox, 2008.

Bernardin, Joseph. *The Seamless Garment.* Kansas City, Mo.: National Catholic Reporter, 1984.

Berry, Jeffrey M. *The New Liberalism: The Rising Power of Citizen Groups.* Washington, D.C.: Brookings Institution Press, 1999.

———. *Surveying Nonprofits: A Methods Handbook.* Washington, D.C.: Aspen Institute, 2003.

Berry, Jeffrey M., and Clyde Wilcox. *The Interest Group Society.* 4th ed. New York: Pearson Longman, 2007.

Berry, R. J., ed. *The Care of Creation: Focusing Concern and Action.* Downers Grove, Ill.: InterVarsity, 2000.

Bliss, Lowell. "Environmental Missions: An Introduction." In *Creation Care and the Gospel: Reconsidering the Mission of the Church,* ed. by Colin Bell and Robert S. White, 53–70. Lausanne Library. Peabody, Mass.: Hendrickson, 2016.

———. *Environmental Missions: Planting Churches and Trees.* Pasadena, Calif.: William Carey Library, 2013.

Bolce, Louis, and Gerald De Maio. "Secularists, Antifundamentalists, and the New Religious Divide in the American Electorate." In *From Pews to Polling Places: Faith and Politics in the American Religious Mosaic,* edited by J. Matthew Wilson, 251–85. Washington, D.C.: Georgetown University Press, 2007.

Bosso, Christopher J. *Environment, Inc.: From Grassroots to Beltway.* Lawrence: University Press of Kansas, 2005.

Bouma-Prediger, Steven. *For the Beauty of the Earth: A Christian Vision for Creation Care.* Grand Rapids: Baker, 2001.

Boyer, Paul S. *When Time Shall Be No More: Prophecy Belief in Modern American Culture.* Cambridge, Mass.: Harvard University Press, 1992.

Brown, Edward R. *Our Father's World: Mobilizing the Church to Care for Creation.* 2nd ed. Downers Grove, Ill.: IVP Books, 2008.

Bruce, Steve. *The Rise and Fall of the New Christian Right: Conservative Protestant Politics in America, 1978–1988.* Oxford: Oxford University Press, 1988.

Brulle, Robert J. *Agency, Democracy, and Nature: The U.S. Environmental Movement from a Critical Theory Perspective.* Cambridge, Mass.: MIT Press, 2000.

———. "Institutionalizing Delay: Foundation Funding and the Creation of U.S. Climate Change Counter-movement Organizations." *Climatic Change* 122 (2014): 681–94.

Bullard, Robert D. *Dumping in Dixie: Race, Class and Environmental Quality*. 3rd ed. Boulder, Colo.: Westview Press, 2000.

Cahn, Robert, and Patricia Cahn. "Did Earth Day Change the World?" *Environment* 32, no. 7 (1990): 16–42.

Carpenter, Joel A. *Revive Us Again: The Reawakening of American Fundamentalism*. New York: Oxford University Press, 1997.

Carson, Rachel L. *Silent Spring*. Boston: Houghton Mifflin, 1962.

Cizik, Richard. Foreword to *The Future of Faith in American Politics: The Public Witness of the Evangelical Center*, by David P. Gushee. Waco, Tex.: Baylor University Press, 2008.

————. "A History of the Public Policy Resolutions of the National Association of Evangelicals." In *Toward an Evangelical Public Policy: Political Strategies for the Health of the Nation*, edited by Ronald J. Sider and Diane Knippers, 35–63. Grand Rapids: Baker, 2005.

Cook, John, Dana Nuccitelli, Sarah A. Green, Mark Richarson, Bärbel Winkler, Rob Painting, Robert Way, Peter Jacobs, and Andrew Skuce. "Quantifying the Consensus on Anthropocentric Global Warming in the Scientific Literature." *Environmental Research Letters* 8, no. 2 (2013): 024024.

Crichton, Michael. *State of Fear*. 2004. Reprint, New York: HarperCollins, 2013.

Cromartie, Michael, ed. *A Public Faith: Evangelicals and Civic Engagement*. Lanham, Md.: Rowman and Littlefield, 2003.

Crouch, Andy. *Culture Making: Recovering Our Creative Calling*. Downers Grove, Ill.: IVP Books, 2008.

Cumbey, Constance E. *Hidden Dangers of the Rainbow: The New Age Movement and Our Coming Age of Barbarism*. Shreveport, La.: Huntington House, 1983.

Danielsen, Sabrina. "Fracturing Over Creation Care? Shifting Environmental Beliefs Among Evangelicals, 1984–2010." *Journal for the Scientific Study of Religion* 52 (2013): 198–215.

De Bell, Garrett, ed. *The Environmental Handbook*. New York: Ballantine/Friends of the Earth, 1970.

DeWitt, Calvin B. "Creation's Environmental Challenge to Evangelical Christianity." In *The Care of Creation: Focusing Concern and Action*, edited by R. J. Berry, 60–73. Downers Grove, Ill.: InterVarsity, 2000.

————. "Knowing and Doing: The Science-Ethics-Praxis Triad and the Human Predicament." *Green Cross* (Winter 1997).

————. "The Place of Creation in Today's Missionary Discourse: Evangelical Environmentalism in America." In *Missiology and the Environment*, edited by Lukas Vischer, 174–204. Geneva, Switzerland: John Knox Center, 2007.

————. "Reading the Bible through a Green Lens." In *The Green Bible*, I-25–I-34. New York: HarperOne, 2008.

———. "Science, Scripture, and Con-serving Creation." In *Holy Ground: A Gathering of Voices on Caring for Creation*, edited by Lyndsay Moseley, 74–87. San Francisco: Sierra Club Books, 2008.

———. "The Scientist and the Shepherd: The Emergence of Evangelical Environmentalism." In *The Oxford Handbook of Religion and Ecology*, edited by Roger S. Gottlieb, 568–87. Oxford: Oxford University Press, 2006.

———. "You Can Make Your Church a Creation Awareness Center." *Green Cross.* Winter 1995.

DeWitt, Calvin, and Susan Drake. "Resolution on the Care and Keeping of Creation and Its Living Species." *Green Cross.* Winter 1996.

Diamond, Sara. *Roads to Dominion: Right-Wing Movements and Political Power in the United States.* New York: Guilford Press, 1995.

———. *Spiritual Warfare: The Politics of the Christian Right.* Boston: South End Press, 1989.

Dowie, Mark. *Losing Ground: American Environmentalism at the Close of the Twentieth Century.* Cambridge, Mass.: MIT Press, 1995.

Dowland, Seth. "American Evangelicalism and the Politics of Whiteness." *Christian Century* (June 19, 2018). https://www.christiancentury.org/article/critical-essay/american-evangelicalism-and-politics-whiteness (accessed February 25, 2019).

Dryzek, John S. *The Politics of the Earth: Environmental Discourses.* 2nd ed. Oxford: Oxford University Press, 2005.

Dryzek, John S., David Downes, Christian Hunold, and David Scholsberg, with Hans-Kristian Hernes. *Green States and Social Movements: Environmentalism in the United States, United Kingdom, Germany, & Norway.* Oxford: Oxford University Press, 2003.

Dunlap, Riley E., and Aaron M. McCright. "Organized Climate Change Denial." In *The Oxford Handbook on Climate Change and Society*, edited by John S. Dryzek, Richard B. Norgaard, and David Schlosberg, 144–60. Oxford: Oxford University Press, 2011.

———. "Social Movement Identity: Validating a Measure of Identification with the Environmental Movement." *Social Science Quarterly* 89, no. 5 (2008): 1045–65.

Eckberg, Douglas Lee, and T. J. Blocker. "Varieties of Religious Involvement and Environmental Concern." *Journal for the Scientific Study of Religion* 28 (1989): 509–17.

Ehrlich, Paul R. *The Population Bomb.* New York: Ballantine Books, 1968.

Elisha, Omri. "All Catholics Now? Specters of Catholicism in Evangelical Social Engagement." In *The New Evangelical Social Engagement*, edited by Brian Steensland and Philip Goff, 73–93. New York: Oxford University Press, 2014.

Ellingson, Stephen. *To Care for Creation: The Emergence of the Religious Environmental Movement.* Chicago: University of Chicago Press, 2016.

Emerson, Michael O., and Christian Smith. *Divided by Faith: Evangelical Religion and the Problem of Race in America*. New York: Oxford University Press, 2000.

Evans, John H., and Michael S. Evans. "Religion and Science: Beyond the Epistemological Conflict Narrative." *Annual Review of Sociology* 34 (2008): 87–105.

Eyerman, Ron, and Andrew Jamison. *Social Movements: A Cognitive Approach*. University Park: Penn State University Press, 1991.

Falwell, Jerry. "An Agenda for the 1980s." In *Piety and Politics: Evangelicals and Fundamentalists Confront the World*, ed. Richard John Neuhaus and Michael Cromartie. Washington, D.C.: Ethics and Public Policy Center, 1987.

———. "Introduction by Jerry Falwell." In *The New Right: We're Ready to Lead*, by Richard A. Viguerie. Falls Church, Va.: Viguerie, 1980.

Fetzer, Joel, and Gretchen S. Carnes. "Dr. Ron Sider: Mennonite Environmentalist on the Evangelical Left." In *Religious Leaders and Faith-Based Politics: Ten Profiles*, edited by Jo Renee Formicola and Hubert Morken, 159–73. Lanham, Md.: Rowman & Littlefield, 2001.

Fiorina, Morris P., with Samuel J. Adams and Jeremy C. Pope. *Culture War? The Myth of a Polarized America*. 3rd ed. New York: Pearson Longman, 2010.

FitzGerald, Frances. *The Evangelicals: The Struggle to Shape America*. New York: Simon & Schuster, 2017.

Fowler, Robert Booth. *The Greening of Protestant Thought*. Chapel Hill: University of North Carolina Press, 1995.

———. *A New Engagement: Evangelical Political Thought, 1966–1976*. Grand Rapids: Eerdmans, 1982.

Fowler, Robert Booth, Allen D. Hertzke, Laura R. Olson, and Kevin R. den Dulk. *Religion and Politics in America: Faith, Culture, and Strategic Choices*. 3rd ed. Boulder, Colo.: Westview, 2004.

Franzen, Jonathan. *Freedom*. New York: Farrar, Straus and Giroux, 2010.

Freeman, Jo. "On the Origins of Social Movements." In *Waves of Protest: Social Movements Since the Sixties*, edited by Jo Freeman and Victoria Johnson, 7–24. Lanham, Md.: Rowman and Littlefield, 1999.

Gerson, Michael J. *Heroic Conservatism: Why Republicans Need to Embrace America's Ideals (And Why They Deserve to Fail If They Don't)*. New York: HarperOne, 2007.

Gore, Al. *Earth in the Balance: Forging a New Common Purpose*. London, UK: Earthscan, 1992.

Gottlieb, Roger S. "Earth 101." *Worldviews* 8, nos. 2/3 (2004): 377–93.

———. *A Greener Faith: Religious Environmentalism and Our Planet's Future*. Oxford: Oxford University Press, 2006.

Graham, Billy. *Approaching Hoofbeats: The Four Horseman of the Apocalypse*. Minneapolis, Minn.: Grason, 1983.

———. *Just As I Am: The Autobiography of Billy Graham*. New York: Harper Collins, 1997.

Gray, Virginia, and David Lowery. *The Population Ecology of Interest Representation: Lobbying Communities in the American States.* Ann Arbor: University of Michigan Press, 1996.

Green, John C. "Evangelical Protestants and Civic Engagement: An Overview." In *A Public Faith: Evangelicals and Civic Engagement,* edited by Michael Cromartie, 11–29. Lanham, Md.: Rowman and Littlefield, 2003.

———. "Seeking a Place: Evangelical Protestants and Public Engagement in the Twentieth Century." In *Toward an Evangelical Public Policy: Political Strategies for the Health of the Nation,* edited by Ronald J. Sider and Diane Knippers, 15–34. Grand Rapids: Baker, 2005.

Griffith, R. Marie. *God's Daughters: Evangelical Women and the Power of Submission.* Berkeley: University of California Press, 1997.

Griffith, R. Marie, and Melani McAlister. "Is the Public Square Still Naked?" *American Quarterly* 59, no. 3 (2007): 527–63.

Guha, Ramachandra. *Environmentalism: A Global History.* Oxford: Oxford University Press, 2000.

Gushee, David P. *The Future of Faith in American Politics: The Public Witness of the Evangelical Center.* Waco, Tex.: Baylor University Press, 2008.

Guth, James L., John C. Green, Lyman A. Kellstedt, and Corwin E. Smidt. "Faith and the Environment: Religious Beliefs and Attitudes on Environmental Policy." *American Journal of Political Science* 39 (1995): 364–82.

Hackett, Conrad, and D. Michael Lindsay. "Measuring Evangelicalism: Consequences of Different Operationalization Strategies." *Journal for the Scientific Study of Religion* 47, no. 3 (2008): 499–514.

Hamlin, Christopher, and John T. McGreevy. "The Greening of America, Catholic Style, 1930–1950." *Environmental History* 11 (2006): 464–99.

Hand, Carl M., and Kent D. Van Liere. "Religion, Mastery-Over-Nature, and Environmental Concern." *Social Forces* 63 (1984): 555–70

Harrington, Jonathan. "Evangelicalism, Environmental Activism, and Climate Change in the U.S." *Journal of Religion and Society* 11 (2009): 1–24.

Hart, D. G. *That Old-time Religion in Modern America: Evangelical Protestantism in the Twentieth Century.* The American Ways Series. Chicago: Ivan R. Dee, 2002.

Hatch, Nathan O. *The Democratization of American Christianity.* New Haven, Conn.: Yale University Press, 1989.

Hawken, Paul. *Blessed Unrest: How the Largest Social Movement in History Is Restoring Grace, Justice, and Beauty to the World.* New York: Penguin, 2007.

Hayek, F. A. *The Road to Serfdom.* Vol. 2 of *The Collected Works of F. A. Hayek,* edited by Bruce Caldwell. New York: Routledge, 2008.

Hayhoe, Katharine, and Andrew Farley. *A Climate for Change: Global Warming Facts for Faith-Based Decisions.* New York: FaithWords, 2009.

Hays, Samuel P. *Beauty, Health, and Permanence: Environmental Politics in the United States, 1955–1985.* Cambridge: Cambridge University Press, 1987.

Hedges, Chris. *American Fascists: The Christian Right and the War on America.* New York: Free Press, 2006.

Heelas, Paul. *The New Age Movement: The Celebration of the Self and the Sacralization of Modernity.* Oxford: Blackwell, 1996.

Hendricks, Stephenie. *Divine Destruction: Wise Use, Dominion Theology, and the Making of American Environmental Policy.* Melville Manifestos. Hoboken, N.J.: Melville House Publishing, 2005.

Herberg, Will. *Protestant-Catholic-Jew.* Garden City, N.Y.: Doubleday-Anchor, 1955.

Hertzke, Allen D. "American Religion and Politics: A Review Essay." *The Western Political Quarterly* 41, no. 4 (1988): 825–38.

Hescox, Mitch, and Paul Douglas. *Caring for Creation: The Evangelical's Guide to Climate Change and a Healthy Environment.* Bloomington, Minn.: Bethany House Publishers, 2016.

Heyrman, Christine Leigh. *Southern Cross: The Beginnings of the Bible Belt.* Chapel Hill: University of North Carolina Press, 1997.

Hitzhusen, Gregory E. "Judeo-Christian Theology and the Environment: Moving Beyond Scepticism to New Sources for Environmental Education in the United States." *Environmental Education Research* 13, no. 1 (2007): 55–74.

Hofrenning, Daniel J. B. *In Washington but Not of It: The Prophetic Politics of Religious Lobbyists.* Philadelphia: Temple University Press, 1995.

Hunter, James Davison. *American Evangelicalism: Conservative Religion and the Quandary of Modernity.* New Brunswick, N.J.: Rutgers University Press, 1983.

———. *Culture Wars: The Struggle to Define America.* New York: Basic Books, 1991.

———. "Operationalizing Evangelicalism: A Review, Critique, and Proposal." *Sociological Analysis* 42 (1982): 363–72.

Hunter, Joel C. *A New Kind of Conservative.* Ventura, Calif.: Regal, 2008.

———. *Right Wing, Wrong Bird: Why the Tactics of the Religious Right Won't Fly with Most Conservative Christians.* Longwood, Fla.: Distributed Church Press, 2006.

Hurlburt, Heather, with Chayenne Polimedio. "Can Transpartisan Coalitions Overcome Polarization? Lessons from Four Case Studies." *Newamerica.org.* Washington, D.C.: New America, 2016. https://www.newamerica.org/political-reform/policy-papers/can-transpartisan-coalitions-overcome-polarization/ (accessed May 26, 2019).

Illyn, Peter. "Belly-Button Christianity." *Notre Dame Journal of Law, Ethics & Public Policy* 23, no. 2 (2009): 605–21.

Ingersoll, Julie J. *Building God's Dominion: Inside the World of Christian Reconstructionism.* New York: Oxford University Press, 2015.

Jacobs, Anton K. "The New Right, Fundamentalism, and Nationalism in Postmodern America: A Marriage of Heat and Passion." *Social Compass* 53, no. 3 (2006): 357–66.

Jacques, Peter J. "The Rearguard of Modernity: Environmental Skepticism as a Struggle of Citizenship." *Global Environmental Politics* 6, no. 1 (2006): 76–101.

Jacques, Peter J., Riley E. Dunlap, and Mark Freeman. "The Organisation of Denial: Conservative Think Tanks and Environmental Scepticism." *Environmental Politics* 17, no. 3 (2008): 349–85.

Jasper, James M. *The Art of Moral Protest: Culture, Biography, and Creativity in Social Movements.* Chicago: University of Chicago Press, 1997.

Johnston, Hank, and Bert Klandermans. "The Cultural Analysis of Social Movements." In *Social Movements and Culture*, edited by Hank Johnston and Bert Klandermans, 3–24. Minneapolis: University of Minnesota Press, 1995.

Jones, Peter. "The Antithesis: Ephesians 4:17–20." In *On Global Wizardry: Techniques of Pagan Spirituality and a Christian Response*, edited by Peter Jones, 258–71. Escondido, Calif.: Main Entry Editions, 2010.

Jones, Peter, ed. *On Global Wizardry: Techniques of Pagan Spirituality and a Christian Response.* Escondido, Calif.: Main Entry Editions, 2010.

Jordan, James B. "Making a Difference." *The Coral Ridge Encounter* 3 (May 1990).

Kanagy, Conrad L., and Hart M. Nelsen, "Religion and Environmental Concern: Challenging the Dominant Assumptions." *Review of Religious Research* 37, no. 1 (1995): 33–45.

Kang, Seok, and Hanna E. Norton. "Nonprofit Organizations' Use of the World Wide Web: Are They Sufficiently Fulfilling Organizational Goals?" *Public Relations Review* 30 (2004): 279–84.

Kearns, Laurel. "Green Evangelicals." In *The New Evangelical Social Engagement*, edited by Brian Steensland and Philip Goff, 157–78. New York: Oxford University Press, 2014.

———. "Noah's Ark Goes to Washington: A Profile of Evangelical Environmentalism." *Social Compass* 44 (1997): 349–66.

———. "The Role of Religious Activism." In *The Oxford Handbook on Climate Change and Society*, edited by John S. Dryzek, Richard B. Norgaard, and David Schlosberg, 414–28. Oxford: Oxford University Press, 2011.

———. "Saving the Creation: Christian Environmentalism in the United States." *Sociology of Religion* 57 (1996): 55–70.

———. "Saving the Creation: Religious Environmentalism." Ph.D. diss., Emory University, 1994.

Kellstedt, Lyman, John Green, Corwin Smidt, and James Guth. "Faith Transformed: Religion and American Politics from FDR to George W. Bush." In *Religion and American Politics: From the Colonial Period to the Present.* 2nd ed. Edited by

Mark A. Noll and Luke E. Harlow, 269–95. Oxford: Oxford University Press, 2007.

Kennedy, D. James. "To Tend the Earth: Our Christian Responsibility." *The Coral Ridge Encounter* 3 (May 1990).

Kennedy, D. James, and Jerry Newcombe. *How Would Jesus Vote? A Christian Perspective on the Issues*. Colorado Springs, Colo.: WaterBrook Press, 2008.

Killingsworth, M. Jimmie, and Jaqueline S. Palmer. "Millennial Ecology: The Apocalyptic Narrative from *Silent Spring* to *Global Warming*." In *Green Culture: Environmental Rhetoric in Contemporary America*, edited by Carl G. Herndl and Stuart C. Brown, 21–45. Madison: University of Wisconsin Press, 1996.

Kjos, Berit. *Under the Spell of Mother Earth*. Wheaton, Ill.: Victor Books, 1992.

———. *Your Kid and the New Age*. Wheaton, Ill.: Victor Books, 1990.

Klein, Naomi. *This Changes Everything: Capitalism vs. the Climate*. New York: Simon and Schuster, 2014.

Kline, Benjamin. *First Along the River: A Brief History of the Environmental Movement*. 3rd ed. Lanham, MD: Rowman & Littlefield, 2007.

Kohut, Andrew, John C. Green, Scott Keeter, and Robert C. Toth. *The Diminishing Divide: Religion's Changing Role in American Politics*. Washington, D.C.: Brookings Institution, 2000.

Kovaleski, Kevin. "Warming Up to Environmentalism: A Changing Climate in the Politics of Evangelicals." *Responsive Philanthropy* 3 (2006): 1–5.

Kuhn, Thomas S. *The Structure of Scientific Revolutions*. 4th ed. Chicago: University of Chicago Press, 2012.

Lanham, Robert. *The Sinner's Guide to the Evangelical Right*. New York: New American Library, 2006.

Larsen, David K. "God's Gardeners: American Protestant Evangelicals Confront Environmentalism, 1967–2000." Ph.D. diss., University of Chicago, 2001.

———. "God's Wilds: John Muir's Vision of Nature by Dennis C. Williams." *The Journal of Religion* 83, no. 2 (2003): 284–85.

Larson, Edward J. *Summer for the Gods: The Scopes Trial and America's Continuing Debate Over Science and Religion*. New York: Basic Books, 1997. Reprinted with new afterword, 2006.

Lausanne/WEA Creation Care Network. "The Jamaica Call to Action." In *Creation Care and the Gospel: Reconsidering the Mission of the Church*, edited by Colin Bell and Robert S. White, 7–10. Peabody, Mass.: Hendrickson, 2016.

Lewis, C. S. *Mere Christianity*. Rev. ed. New York: HarperOne, 2001.

Liebman, Robert C., and Robert Wuthnow. *The New Christian Right: Mobilization and Legitimation*. New York: Aldine, 1983.

Lindsay, D. Michael. "Elite Power: Social Networks within American Evangelicalism." *Sociology of Religion* 67, no. 3 (2006): 207–27.

————. *Faith in the Halls of Power: How Evangelicals Joined the American Elite.* Oxford: Oxford University Press, 2007.

Lindsell, Harold. *The Battle for the Bible.* Grand Rapids: Zondervan, 1976.

Livingstone, E. A. *The Concise Oxford Dictionary of the Christian Church.* Rev. 2nd ed. Oxford: Oxford University Press, 2006.

Lowe, Ben. *Green Revolution: Coming Together to Care for Creation.* Downers Grove, Ill.: InterVarsity, 2009.

Lowery, David, and Holly Brasher. *Organized Interest and American Government.* New York: McGraw Hill, 2004.

Maltby, Paul. "Fundamentalist Dominion, Postmodern Ecology." *Ethics & the Environment* 13, no. 2 (2008): 119–41.

Malthus, T. R. *An Essay on the Principle of Population,* edited with introduction and notes by Geoffrey Gilbert. New York: Oxford University Press, 2008.

Marsden, George M., ed. *Evangelicalism and Modern America.* Grand Rapids: Eerdmans, 1984.

Marsden, George M. "The Evangelical Denomination." Introduction to *Evangelicalism and Modern America,* edited by George Marsden, vii-xix. Grand Rapids: Eerdmans, 1984.

————. *Fundamentalism and American Culture: The Shaping of Twentieth Century Evangelicalism, 1870–1925.* New York: Oxford University Press, 1980.

————. *Understanding Fundamentalism and Evangelicalism.* Grand Rapids: Eerdmans, 1991.

Martin, William. *With God on Our Side: The Rise of the Religious Right in America.* Rev. ed. New York: Broadway Books, 2005.

Marty, Martin E. "The Years of the Evangelicals." *The Christian Century.* February 15, 1989.

Mauch, Christof, Nathan Stoltzfus, and Douglas R. Weiner. Introduction to *Shades of Green: Environmental Activism Around the Globe,* edited by Christof Mauch, Nathan Stoltzfus, and Douglas R. Weiner, 1–12. German Historical Institute Studies in International Environmental History. Lanham, Md.: Rowman & Littlefield, 2006.

McCammack, Brian. "Hot Damned America: Evangelicalism and the Climate Change Policy Debate." *American Quarterly* 59, no. 3 (2007): 645–68.

McCarthy, John D., and Mayer N. Zald. "Resource Mobilization and Social Movements: A Partial Theory." *American Journal of Sociology* 82, no. 6 (1977): 1212–41.

McCright, Aaron M., and Riley E. Dunlap. "Challenging Global Warming as a Social Problem: An Analysis of the Conservative Movement's Counter-claims." *Social Problems* 47, no. 4 (2000): 499–522.

McDuff, Mallory. *Natural Saints: How People of Faith Are Working to Save God's Earth.* New York: Oxford University Press, 2010.

McFarland, Andrew. *Neopluralism: The Evolution of Political Process Theory.* Lawrence: University Press of Kansas, 2004.

————. *Public Interest Lobbies: Decision Making on Energy.* Washington, D.C.: American Enterprise Institute, 1978.

————. "Public Interest Lobbies vs. Minority Faction." In *The American Polity Reader,* edited by Ann G. Serow, W. Wayne Shannon, and Everett C. Ladd, 414–21. 2nd ed. New York: W. W. Norton, 1993.

McGirr, Lisa. *Suburban Warriors: The Origins of the New American Right.* Princeton, N.J.: Princeton University Press, 2001.

McNeill, J. R. *Something New Under the Sun: An Environmental History of the Twentieth-Century World.* London: Penguin, 2000.

Meadows, Donella H., Dennis L. Meadows, Jørgen Randers, and William W. Behrens. *The Limits to Growth. A Report for the Club of Rome's Project on the Predicament of Mankind.* New York: Universe Books, 1972.

Melucci, Alberto. *Challenging Codes: Collective Action in the Information Age.* Cambridge: Cambridge University Press, 1996.

————. "The Process of Collective Identity." In *Social Movements and Culture,* edited by Hank Johnston and Bert Klandermans, 41–63. Social Movements, Protest, and Contention. London: Routledge, 1995.

Merchant, Carolyn. *American Environmental History: An Introduction.* New York: Columbia University Press, 2007.

————. *Radical Ecology: The Search for a Livable World.* New York: Routledge, 1992.

Merritt, Jonathan. *Green Like God: Unlocking the Divine Plan for Our Planet.* New York: FaithWords, 2010.

————. "Uplink." In *Green Revolution: Coming Together to Care for Creation,* edited by Ben Lowe, 164–65. Downers Grove, Ill.: IVP Books, 2009.

Meyer, David S., and Suzanne Staggenbord. "Movements, Countermovements, and the Structure of Political Opportunity." *American Journal of Sociology* 101, no. 6 (1996): 1628–60.

Micheletti, Michele, Andreas Follesdal, and Dietlind Stolle. *Politics, Products, and Markets. Exploring Political Consumerism Past and Present.* Rutgers, N.J.: Transaction Publishers, 2003.

Miller, Donald. *Blue Like Jazz: Nonreligious Thoughts on Christian Spirituality.* Nashville, Tenn.: Thomas Nelson, 2003.

Moberg, David O. *The Great Reversal: Evangelism and Social Concern.* Philadelphia: Lippincott, 1977.

Mooney, Chris. *The Republican War on Science.* New York: Basic Books, 2005.

Mosely, Lyndsay. "Editors' Preface." In *Holy Ground: A Gathering of Voices on Caring for Creation,* edited by Lyndsay Moseley and the staff of Sierra Club Books, 9–13. San Francisco: Sierra Club Books, 2008.

Murdock, John A. "Creation Careless: Looking for a Green Path in the Age of Trump." *First Things*. March 10, 2017. https://www.firstthings.com/web-exclusives/2017/03/creation-careless (accessed June 2, 2017).

Naess, Arne. *Ecology, Community, and Lifestyle: An Outline of Ecosophy*. Cambridge: Cambridge University Press, 1989.

———. "The Shallow and the Deep, Long-Range Ecology Movement: A Summary." In *Debating the Earth: The Environmental Politics Reader*, edited by John S. Dryzek and David Schlosberg, 343–47. 2nd ed. Oxford: Oxford University Press, 2005.

Nagata, Judith. "Beyond Theology: Toward an Anthropology of 'Fundamentalism.'" *American Anthropologist* 103, no. 2 (2001): 481–98.

Nagle, John Copeland. "The Evangelical Debate Over Climate Change." *University of St. Thomas Law Journal* 5, no. 1 (2008): 53–86.

Nash, Roderick Frazier. *The Rights of Nature: A History of Environmental Ethics*. History of American Thought and Culture, edited by Paul S. Boyer. Madison: University of Wisconsin Press, 1989.

Neuhaus, Richard John. *In Defense of People: Ecology and the Seduction of Radicalism*. New York: Macmillan, 1971.

———. *The Naked Public Square: Religion and Democracy in America*. Grand Rapids: Eerdmans, 1984.

Neuhaus, Richard John, and Michael Cromartie, eds. *Piety and Politics: Evangelicals and Fundamentalists Confront the World*. Washington, D.C.: Ethics and Public Policy Center, 1987.

Newport, John P. *The New Age Movement and the Biblical Worldview: Conflict and Dialogue*. Grand Rapids: Eerdmans, 1998.

Niebuhr, H. Richard. *Christ & Culture*. Expand. ed. San Francisco: HarperSanFrancisco, 2001.

Noll, Mark A. *American Evangelical Christianity: An Introduction*. Malden, Mass.: Blackwell, 2001.

———. *The Old Religion in a New World: The History of North American Christianity*. Grand Rapids: Eerdmans, 2002.

Noll, Mark A., and Luke Harlow, eds. *Religion and American Politics: From the Colonial Period to the Present*. 2nd ed. Oxford: Oxford University Press, 2007.

Numbers, Ronald L. *The Creationists: From Scientific Creationism to Intelligent Design*. Exp. ed. Cambridge, Mass.: Harvard University Press, 2006.

Ohlman, Dean. "The Evangelical Christian's Relationship to Governments and to Individuals that Influence Economic Policy." Dean Ohlman Private Papers, Grand Rapids, Mich.

———. "Finding the Lost Fundamental." Dean Ohlman Private Papers, Grand Rapids, Mich.

———. "Green Cross Bible Study." *Green Cross* (Fall 1997).

———. "This Is Our Father's World—a Christian View of Ecology." In *Under the Spell of Mother Earth*, by Berit Kjos, 161–69. Wheaton, Ill.: Victor Books, 1992.

Olson, Laura R. "The Religious Left in Contemporary American Politics." *Politics, Religion & Ideology* 12, no. 3 (2011): 271–94.

Opie, John. *Nature's Nation: An Environmental History of the United States.* Orlando, Fla.: Harcourt Brace, 1998.

Paehlke, Robert C. *Environmentalism and the Future of Progressive Politics.* New Haven, Conn.: Yale University Press, 1989.

Pally, Marcia. *Die Neuen Evangelikalen: Freiheitsgewinne durch fromme Politik.* Berlin: Berlin University Press, 2010.

———. *The New Evangelicals: Expanding the Vision of the Common Good.* Grand Rapids: Eerdmans, 2011.

Payne, Daniel G. *Voices in the Wilderness: American Nature Writing and Environmental Politics.* Hanover, N.H.: University Press of New England, 1996.

"Peter Illyn, Restoring Eden." *Grist.* March 10, 2003. http://grist.org/article/illyn-restoringeden/full/ (accessed February 10, 2020).

Pierard, Richard V., and Robert D. Linder. *Civil Religion & the Presidency.* Grand Rapids: Academie Books, 1988.

Pierard, Richard V. "The New Religious Right in American Politics." In *Evangelicalism and Modern America,* edited by George M. Marsden, 161–74. Grand Rapids: Eerdmans, 1984.

Pike, Sarah M. *New Age and Neopagan Religions in America.* New York: Columbia University Press, 2004.

Poewe, Karla. *New Religions and the Nazis.* New York: Routledge, 2005.

Pooley, Eric. *The Climate War: True Believers, Power Brokers, and the Fight to Save the Earth.* New York: Hyperion, 2010.

Pritchard, Rusty. "The Danger of Derivatives." *Prism.* 2009.

———. "The Myth of Overpopulation." *Flourish.* Winter 2011. http://www.flourishonline.org/2011/01/the-myth-of-overpopulation/ (accessed July 11, 2017).

———. "The Other Environmental Crisis." *Flourish: Deep Down Things.* June 16, 2010. http://www.flourishonline.org/2010/06/the-other-environmental-crisis/ (accessed July 10, 2017).

———. "The Real Earth Day," *Flourish.* November 24, 2011. http://www.flourishonline. org/2010/11/the-real-earth-day/ (accessed July 25, 2017).

Putnam, Robert D., and David E. Campbell. *American Grace: How Religion Divides and Unites Us.* New York: Simon & Schuster, 2010.

"Rachel Carson Warns of a Silent Spring, 1962." In *Major Problems in American Environmental History: Documents and Essays,* edited by Carolyn Merchant, 437–40. 2nd ed. Boston: Wadsworth Publishing, 2006.

Ravetz, Jerome R. "What Is Post-Normal Science." *Futures* 31, no. 7 (1999): 647–53.

Rodin, Scott R. *Stewards in the Kingdom.* Downers Grove, Ill.: InterVarsity, 2000.

Roberts, David. "An Interview with J. Matthew Sleeth, Evangelical Environmentalist and Author." *Grist*. October 6, 2006. http://grist.org/article/sleeth/ (accessed August 4, 2017).

Ross, Tracy. "Hike. Pray. Protest." *Backpacker Magazine*. March 2011. http://www.backpacker.com/hiking-praying-protesting/destinations/15315 (accessed October 14, 2019).

Rushdoony, Mark R. Foreword to *The Mythology of Science* by Rousas John Rushdoony. 1967. Reprint, Vallecito, Calif.: Ross House Books, 2001.

Rushdoony, Rousas John. *The Mythology of Science*. 1967. Reprint, Vallecito, Calif.: Ross House Books, 2001.

Sabin, Scott C. *Tending to Eden: Environmental Stewardship for God's People*, edited by Kathy Ide. Valley Forge, Pa.: Judson Press, 2010.

Samuels, Mike, and Hal Zina Bennett. *Well Body, Well Earth: The Sierra Club Environmental Health Sourcebook*. San Francisco: Sierra Club Books, 1983.

Schaeffer, Francis A. *Pollution and the Death of Man: The Christian View of Ecology*. London, UK: Hodder and Stoughton, 1970.

Scott, Eugenie C. *Evolution vs. Creationism: An Introduction*. 2nd ed. Berkeley: University of California Press, 2009.

Shabecoff, Philip. *American Environmentalism in the 21st Century*. Washington, D.C.: Island Press, 2000.

Sider, Ronald J. "Biblical Foundations for Creation Care." In *The Care of Creation: Focusing Concern and Action*, edited by R. J. Berry, 43–49. Downers Grove, Ill.: InterVarsity, 2000.

————. *Completely Pro-Life*. Downers Grove, Ill.: InterVarsity, 1987.

————. "ESA's History: A Reflection." *Evangelicalsforsocialaction.org*. http://www.evangelicalsforsocialaction.org/about/history/ (accessed October 7, 2019).

————. "The Place of Humans in the Garden of God." *Green Cross*. Summer 1995.

————. *Rich Christians in an Age of Hunger*. Downers Grove, Ill.: InterVarsity, 1977.

Simmons, J. Aaron. "Evangelical Environmentalism: Oxymoron or Opportunity?" *Worldviews* 13 (2009): 40–71.

Sleeth, Emma. *It's Easy Being Green: One Student's Guide to Serving God and Saving the Planet*. Grand Rapids: Zondervan, 2008.

Sleeth, Matthew. *24/6: A Description for a Healthier, Happier Life*. Carol Stream, Ill.: Tyndale House, 2012.

————. *The Gospel According to the Earth: Why the Good Book Is a Green Book*. New York: HarperOne, 2010.

————. "Introduction: The Power of a Green God." In *The Green Bible*, I-17-I-24. San Francisco: HarperOne, 2008.

————. *Serve God, Save the Planet: A Christian Call to Action*. Grand Rapids: Zondervan, 2006.

Sleeth, Nancy. *Almost Amish: One Woman's Quest for a Slower, Simpler, More Sustainable Life*. Carol Stream, Ill.: Tyndale House, 2012.

———. *Go Green, \$ave Green: A Simple Guide to Saving Time, Money, and GOD'S Green Earth*. Carol Stream, Ill.: Tyndale House, 2009.

Smith, Christian. *Christian America? What Evangelicals Really Want*. Berkeley: University of California Press, 2000.

———. "Correcting a Curious Neglect, or Bringing Religion Back In." In *Disruptive Religion: The Force of Faith in Social Movement Activism*, edited by Christian Smith, 1–25. London: Routledge, 1996.

Smith, Christian, with Michael Emerson, Sally Gallagher, Paul Kennedy, and David Sikkink. *American Evangelicalism: Embattled and Thriving*. Chicago: University of Chicago Press, 1998.

Smith, Nicholas, and Anthony Leiserowitz. "American Evangelicals and Global Warming." *Global Environmental Change* 23 (2013): 1009–17.

Soper, Christopher J. "Differing Perspectives on Politics among Religious Traditions." In *In God We Trust? Religion and American Political Life*, edited by Corwin E. Schmidt, 13–34. Grand Rapids: Baker Academic, 2001.

Sorley, Craig. "Creation Care and the Great Commission." In *Creation Care and the Gospel: Reconsidering the Mission of the Church*, edited by Colin Bell and Robert S. White, 71–83. Lausanne Library. Peabody, Mass.: Hendrickson, 2016.

Steensland, Brian, and Philip Goff, eds. *The New Evangelical Social Engagement*. New York: Oxford University Press, 2014.

Steensland, Brian, and Philip Goff. "Introduction: The New Evangelical Social Engagement." In *The New Evangelical Social Engagement*, edited by Brian Steensland and Philip Goff, 1–27. New York: Oxford University Press, 2014.

Stoll, Mark. *Protestantism, Capitalism, and Nature in North America*. Albuquerque: University of New Mexico Press, 1997.

Stott, John. *Evangelical Truth: A Personal Plea for Unity, Integrity and Faithfulness*. 2003. Reprint, Carlisle, UK: Langham Global Library, 2013.

Swartz, David R. "Left Behind: The Evangelical Left and the Limits of Evangelical Politics, 1965–1988, Volume One." Ph.D. diss., University of Notre Dame, 2008.

———. *Moral Minority: The Evangelical Left in an Age of Conservatism*. Philadelphia: University of Pennsylvania Press, 2012.

Sweet, Leonard I. "The 1960s: The Crises of Liberal Christianity and the Public Emergence of Evangelicalism." In *Evangelicalism and Modern America*, edited by George M. Marsden, 29–45. Grand Rapids: Eerdmans, 1984.

Taylor, Bron. *Dark Green Religion: Nature Spirituality and the Planetary Future*. Berkeley: University of California Press, 2010.

Taylor, Verta. "Mobilizing for Change in a Social Movement Society." *Contemporary Sociology* 29, no. 1 (2000): 219–30.

Tindall, George Brown, and David E. Shi. *America: A Narrative History.* New York: W. W. Norton, 1993.

Tucker, Mary Evelyn. "Religion and Ecology: Survey of the Field." In *The Oxford Handbook of Religion and Ecology*, edited by Roger S. Gottlieb, 398–418. Oxford: Oxford University Press, 2006.

Turner, James Morton, and Andrew C. Isenberg. *The Republican Reversal: Conservatives and the Environment from Nixon to Trump.* Cambridge, Mass.: Harvard University Press, 2018.

Unnever, James D., John P. Bartowski, and Francis T. Cullen. "God Imagery and Opposition to Abortion and Capital Punishment: A Partial Test of Religious Support for the Consistent Life Ethic." *Sociology of Religion* 71, no. 3 (2010): 307–22.

Vaillancourt, Jean-Guy. "Environment." In *Conservation and Environmentalism: An Encyclopedia*, edited by Robert Paehlke. London: Fitzroy Dearborn, 1995.

Veith, Gene Edward, Jr. *Fascism: Modern and Postmodern.* Mussoorie, U.P., India: Nivedit Good Books Distributors, 2000.

Veldman, Robin Globus. "What Is the Meaning of Greening? Cultural Analysis of a Southern Baptist Environmental Text." *Journal of Contemporary Religion* 31, no. 2 (2016): 199–222.

Viguerie, Richard A. *The New Right: We're Ready to Lead.* Falls Church, Va.: Viguerie, 1980.

Wald, Kenneth D., Adam L. Silverman, and Kevin S. Fridy. "Making Sense of Religion in Political Life." *Annual Review of Political Science* 8 (2005): 121–43.

Walker, Jack L. *Mobilizing Interest Groups in America: Patrons, Professions, and Social Movements.* Ann Arbor: University of Michigan Press, 1991.

Warner, R. Stephen. "Evangelicals of the 1970s and 2010s: What's the Same, What's Different, and What's Urgent." In *The New Evangelical Social Engagement*, edited by Brian Steensland and Philip Goff, 280–91. New York: Oxford University Press, 2014.

Warren, Rick. *The Purpose-Driven Life: What on Earth Am I Here For?* Grand Rapids: Zondervan, 2002.

Weber, Max. *The Protestant Ethic and the Spirit of Capitalism.* Translated by Talcott Parsons. New York: Charles Scribner's Sons, 1958.

White, Lynn, Jr. "The Historical Roots of Our Ecologic Crisis." In *Machina Ex Deo: Essays in the Dynamism of Western Culture*, edited by Lynn White Jr., 75–94. Cambridge, Mass.: MIT Press, 1968.

Whitehead, Andrew L., Samuel L. Perry, and Joseph O. Baker. "Make America Christian Again: Christian Nationalism and Voting for Donald Trump in the 2016 Presidential Election." *Sociology of Religion* 79, no. 2 (2018): 147–71.

Whitney, Elspeth. "Christianity and Changing Concepts of Nature: An Historical Perspective." In *Religion and the New Ecology: Environmental Responsibility in a World in*

*Flux*, edited by David M. Lodge and Christopher Hamlin, 26–52. Notre Dame, Ind.: University of Notre Dame, 2006.

———. "Lynn White, Ecotheology, and History." *Environmental Ethics* 15 (1993):151–69.

Wilcox, Clyde. *God's Warriors? The Christian Right in Twentieth-Century America*. Baltimore, Md.: Johns Hopkins University Press, 1992.

Wilcox, Clyde, and Carin Larson. *Onward Christian Soldiers?: The Religious Right in American Politics*. 3rd ed. Boulder, Colo.: Westview, 2006.

Wilkinson, Katharine K. *Between God & Green: How Evangelicals Are Cultivating a Middle Ground on Climate Change*. Oxford: Oxford University Press, 2012.

Wilkinson, Loren E., ed. *Earthkeeping: Christian Stewardship of Natural Resources*. Grand Rapids: Eerdmans, 1980.

———., ed. *Earthkeeping in the '90s: Stewardship of Creation*. Revised ed. Grand Rapids: Eerdmans, 1991.

———. "The Making of the Declaration." In *The Care of Creation: Focusing Concern and Action*, edited by R. J. Berry, 50–59. Downers Grove, Ill.: InterVarsity, 2000.

Williams, Daniel K. "Prolifers on the Left: Progressive Evangelicals' Campaign Against Abortion." In *The New Evangelical Social Engagement*, edited by Brian Steensland and Philip Goff, 200–220. New York: Oxford University Press, 2014.

Wilson, E. O. *The Creation: An Appeal to Save Life on Earth*. New York: W. W. Norton, 2006.

Withrow King, Sarah. *Vegangelical: How Caring for Animals Can Shape Your Faith*. Grand Rapids: Zondervan, 2016.

Wolfe, Alan. "The Evangelical Mind Revisited." *Change: The Magazine of Higher Learning* 38, no. 2 (2006): 9–13.

Wolkomir, Michelle, Michael Futreal, Eric Woodrum, and Thomas Hoban. "Denominational Subcultures of Environmentalism." *Review of Religious Research* 38 (1997): 325–43.

Worthen, Molly. *Apostles of Reason: The Crisis of Authority in American Evangelicalism*. New York: Oxford University Press, 2013.

———. "The Chalcedon Problem: John Rousas Rushdoony and the Origins of Christian Reconstructionism." *Church History* 77, no. 2 (2008): 399–437.

Wuthnow, Robert, ed. *The Encyclopedia of Politics and Religion*. Washington, D.C.: CQ Press, 1998.

———. "Quid Obscurum: The Changing Terrain of Church-State Relations." In *Religion and American Politics: From the Colonial Period to the Present*, 2nd edition, edited by Mark A. Noll and Luke E. Harlow, 441–58. Oxford: Oxford University Press, 2007.

———. *The Restructuring of American Religion: Society and Faith since World War II*. Princeton, N.J.: Princeton University Press, 1988.

———. *The Struggle for America's Soul: Evangelicals, Liberals, and Secularism*. Grand Rapids: Eerdmans, 1989.

Zald, Mayer N., and John D. McCarthy. *The Dynamics of Social Movements: Resource Mobilization, Social Control, and Tactics.* Cambridge, Mass: Winthrop, 1979.

Zaleha, Bernd, and Andrew Szasz. "Keep Christianity Brown! Climate Denial on the Christian Right in the United States." In *How the World's Religions Are Responding to Climate Change: Social Scientific Investigations*, edited by Robin G. Veldman, Andrew Szasz, and Randolph Haluza-DeLay, 209–28. New York: Routledge, 2014.

Zelko, Frank. "Challenging Modernity: The Origins of Postwar Environmental Protest in the United States." In *Shades of Green: Environmental Activism Around the Globe*, edited by Christof Mauch, Nathan Stoltzfus, and Douglas R. Weiner, 13–40. German Historical Institute Studies in International Environmental History. Lanham, Md.: Rowman & Littlefield, 2006.

# INDEX